REASON AND REVELATION BEFORE HISTORICISM:
STRAUSS AND FACKENHEIM

SHARON PORTNOFF

Reason and Revelation before Historicism

Strauss and Fackenheim

UNIVERSITY OF TORONTO PRESS
Toronto Buffalo London

ISBN 978-1-4426-4307-9

♾

Printed on acid-free, 100% post-consumer recycled paper with
vegetable-based inks.

Library and Archives Canada Cataloguing in Publication

Portnoff, Sharon
Reason and revelation before historicism : Strauss and Fackenheim /
Sharon Portnoff.

Includes bibliographical references and index.
ISBN 978-1-4426-4307-9

1. Strauss, Leo.   2. Fackenheim, Emil L., 1916– .   3. Philosophy and
religion.   4. Historicism.   5. Judaism and philosophy.   6. Philosophy,
Modern.   I. Title.

BL51.P67 2011   210   C2011-906382-4

University of Toronto Press acknowledges the financial assistance to its
publishing program of the Canada Council for the Arts and the Ontario
Arts Council.

Canada Council   Conseil des Arts   ONTARIO ARTS COUNCIL
for the Arts   du Canada   CONSEIL DES ARTS DE L'ONTARIO

University of Toronto Press acknowledges the financial support of the
Government of Canada through the Canada Book Fund for its publishing
activities.

This book is dedicated to the memory of Laurence Berns, may his memory be for a blessing. Without his generosity and inquisitive mind, this book would not exist.

Contents

Acknowledgments

I would like to gratefully acknowledge by name those individuals to whom I owe a special debt in the preparation of this book. I begin with Emil Fackenheim, *zikhrono li-verakhah*, who generously devoted time to me on my two visits to Jerusalem in the winter of 2002 and the summer of 2003. Without his having coaxed and inspired me, I would not have encountered Strauss fully. There are numerous other individuals who guided, inspired, pushed, and challenged me in this project. Among them are Gisela Berns, James A. Diamond, Oona Eisenstadt, Patricia Fenton, Abigail Gillman, Neil Gillman, Kenneth Hart Green, Zayn Kassam, Catherine Lasser, Shaul Magid, Alan Mittleman, Joshua Parens, Martin J. Plax, Ted Richer, Alan Udoff, and Martin D. Yaffe. I am very grateful for their continual feedback, encouragement, and criticism.

I would also like to gratefully acknowledge the Jewish Theological Seminary of America, Pomona College, and Connecticut College for their support, financial and otherwise, which made it possible for me to work on this book and bring it to fruition. I am especially grateful to the program and the community of St. John's College, Annapolis, which inspired in me a lifelong passion to seek and which helped me to recognize that wisdom is the asking of the right questions.

REASON AND REVELATION BEFORE HISTORICISM:
STRAUSS AND FACKENHEIM

1 Background and Introduction

Introduction

It is well known that the work of Emil L. Fackenheim was influenced by Rosenzweig and Buber. Less well known is the tremendous impact that Leo Strauss had on his work. As a young scholar in Toronto, Fackenheim visited New York to converse with Strauss. He sought him out, not so much to learn what various thinkers had thought, but rather to learn whether what these thinkers had written 'was right.'[1] This was not simply the loneliness of one German Jewish exile seeking out another: both men were keenly aware of what they had identified as the failures of modern philosophy. And Strauss was in the process of tracing the failures to an inadequate understanding of the relationship between reason and revelation, to the consequent inability to take seriously enough either reason or revelation, and to the resultant loss of common sense. The loss of common sense manifests itself as an idealistic blindness to the surface of things, brought on initially by an unbounded belief in progress and ending in the 'deep pit beneath the cave'[2] – historicism. While both Strauss and Fackenheim sought to refute historicism – or at any rate to respond to it – each utilized a different means. For Strauss, the return to philosophy conceived as a never-ending quest for natural right would enable us to discover the possibility of revelation as beyond philosophy's purview. Fackenheim was more concerned with the reaffirmation of the possibility of Jewish revelation in the context of the secular world, even as he recognized the impact of thought on history – and specifically, the reality of evil. For Fackenheim, it was impossible to return to a pre-modern conception of reality, but it was possible to return to and continually engage with the thinker most responsible for the shift from nature to history as the basis of thought: Hegel.

Strauss taught at the New School for Social Research beginning in 1938, a year after his arrival in the United States, and ending in 1948, at which time he received an appointment at the University of Chicago, where he taught until the late 1960s. In 1968 he settled at St. John's College, Annapolis, with a curtailed teaching schedule, until his death in 1973. He was born to an Orthodox Jewish family in Kirchhain, Germany, and received his PhD from the University of Hamburg in 1921. In 1925 he became a research assistant at the *Akademie für die Wissenschaft des Judentums*, where he studied, primarily, Hobbes and Spinoza. He received a Rockefeller Grant in 1932 that enabled him to leave Germany for France and then England. During this time, he studied Jewish and Islamic medieval philosophy and continued his work on Hobbes.[3] In 1937 he was able to leave Europe altogether for the United States. He was a research fellow at Columbia University until his appointment to the New School.

Fackenheim was not so fortunate. He was born in 1916 in Halle, Germany, and in 1935, the year of the Nuremberg Laws, he began his rabbinic studies at the *Hochschule für die Wissenschaft des Judentums* in Berlin. On *Kristallnacht*, 9–10 November 1938, he was arrested and taken to Sachsenhausen, where he remained for three months. Although on his release he was told to leave Germany immediately, he returned to Berlin to receive his ordination (Reform) in April 1939.[4] Finally, in May of that year, he fled to Scotland, where he began studies at the University of Aberdeen. Shortly thereafter, he was interned in camps for sixteen months, ending up in one in Canada. Upon his release, he entered the doctoral program at the University of Toronto. Concurrently, he took a pulpit for five years at Temple Anshe Shalom in Hamilton. He received his PhD from the University of Toronto in 1945 and remained there teaching until moving to Jerusalem in 1984, where he died in 2003.

By Fackenheim's own account,[5] Strauss's *Philosophy and Law* strongly influenced his doctoral dissertation, which was in the field of medieval Islamic thought. These beginnings had a profound lifelong affect on him, and he devoted his intellectual life to the question – raised by Strauss – whether it was possible for belief in revelation to survive within the context of modern thought. His *magnum opus*, *To Mend the World* (1982), is dedicated to Strauss's memory; and he studied and cited various of Strauss's works, including his writings on Rosenzweig and his few but poignant insights regarding the Nazis.[6] Michael L. Morgan recounts that Fackenheim read Strauss's *Philosophy and Law* (1935) in Nazi Berlin and 'had sensed an urgency about revelation and the challenges to it from Enlightenment rationalism ... Strauss's questions became lifelong interests, consuming interests, for Fackenheim, signs on a journey to clarify what revelation is and why it is necessary for any authentic Jewish belief.'[7] Fackenheim considers his *Encounters between Judaism and Modern Philosophy* (1973) to be a response to Strauss's 'Preface.' He also begins his exploration of Spinoza in *To Mend the World* under the direction of both Strauss's 'Preface' and 'How to Study Spinoza's *Theologico-Political Treatise'* in *Persecution and the Art of Writing*[8] and refers to Strauss in many of his other books.[9] Yet in terms of writing solely about Strauss's thought, Fackenheim produced only a single short essay, 'Leo Strauss and Modern Judaism.'[10] This would seem to indicate a profound respect for Strauss but may also suggest a deep disagreement with his thought.

Strauss sought to rediscover standards of morality, and later so would Fackenheim. The standard that Strauss sought to articulate is derived from a return to the original concept of natural right. What is 'by nature just' is not identical with the dictates of right reason: Greek philosophical thought seeks to discover what is by nature just by beginning with things as they appear to *us;* it therefore begins from the surface of things – in the various and conflicting opinions regarding what is the right way of life – and seeks to ascend beyond that surface. Philosophically, one can hope to ascend beyond the surface of things; but although Plato and Aristotle aim to arrive at knowledge, the best one can hope for politically is generally accepted opinion that approximates the dictates – the 'laws' – of right reason.[11] Strauss's return to the unfettered inquiry into opinions about the right way of life entails the necessary distinction between the natural and the conventional, but natural right is not necessarily exclusive of divine law: while philosophy and revelatory theology remain distinct insofar as either may issue in laws for human action, the notion of natural law 'is not coeval with human thought'[12] because nature had to be discovered.[13] The discovery of natural right allows the philosopher to ask whether or how far one might understand divine law by one's own unassisted efforts so that one might have some knowledge of whom one obeys (or against whom one rebels), but one cannot have complete knowledge of divine law. As Strauss points out, 'there is no natural law teaching, for instance, in the Old Testament [*sic*].'[14] Most pressing in Strauss's articulation of his return to natural right is its implicit non-dogmatism. Socrates says that he knows nothing; Strauss's rediscovery of Platonic ideas reveals the truth that the *idea* of justice is the *problem* of justice. Fackenheim seeks to reaffirm a standard of morality through a reassessment of the biblical/ rabbinic tradition[15] in light of Strauss's work, or an encounter between the revelatory tradition and philosophy.

In their efforts to rediscover a definite standard of morality, even while avoiding the tyranny that can result from any form of absolutism, both Strauss and Fackenheim made it their main goal to discover a means by which reason and revelation might coexist, each in its own terms – a means that might serve both as an alternative to modern secularism, which Strauss defines as 'the preservation of thoughts, feelings, or habits of biblical origin after the loss or atrophy of biblical faith,'[16] and also, for Fackenheim, as a mending of the rupture in Judaism caused by the Holocaust. In both thinkers' work, this definite standard of morality takes the form of a theoretic 'openness' of each reason and revelation to the claims of the other within the *practical* choice of either philosophy or revelatory theology.[17] At the same time, each thinker recognizes that human existence must be informed by this definite thought: Strauss will recommend a return to Greek philosophical thought understood as a never-ending quest for justice, even as he recognizes that what is most necessary now to safeguard philosophy and the state is the eradication of dogmatism in all its forms.[18] Fackenheim will promote a 'quasi-historicism'[19]: historicism, insofar as it incorporates the idea that changes in human thinking literally change the object of thought; but only *quasi*-historicism, because it limits the extent to which those changes can occur.[20] His quasi-historicism will serve as the basis for an openness to the possibility of the revelation of the one true God *and* for a closedness to all false gods.

Strauss's question – Is the revelatory tradition reliable? – became the starting point for Fackenheim's work. Fackenheim adopted Strauss's critique of liberalism and idealism, his recognition that the crisis of modernity stems from the syntheses and attempted syntheses of reason and revelation – which syntheses nullified the authority of both, and his discovery that knowledge or wisdom is the activity in which one engages in the quest for the right way of life. Strauss's thought remains outside the revelatory tradition in order to leave open the question of its reliability – even as he relies on our elementary experiences of right and wrong – whereas Fackenheim begins within the stance of covenantal affirmation,[21] though he does not define the content of that affirmation. For the one, what is primary is not to defend but rather to understand Judaism – though this may concomitantly issue in a defence of Judaism; for the other, the Jewish revelatory tradition must begin in Jewish election and as committed experience. At the same time, however, Fackenheim recognizes that this experience must be grounded in contemporary concerns: if God is the God of history, He is the God of contemporary history as well – He must, that is, have the ability to intervene in the events of history – and both liberal secularism and the Holocaust have severely tested the authenticity of this commitment. To perpetuate the Jewish revelatory tradition, even as he leaves its reliability uncertain, Fackenheim translates contemporary idealism into hope as a transcendent principle and reaffirms the authority of both personal experience and ultimate (though not final[22]) mystery.

In his essay on Strauss, Fackenheim both acknowledges his debt to him and also criticizes him for what he considers to be his 'excessive restraint in dealing with radical evil.'[23] He goes on to specify the Holocaust as an evil beyond the scope of Platonic philosophy: in the Holocaust, evil became a transcendent principle that resulted in the reformulation the Platonic *question* – What is justice? – into an *answer*: committed action against the Nazi evil. Implicit to his criticism, as the Straussian scholar Kenneth C. Blanchard has pointed out,[24] is Fackenheim's acceptance of historicism,[25] albeit a qualified one, as we shall see. So, for instance, one might recognize that human slaughters have a long history and that the events of this history do not necessarily direct us to reformulate the theoretic question of what justice is.[26] Yet Strauss's return to Plato is not itself unqualified; it too is informed by contemporary concerns.[27] While both thinkers seek a return to beginning in the surface of things, to the authority of political context,[28] the very nature of return qualifies its goal. Strauss characterizes this as the extreme difficulty of Jewish *t'shuvah* – 'return,' 'repentance' – after the break effectuated by Spinoza.[29] To overcome this difficulty, Strauss proposes an 'unqualified return to Jewish orthodoxy'[30] – to an orthodoxy that would provide the terms by which to understand, for instance, not how *we* understand them, but rather how the biblical authors understood themselves.[31] For Fackenheim, Strauss's reduction of Torah ('instruction') to (primarily) Law is not optimistic enough: Judaism cannot persist without its teaching of hope. Furthermore, in Fackenheim's thought, return is not a possibility because there was a twelve-year period in history – the Holocaust – during which a world view was adopted that was both radically evil and also unintelligible.[32] Philosophy, Christianity, and Judaism have been ruptured, and human resistance to radical evil is required to effectuate a mending. For Fackenheim, Strauss's lack of attention to the Holocaust as an instance of radical evil is too optimistic.

Except for the essays of Fackenheim and Blanchard, there has been, to my knowledge, no extensive treatment comparing the thought of Strauss and Fackenheim. Morgan was a student and friend of Fackenheim and has also responded to Strauss,[33] yet he has not written extensively in connection with both thinkers. Kenneth Hart Green, however, recognizes the importance of Strauss's influence on Fackenheim's thought as cause to 'see Strauss in a new and different light'[34]; and Allan Arkush recognizes in his essay 'Leo Strauss and Modernity'[35] both the indebtedness of Fackenheim to Strauss and their divergent thinking. Yet despite what Arkush calls their 'deep spiritual kinship' and 'strong intellectual affinity,'[36] Strauss and Fackenheim disagreed with each other about the means to secure the future viability of Judaism and of philosophy. An in-depth study of their affinities and differences is long overdue.

PART II. GENERAL BACKGROUND

Why Is There a Tension between Philosophy and Revelatory Theology?

The tension between philosophy and revelatory theology arose concurrent in the West with the beginnings of philosophy. For the purposes of this book, 'revelatory theology' is to be distinguished from natural theology, which properly is a branch of philosophy, and is to be understood as the placing of revelatory experience within a theological framework in accordance with some idea of nature.[37] Philosophy was brought into existence through its separation from myth: both philosophy and myth seek to discover the origin of things, but philosophy does so in the light of the idea of nature, while myth does so in the light of ideas about gods.[38] More specifically, when philosophy replaced the ancient concept of fate with the idea of nature, which bore with it intelligible necessity, so too the quest for beginnings became intelligible. It was then understood that there were eternal verities and that one could strive toward knowledge of them. Strauss discovered that, once the idea of nature was recognized as the necessary, as what is intrinsic to things, gods were not required as the means by which to formulate the laws by which to live the good life. But philosophy's separation from myth, and ultimately from revelatory religion, is possible only through beginning with the presupposition that the belief in gods is a product of 'custom,' in the sense of a pre-philosophic equivalent of 'nature'[39]: powers in things as ordained by gods.[40] Consequently, as Plato recognizes – especially in *The Republic* and *Laws* 10 – though the goal is wisdom, one can never achieve completed knowledge: philosophy accounts for myth non-mythically, in terms that are alien to myth. Myth is not refuted, and 'philosophy consists, therefore, in the ascent from opinions to knowledge or to the truth, in an ascent that may be said to be guided by opinions.'[41] One can, however, achieve the human wisdom of one's ignorance and thus one's need to continue philosophizing: individual progress in understanding the 'fundamental alternatives' is not ruled out, but 'there is no guaranty [*sic*] that the [philosopher's] quest ... will ever legitimately go beyond the stage of discussion or disputation and will ever reach the stage of decision.'[42]

Biblical thought, on the other hand, insofar as it includes moments illustrative of its adherents' desire to know something about whom they serve, also cannot account for the whole. Its focus on God's incomprehensibility puts the Bible at odds with philosophic thought because the Bible, for the most part, seeks to impart not wisdom, but rather what it means to live with God.[43] Strauss discovers that the 'basic premise [of the Old Testament] may be said to be the implicit rejection of philosophy.'[44] Biblical thought is born with the revelation of God at Sinai; philosophical doubt is irrelevant, if not sinful. What is required is to know God through His actions, to recognize God and the code given at Sinai as unique, and to live with God through a covenant of faith and hope. The concept of nature as the foundation of knowledge is at the very least discouraged, though the worship of nature seems to be a temptation.[45] While the Bible's primary intention may be to preclude the necessary bases of philosophical thought – such as knowledge based on the idea of nature – from its world view, there appear in the Bible (e.g., in Ecclesiastes) instances of a denial of its providential world view.[46] And while kalamists might claim that reasoning and sense perception are, consequently, precluded as well from the biblical world view, Strauss shows that the powers 'separated' at the beginning of Genesis are separated intelligibly.[47]

While there may be a theoretic reconciliation between Greek philosophic and biblical thought – hinted at, perhaps, by the need to explain the *almost* universal belief in gods in Greek philosophic thought and the vestiges in the Bible of the temptation toward the worship of nature[48] –

Greek philosophic and biblical thought admit of no practical reconciliation between them: the one begins in human doubt and the quest for knowledge of natural necessity, and the other in hope, or fear, and the obedience of human beings to God. Nevertheless, Strauss argues that both reason and revelation claim to provide the right way of life and that in fact, because both stances of thought inform Western civilization and are the bases of it, there is a sort of living reconciliation between them.[49]

Both Strauss and Fackenheim (following him) recognize that neither Greek philosophic nor biblical thought manages to dismiss entirely the claims of the other. Nor can philosophy 'progress' to the point where it can. Refutations of philosophy presuppose belief in revelation, while those of revelation by philosophy presuppose unbelief in revelation.[50] Pascal, for instance, presupposes faith when he proves that the life of a philosopher is tragic. As Fackenheim frames it, the Commanding Presence of God remains silent and absent to those whose stance toward reality precludes either God or, alternatively, recognition of the contingent. Revelatory theology is pertinent only to those who through both *their* actions and *its* guidance make it meaningful. Regarding modern refutations of revelation, Strauss argues that they presuppose natural theology – both the impossibility of miracles and also knowledge of God – which in turn presupposes that God's nature is comprehensible. Yet for God's nature to be altogether comprehensible, the completion of a system – knowledge of the whole – must be presupposed. This knowledge is, of course, impossible, and the dogmatic exclusion of miracles that underlies the historical and scientific attack against revelation in the seventeenth and eighteenth centuries does not in any sense refute the truth of revelation. While some notion of the whole is presupposed by any philosophy, the serious philosopher tries to arrive at the best supported opinion about the whole, or to understand the best supported alternative opinions about the whole – that is, the fundamental problems.

The Tension between Philosophy and Revelatory Theology in Modern Western Thought

Much of modern thought has attempted to reconcile the tension between philosophy and revelatory theology. During the early modern period, in thinkers such as Machiavelli, Hobbes, and Spinoza, religion was recast, on the surface, as a tool of the state – a recasting that obfuscated the truth claims of revelatory theology. This obfuscation, however, did not constitute a philosophic disproof; rather, the change from the physiocentric or theocentric world view to the anthropocentric rendered it irrelevant to address the truth claims of revelatory theology beyond the assertion that, as Hobbes put it, the moral laws are 'also divine laws in respect of the author thereof, God Almighty; and ought to agree with, or at least not be repugnant to, the word of God revealed in Holy Scripture.'[51] These thinkers either subordinated theology to politics (Machiavelli), or, at least on the surface, integrated philosophy and theology (Hobbes and Spinoza).

Machiavelli, Hobbes, and Spinoza successfully carved out an artificial space that is secular – or, more specifically, defined revelatory religion as outside the boundaries of the secular but essential for political life. As a replacement for revelatory theology, to guide moral action, natural law was posited. These modern thinkers attempted to return to philosophy independent of ecclesiastical authority (as, for instance, Plato understood philosophy) or to subordinate ecclesiastical authority to philosophic authority. Natural law, however, as distinct from natural right, was not the central issue for the Greek philosophers: ancient thought was more interested in identifying the source – nature or convention – of what were recognized as universal rights.[52] Aquinas's natural law sidestepped this issue by equating nature with convention – or, more precisely, by glossing over the distinctions between 'custom' and 'law,'[53] so that the natural law emanates from the eternal law. For Aquinas, as Strauss formulates it, natural law begins 'with the hierarchic order of man's natural ends ... [Hobbes, however, started] with the lowest of those ends (self-preservation) which could be thought to be more effective than the higher ends.'[54] Hobbes adopted the idea of nature as solely accessible to reason – even as passion is to be relied upon. Moreover, by rejecting the eternal law, he made nature subject to manipulation.

Machiavelli had provided for Hobbes the shift in viewpoint – from how human beings ought to live to how human beings do live – that enabled him to understand the human being as able to use 'mere calculation'[55] to mould society and himself as a social being. For early modern philosophers, the possibility of the emergence of natural law was based in their anthropocentrism: law can be 'natural' because the human being can 'conquer' nature. The new science was understood as revealing clear and evident principles of nature.

Bacon validated the new scientific method in his attempt to separate religion from philosophy. This separation would, he argued, avoid heretical religion and fabulous philosophy: his identification of the 'idols of the mind' had as its (unachievable) goal the 'exhibit[ion of] the matter naked to us so that we may use our own judgment.'[56] His introduction of the possibility of 'command[ing] nature' conceals the less sanguine aspects of humanity. By adopting an idea of nature as a totality, or as a hermetic system – one that by being 'obeyed'[57] can be known and manipulated – Bacon renders it necessary to argue for history as the means by which the human being separates himself from nature's mechanism. Kant adopted the anthropocentric world view, within which he developed his concept of autonomous reason. He was interested in establishing a philosophic grounding for morality; he therefore critiqued revelatory theology, but only insofar as its results might contradict the conclusions of autonomous reason, which he equated with morality. Kant understood morality as the highest truth to which autonomous reason can aspire, but in Fackenheim's reading of him, he did not leave it at that: Kant also wanted to know whether there could be room for revelation after reason had bounded religion to morality.[58] Each of the chapters of *Religion within the Bounds of Reason Alone*, and each of his three *Critiques*, ends with religious questions.[59] Kant exposed revelatory theology to reason in terms appropriate to revelatory theology. At the same time, he did not assimilate revelatory theology into autonomous reason: the religious questions remain unresolved but also unavoidable.

The attempt to synthesize reason and revelation, which followed the early moderns, emerged as a result of the failure of their successors to recognize that Machiavelli, Hobbes, and Spinoza had succeeded in freeing themselves from ecclesiastical authority. Although the battle had been won, Hegel and Heidegger, as philosophers, had to attempt to subjugate revelation to the demands of the new anthropocentric philosophy. The syntheses that resulted would end, first, in what Fackenheim labels a Christian Constantinianism – a form of supersessionism – or second, in the reformulation of the revelatory God as Being itself. In both cases, human knowledge became both clear and evident and also revealed, both progressive and also certain.

Before the modern project of reconciling reason and revelation reached its height in Hegel and Heidegger, Fichte and the early Schelling, recognizing the implicit contradiction in Kant's thought, adopted his absolute standpoint in an attempt to assimilate revelatory theology into philosophic thought without relinquishing autonomy. When it became clear, in other words, that revelation had never been refuted but only thrust outside the boundaries of philosophy, the attempt to explicitly reintroduce revelatory theology into this philosophy was made. But the victory of the early moderns over ecclesiastical authority was misunderstood by the later moderns to be a victory over revelation itself. The synthesis between philosophy and revelatory theology that followed the latter's removal from the sphere of thought retained the translation of revelation into the terms of political philosophy. Early modern thought affirms the primacy of reason over revelation as a means of freeing the human being to progress; later modern thought, even as it reintroduced the claims of revelation, did not disillusion itself of the claim to progress.[60] The result was a synthesis, without validation, between reason and revelation – or, alternatively, an internalization of the claims of revelation in the name of historical progress. The later Schelling recognized – or alleged – in what will become important for Fackenheim's thought, that a synthesis between philosophy and revelatory theology may be grounded in history, in existentialism.[61]

The two most important thinkers representing the trend toward the synthesis of philosophy and revelatory theology in modern thought are Hegel and Heidegger. Hegel attempted a synthesis through the medium of history: absolute truth may be 'revealed' because it may gradually unfold in the religious consciousness of human beings – ultimately as philosophy (Idea). Philosophy and revelatory theology are therefore synthesized in the sense that each moment in the past is philosophically reconstructed according to its purposiveness toward an ultimate theological truth. While Hegel's synthesis was accomplished through history, Heidegger's synthesis – so Heidegger claimed – occurs through Being itself. Heidegger, rather than reframing as Plato did the divine as the rational, instead defined the revelatory realm as the subject matter of philosophical inquiry. Heidegger's Being took on the character of the biblical God, even while he affirmed the necessity of temporality in order for Being to articulate itself. In Heidegger's language, the philosophical tradition had lost account of Being, which must become the foundation of philosophical inquiry. By making the revelatory realm the subject matter of philosophy, Heidegger brought the autonomy established in the philosophical realm to bear on revelatory theology. He attempted (unsuccessfully, according to Fackenheim) to address the problem caused to the traditional conception of God; but philosophy, as Heidegger conceived it, could no longer uncover knowledge of nature. It could neither identify myth nor recognize the traditional God. Philosophy itself was led on a path to self-destruction.[62]

Strauss and Fackenheim on the Tension between Philosophy and Revelatory Theology in Modern Western Thought

In Strauss's formulation, early modern thought, impelled by the need to explain the partial intelligibility of the world, attempted to carve out a religion free of superstition. In medieval thought, philosophy could be validated by revealed religion as but one of the Creator God's gifts to humanity and could therefore be reconciled, albeit with tension, with revealed religion without distorting either. But in the early modern period, the medieval concept of rebellion – removing oneself from God's estate – was recast as 'freedom,' and the medieval 'polarity faithfulness-rebellion,' which existed within the theological construct of obedience to God, was replaced with the 'polarity prejudice-freedom.'[63] Obedience to God in the traditional sense now became a prejudice; but more important, freedom, which was understood once as rebellion from God, became a means of serving God.[64] Philosophy in effect took on a theological function: one serves God through one's autonomy.

When nature was reformulated by Bacon as something to be manipulated or controlled, the replacement of necessity with freedom was made possible. This entailed also the replacement of natural law or human nature with history.[65] Philosophy was reformulated, ostensibly, as independent of a revealed God or His gifts, grounded exclusively in human reason. To validate the authority of reason, Hobbes, for instance, attempted a synthesis of political idealism and an 'atheistic view of the whole.'[66] Synthesis, as Strauss defines it, is the 'transition of thought from the plane of the original positions to an entirely different plane.'[67] The different plane to which philosophy and revelatory theology are transitioned is an idealistic *and* materialistic philosophy, or, alternatively, a philosophically established and created religion that retains neither natural necessity nor the terms appropriate to revelation.

Strauss recognizes in the above process the crisis of modernity: as a consequence of the synthesis of philosophy and revelation and the consequent loss of the recognition of the permanent tension between reason and revelation, modern philosophy articulates a historical relativism that cannot answer how we are to orient ourselves intellectually and morally. When historicism emerged, history was understood to demonstrate that values change with time and place. History, rather than an 'inquiring,' or a quest, became itself the object of inquiry in the realms of both reason and revelation. Strauss attempts to counter this by spelling out the practical irreconcilability of reason and revelation – the need for a particular understanding of custom – even while he redis-covers the theoretic common ground between them. He articulates the distinction between philosophy and state-sanctioned religion – political philosophy – in order to rediscover the doubt of authority at the basis of philosophy. Furthermore, he attempts to rediscover the claims of revela-tion by arguing for both its distinction from all human authority (both of the state and of the church) and also its relevance to modern thought.

Building on Strauss's work, Fackenheim focuses on the distortion of revelation as a result of the failure of the synthesis between reason and revelation. According to him – who, as we recall, proceeds from a 'qua-si-historicist' stance – the development of modern Western philosophy, from Spinoza to Heidegger, was a movement toward a more and more internalized God. Because this movement translates the transcendent God into a product of human reason, or human reason itself, the issue can be reframed as a submersion of revelatory theology into philoso-phy. In Fackenheim's formulation, the internalization was a process, beginning with Spinoza, who, for the purpose of establishing reason as authority, separates out revelation from philosophy, and culminating in Hegel, whose God exists in immanence through history as the *Zeitgeist*. With the internalization of God comes the identity of revelatory theol-ogy and philosophy; this identity enables Heidegger to eliminate from his thought the God who had been acknowledged as Being outside the context of temporality.[68] Heidegger's elimination is built on a synthesis that fails to recognize the terms appropriate to revelatory theology and has no rational basis.

Both Strauss and Fackenheim recognize the failure of the modern attempt to synthesize philosophy and revelatory theology – or, alter-natively, to internalize God – as implicit in the attempt itself. Just as Strauss recognizes that with the introduction of the modern concept of freedom – as Hegel writes, 'the Concept is the principle of freedom, the power of substance self-realized'[69] – came the abandonment of the medieval possibility of reconciling reason and revelation, so too Fack-enheim recognizes the rejection of the medieval assumptions that made the reconciliation possible. The fundamental medieval assumption, ac-cording to Fackenheim, is the irreducibility of reason to revelation, or *vice versa* – an assumption that leads to 'these additional ones: that rea-son and revelation cover at least in part the same ground; that there is at least some apparent conflict between them; and that the conflict is apparent only – that it can be resolved without violence to either reason or Judaism.'[70] In the medieval reconciliation, the ceremonial laws of

Judaism could be retained as being among those things of the eternal law that are beyond the capacity of human comprehension. Spinoza was forced both to renounce the Jewish ceremonial laws as being external to Hobbes's 'fundamental' religion – that 'Jesus is the Messiah, the Christ'[71] – and also to defend, against Maimonides, the reasonableness of Judaism.[72] Spinoza's Judaism lost its core: revelation as irreducible to reason, and the content of that revelation (i.e., Law).[73]

To illuminate this point, Fackenheim on several occasions[74] contrasts the nature of the modern challenge to its ancient and medieval variants. In *Religious Dimension*, for instance, he summarizes the transition as follows. The rift between thought and life was created in the ancient world, which, since it failed to inform thought with the contingent, destroyed itself.[75] Christ was understood in the medieval world as resolving the rift in principle only; the world was inverted, the world of idea was understood as real, while the contingent was understood as illusory.[76] The modern world is a reversal of the ancient philosophical flight from the world. In the early modern period, in order to reconnect the world of idea with the world of the contingent, the 'Catholic heaven' was redefined as the 'Protestant heart on earth.'[77] This redefinition, by in effect infusing the contingent with the absolute, validates the world of the contingent, the secular world, as a realm of infinite self-confidence.[78] In Fackenheim's view, this radical self-confidence played a role in the Nazis' overreaching of human existence[79] as well as in the failure of many German Jews to recognize the limitations of their participation in German world culture.[80]

The Tension between Philosophy and Revelation in Jewish Philosophy

As in general philosophy, so too the tension between philosophy and revelatory theology exists in Jewish philosophy. The foundational source of the tension is the Bible, which excludes – or attempts to exclude – the bases of philosophy from its theology.[81] God is communicated to be beyond human speech or comprehension: He is transcendent, the Law-Giver and the Creator; He has contravened reason by making something come into being out of nothing. But the images of God in the Bible include characteristics that are comprehensible and admirable to human beings, so that something about God may be communicated and a religion based on Him can be attractive: it is reasonable that human beings should want to have knowledge of Him whom they obey.

This dual loyalty – to obey and to know – is an underlying conflict between philosophy and revelatory theology that emerges in the Jewish philosophical tradition in late antiquity with Philo and in the Middle Ages. Complicating that conflict is the desire to respond to or ameliorate the Jewish political situation.

Modern Jewish thought, like general Western thought, defines a 'history' of the attempt to first separate out revelatory theology from philosophy and then to reintroduce it. The reintroduction was particularly problematic for Jews because the most fundamental biblical prohibition – against idolatry, which implies the Otherness of God – cannot coexist as a *practical* unity with autonomy: theoretically, autonomy and obedience may and do exist in relational tension with each other, but because autonomy presumes the validity of only self-legislation, it is in practical conflict with transcendent legislation.[82]

Because Spinoza alone makes a break with Judaism,[83] his thought introduces the idea of progress to Jews and consequently sets the agenda for all subsequent Jewish thought. His stated goal in writing the *Treatise* is to separate revelatory theology and philosophy in order to establish a universal philosophy. Although the revelatory theology of Judaism differs from that of Christianity in the decisive respect of rejection or acceptance of the Incarnation, Spinoza attempts to construct a secular realm wherein Jews and Christians might unite in thought. On its surface, he denies the Sinaitic revelation by labelling it a form of temporal government exclusively, which, now that the Jewish kingdom has been destroyed, is no longer valid. The text of the Old Testament, while containing within itself true religion is both anachronistic and also purely a particularistic and carnal interpretation of true religion. Judaism, at least ostensibly for Spinoza, is either purely a religion of reason,[84] or alternatively, an empty ritualism unwilling to accept the Incarnation. Likewise the text of the New Testament is interpretation. Yet Christians need not give up belief in the Incarnation: it is precisely the Incarnation that *is* the true religion and that defines Christianity as the 'universal religion.'[85] Because Jesus the Christ no longer reveals himself as a human being, however, Christians are in no better position than Jews to distinguish between true religion and interpretation. Through this ingenious argument, Spinoza is able to argue that Jews and Christians can join forces in the common goal of knowing true religion through the method of biblical criticism.

By replacing traditional with hermeneutical biblical interpretation, Spinoza not only unites Jews and Christians in thought but also attempts to unite them in practice. The form this will take is a modern liberal democracy. Since Judaism, according to his overt argument, has been reduced to a religion of reason, and since democracy is the most reasonable form of government,[86] it is not difficult for Jews to adopt democracy: in order to avoid the problem of serving two masters (as Hobbes puts it), they need only give up the ceremonial laws.[87] Christians, meanwhile, need only recognize that true religion is inscribed on the heart and that in order to be truly pious, they must privatize their religion.[88] Democracy, because it is the most 'natural' form of government and the form of government 'most consonant with individual liberty,'[89] is the best translation of internal religion – God's inscription on the human heart – to external religion – the divine law given the force of human law.[90] By uniting Jews and Christians in a democratic form of government, Spinoza – while establishing a universal realm of thought – can also ameliorate the empirical situation of the Jews.

But two problems emerge from Spinoza's project. First, he does not deny all revelation, but, at least overtly, only revelation as it may appear as part of the historical process. The Sinaitic revelation and the revelations as presented in the Old and New Testaments are discounted as interpretative only of true revelation. But the Incarnation, as a moment that has once entered the human realm but that cannot be built into rites or external signs within the historical process, not only is not overtly denied but rather becomes the overt basis for Spinoza's argument that Christians need to privatize their religion. In Fackenheim's formulation, Spinoza uses Jewish 'Old Testament' revelation to represent the necessity of dismissing all revelation except the revelation that is the very foundation of Christianity. In Fackenheim's historicist or quasi-historicist reading, the unequal use of Old and New Testament revelation and citations, and Spinoza's reconciliation of the teachings of Jesus and Paul with his own philosophy of liberal democracy, translate anti-Jewish bias into the modern liberal state.[91] Strauss argues something more fundamental: Spinoza created the problem of historical consciousness for Jews because the belief in progress that is implicit to Spinoza's biblical criticism is antithetical to the Jewish biblical concept of *t'shuvah*, which presumes that the beginning was 'perfect.'[92]

The second problem to emerge from the project is, more generally, that Spinoza dispenses with the need to provide an explicit philosophical refutation of revelation because the goal of diminishing the power of the medieval Church itself stands for such a refutation. His refutation of revelation consists, Strauss discovers, in his providing a 'clear and distinct account of the whole,' which, by virtue of its being clear and distinct, will be chosen over more obscure accounts, including the biblical account.[93] But this is not a proof: Spinoza presumes the refutation without explicitly providing it.[94]

By adopting Spinoza's exoteric thought – or more precisely, misconstruing or ignoring the political motivation of Spinoza's work – Mendelssohn perpetuates the unfounded presumption. His construction of an encounter between Judaism and philosophy, or revelation and reason, presumes already the superiority of reason. Judaism is therefore fully exposed to philosophy and is already in the inferior position. Mendelssohn adopts Spinoza's model of reason without recognizing that the Spinoza he adopts – because he does not refute reason's greatest adversary revelation – is not, at least ostensibly, fully reasonable. He did not, Strauss might formulate it, understand Spinoza as closely as possible to how Spinoza understood himself. The modern philosophical judgment of Judaism, insofar as it describes a 'progression,' is prejudgment because no refutation of revelation is offered before Judaism subjects itself to philosophical scrutiny.

Hermann Cohen zeroed in on the problem: the conflict between reason and revelation had never been resolved.[95] Cohen attempts to reintroduce traditional Jewish revelation into the modern philosophical project, but his resolution is painfully inadequate: Kant's 'reality' principle[96] is absent. Judaism becomes a 'religion of reason' rather than a living human–God connection in the world. Although he affirms the Jewish understanding of covenant as the guarantee for moral action, only by dissolving the human–God connection can Cohen define the human role as autonomous. The synthesis between philosophy and revelatory theology is possible for Cohen only by ridding Judaism of the relational aspect – between human beings and a living God – of its covenantal theology.

It is at this point in this history of philosophy that a question introduced itself: Can revelatory theology, the formulation of the possibility of encounters with a living God, inform philosophy? And if so, how? Rosenzweig affirms that revelation can inform philosophy through an existential 'leap to life'; yet because his thought begins in philosophy, Strauss sees his teaching as an accommodation of, or concession to, a presumed superior philosophy. Rosenzweig relied on Hegel's transfiguration of history as an 'inquiring' into History as a determinate succession of events whose laws are proper objects of scientific inquiry.

The history of Jewish revelatory experience with the transcendent falls outside those objects of inquiry. And so, as Fackenheim formulates it, Rosenzweig removes Judaism and Jews from 'history.'

With Rosenzweig's historicist exclusion of Jews from 'history' and the modern philosophical project, it now becomes clear that the Western attempt to reintroduce revelatory theology into a philosophy guided by historicism culminated in a specifically post-Christian political philosophy because first, in Jesus, the Creator God of the Universe was united with human being, and second, this now post-Christian stance was the perspective from which the events of 'history' are believed to be defined. The Jewish political situation was not ameliorated, and the 'comprehensive truth' of modern philosophy perpetuates the Christian anti-Jewishness that may have prompted, or at least defined the methodology of, Spinoza's initiation of the project.[97]

The Dead End of Resolving Tension

The synthetic project failed because a fundamental tension exists between traditional philosophy and revelatory theology: while philosophy seeks the life of 'autonomous knowledge,' revelatory theology affirms the life of 'obedient love.'[98] When the successors to Machiavelli, Bacon, Hobbes, and Spinoza failed to recognize that those thinkers wrote esoterically, they initiated a project that ended in historicism, in the 'pit beneath the cave,' a position from which neither the original meaning of history nor the permanence of the tension between reason and revelation can be seen.[99] More broadly, in the realm of general philosophy, the failure of the synthetic project may be traced to the inability of traditional philosophy to be synthesized with any theology but one that identifies divinity with fullness and purity of goodness (a position one can see in both Plato and Kant, indicating the *permanence* of the problem); this, in conjunction with the idea of progress, which suggests that the problem has been – or can be – solved. But if philosophy were to conform to revelatory theology in the latter's own terms – terms that include interpretations of experiences of moments of transcendence – traditional philosophy, as Spinoza argued, would prompt its own destruction by creating the paradox of using reason to prove its own inadequacy.[100] As Strauss writes: 'The knot which was not tied by man could not be untied by man.'[101]

Likewise, the failure of the synthetic project in Jewish thought results from the use of a theology that rationalizes – or as Fackenheim

formulates it, internalizes – God to synthesize revelatory theology and
philosophy. More specifically: in the synthetic project, Jewish revelation is transferred to the realm of idea – as in the thought, for instance,
of the later Hermann Cohen – but the recording of actual Jewish revelatory experience with a transcendent God is precluded. Rosenzweig
reaffirms Jewish revelatory experience, but, because historicist philosophy cannot recognize the permanence of the tension between reason
and revelation, the record of the transcendent revelatory experience
remains outside the realm of 'history' as the modern philosophical
project has defined it. More pressingly for Fackenheim, this exclusion
destroys Jewish revelation because it precludes history as the future
meeting place of Jews and the God of Sinai.

Implicit in Strauss's critique of the modern project of synthesizing
philosophy and revelatory theology is the critique of historical consciousness – specifically, the notion of freedom or progress.[102] It is this
notion that initiated and guided the project, and it is this notion that
perpetuates anti-Jewish animus. Judaism, the oldest of the Western religions, is initially presumed, and continually claimed to be, inferior,
not only to Christianity but now also to political philosophy.[103] Denied
is the concept of t'shuvah by the idea of progress; denied, too, is the attempt to return to Judaism after Spinoza's historical critique, which contains within itself already a break with the concept of t'shuvah. What is
more, the modern idea of progress presumes a concept of universalism
that both precludes the Jewish concept of election and also fosters in
Jews an idealism that is quite at odds with the reality of their social exclusion. Jewish historical consciousness has been a hermeneutic of self-
destruction.

Strauss argues that the modern relationship between philosophy and
revelation in historicist terms results in the obfuscation of the possibilities of both philosophy's eternal (or permanent) verities and religion's
revelation; the consequence of this is a political realm in which tyranny
can flourish and the modern liberal state proves ineffectual to overcome it. Because it has constructed a private realm, the modern liberal
state is unable to rectify, or even address, the issue of Jew hatred. What
is more, the idea of progress, on which the modern liberal state is built,
cannot secularize or succeed Judaism because biblical thought is built
on the ever returning of the human being to God. Jews as Jews continue
to be the targets of state-tolerated hatred. It is vital, therefore, that Jews
not place their trust exclusively in the modern liberal state – that they
keep open the possibility of an unqualified return to orthodoxy, be it in

the philosophic questing of Socrates or within the terms of revelatory theology.

Fackenheim recognizes the problem of the preclusion of both Jews as Jews from the modern liberal state and also of Jews and Judaism from the idea of history at the inception of the modern synthetic project. However, because Judiasm – both biblical and rabbinic – conceives of the relationship between its God and His people as existing within the realm of what he calls flesh-and-blood history, he does not agree with Strauss's argument that historical consciousness – and, when accompanied by the thought that modern thought is superior to the thought of the past, the historicism to which it might lead – be recognized as a modern prejudice that informs, not the eternal truths, but merely the way in which the eternal truths and problems are interpreted in a sequence of philosophic texts.[104] From Fackenheim's perspective, the possibility of the flesh-and-blood Jews encountering the specific God who revealed Himself at Sinai must include recognition of the 'history' into which we have thought ourselves; this is because, to put it simply, flesh-and-blood Jews continued to live during the period of the synthetic project. Fackenheim's primary concern, then, is whether Jewish thought can respond effectively to its exposure to modern (and post-Christian) philosophy.[105] He traces the religious dimension in modern thought in order to expose that its synthesis of philosophy and revelatory theology is not simply a rejection of a revelatory God; rather, it is a development of the Protestant God into thought. He does not argue that modernity continues traditional Protestant theology; he does argue that a specifically anti-Jewish animus is built into modern thought. This occurs on two levels. First, regarding Catholic, Protestant, or Jewish theology: Jewish theology, which denies the Incarnation, becomes representative of a theology that *cannot develop* toward the espousal of a God who is exclusively on earth. Understood another way, one sees, for instance, in Spinoza, ostensibly, that in order to pave the way for a reason autonomously capable of establishing a moral political state, Jews and the Jewish God are eliminated from the historical events that have been defined as the objects of inquiry.[106] This elimination becomes explicit in the thought of Rosenzweig. Second, Judaism exposed itself wholly to philosophy and to the possibility of being part of the modern liberal state; neither Catholicism nor Protestantism did so, nor did they have to. Fackenheim notes, 'Spinoza can hope to free Christians from their prejudices only by appealing to them. And since these include prejudices against Judaism, he resorts to the tactic of making the Jewish elements in Christianity, and more specifically, the "Old Testament, the scapegoat for everything he finds objectionable in actual Christianity." ... Spinoza spiritualizes the Hebrew prophets, thus exempting them from his general strictures against the "carnal" Old Testament, unlike these heirs he attributes to them a morality no less exalted than that of Jesus and the Apostles, and a universality restricted not in quality but only in the accidental scope of their audience ... This is not to say, however, that Jews and Christians must pay an equal price in order to achieve the civic virtue referred to. Christians need only shed their bigotry: they must privatize their religious beliefs insofar as they go beyond the seven dogmas [Spinoza's dogmas of universal faith]. In contrast (since the religion of Moses is a political constitution also, and Jews cannot be members of two nations) Jews must abandon rather than privatize the "ceremonial laws" of Moses that once made them a nation.'[107]

Both Strauss and Fackenheim agree, however, that there is a need for a re-evaluation of Judaism's relationship to philosophy: the philosophical history from Spinoza to Cohen or Rosenzweig is a history of Jewish defeatism. The modern attempt to reincorporate revelation into philosophy – in the work of Rosenzweig or of Heidegger, for instance – continues to cast Judaism as irrational (as a special case of rationality) or worse. In Heidegger, what had defined philosophy – its quest for wisdom and its discovery of the eternal verities – is abandoned, and in this abandonment philosophy begins the process of destroying itself (philosophy is transcended by 'thinking'). Allegedly, revelatory theology gains a voice equal with philosophy only through the self-destruction of both philosophy and revelation. Since Rosenzweig's thought begins in Hegelian philosophy, it is grounded in a theology of supersessionism, a theology from which Jews, because they have been superseded, cannot 'leap to life.' Insofar as the modern project of publicizing philosophy and making it practical was successful, in Rosenzweig's thought the people of the covenant themselves become transcendent, excluded from philosophical inquiry, the history of their events with the transcendent excluded as proper objects of study.

Strauss and Fackenheim: Two Options to Restore Reason and Revelation

Strauss and Fackenheim represent two alternatives by which to restore the authority of reason and revelation and, concomitantly, the tension between them. Since modern historicist philosophy begins by adopting the unreasonable affirmation that philosophy can refute revelation, is the attempt to inform (historicist) philosophy with revelatory theology in principle a failure because it presupposes revelatory theology's inferiority? Strauss argues that it is. Or has historicist philosophy informed history itself, and must it therefore continue, but now qualified by personal knowledge of the possibility of revelation? So argues Fackenheim, who is also aware of its unreasonable basis. Strauss seeks to articulate what would be meant by an unqualified orthodoxy – by which he means a return to the possibility of revelation, to an understanding of the biblical authors as they understood themselves. His purpose in this is to counter the idealistic, at times fanatical, this-worldly messianism that results from beginning one's thought, not in the surface of things, or things as they appear to us, but rather in interpretations of that surface or appearance. By contrast, Fackenheim's return to revelation seeks to incorporate, as the surface of the thing, the singled-out Jewish experience in both its extremes: the Sinaitic revelation, when for an instant all Jews became prophets; and the Holocaust, when for an eternity all Jews became *Muselmaenner*.[108]

Both thinkers recognize the need for a return to the sources from which the tension between reason and revelation arose and were purportedly synthesized. What this means primarily, for both thinkers, is that they extricate themselves from the circle of idealism that has defined modern philosophy. Strauss identifies the adoption of the historical sense as the root of modern idealism because that sense asserts itself as a context prior to the experience of history itself. His critique of this effect indicates to him that, in order for a reader to assess appropriately a text's meaning, he must begin with the surface of the text, which will reveal the context that the text itself establishes. This context may or may not be historically based, but it cannot be presupposed to assume a fully known historical context.

Strauss argues that Westerners might recognize that the vitality of their culture is embedded in the persistent tension between philosophy and revelatory theology and that this tension should be preserved. He dramatizes this vitality in a discussion of Epicureanism and of the battle between reason and revelation waged by Spinoza, characterizing 'atheism' as 'the heir and judge of the belief in revelation, of the secular struggle between belief and unbelief, and finally of the short-lived but by no means therefore inconsequential romantic longing for the lost belief, confronting orthodoxy in complex sophistication formed out of

gratitude, rebellion, longing, and indifference, and in simple probity.'[109]
At an early point, Strauss had argued that Spinoza had not disproved
revelation; yet ultimately, Strauss finds it necessary to return to Maimonides because, by proving that Spinoza had not refuted revelation,
he had proved too much. He had 'effectively insulated any form of orthodoxy (or, we might even say, any explicitly irrational commitment)
from rational criticism.'[110] Again, Strauss suggests that we preserve
reason *and* revelation as the means by which to assure that *each* stops
short of a fanatical teaching. Because philosophy, in its classical form,
derives its meaning from its awareness that it does not comprehend the
whole, the possibility of an unqualified return to Jewish orthodoxy as
the means by which to gain this awareness must remain open if philosophy is to have meaning.[111]

Strauss, in order to break through the circle of idealism that is implicit
in the modern liberal state, attempts to rediscover what ancient philosophers were thinking about the relationship between public or political
thought and (private) philosophy.[112] He draws a distinction between,
in modern terms, political science and political philosophy: the latter
seeks to uncover, not the appropriate laws for the state, but rather the
basis for those laws. So, for instance, Strauss's work on Machiavelli,
Hobbes, and Rousseau suggested to him that the adoption of the osten-
sible denial of revelation without refutation precludes understanding
the state as Plato did (i.e., as an integration of the aims of the few with
the many), rather than, for instance, 'Nietzsche's attempt to synthesize
master and slave morality.'[113] Nietzsche's attempted synthesis denies
the claims of, for instance, both Aristotle's great-souled man and also
Maimonides's prophet; it also leaves the political realm open to both
the tyranny of a demagogue[114] and also the vulnerability of the modern
liberal state.

Fackenheim adopts from Strauss the recognition that political authority is necessary for political thought; but he rejects the possibility of
a context accessible exclusively to human beings as human beings that
can include Jews as Jews.[115] He works within a stance of 'covenantal affirmation'[116] as the source of authority of both philosophic and biblical
texts for Jewish thinkers. At the same time, he recognizes that in order
for the rabbinic tradition to be authoritative in the era of the Holocaust
and 'subjectivist reductionism'[117] – or in order for the rabbinic tradition
to remain accessible to Jews as human beings – secular doubt must be
incorporated into that tradition.[118] What is accessible to Jews as Jews is
no longer, according to Fackenheim, solely the authority of the rabbinic

tradition as it is practised in Jewish life; it now includes also the authority of Jewish existence, which is ever more precarious in the modern world (due to the loss of the possibility of martyrdom in the Holocaust and the accessibility of weapons of mass destruction), but which is also – either as imposed by the Nazis or as self-imposed by the natural sciences[119] – accessible to Jews as Jews. The perpetuation of the rabbinic tradition calls for a reassessment of the political authority within which the rabbis wrote and within which Jews read.

The most obvious difference between Strauss and Fackenheim is their choice of project. Strauss worked on decidedly Jewish thinkers – for instance, on Mendelssohn and Cohen – but he carried out that work primarily while employed at the *Akademie für die Wissenschaft des Judentums*. After leaving Germany in 1932, he wrote almost exclusively in the field of political philosophy.[120] Fackenheim's project, while beginning in the surface of things, on the level of political authority, is to provide a means by which to perpetuate the rabbinic tradition and the possibility of a revelation of the Sinaitic God as a reality. The problem with adopting Strauss's return to the surface of texts is that for Fackenheim the claims of revelation include historical consciousness, and this must include (though not exclusively) the historical consciousness that modern thought has largely adopted historicism.[121] So, for instance, he understands Hegel as preserving the separate claims of reason and revelation insofar as Hegel sought to synthesize not all of reality, but only the philosophic concern for eternity with the religious concern for history.[122] Strauss ironically suggests that 'Hegel's synthesis of classical and Biblical morality effects the miracle of producing an amazingly lax morality out of two moralities both of which made very strict demands on self-restraint.'[123] The fundamental difference between these two thinkers seems to concern the proper understanding of 'history.' When one compares them on their positions with regard to historicism, one must bear in mind that Strauss works outside, and Fackenheim works within, a stance of covenantal affirmation.[124]

This book explores the similarities and differences between Strauss and Fackenheim in their attempts to address the issue of the modern misappropriation of revelation by reason and to redirect (future) thought. For both thinkers, a reassessment is required: for the one, a reassessment of the great philosophic texts of the past within their political contexts; for the other, a reassessment of the relationship between the great texts of philosophy and of religion and their political results. The similarities between these two thinks are their diagnosis of the problems of modern philosophy, their recognition of the mutual ir-refutability of reason and revelation, and, perhaps also important, that each was a German Holocaust refugee who eventually settled in North America[125] Both thinkers recognize the possibility that political weakness is built into the modern liberal state, and both deny that it is appropriate to include commitment – in Heidegger's sense of the term – as a basis of philosophical thought. Strauss argues that modern thought should recognize that historicism – and the idealism that grows out of it – may be only a prejudice. Without necessarily affirming that it is possible, he argues that it may be possible to return to philosophy that is not based on historical consciousness, beginning with a history of philosophy as the tool through which we come to see our prejudice. Fackenheim, for his part, argues that such a return is neither possible nor desirable: instead, philosophy must question the existence of its permanent verities in order to confront the Holocaust, and revelatory theology must accept historical consciousness in order to provide a means to affirm both the continued existence of the Sinaitic God and also the possibility of God's presence in history after the Holocaust.

Strauss bases his political philosophy on natural necessity rather than revelatory religion; Fackenheim bases his new theology on the religio-secularism of Hegel.[126] Each thinker, however, recognizes the necessity of a theoretic openness to both philosophy and revelatory theology.[127] So, for instance, the central chapter of Strauss's last book, published posthumously, is an essay on the Bible reworked through Plato, 'Jerusalem and Athens.'[128] While Strauss makes the practical choice of philosophy, the philosophy he chooses is that of Plato, which recognizes itself as having been born from its separation from myth, and which, while seeking knowledge of the whole, acknowledges its perpetual inadequacy in achieving it. His philosophy has a fundamental commitment to revelatory theology as a means by which to recognize the ultimate limits of philosophic knowledge; that commitment, however, in no way forces a synthesis with revelatory theology. Fackenheim's new thinking, while based in revelation, is open both to philosophic and historical scrutiny.

For Strauss, the return to (or rediscovery of) Plato signals the rejection of historicism and an understanding of God as the Good. Fackenheim rejects this position because Plato's God, in its exclusive concern with eternity, denies the existence of both holiness and unholiness. Only knowledge attained in the sight of God can 'prove' God's existence; and, what is more, in its 'proof,' it fights evil rather than simply

discounting it as unreal.[129] Fackenheim accepts this qualified historicism as philosophically, theologically, and ethically mandated after the
Holocaust.[130] For him, the confrontation between revelatory theology
and philosophy is the confrontation between Buber-Rosenzweig and
Hegel: the former theology is open already to philosophic autonomous
interpretation, the latter philosophy is open already to the actuality of
revelation in history. One might, in short, address the differences between Strauss and Fackenheim as the differences between Plato and
Hegel, each of whom took seriously both God and philosophy.[131]

   Fackenheim argues that a synthesis – this time between philosophy
and a specifically Jewish theology – can be accomplished in a theology
based in the new thinking. Philosophy should be informed by personal
knowledge of the possibility of revelation as a general principle. By
joining philosophy with a covenantal theology, the whole truth, as it
were, can be understood in and as moments of experience. In addition,
a 'new' Judaism, one that begins in history, with the Jewish people,
and that includes both non-believers and believers, must be forged in
the wake of the Holocaust – a strategy whose precedence Fackenheim
takes from the ancient rabbis, who, in the wake of the Destruction of the
Second Temple forged a 'new' (rabbinic) Judaism. For Jews to 'return
into history,' they must bring their theology to practical life through the
filter of philosophy. This requires the input of all Jews: since, despite
the introduction of the new science, and after the Holocaust, Jews know
themselves to be defined as Jews regardless of belief or non-belief, post-
Holocaust Judaism is religio-secular and must include both revelatory
theology and philosophy. Because in any moment of lived experience,
human beings and their knowledge are not partial, because 'the intrinsic value of human personality ... is ... forever regiven and reappro-
priated,'[132] Fackenheim finds in a theologico-philosophy the means by
which to receive and accept the only knowledge that is of value: the full
openness of the integrated human being to accept God's love. By recognizing the informing of thought with historical experience, which establishes the partiality of knowledge at any given moment, Fackenheim
argues that philosophy and revelatory theology may be synthesized
with an openness to a necessarily informed and ethical future.

   The historical realm becomes for Fackenheim the realm in which philosophy and revelatory theology may be synthesized, each retaining its
own terms. Yet he argues that Jews cannot follow the modern Western
philosophical model of synthesis: the conforming of revelatory theology to philosophy begins a process of secularization that, because it is

an internalization of God – or, alternatively, because it does not recognize the singled-out condition of Jewish existence – is specifically post-Christian. In its finest moment in Hegel, according to Fackenheim, the synthetic project fails because, to borrow a phrase from Yeats, 'the centre cannot hold':[133] Hegel's dialectic cannot sustain the simultaneity of the human being–God / God–human being relationship. Fackenheim argues that by returning to Hegel and reinvesting his thought with the Jewish concept of covenant – with a theology built on the enduring tension of the relationship between the immanent and the transcendent – one can successfully synthesize ('put or place together') philosophy and revelatory theology. Philosophy is thereby preserved as a continual quest; the historical realm and theology are informed with transcendence; and the construction of a post-Jewish (i.e., post-Holocaust) Judaism is begun.

For Fackenheim, Jews need secularism as a means of witnessing, against Hegel and against Hitler, to the Jewish presence *in* history, not simply above history.[134] For him, an intimate connection exists between reality and experience: the political realm shapes reality. Hitler, therefore, was not simply another demagogue, but rather a particular and profoundly unique instance of the reality of radical evil. The return to either Greek philosophy or traditional Jewish theology is equally problematic: the awareness of the 'ruptures' in both philosophy and revelatory theology created by historical consciousness and the brokenness of the covenant experienced through the Holocaust have together forced human consciousness into empirical, immanent history. Fackenheim argues that if we are to preserve both the meaningfulness of philosophy as relevant to current human experience and also the immediacy of a relationship with God, we must recognize the possibility of their syntheses in moments of empirical history. For him, the only means by which post-Holocaust Jewish theology can persist is through a philosophical, systematic and 'unfanatical'[135] affirmation of its continuity from the Sinaitic revelation *and also* its theological affirmation of the possibility of that same God's present action in history.

Along these lines, one may suggest that, while Strauss's primary concern was to preserve philosophy from the vagaries of politics, Fackenheim's was to preserve Jewish faith amidst the trauma of the disaster. This, however, would be a simplification. Strauss remarks of Spinoza that he sells his ancient birthright for a mess of modern pottage. One need, in addition, only consider the number of scholarly books and articles devoted to assessing Strauss's relationship to, and concern for, the survival of Judaism.[136] And one must, when reading Fackenheim's work – even what one would consider to be exclusively his theology – remain constantly aware of the great philosophical mind that infuses his teachings and of his attempt to establish a framework that defines the continuity between pre- and post-Holocaust Jewish thought. Yet it seems clear that Strauss's primary concern was to teach philosophy in such a way that his students might discover, by thinking it through for themselves, what great thinkers and scholars have written and said.[137] This discovering safeguards philosophy, and revelation as well, from the inadequacies of the modern liberal state – indeed, any state. Fackenheim is more obviously concerned with the reformulation of revelatory theology in such a way that modern human beings can, despite the devastating critique of it, honestly believe in it and live in accordance with it. While it would be untrue to argue that his desire to preserve Judaism after the Holocaust is but a specialized case of his desire to preserve revelation for all modern believers, still, one detects in his later focus on Christian–Jewish relations strands of that as well[138]: the survival of Judaism within the modern secular state requires, at least in part, the reaffirmation of the mystery of Christianity's traditional revelation.

What Strauss labels the political naivety of the modern liberal state, Fackenheim traces to its post-Christianity,[139] to Hegel's inability to account for the contingent in terms of the contingent, or to Heidegger's denial of the one eternal standard of idolatry or, more generally, his unwillingness to differentiate among gods.[140]

PART III. DEVELOPMENT OF ARGUMENT IN CHAPTER FORM

Overview of Book in Chapter Form

The book began with a brief overview of the tension between philosophy and revelatory theology in Western thought. After establishing the tension's roots in Plato, the book proceeded directly to the Western philosophical context of Strauss and Fackenheim's thought. It then presented a brief overview of the tension in modern Jewish thought, from Spinoza to Rosenzweig. This overview suggests that the inherent tension between philosophy and revelatory theology cannot be resolved and that attempts to do so in the modern period have destroyed the foundations of both philosophy – its beginning in doubt and wonder – and revelatory theology – the obeying of an Other Who prescribes human action.

Chapters 2 and 3 will explore how Strauss and Fackenheim respectively formulate the crisis of modernity. Chapter 2 will analyse Strauss's position in depth by focusing on his thought regarding individual thinkers: first, general Western thought, including the ancients, Machiavelli, Hobbes, and Heidegger; and then Jewish thought, including the Bible, Spinoza, Cohen, and Rosenzweig. Strauss traces the development of the crisis in order to provide the tools by which we might extricate ourselves from historicist thought. The adoption of these tools is a temporary measure, to be abandoned once thought can return to Plato's original cave. Strauss's history of philosophy might begin in the Christian medieval synthesis of philosophy and revelatory theology, which placed philosophy under ecclesiastical authority. Machiavelli and Hobbes (and Spinoza) rebel against authority in the name of philosophy but are not free to do so openly. They adopt, yet also revolutionize, the art of esoteric writing in order to preserve for the masses the political stability that issues from the public adoption of natural theology. What existed with the ancients as the private sphere of philosophy – in dialectical relationship with the public sphere of political philosophy – was disseminated to the public in early modernity as the means by which to overthrow ecclesiastical authority. The problem, however, became critical when the art of esoteric writing was lost; the victory over ecclesiastical authority accomplished by the early moderns was misunderstood to be a victory over revelation itself, and the permanence of the problem of the mutual irrefutability of reason and revelation was obfuscated.

Strauss traces the crisis to the rise of secular atheism, as opposed to pre-modern disbelief, which used esoteric writing to preserve religious categories as the means of sustaining political harmony, as in the work of Machiavelli, Hobbes, and Spinoza.[141] This particularly modern form of disbelief led to the recognition that one could, in Bacon's terms, conquer nature.[142] Since it is progressive – since it builds toward ever more comprehensive knowledge – the new science by which to conquer nature abandons guiding standards for ethical action. From this recognition, the fateful step into historicism – a step that replaced the 'delusion' of pre-modern religious belief with the delusion of modern idealistic belief – was made. Furthermore, for instance, Dilthey's distinction between human and natural sciences gave rise to the human being as subject matter of inquiry. The shift in perspective destroyed values, replacing them with 'facts,' from which it became impossible to extricate one's thought.[143] As Deutsch and Nicgorski formulate it, citing Strauss:

The modern unbelief effected by Hobbes, Machiavelli, and Spinoza led to 'the epoch making change' of 'political atheism.' Such political atheists have 'grown active, designing, turbulent and seditious.' Premodern atheists never 'doubted that social life required belief in, and worship of God, or gods.' According to Strauss, modern unbelief – by undermining those comforting 'religious delusions' – leads to the recognition that human beings can become 'the master and owner of nature. But this whole enterprise requires, above all, political action, revolution, a life and death struggle.'[144]

The seditiousness of the modern political atheists is the exoteric dissemination of philosophy – a dissemination that undermines the authority of religion and thus political stability. In this light, as will be discussed in chapter 5, the question of Strauss's defence of revelation, or of revelatory Judaism, takes on an added dimension: Is that defence inspired by a belief in the possibility of revelation, or is it an esoteric device meant both to preserve political stability and also to curtail philosophy's self-destruction?

Chapter 3 will analyse in depth Fackenheim's position by focusing on his thought regarding individual thinkers: first, Western thought, including Kant, Hegel, Schelling, and Heidegger; and then Jewish thought, including the Bible, Spinoza, Rosenzweig, and Buber. The chapter will trace the means by which Fackenheim concludes that the attempt to synthesize philosophy and revelatory theology has been a failure, and his consequent argument that thought – both philosophical and religious – may ground itself in 'history' as a means of both bringing unity to the thinker and also of retaining the integrity of each philosophy and revelatory theology. Fackenheim's work as a philosopher is a continuation – or theological correction – of Hegelian thought, while his work as a theologian continues the work of Buber, affirming the necessity of informing revelatory theology with philosophic thought. For Fackenheim, the synthesis of philosophy and revelatory theology remains dialectical; each is open to the other *through* time but exclusive of the other *in* any given moment. While affirming the necessity of philosophic systems in order to avoid the problem of what Bacon called heretical religion, or revelatory self-validation, Fackenheim affirms also the priority of historical experience to any system of thought. Both philosophy and revelatory theology are necessary to allow the Jewish God – Who once revealed His Laws – to be recognized – should He command again in the present – as the Sinaitic God.

Fackenheim's work addresses the contemporary crisis of faith. This crisis is a result of arguments springing from the advent of modern science and the lack of hierarchy in the universe that destroys of values.[145] Both arguments, he contends, are mistaken because empirical fact cannot refute faith since it is qualitatively different from faith. He argues that faith has been undermined for two reasons. First, because modernity has demonstrated that religious authority can be accepted only by one who has faith already, modern thinkers have recognized the circularity involved in thinking about faith. Second, faith has been dismissed through the method of 'subjectivist reductionism,' which is itself based on an *a priori* philosophical argument and not on empirical evidence. In subjectivist reductionism, first faith is redefined as a feeling of standing in relation with God, from which one infers that there is a God. Then, using either the logic of Ockham's razor or Kant's delegitimization of moving from natural effect to supernatural cause, the inferred God is dismissed as unnecessary and unwanted. God, through this process, is redefined as an unconscious projection.[146] Fackenheim concludes that subjectivist reductionism is a philosophically invalid argument, and further that, when one redefines the question whether an Other exists to knowledge of Who He is, one's subjectivist reductionism is a 'subjectivist prison.'[147]

The crisis of modernity reaches its apex in the modern doctrine of historicism. What was begun in Machiavelli, who, by arguing for human freedom, laid the foundation for the idea of history, was developed to its height by Heidegger, who argued that human freedom extends to human self-creation. Because the fundamental disagreement between Strauss and Fackenheim relates to whether historicism should be rejected or adopted, chapter 4 will compare their positions with regard to historicism. This comparison will emerge through close readings of Strauss's 'Natural Right and the Historical Approach' and two essays by Fackenheim: 'Metaphysics and Historicity' (written specifically in response to Strauss's challenge) and, more briefly, 'Judaism and the Meaning of Life.' For Strauss, the acceptance of any form of historicism obscures the validity of both the eternal (or perhaps merely permanent) verities of philosophy and the revelation of biblical religion. For Fackenheim, only by philosophically validating a theology that includes revelatory transcendence, or by somehow uniting philosophy with such a theology, can the specifically Jewish return into history be validated. In chapter 4, I could only point to Fackenheim's later work on the Holocaust and Christian–Jewish relations.[148] Instead, I focus on his thought on historicism because in that thought, one sees Strauss's strongest influence on Fackenheim. This influence includes Fackenheim's formulation of the problem of authority: the uncritical or dogmatic acceptance of liberalism – and of historicism in particular – has led to the loss of common sense. What is more, the acceptance of historicism has, according to Strauss, induced a blindness from which its adherents cannot escape – that is, a blindness both to the meaning of a given philosophical text and also to the contextual authority in which the text arose. Strauss seeks to understand the distinct claims of the two bases of Western thought, reason and revelation, and Fackenheim follows this path. But for Fackenheim, the return to reason and revelation must be undertaken within a stance of 'covenantal affirmation.'[149]

Both Strauss and Fackenheim recognize, to put it in the simplest terms, that the modern crisis in philosophy stems from the lack of a definite standard by which to judge morality. At the same time, both thinkers recognize that there is a risk to reaffirming a definite standard; such an affirmation can (and did) lead to political tyranny.[150] As will be discussed in chapters 4 and 5, while each seeks to discover a root for thought, also each recognizes that it is ultimately beyond human comprehension: the standard is the living of the right way of life. While Strauss makes the *practical* choice of philosophy, and Fackenheim chooses to begin his thinking from within the stance of covenantal affirmation, each thinker recognizes the ultimate insufficiency of his results. Furthermore, as a consequence of this ultimate insufficiency, Strauss's rejection of historicism is qualified by the contemporary need to, as he puts it, ascend from the pit beneath philosophy's original cave – that is to say, the need to engage in historical studies as the tool by which to critique historicism; for his own part, Fackenheim's return to Judaism is a return to a stance of relationship that may or may not involve God and commandment.

Chapter 5 will discuss the conclusion reached by both Strauss and Fackenheim that to adequately represent human experience and knowledge, one must be open in a fundamental way to the alternative position. Again, Strauss seeks to suggest that the secret of continued Western vitality lies in our maintaining the tension between philosophy and revelatory theology.[151] Fackenheim's primary goal is to resolve Rosenzweig's dilemma – which is, to philosophically validate the 'return' of Jews into history. He understands the failure of the modern project as the loss of openness in favour of systems of thought: because, unlike medieval thought, modern thought does not take seriously revealed authority, modern thought may (seemingly) lay claim to comprehensiveness. At the same time, empirical history refutes this comprehensiveness and refutes the validity of philosophical systems. Modern thought must understand itself as fragmented, must renounce its claim to comprehensiveness.[152]

Chapter 5 will explore the precise nature of the relationship between reason and revelation, or Athens and Jerusalem, as Strauss understands. it. While he recognizes the practical necessity of choosing one or the other as the means to the right way of life, he discovers the common ground of Greek philosophy and the Bible as a theoretic reality: both strive to inform one's life with justice. Next, the chapter will explore some of the reasons that Fackenheim rejects what he understands as Strauss's return to Plato as well as some of the results of beginning with Fackenheim's position. For Strauss, the means by which to rediscover the validity of philosophy – and, concomitantly, of revelatory theology – is to establish it as in tension with the practical application of government. But to Fackenheim, Strauss's resolution evades the import of the Holocaust, or more generally, the problem of evil. Because, on the one hand, normative Judaism brings thought into historical application – or alternatively, does not separate faith from action – and on the other, history informs Jewish thinking, Fackenheim concludes that modern Jewish thought must encounter and confront the Holocaust in order to remain valid. Accordingly, philosophy and/or revelatory theology cannot be made distinct from human action, or indeed from governmental action.

The book will conclude with a brief statement of the present writer's position. I will suggest that, while Strauss's Jewish thought – as indeed all Jewish thought – should be included in the reconstruction of Jewish categories, Fackenheim's model of committed openness, notwithstanding the criticisms levelled against it, is the model better suited for Jewish thought – indeed, Strauss himself suggests this[153] – at least for the moment. Paradoxically, it may be that, if Fackenheim's project were to succeed – if he were to sustain Jewish faith through this moment in history – it would be possible for Jews to rediscover a theoretic model more closely resembling Strauss's.

Strauss and Fackenheim: A Note on Methodology

Each thinker, Strauss and Fackenheim, before addressing the difficult relationship between philosophy and revelation in modern thought, explores the roots of the relationship in medieval thought. The exploration is necessary in order to disentangle the one from the other in modern thought – or at any rate, to uncover alternative ways of bringing into relationship reason and revelation. Furthermore, the undertaking of the exploration suggested implicitly each thinker's belief that one must reassess old texts, subjecting them to careful and perhaps new interpretations, in order to recognize the roots of the results of the relationship. For Strauss, one must read the text not with *more* understanding than their original authors, but rather, as far as possible, with the *same* understanding.

My discussion of Strauss's readings of various thinkers in chapter 2 of this book is fraught with difficulties. First, Strauss writes both subtly and densely. In addition, he often writes as though in internal dialogue with and about the thinkers with whom he is engaged. Disentangling his thought from the thought of the thinker about whom he writes is therefore a challenge. But I do not believe that he is unaware of this challenge: one cannot separate Strauss's thought from the thought of his subject without approaching the subject independently of Strauss. He is suggesting to his readers that each of us approach these great thinkers independently, not *through* his thought. Paradoxically, in order to read according to Strauss's teaching, one must read independently of Strauss's interpretations. This paradox becomes obvious when one accepts as a starting point the need to read texts as though their writers were speaking between the lines, so to speak, of their words, and also when Strauss himself insists on this method of reading when one approaches his own texts. Strauss teaches by example.[154]

In addition, Strauss's work is an intellectual journey, marked by the ability to read texts more and more 'literally.'[155] To read literally is to ground oneself in an understanding of the political (in the broadest sense of the word) context in which the author wrote. By reading literally, in Strauss's sense, one eliminates, or hopes to eliminate, not only the contingent garb in which the permanent philosophical problems appear, but also any vestiges of the specifically modern form of idealism, which, as a matter of *fact*, is a development from the modern prejudice in favour of historical consciousness. In this regard, Strauss discovers that 'the problem inherent in the surface of things is the heart of things.'[156] His famous discovery of esoteric writing is a reflection of the profound literalism that he learned to identify in the authors he read.

Fackenheim recognizes that the course taken by modern philosophy has been disastrous: modern philosophy, by internalizing revelation, leads to the possibility of radical evil, evil beyond the restraints of natural or biblical law.[157] So, for instance, the Holocaust demonstrated to him that human nature can be unfixed from all rational boundaries, can be altered to indicate senseless destruction, both of self and of other, while so too transgressions of the biblical law against idolatry can take on new, modern forms. He disagrees with Strauss, however, about the appropriate remedy. For him, the return to pre-modern thinking, or the 'old thinking, would make the Holocaust humanly intelligible, and this intelligibility would perpetuate the modern faith in reason and allow thought to remain immune to the reality of the Holocaust's unique evil. As we shall see in chapter 3, Fackenheim reads the texts in the light of the new thinking: with a recognition that the only means by which to save philosophy from the effects of its internalization of revelation is by reading texts *both* systematically *and* from the unique personal and historical vantage point of the reader.[158] While Strauss argues for reading texts as far as possible with the same understanding as their authors, Fackenheim argues for reading texts retrospectively: as we read, we must remain aware that we are encountering texts as post-Holocaust Jews and Christians,[159] committed not to philosophy but to the historical dimensions and implications of our beliefs.

In response to modern philosophy's dismissal of Judaism as a valid source of religious inspiration, Fackenheim attempts to reveal the partiality of modern thought by putting it into dialogue with Judaism. His position will undergo a transition between his early and later thought, a transition that reflects a (seeming) reversal of his position: a movement away from grounding his theological thought in philosophy and philosophical discourse toward basing his philosophical thought in theology. The transition will be occasioned by his insight that, because thought and action are integrated when philosophy and revelatory theology are integrated, thought itself has consequences. One's thought must be guided by ethical action. Ideas alone can neither reveal nor inform truth.

2 Strauss's Formulation of the Relationship between Reason and Revelation in Modern Thought and His Rejection of a Practical Synthesis

Introduction

> 'Do you know?' he continued, again diverging from the point, 'our provincial institutions put me in mind of the little sprigs of birch we stick into the ground on Trinity Sunday and make believe that it is a real European forest. I have no faith in these sprigs and cannot for the life of me water them.'[1]

The methodology of reading is of paramount importance to Strauss: for readers to extricate themselves from the delusion created by the acceptance of the modern idea of history, they must learn to read with the greatest of attention to the surface of the text. But as Janssens points out, Strauss, and the writers on whose texts he wrote, were aware that 'not all readers are equally thoughtful, perspicacious, patient, and learned.'[2] Consequently, he could not, he indicated, provide adequate interpretations of the texts he studied, which would require of the reader protracted and first-hand study, taking, perhaps, a lifetime, but could only point to the initial steps to a more adequate interpretation.[3] He argues that one must read according to the terms that the thinkers themselves assign. For instance, Spinoza based his argument on historical conditions, therefore to understand his proposal for the solution of the problem of Jewish exile, one must understand his historical circumstances. Reading, then, partly involves discovering those terms, and it is complicated by the fact that in ancient philosophy those terms are non-historicist, whereas in later modern philosophy, they are often not. Only through learning to read again may modern thinkers begin the process of freeing themselves from the modern historical prejudice – that they understand pre-modern writers better than those writers understood themselves – and attempt to address again the permanent problems. Strauss reads the great thinkers of the past – ancient, medieval, and early modern – to investigate how they address the theologico-political problem, a problem that is permanent and that had gripped him at an early age.[4]

It was through the idea of history that modern thinkers came to believe they had resolved the theologico-political problem. This chapter explores the break between the ancients and the moderns that Strauss sees as the foundation for this idea. The first part of the chapter explores his thought on Western philosophy, beginning with Greek philosophy, which, he discovers, provides an ideal – justice – by which to guide philosophy as well as a context for that ideal within the practical aspect of the state. The chapter then proceeds to account for the break itself, beginning with the writings of Machiavelli and Hobbes. These thinkers (among others) attempted to carve out an atheistic realm in which the state might operate separate from ecclesiastical authority. The success of their enterprise, however, was not recognized: their victory over ecclesiastical authority was taken to indicate the victory of reason over revelation itself.

Strauss traces the mistake to the loss of the art of esoteric writing. With careful attention to the surface of philosophical texts, he is able to recognize in certain pre-modern and early modern thinkers the distinction between their 'political' philosophy – that is, their exoteric speech, intended to preserve the social order – and their esoteric speech, which is intended to claim for philosophy freedom from religious authority.[5] By recapturing the art of esoteric writing – by becoming readers good enough to recognize that Machiavelli and Hobbes, for instance, wrote esoterically – it becomes possible for us to recognize that modern philosophy's claim that it has refuted revelation is unsubstantiated. Furthermore, doing so frees philosophy, understood as the private quest for the right way of life, from the authority of the public sphere – even as it enables philosophers to uphold the laws of the state. Strauss argues for a rereading of the works of Machiavelli, Hobbes, and Spinoza in order that we may recognize, in their conception of the need for esoteric writing (subsequently lost), their recognition of the permanent problem of the mutual irrefutability, and mutual dependence, of reason and revelation.

The loss of esoteric writing was initiated by Machiavelli, who revealed the content of the esoteric as, not the hidden knowledge of the ancients that their utopia both should be sought and also is unrealizable, but rather, solely that it is unrealizable. As if revealing the secret wisdom of the Greeks, Machiavelli reveals only that part of their wisdom which is effectual; he also contradicts himself by denying the authority of human aspiration, which grounds their wisdom's effectuality. The successors to Machiavelli and Hobbes did not recognize that Hobbes wrote esoterically because these successors, having claimed victory over ecclesiastical authority, no longer required esoteric writing. Not only was reason thus made irrational, insofar as it based itself on the irrational assertion that it had disproved revelation, but also this irrational reason was publicly disseminated. The romantic longing to reincorporate revelation into reason reached its apex in Heidegger, who is the thinker treated next in this chapter. The result was a radical historicism in which Being took on the attributes of the biblical God. Even so, Heidegger is important to Strauss's work because, like him, Heidegger recognized that the conception of a tradition of philosophy must be reinvestigated.

One might include Spinoza in the development of this modern break. Hobbes remarked that Spinoza's work, though along similar lines of thought, was far more overt than his. However, I have included Spinoza in the second part of this chapter, 'Strauss on Jewish Philosophy' because Strauss considers Spinoza's work to be in the tradition of Maimonides. This is not to say that he considered Spinoza a good Jew – he did not – but Spinoza's work establishes the context for all subsequent Jewish thought. More specifically, if we are to rediscover the possibility of revelation, Spinoza must be proved wrong in every respect. Strauss reads the Bible in order to discover in it, not its interpretations of revelation, but rather, through these interpretations, revelation itself. Revelation itself, in the orthodox view, is unqualified by modern historicism, modern attempts to synthesize reason and revelation, and subsequent critiques of this synthesis; therefore this view can give access to how the biblical authors understood themselves. With the rediscovery of the possibility, and the authority, of revelation, Strauss addresses the thought of his immediate predecessors, Cohen and Rosenzweig. In Cohen, Strauss identifies an idealism from which Cohen could not break, an idealism implicit in much modern philosophy; in Rosenzweig, he identifies an attempt to inform reason with the non-rational. Both thinkers, in his account, were unable to break through the circle of idealism because they did not read literally enough: one may ascend to the ideal, but only if one holds fast to the surface of things within which the idea was suggested. As Strauss writes: 'The problem inherent in the surface of things, and only in the surface of things, is the heart of things.'[6]

Strauss on the Ancient Philosophers

Strauss's thought moves from the medieval thinkers to the ancients. From this return, he seeks to draw inspiration for his critique of modern philosophy generally, and, more specifically, for his critique of the hermeneutics that arise from the historicist viewpoint.[7] His chief aim is to understand thinkers, ancient and modern, in their own terms; his battle is against a dogmatically thoughtless acceptance of the doctrines of any thinker, ancient or modern. In modern times, however, the thoughtless acceptance of modern doctrines is obviously more pre-eminent, more obviously calling for criticism. His return to the 'dusty old books' of the ancients resulted in the rediscovery of both classic natural right and also the art of esoteric writing. Yet the confirmation of his discovery of the long tradition of esoteric writing reveals to Strauss a paradox at the heart of classic natural right:[8] on the one hand, the quest for wisdom is essentially a private matter that must be safeguarded from public dogma or societal convention; on the other, public dogma or societal convention must be safeguarded from the political instability that can result from the dissemination of philosophy. The use of esoteric writing enables the preservation of a right deemed superior to the positive rights of any state, even as it is recognizes that this private right depends on the rights of the state for its existence. The modern loss of the art of esoteric writing resulted in the loss of this paradox at the heart of philosophy and the loss of a proper understanding of philosophy itself.

Strauss understands ancient philosophy as a quest:[9] human beings both dwell in the particulars and also have within themselves innate excellence; according to Plato, human beings can, by their own efforts, seek wisdom. Yet at the same time, ideas for Plato have an independent existence that is ultimately separate from any possible human *qua* human achievement. The ascertainment of wisdom is eternally beyond human possibility. Plato offers not simply an intellectual explanation or depiction of reality, but – more important to Strauss – a means of life: by living in the pursuit of wisdom, one lives in pursuit of the good. Ancient philosophy offers ethics that are alternative to what is offered by biblical religion,[10] and one may privately question the value of the religious tradition even as one continues to live a life of right action.

Strauss acknowledges that it is difficult to recognize that ideas as such may have an independent existence. Nevertheless, Plato, he argues, may teach us that ideas, though not eternal, are *permanently* connected to political circumstances, just as they were for him. Throughout the philosophical tradition, ideas are never simply ideas pure and simple; rather, the philosophical expressions of ideas exist forever bound to the political circumstances that gave rise to them and that also may have constrained their exposure. It seems that the permanent human problem is this: ideas are bound to political or religious exigency, or to the surface of things,[11] knowledge of which is accessible to every human being *qua* human being; yet at the same time, ideas suggest within themselves the possibility of an ascension from this surface of things, to a realm of permanent existence.[12] Strauss argues that, though a return to Plato may not be possible, there may exist an independent standard that can reveal, if not the eternal, then at least the permanent human condition. This standard is conveyed through the art of esoteric writing.

Strauss traces the emergence of philosophy to the discovery of nature. In its pre-philosophic conception, nature is understood as custom or way, which, by virtue of its dominance over political life, carries with it authority. He points out that authority is consequently pre-decided in favour of a particular custom or way. Because authority is bestowed on one's own customs, the ancestral becomes equated with the good and thus becomes either confused with the gods or identified with students of the gods. From this extrapolation, authority came to be conceived as resting in divine law. In Strauss's account, belief in revelation's authority determines, in the pre-philosophical mind, belief in revelation.

When the ancients discovered nature, they were able to free themselves from basing their ideas on authority. In a point that is important to his conception of ancient philosophy, Strauss emphasizes that the ancients' discovery of nature is not the discovery of nature as either an idea or a totality.[13] Rather, the original form of the discovery of nature is as the separation of phenomena that are natural from those that are not. Were the ancient philosophical conception of nature an *idea*, the ancient philosophers would have remained bound to the conclusion that authority determines the good. Only when authority is doubted can philosophical thought begin.[14] This doubt must take place apart from rulers and gods, and Strauss provides examples from Plato – written by Plato esoterically – to point to the emergence of the esoteric writing of philosophy.[15] While philosophy emerges as the quest for beginnings, conducted in private, and both antagonistic to and dependent on the state, revelatory theology is associated by Strauss with authority, is affirmed and enacted in full public view, and is both antagonistic and open to philosophy. Strauss argues for the necessity of both the privacy of philosophical thinking and also the authoritative and passion-breeding opinions in support of the law of the state.[16] The source of the development of the art of esoteric writing is the tension between philosophy and the state, or reason and revelatory theology.

Strauss argues that to rediscover the philosophic thought of the ancients and the 'common sense'[17] that guided their thinking, modern philosophy must begin by doubting authority: both its own authority and the authority of revelatory theology. Only when authority is doubted can nature in its original form as phenomena, as the surface of things, be discovered; only when nature in its original form is discovered can philosophic thought return to Plato's cave from the deep pit of historicism beneath the cave. Because modern thought has tended to synthesize philosophy and revelatory theology, Strauss's goal – like Spinoza's – is to return to a model wherein the two remain in tension and mutually interdependent in their tension.[18]

Strauss's discovery of Socrates's return, from its extrapolation, to the political itself, provides him with the means by which to counter revelation with philosophical doubt – not doubt of revelation *per se*, but rather doubt of the primacy of one's own customs.[19] So, for instance, to understand Plato or Aristotle, a modern thinker must understand, not their solutions to permanent problems, but rather the problems as they saw them. To understand the relationship between practical and speculative wisdom in Aristotle's thought, one does not too quickly accept his reconciliation of the two as ultimately one human end. Rather, the modern philosopher must ponder the very real problem that Aristotle faced: What is the relationship between the practical life and the speculative life? What is the relationship between doing good acts and being good? Only by beginning with his *problem*, and not with his *solution*, can we avoid being led astray by authority and can we think philosophically.

According to Strauss, Socrates was the founder of the classic natural right doctrine.[20] This doctrine was in turn developed by Plato and, with variations,[21] by Aristotle, the Stoics, and Thomas Aquinas.[22] Socrates's founding of his natural right doctrine was accomplished by introducing a new approach to understanding the permanent problems: instead of reducing human things to natural or divine things, he focuses on human things as the result of a process. This focus supplies information about both the permanent problems for human beings, what is first for us, and also the process itself from which the human things arose.[23] He proposes beginning with human things *as they appear to us*.[24] Neither nature as idea, nor the divine, can serve as the intellectual world view; rather, 'the "surface" of things'[25] can define for human beings the one common world of phenomena from which human beings derive both the process from which human things came and also the whole of which they are parts.[26] Strauss's recognition of the surface of things provides a key element for his esoteric reading: access to the particular rules by which an author intends his text to be read.[27]

The ancients discovered natural religion, or religion defined through the discovery of distinctions among the customs of various peoples, and then extrapolated to a distinction between the necessary and the contingent.[28] The necessary was understood as intrinsic to things themselves, or as nature; the contingent was understood as convention or law, as things derived from thought. Natural religion was the quest for the good within the bounds of the necessary. It sits in opposition to revelatory theology because it remains rooted in the doubt of authority, even while it fulfils one function of revelatory theology by providing the basis from which to define ethical action: by reflecting on nature, philosophy was able to identify and know the good life.[29] As we shall see, Strauss argues that, although natural religion is at odds with biblical religion, natural religion provides an ethical framework, one that enables it to move in accordance with biblical religion.[30]

Strauss, both because one's thought must arise from the necessary – in the surface of things – and also because human problems that are permanent do in fact exist, discovers the existence of both esoteric writing and also natural right. The modern loss of the ability to see either nature as phenomena or the human world view out of which we view things has resulted in our loss of the ability both to use and to recognize esoteric writing. In his discussion of the formation of historicism, for instance, Strauss points to the critiques of natural right levelled by the moderns, as opposed to the critique offered by the classical conventionalists.[31] The former critique is based on a fundamental misunderstanding: the moderns define natural right as both discernible by human reason and also universally acknowledged. They conclude that, since there are many forms of natural right, there are no 'immutable principles of justice.'[32] Strauss points to three basic reasons that the modern critique is misguided. First, it has always been known that different ideas of justice exist at different times and in different places. This knowledge does not in and of itself suggest that natural right does not exist; rather, it may – as it did, for instance, for Aristotle[33] – become the impetus for the quest for natural right. The modern critique's second misunderstanding is that it presumes the *idea* of history in order to prove its argument in favour of history. The critique uses a quasi-historical argument that is not based on historical experience.[34] Third and finally, this modern critique of natural right, with its historical sense, argues that, because it is not universally knowable, natural right does not exist. But this too has always been known and did not lead the ancients to reject the existence of natural right.[35]

As mentioned above, the classical conventionalists – and Strauss points to Aristotle as an example – also critique natural right, but they come to a different conclusion. The primary distinction between the critiques of the modern thinkers and those of the classical conventionalists is that the latter make fundamental the distinction between convention and nature, with nature of a higher dignity than convention. The quest for understanding the natural is the quest for understanding the eternal. Because this understanding must, from the point of view of the eternal, always be inadequate, Aristotle rejects the knowability of natural right.[36] Yet like Plato, he does not reject the fundamental distinction between convention and nature. Philosophy remains a possibility, and natural right remains a reality, because Aristotle continues to recognize the possibility of ascending from convention, opinion, or Plato's cave to knowledge or nature.[37] Because modern historical consciousness rejects natural right – based on either the dismissal of the distinction between convention and nature or the trivializing of nature in favour of convention[38] – so too the possibility of philosophy is thwarted. The historicist exaltation of universal human creativity reduces human thought to the lowest common denominator.

As suggested above, Strauss seeks to rediscover philosophy as a quest or way of life.[39] Philosophy is the activity in which one engages as a philosopher. It does not have an end outside the very act of philosophizing. If the right kind of pleasure, as Aristotle suggests, is a sign of morality or perfection of character, and if one's life as activity is intensified by the explicit 'blossom' of its accompanying pleasure, then one's life is not a process, or a motion, toward an end. One does not accumulate knowledge of the philosophical tradition as a means of advancing the cause of knowledge – though, as Strauss argues, there is a temporary need for the study of the history of philosophy in order to return us to the possibility of rediscovering philosophy as understood by the ancients. Philosophy must remain a quest in order to be a means by which human beings perform their proper function as rational beings. Human beings do not engage in a process of becoming more like the divine; rather, they manifest the divine in themselves by acting in a manner akin to the gods. In practical terms, this means two things. First, philosophy has no tradition in the sense of its being on a path that over time more fully completes perfect knowledge.[40] Second, no number of readings of a particular philosophical text will yield results: it is the activity of one's engagement with the text that yields the only result possible for philosophy, the philosophical life.

The modern concept of progress is simply a prejudice. One can conceive of a world where non-progressive motion takes place, where, even as one develops one's character toward its alignment with the eternal (or permanent) verities, such motion may take place, as it were, intransitively. Alternatively, one can conceive of a world that more closely approaches wisdom even as wisdom remains permanently outside one's reach. From this vantage point, modernity's idealistic concept of progressive history seems a prejudice even more destructive of Jewish thought than Greece's concept of 'know thyself': the former must dismiss Judaism's directive of 'return' as, at the least, anachronistic; whereas the latter, while in tension with Jewish thought, can allow its coexistence.[41]

Strauss on Machiavelli

According to Strauss, Machiavelli, by introducing the concept of freedom, begins the crisis that culminates in both historicism and the loss of authority. While freedom continues in Machiavelli to be connected to the classical concept of *fortuna*, his introduction of the idea of history is revolutionary. History becomes the locus in which freedom is realized; Machiavelli reverses the traditional stance of thought, from theocentrism, which upheld the idea of God's estate, to anthropocentrism. He was not, however, unaware of this reversal: he writes in the Dedicatory Letter of *The Prince*: 'For just as those who sketch landscapes place themselves down in the plain to consider the nature of mountains and high places and to consider the nature of low places place themselves high atop mountains, similarly, to know well the nature of peoples one needs to be prince, and to know well the nature of princes one needs to be of the people.'[42]

The importance of Machiavelli to Strauss's thought should not be underestimated.[43] Strauss argues that 'in the course of the sixteenth century there was a conscious break with the whole philosophic tradition, a break that took place on the plane of purely philosophic or rational or secular thought. This break was originated by Machiavelli, and it led to the moral teachings of Bacon and Hobbes ...'[44] By recognizing the break between the modern and pre-modern traditions, Strauss affirms the possibility of retracing the loss of the art of esoteric writing, and of reading texts in their own terms – this is, in terms of awareness of the relation between philosophy and the state that existed when they were written. The reading of texts in their self-defined contexts affords the possibility of re-establishing the conversation through time about the permanent human problems.[45]

While the ancients had understood the political as both necessary for and antagonistic to philosophy, for Machiavelli, the political is the means toward effectual truth, the means to achieve justice. Paradoxically, he argues for the priority of justice even as he redefines entirely the concept of justice. The classical idea of justice had been based in the view of the cosmos as an order, a harmony, in which human beings hold a fixed place. Justice was understood as the aspiration toward how human beings ought to live, even while it was recognized that this ideal was utopian.[46] Machiavelli, minimizing the fixity of both human nature and the cosmological order, understands justice as beginning with how human beings do in fact live. The foundation for Hobbes's replacement of the classical concern for the end of human beings with concern for their beginning, is laid by Machiavelli.[47] According to Machiavelli, fortune is not blind, as the ancients presumed; rather, human beings, through recognizing and taking advantage of the opportunities provided by fortune, may succeed in moulding necessity.[48] Machiavelli destroys the classical understanding of philosophy in order argue for a new philosophy that operates autonomously in a sphere from which classical morality is excluded.

Strauss discovers in Machiavelli the beginnings of the process of establishing an autonomous sphere in which political science can be practised.[49] Even as he seeks to break with it, Machiavelli takes his bearings from the classical tradition. So, for instance, while displacing religion from the public realm, he, like the ancients, remains concerned about political stability; and, while transforming philosophy from the quest

for the ideal beyond human attainment into philosophy based in effectual truth, he remains concerned with the permanent human problems.
Machiavelli, ostensibly, is little concerned with justice: his refashioning
of Aristotle's moral virtues in chapter 15 of *The Prince* omits justice altogether. But Strauss argues against this position, claiming that Machiavelli is concerned with justice: 'no one of consequence ever doubted
that Machiavelli's study of political matters was public spirited.'[50] He
continues to be guided by classical thought[51] even as he substitutes human worldly experience for the classical concept of justice, and political
virtue for moral virtue. But his public spiritedness is countered with
an equal dose of anti-classical thought: the standards of human excellence are lowered in order to ensure human achievement. The purpose
of philosophy for Machiavelli becomes 'to relieve man's estate or to
increase man's power or to guide man toward the rational society, the
bond and the end of which is enlightened self-interest or the comfort-
able self-preservation of each of its members. The cave becomes "the
substance."'[52] In Machiavelli, philosophy moves to the public realm,
while religion becomes a private matter. The classical assumption that
the state requires its citizens to believe in God or the gods in order to
achieve justice is abandoned, yet Machiavelli does not offer a standard
by which to define what is just, or rather, the standard offered is tied
to the exigencies of the state.[53] As Strauss puts it, Machiavelli well understood that 'the jump from the realm of necessity into the realm of
freedom will be the inglorious death of the very possibility of human
excellence.'[54]

Strauss argues that Machiavelli is a 'teacher of evil,' neither a 'patriot' nor a 'scientist,' but, more dangerously, a man who teaches the
'virtue' of 'collective selfishness' yet who remains always attentive to
the surface of things.[55] Machiavelli's evil teaching is, at its root, that
philosophy – and only its effectual aspect – be disseminated to the public. This dissemination will destroy the art of esoteric writing, creating a delusional hermeneutic around the issue of the idea of history;[56]
furthermore, it will tie philosophical thought to the exigencies of the
state. As Strauss argues elsewhere,[57] the state, once the cave – that is,
both open and closed to philosophy – now becomes the pit beneath the
cave, completely closed off to philosophy.[58] Machiavelli is a blasphemer against religion, but he blasphemes covertly. Because it is covert, his
blasphemy, in Strauss's assessment, is all the more insidious: the attentive reader, rather than shuddering at the blasphemy, will be compelled
'to think the blasphemy by himself and so to become an accomplice of

the blasphemer.'[59] To understand Machiavelli as he understood himself, to abandon the modern presumption – introduced by Machiavelli himself – that religion is a private matter, readers must begin with the pre-modern thought from which his thinking emerged.[60] To understand Machiavelli, one must return to his pre-modern bases: classical thought and biblical thought.

With regard to biblical thought, Machiavelli ostensibly praises religion even while he is, Strauss argues, both irreligious and immoral. Most simply, Machiavelli blames religion for making human beings weak and for making good human beings prey to bad ones. Yet his characterization of religion is more subtle than that: the revolutionary character as well as the insidiousness of his teaching are evident in his use of traditional religious vocabulary in radically new meanings. For instance, he writes: 'And he [Savonarola] who said that our sins were the cause of [the seizure of Italy by Charles] spoke the truth. But the sins were surely not those he believed, but the ones I have told of.'[61] Strauss stresses that, while to the ears of those in the post-Machiavelli world, this sentence may not be shocking, one must, in order to recognize how truly shocking it is, and how easily such use of language can lull and delude the reader, recall the biblical meaning of sin and punishment. It may be true that the failures of the Italians allowed the seizure by Charles; but to equate linguistically these failures with human failures toward God is shocking: Machiavelli blasphemes against religion, yet for those readers who do not pay close attention, he is merely using religion as a measure against which to understand contemporary history.

Machiavelli blasphemes against religion in other ways as well, without revealing clearly his intention. His use of the term 'unarmed prophet' immediately calls to mind Jesus, who in Machiavelli's estimation is 'ruined' of necessity.[62] Furthermore, in *The Prince*, he changes the measure of human excellence from man–God to man–horse.[63] Christ is replaced by the mythological (or imaginary) Chiron as the teacher of humankind.[64] Yet at the same time, Machiavelli puts himself in the role of teacher with regard to Lorenzo de' Medici, and, more esoterically, to 'whoever understands it.'[65] By replacing Christ with Chiron, and by paralleling that replacement with his own role toward Lorenzo, Machiavelli denies the transcendent aspect of Christ; he and other 'centaurs' may effectually assume God's position.[66] The effectual replacement of the perspective of the human being from a fixed position in the order of things – a stance held in common by both biblical religion and pre-modern thought – with that of the human being as able to climb a mountain to view the valley, or descend a valley to view the mountain,[67] is, Strauss discovers, Machiavelli's most revolutionary teaching. Strauss points out that Machiavelli is not the first to recognize the bestiality of human government and the bulk of humanity reduced to beasts, to 'fox-lions.'[68] Xenophon, for example, had recognized the bestiality of Simonides and had used a similar method of esoteric writing to instruct regarding that which cannot be instructed.[69] The difference between Machiavelli and Xenophon's works, however, is substantial: while Xenophon represents the beast as a character in a dialogue, Machiavelli puts his name on a guidebook for evil. It is, Strauss argues, at one and the same time, a continuation and a revolution of esoteric speech.

Notwithstanding his revolutionary change in human perspective, Machiavelli's work, like all esoteric writing, remains concerned with political stability. He does not simply dismiss the truth of religion: his use of religion as a tool of the state reveals his concern for stability or fixity. His concern for the fatherland assumes the model of his concern for the soul; his concern for the soul is made evident by his appeal 'to all thinking men regardless of time and place.'[70] For Strauss, Machiavelli's concern for the fatherland does not make him simply a patriot: because he seeks to change not the *content* of revelatory religion but rather the *perspective* from which the attentive reader views revelatory religion, Machiavelli's thought 'presupposes a comprehensive reflection.'[71] This change in world view is accomplished through his proposal that those who can understand should recognize their authority over revelatory religion.[72] But it is not a dismissal of revelatory religion: it retains revelatory religion even as it eliminates its authority over human action. Machiavelli is at once concerned with stability and human authority. His comprehensive reflection, his stance that is neither entirely religious nor entirely irreligious,[73] that is concerned entirely neither with his fatherland nor with his soul, comprises the 'core of Machiavelli's thought.'[74] Ultimately Strauss denies that Machiavelli can salvage the strand of his thinking that, even as it limits those to whom it applies, retains the higher aspiration of human beings.

Machiavelli's 'covert' teaching, to which he gently directs the attentive reader of *The Prince*[75] – that he replaces God as the teacher of humankind – is suggested also by his references to Moses. Moses is first mentioned in *The Prince* in connection with those of great 'virtue,' who used their 'own arms,' who did not require the help of fortune for success.[76] One notices immediately that two of the names on Machiavelli's list are either mythological (Romulus) or legendary (Theseus), which intimates that Moses did not exist apart from the human imagination. In chapter 6, he suggests that Moses cannot be treated as all the others; but later on, in chapter 26 – a number of great interest to Strauss[77] – he does in fact treat Moses as all the others are treated,[78] writing that 'it was necessary for anyone wanting to see the virtue of Moses that the people of Israel be enslaved in Egypt, and to learn the greatness of spirit of Cyrus, that the Persians be oppressed by the Medes.'[79] What is more, he refers to the movement he is hoping to inspire as a 'redemption.'[80] Ironically, just as in the case of Christ, where he praises religion only to render it a merely effectual truth, so too in the case of Moses he praises an aspect of religion not previously overtly lauded: Moses is all the greater because there was no God for whom he was merely 'executor.'[81] Strauss discovers that Machiavelli's 'praise of religion is only the reverse side of what one might provisionally call his complete indifference to the truth of religion.'[82]

Just as Machiavelli shifts the meaning of the biblical vocabulary, so too he shifts the meaning of the vocabulary of pre-modern philosophic thought. Indeed, as mentioned above, *The Prince* is a refashioning of Aristotle's *Ethics*.[83] Chapter 15 reframes Aristotle's moral virtues, while the end of chapter 21 and the first half of chapter 25 comprise almost a direct critique of Aristotle. With his redefinition of virtue as virility within the worldly context, Machiavelli effectively separates human existence from the eternal ideas. In his thought, ideas lose their anchor in either nature or natural law.[84] So too the fixity of human nature is abandoned in favour of the idea of at least partial self-creation, an idea that lacks directionality, limitation, and the possibility of connection between the eternal and the contingent.[85]

To accomplish the goal of establishing an autonomous sphere in which political science can be practised, Machiavelli must upend the classical understanding of the city as the cave *qua* closed to philosophy,[86] even as he upholds the classical sense of the city's importance as the realm of public stability. As an example of the means by which he undermines classical thought while seeming to perpetuate it, I cite the following: 'I believe, therefore, that he is happy who adapts his mode of proceeding to the qualities of the times; and similarly, he is unhappy whose procedure is in disaccord with the times. For one sees that in the things that lead men to the end that each has before him, glories and riches.'[87] One is struck by Machiavelli's refashioning of what it is to be happy, which replaces Aristotle's understanding of happiness as the quality of a person's nature with the qualities of the times. To underscore this point, Machiavelli denies Aristotle's idea of teleology, of the human being's having an end, by suggesting that each human being has the same end of glories and riches. Two things are occurring here. First, history is replacing the natural order as the measure of human worth;[88] and second, in order to argue for some fixity in human worth, Machiavelli preserves the idea of a common end for human beings. In the larger sense, his concern is with the beginning of human life rather than with its goal or end.

The biblical and pre-modern philosophic positions have in common the positing of the human being in a fixed position in the order of things. What Machiavelli argues – rather shockingly, since in the Bible, to have virtue is to recognize one's responsibilities to God, and for Aristotle, to have virtue is to actualize one's teleological position in the cosmos – is that the human being's position is fixed only for those who have no virtue. This is an exact reversal of the traditional positions. Strauss discovers that Machiavelli's primary instruction to those who read attentively is that 'what ought not to be said cannot be said.'[89]

By refashioning both the biblical and the classical philosophic attitudes, Machiavelli lowers the standards of human excellence. He does this, Strauss argues, to ensure success. The lowering is done in two senses: first, human beings can *aspire* to only human goals, whether those goals are experiential or imaginary; and second, those goals are *defined* from a perspective that is circumscribed by merely human existence or imagination. Because Machiavelli makes his thought hermetic – one's goals are both achievable and self-created, and also self-created and achievable – the inattentive reader may not notice that Machiavelli's thought shares in self-evidence only because he has presumed already Machiavelli's premises. Most important for Strauss, Machiavelli's arguing for the informative value of history to truth is the means by which he attempts to resolve the theologico-political problem; it need not and does not solve the problem permanently. Strauss argues against what will later in Western thought become historicism.[90]

Strauss on Hobbes

The break between the ancients and the moderns was further developed by Hobbes, both in his concern for the beginnings of human beings and in his moral teachings. Strauss attempts 'to prove that Hobbes['s] view of human nature marked a complete breach with classical tradition, including Thucydides, to whom Hobbes owed a great deal.'[91] The proof of this complete breach is important to Strauss because with it, and with his demonstration of the internal contradictions of the new 'comprehensive reflection,' he can undermine the modern project of displacing classical philosophy – especially classic natural right theory – and biblical revelation, from thought.[92] Furthermore, once the non-validated displacement is recognized, also recognized is the arbitrary bases of the shift to the anthropocentric world view and of the belief in progress.[93] The later modern project of synthesizing philosophy and revelation – or of reintroducing revelatory thought into philosophy, as seen in Heidegger[94] – may be seen as serving to pre-emptively and progressively obfuscate from view natural right and the revelatory God.

Hobbes builds on the thought of Machiavelli by continuing the project of the autonomous creation of a political order. Just as Machiavelli redefines justice in order to achieve the good state, so too Hobbes, Strauss argues, redefines wisdom in order to achieve certainty. Hobbes finds his predecessor's thought deficient in that it does not base its political morality on natural morality, which basis would give his thought a foundation of certainty.[95] The one realm in which traditional philosophy has not failed, in which it has yielded certain results, Hobbes argues, is the realm of mathematics. By creating a mathematical 'artificial world,' he can establish a progressive materialism that has certainty. This artificial world, in answer to all scepticism, can catalogue the achievements of human creation. Hobbes 'defines mathematical objects operationally rather than theoretically ... A line is what is generated by the path of a moving point, rather than a breadthless length. The intuition is *a priori*, because we, through our imagination, supply it.'[96] Hobbes argues that human beings have certainty in mathematics because they can be certain of their judgments on natural phenomena, on things as they appear to us. For Strauss, Hobbes's argument from things as they appear to us continues the basis of the natural right tradition as it appears in Plato; and it supplies, as shall be seen below, the basis for Hobbes's esoteric writing.

Strauss discovers that Hobbes cannot be understood unless he is read as an esoteric writer: Hobbes's goal is to free human beings from ecclesiastical authority; or, more precisely, his goal is to change the *perspective* from which one views revelatory religion without necessarily changing its *content*. Once this goal is obscured – and ironically, it is his success in this matter that has made it difficult for modern readers to recognize his goal – one can no longer recognize Hobbes's concern with political stability and the pre-modern understanding of virtue. When

Hobbes is read exoterically, there is no higher aspiration to which his ideas may ascend.[97]

Strauss argues that Hobbes ignores all strains of philosophy but the idealistic one. As a consequence, he understands political philosophy as necessarily 'public spirited.'[98] His goal was to preserve natural right, even as he enlarged its meaning: the theology of Hobbes's self-created artificial world becomes a subcategory of a new philosophy of idealistic materialism, or the effectuation of a commonwealth built on universal reason. For Plato the human soul, or human nature, provides the authority by which one shapes and judges political action. Hobbes continues the understanding of nature as the necessary by which one shapes and judges the political community. The political community serves as 'protection against man's natural malice.'[99] For Strauss, the political community must remain grounded in the permanent human condition, a condition that requires – as the pre-modern philosophers readily acknowledged – the guidance of political authority. Political philosophy, and not simply political science, is necessary as the means by which to acquire wisdom, the wisdom to know the difference between the lesser and 'better angels of our nature.'[100]

The breach between the ancients and the moderns is defined by the adoption of the anthropocentric world view: for the ancients, natural law is an 'objective measure ... which man must obey'; for Hobbes, 'natural law represents an ensemble of subjective rights that originate in the human will.'[101] Hobbes's position defines natural law as historically bound. Not only has he effected a break with pre-modern thought, but also he has effectively camouflaged this break behind an esotericism of his own – that is, the modern presupposition that philosophical texts are necessarily bound to their time period.[102] While Hobbes's work affirms the tradition of esoteric writing and in that sense binds his own work to his political exigencies, also it affirms that his text should be read with a historical sensibility. He both breaks with pre-modern thought and also, for his followers – who misunderstood the nature of Hobbes's success – reinforces the break by promoting what Strauss labels a modern prejudice. At the same time, a certain ambiguity, initiated by a reassessment of natural law, remains with regard to history, which continues to be viewed in a 'two-dimensional' perspective.[103]

Unlike Machiavelli, Hobbes offers 'a detailed discussion revealing the harmony between his political teaching and the teaching of the Bible.'[104] Overtly, he argues that Protestant Christianity dictates that, to be a true Christian, one must adhere only to 'fundamental religion'[105] –

that, since 'Jesus is the Christ,'[106] human beings can have no knowledge within the political realm of God. One might argue that Hobbes feared that discrediting religion in favour of the political, as was his true intent, would lead to civil strife. Strauss points out that, while Spinoza was interested in establishing 'a specific Bible *science*,' in Hobbes 'the political preoccupation plainly predominates.'[107] Hobbes sought both to remove religion from the political realm and also to establish a religion that would be acceptable to believers, yet not threaten the state. He uses a theology that would be acceptable to those whom Strauss calls, in relation to Spinoza, potential philosophers among Christians[108] in order to camouflage his true intention of both denying altogether the veracity of traditional revelation and also affirming religion as the means of maintaining social order.

For the purposes of this book, this point – whether or not Hobbes's true intention was to dismiss the value of knowledge gleaned from revelation – is of the utmost importance. On its answer rests not only the viability for and inclusion of Jews of and in the modern secular project, but also the critique of esotericism as a tool of reading. The question may be rephrased as follows: When Hobbes critiques the revelatory tradition, does he stand inside or outside that tradition? Does he critique Christianity from within that tradition, a stance that would establish his fundamental religion as a development of Christianity? Or is his thought informed at its foundation by his contemporary political exigency, an exigency from which he recognizes that the time is ripe, following Machiavelli, to plead, esoterically and from outside the religious tradition, for a political realm that is independent of and autonomous from the religious realm? If Hobbes's exoteric Protestantism is in fact the critique of Protestantism rather than an extension of Protestantism, then the conception of natural right at the basis of the establishment of modern thought is not, as Fackenheim might argue, a return to pre-Christianity and therefore inherently antagonistic to Judaism in particular; rather, it is neutral with regard to Christianity and Judaism.[109] Hobbes argues that Judaism is dead since Jews no longer have a civil order[110] and that Christ is the 'rightful King of the Jews' and 'of Heaven.'[111] But the dangers to Jews of writing esoterically in this way include the possibility of being excluded on principle from participation in the new secular state. How is one to know how not to leave the literal text to begin reading esoterically? If the exoteric meaning of Hobbes's text is that Protestant Christianity teaches the means by which the state may be separated from the Church, or political philosophy from revelatory theology, and if in fact such a reading is plausible, does reading the text esoterically render invisible its explicit antagonism to Judaism? Only, Strauss would argue, for those enmeshed in the historicist delusion: 'The problem inherent in the surface of things, and only in the surface of things, is the heart of things.'[112]

Strauss on Heidegger

Strauss's conception of the break from classical and biblical thought effectuated by Machiavelli (and Bacon) and Hobbes found its basis and fruition in Heidegger.[113] It was he who first recognized the concealment of the roots of modern thought – and indeed, of classical thought – and the consequent misconception of a *tradition*, beginning with Socrates, of philosophy. Furthermore, by arguing that the root of intelligibility is *Dasein*, or the human pre-theoretical understanding of Being, Heidegger is able both to adopt the anthropocentric world view and also to promote a historicism that radicalizes the earlier modern idea of progress.[114]

Putting aside the differences between the earlier and the later Heidegger, we focus on their similarity – what Heidegger calls the question of being. Heidegger's position, which depends on historicism as an organizing principle, is briefly as follows.[115] The problem with both classical and biblical thought is that it presumes that Being endures in things as a property or essence (or in the human being as an image). By beginning our thinking about the being of entities in nature or in God, we ignore the background that constitutes the specific being of a single entity – that is, we ignore the very thing that made intelligible the entity in the first place. On the contrary, an entity is understood by us to have being insofar as it discloses itself to us within a complex of relationships that matter to us in a particular time and place.

In his analytic, Heidegger argues that *Dasein* has three structures in common: facticity, projection, and discourse. His concept of 'facticity' serves to establish that a specific human being is thrown into the world, into a particular time and place. By 'projection,' he indicates that the human being is committed already toward being, insofar as he is acting already. The human being is future directed in the sense that his actions create his identity. He is, furthermore, a being-toward-death – what the human being does 'defines [his] being as a totality';[116] there is no property of being other than *Dasein*'s actions by which to define an identity. 'Discourse' attributes to *Dasein* the fact that human beings discuss the entities that matter to us at a given moment; as the later Heidegger will argue, language gives being to entities originally irrelevant to *Dasein*.[117] *Dasein*, through its intelligibility, clears a space for other beings to enter into notice. Because *Dasein* is thrown into the world, acting already toward its identity and ultimately its death, the clearing unfolds historically. Ultimately, as the later Heidegger argues, Being is mysterious, but insofar as it is intelligible to human beings, from the way in which things appear to us, being is a historical unfolding that has no enduring quality or property.

Although Strauss does not write extensively about Heidegger, Heidegger serves in his thought in a primary way. First, Heidegger's 'destructuring' of the philosophical tradition exposes the roots of that tradition. Heidegger discloses that understanding must begin with how things appear to us, with the surface of things, and that only through that understanding can an individual self-manifest his own being – that is, his understanding. For Strauss, Heidegger provides the clues for how one is to begin to read ancient texts, according to their most literal level, the rules the texts themselves establish. His position with regard to language, however, differs from Heidegger's later position, which argues that language is the *source* of knowledge, rather than that human beings use language to convey intelligibility. Because Strauss questions the necessity of the adoption of the anthropocentric world view, also he questions whether human language alone establishes knowledge. He discovers that a writer uses language as a means to communicate both the exigencies of his political situation and also the means by which a reader is to glean his esoteric meaning. Furthermore, and most important, Heidegger becomes primary for Strauss because he argues for *Dasein* as a temporal process, introducing into thought a radical historicism, which Strauss seeks to challenge. Because Strauss recognizes Heidegger as the historicist 'Master of those who know,'[118] so to speak, one might claim that a major part of the former's work is, if not a refutation of the latter's thought, then an alternative to it.[119]

Strauss studied Heidegger in 'intensive seminars'[120] and attended lectures by him, which he claimed he received usually 'without understanding a word, but [sensing] that he dealt with something of the utmost importance to man as man.'[121] His respect and admiration for Heidegger as a thinker is evident in many places. Regarding his distaste for him as a man, Strauss is more reticent but does on occasion intimate briefly the connection between Heidegger's thought and his politics. The mix of admiration and critique is prevalent in Strauss's writings on him. For instance, he traces the roots of Heidegger's existentialism.

Natural right had been transposed by Machiavelli, Bacon, and Hobbes from the realm of necessity to the realm of freedom. The result was an ethos of seemingly limitless toleration.[122] Strauss argues that human beings created for themselves a vicious circle: 'the more we cultivate reason [i.e., reason's teaching that we cannot know the absolute], the more we cultivate nihilism: the less we are able to be loyal members of society.'[123] And again: 'Heidegger ... surpasses in speculative intelligence all his contemporaries and is at the same time intellectually the counterpart to what Hitler was politically ... By uprooting and not simply rejecting the tradition of philosophy, he made it possible for the first time after many centuries ... to see the roots of the tradition as they are and thus perhaps to know, what so many merely believe, that those roots are the only natural and healthy roots.'[124] Again, these roots are what is accessible to the human being as human being, or the surface of things, and the ascension from this surface to ideas.

The process whereby Heidegger uncovers the roots of the philosophical tradition, and his adoption of historicism as a result of this discovery, are evident in his early work as an existentialist. He discovers that the roots of existentialism are to be found in Nietzsche and not in Kierkegaard.[125] This insight came to Heidegger when he realized that Kierkegaard was understood to be the source of existentialism only because he was read by philosophers who had read and been moulded already by Nietzsche; Kierkegaard, having accepted already historicism and its outgrowth, existentialism, was read within the confines of this thought. His identification of Nietzsche and not Kierkegaard as the root of existentialism marks the beginning of Heidegger's ability to reveal the roots, or the surface, of the philosophical tradition: by identifying the effects of historicism as prior to its cause in any post-Hegelian text, Heidegger was able to see past the many *answers* of philosophy in order to return to the *questions*. The ultimate question is this: Does one use necessity or freedom, nature or history, as the means of organizing knowledge? And having made a choice, what is the relationship between these two organizing principles?[126] Because it is on this point that Strauss parted ways with Heidegger – Strauss, discovering nature or natural right, and Heidegger, history – Strauss devoted himself to exposing the break between ancient and modern thought, a break defined by the modern idea of freedom, or history. Heidegger meanwhile identifies the continuity between the two epochs, reinforcing history and simultaneously negating the validity of nature as an organizing principle.

Strauss defines existentialism as 'the attempt to free Nietzsche's alleged overcoming of relativism from the consequences of his relapse into metaphysics or of his recourse to nature.'[127] Existentialism attempts to resolve the conflict between the natural and the conventional, as first recognized by the classical proponents of natural right, by reaffirming the supremacy of nature, not as an objective, absolute standard but as a standard of subjective will by which one can know the difference 'between the superficial and the profound.'[128] Existentialism teaches that being is ultimately mysterious and that metaphysics, because it presumes that being as such is intelligible, is defective.[129] Ultimately, 'all principles of thought and action [issue from] the experience of nothingness.'[130] The analysis of the experience of nothingness becomes for Heidegger the object of philosophy. He argues that, while one cannot ground one's choices in an eternal verity, one can differentiate between the authentic and the unauthentic, if only on a formal level. In effect, Heidegger replaces nature's authority over human action with an authority in 'man's manner of being.'[131] But because the analysis of one's manner of being begins with a commitment to one's own manner of being, 'the analytics of *Existenz* is necessarily based on a specific ideal of *Existenz*, on a specific commitment; for only committed thought can understand commitment and hence *Existenz*. Existentialist philosophy is subjective truth about the subjectivity of truth or finite knowledge of man's finiteness.'[132]

Heidegger returns to the roots of thought, but despite his return, he changes the question at the heart of philosophy. For him, the object of thought is not the enduring qualities that inhere in an entity, but rather Being itself.[133] In this sense, his project is, as Strauss understands it, an 'attempt to understand being (*Sein*) as a synthesis of the impersonality of Platonic ideas and the elusiveness of the biblical God.'[134] Heidegger establishes a thought that seeks to disclose not the mystery that is God, but rather the mysterious itself: Being has being only insofar as it is bound to the facticity of the historical. One might formulate this differently. Being, in Heidegger, takes on the character of the biblical God. What had been called God's essence is rather God's absence; what had been recognized as the Platonic forms is rather the absence of individual identity. Heidegger provides the apex of the project of synthesizing philosophy and revelatory theology in Western thought: not only is traditional philosophy seemingly destroyed by his position, but so too, as the intimation of Absolute Otherness, is traditional Jewish revelatory theology.[135] His philosophy cannot affirm rational eternal verities;

theology cannot reflect its source in transcendence and becomes a possibility within the realm of the known. The teachings of philosophy and revelatory theology become in Heidegger solely a matter of commitment, which, if it is authentic, if it is mindful of its being-toward-death, has no further standard by which to recommend it.

Heidegger's claim that his anthropocentric version of revelation, now realized solely as an immanent experience of commitment, may be authentic is validated through his positing of a radical historicism: but for human self-creation, there are no eternal verities, nor is there an ultimate Truth. If we limit our search to things human, and if we recognize ourselves, our imaginations, and our wills as self-created, then our understanding, our knowledge, and our actions are by definition *true* to our situation as human beings. By adopting historicism – the idea that changes in human thinking literally change the object of thought or that the foundations of human thought are rooted in particular historical circumstances – one seemingly destroys the eternal verities of traditional philosophy. By claiming that revelation is true only insofar as its source is being-toward-death, one seemingly replaces transcendence with self-congratulatory human consciousness.

Heidegger's anthropocentrism in conjunction with his historicism redefines reason as the glorification of human artistry. According to Heidegger, when one reads a great thinker of the past, one must understand him creatively. This claim leads Strauss to his primary criticism of Heidegger: his implication that he 'understands the great thinkers of the past in the decisive respect [the thinkers' awareness of *Sein*] better than they understood themselves.'[136] Strauss's rejection of him is based not simply on his adoption of a radical historicism, but also on his basic intolerance – on his unwillingness to understand others as they understand themselves, to recognize commitments to manners of being other than his own, and, ironically, to be open to the affirmation of an eternal verity other than a thoroughgoing relativism.

PART II. STRAUSS ON JEWISH PHILOSOPHY

Strauss on the Bible

There are, Strauss argues, two bases for Western civilization: philosophy and the Bible.[137] While the discovery of natural right within the classical philosophical tradition is crucially important to him, the biblical tradition offers its own standard of ethical action. Yet as we shall see, although he discovers that philosophy and the Bible stand in opposition to each other, he discovers also that they share a common ground.[138] To demonstrate their opposition, Strauss suggests that there is no knowledge of natural right in the Old Testament[139] because there is no knowledge of nature.[140] The basis for knowledge of justice in Greek thought is denied by the Old Testament, and furthermore, there is an implicit rejection of philosophy.[141] Just as Strauss returns to Greek philosophical texts as the means of learning to read philosophy in its own terms – including its teachings of the art of esoteric writing – so too he returns to the Bible to read it in its own terms, and this requires his identifying and rejecting the modern tendency toward synthesizing revelatory thought with philosophical thought. Through his argument that one must learn to read both philosophical texts and the Bible within the rules of reading that inhere in each text, Strauss seeks to preserve the tension between reason and revelation as the key to preserving the vitality of Western civilization. Yet at the same time, he undermines this tension: by establishing that one human situation is espoused by both philosophical and biblical thought, that the 'mystery of being' is beyond both, Strauss can argue for a permanent human condition from which the activity of justice or righteousness may be derived.[142]

The tension between the Bible and philosophy is located in their very foundations. The foundations of biblical thought – that there is a particular divine code, one unique God, that this God is beyond knowledge, and that its source is a divinely revealed covenant built on hope – are at odds with the foundations of philosophy – that there is natural right in which all cultures may share, that coming to know, by basing itself on reasoning and sense perception, is essentially a human activity, and that knowledge aspires not to hope, but rather to the identifying of the proper object of knowledge, and not to a righteous or holy life, but to the good life.[143] Because its basis is ultimately beyond the limits of what human beings may seek to know autonomously – knowledge of good and evil – the Bible abounds with contradictions. Philosophy, by contrast, strives for consistency, which it can attain in its books as its authors edit out or include things that are relevant to their arguments.[144] Yet, Strauss argues, 'virtually all the claims of the Biblical critics concerning the differential historical origins of contradictory or stylistically disparate passages in the Bible rest on a presupposed rejection of the possibility of miracles.'[145]

Strauss discovers, however, that there is a commonality between the Bible and philosophy through which they may be compared: since, for instance, the story of creation in the Bible is non-mythological – it suggests an explanation for first things in light of the *idea* of the one God – it may be read, indeed just as philosophy is read, in terms of what is accessible to the human being as human being. Because Strauss takes seriously natural law, it is missing the mark to suggest (as has been done) that he was an atheist.[146] Like Maimonides, he finds valid reasons for reading the Bible in a context separate from, for instance, the rabbinic context; one such reason, as Maimonides argues, is the need to free our minds from the traditions loved in our youth in order to recognize what is demonstrably true.[147] Strauss parts ways with Spinoza's assessment that the Bible is unintelligible: both the Bible and philosophy may be read according to what is accessible to the human being *qua* human being. Both the Bible and philosophy reveal something about the permanent human condition.[148]

Strauss argues that we may read the Bible in order to understand things as they appear to us. Insofar as each philosophy or the Bible attempts only to ask the questions that are imposed on us simply by virtue of our existence within the whole of the permanent human condition, there is no fundamental difference between their accounts. Both know only the permanent human questions; each tries to define the permanent human condition from which the questions arise; and both recognize the human condition as given. Both philosophy and the Bible must be read to discover the pre-scientific and pre-mythological situation that they reveal.[149] For the Bible, the whole is the heaven, the earth, and everything that is within and between them; for philosophy, the whole is the phenomena, or the surface of things. And it is here that the Bible and philosophy reveal their fundamental opposition: the Bible places primary importance on life on earth over heaven – which is the only created thing that is neither called good nor blessed – while philosophy elevates the heaven as primary and looks to cosmology to understand the good.

In his reading of Genesis, Strauss follows the technique of beginning, not with the faith that might preclude direct recognition of the text, but rather with the surface of the text, with what in the text can be made intelligible. Strauss argues that 'the Bible starts then from the world as we know it, and as men always knew it and will know it, prior to any explanation, mythical or scientific.'[150] Beginning from the surface of things, Strauss suggests that we all know what light is 'empirically, ordinarily,'[151] and that all the things created in the Bible are known to us by 'daily sense perception'[152] – he argues that the text is in fact 'accessible to man as man.'[153] Up to this point, his method of finding the text as 'accessible to man as man' seems akin to Kant's reading of Genesis in 'Conjectural Beginnings': Kant's effort to internalize God, or to translate God into human instinct,[154] for instance, by definition results in success – that is, the success of an instinctual reading of Genesis as an account of human instinct. And indeed, Strauss's reading seems to culminate in a dualistic description of creation: things that have no local motion are separated from things that do; things that are like are separated from things that are unlike.[155] His reading seems to culminate in the translation of the foundations of the Bible into philosophy. The lecture hints at such a procedure when, near its beginning, he suggests that by labelling Genesis 1 a mythological account, one 'abandon[s] the attempt to understand.'[156]

The suspicion that Strauss is interpreting the Bible through a philosophical lens, however, is undermined by what Green identifies as Strauss's intentional mis-citation of a misidentified verse: Strauss cites 1:26 rather than the correct 1:27, and when quoting the text of 1:27, repeats the phrase 'in His image' – a repetition not in the original text.[157] Because these errors – seen to be intentional when one remains attentive to the surface of the text – mark the centre of the printed lecture, let us pause for a moment to consider them. Genesis 1:27 reads as follows: 'And God created man in His own image, in the image of God created He him; male and female created He them.' Genesis 1:26: 'And God said: "Let us make man in our image, after our likeness; and let them have dominion over the fish of the sea, and over the fowl of the air, and over the cattle, and over all the earth, and over every creeping thing that creepeth upon the earth."' One might suggest that Strauss cites for the reader, in 1:27, an explanation for why things are the way they are for human beings; human beings exist, exist as male and female, yet have the capacity for both physical and metaphysical motion. On its surface, with regard to what is 'accessible to man as man,' the Bible teaches, first, that human beings have the ability to change their place because they are in the image of God; second, that human beings are limited in their range of motion because God, or He who has knowledge of good and evil, transcends any and all motion they make; and third, that the dualism of human life, male and female, is not overcome on its surface but is overcome only in the oneness of God. Strauss argues that on its surface, the Bible teaches that Genesis 1 replaces the dualism of male and female – the sensual – with the dualism of otherness and local motion – the noetic idea of the one God. But by pointing the reader to 1:26, Strauss at the same time undermines his reading: the human being as human being can have no knowledge of God's intentionality. Furthermore, in 1:26, God is represented, not as a unity, but in the plural; the Bible does not consistently represent the noetic idea of the one God. Strauss's mis-citation suggests that the common ground established between the Bible and philosophy through his philosophic reading of the Bible may not in fact exist.[158]

The suggestion that Strauss esoterically undermines his reading of the Bible as having a common ground with philosophy is reinforced by the second error he makes. By mistakenly repeating the phrase 'in His image' when citing 1:27, he reinforces his argument that, by the Bible's definition, God has two images, an image recognizable on the surface and something other than what is on the surface. One can read the Bible through a lens that acknowledges only what is 'accessible to man as man' to ascertain what is intelligible in order to establish a common ground between them as the surface of things; but in doing so, one does not capture the Bible in its own terms. The Bible does not *limit* itself to knowledge that is accessible to the human being as human being: in order to establish *both* that the human being has motion and *also* that his motion is ultimately limited, the Bible must suggest and reflect *both* a realm that is accessible to the human being as human being and *also* a realm that is not. From the human perspective, God is One in order that human beings may have motion and also that their motion remain local, non-transcended. With regard to wisdom, the human perspective by definition is inadequate.

Strauss ascends in his reading of Genesis from the surface of things to something else. Although some aspects of the Bible are accessible to the human being as human being, and although 'the account of the world given in the first chapter of the Bible is not fundamentally different from philosophic accounts,'[159] knowledge of the createdness of the world is not accessible to the human being as human being. Strauss argues that the opposition between the Bible and philosophy may be summarized as the distinction between depreciating heaven in favour of life on earth and elevating heaven over life on earth.[160] This distinction is the basis for the seeming contradiction of the Bible's stance: its affirmation that it is wrong for the human being 'to find his bearing in the light of what is evident to man as man', and yet its teaching that God created the world, and in His creating depreciated heaven in favour of earth in order to establish a relationship with human beings.[161] While the description of creation in Genesis 1 is not fundamentally dif-

ferent from the cosmologies of philosophy, and while the Bible and philosophy are describing the same permanent human condition, the fact
that the Bible reveals the createdness of the world is neither consonant
with philosophy nor 'accessible to man as man.'

Strauss on Spinoza

Spinoza begins for Strauss his lifelong pursuit of what it means to read
literally. The goal of literal reading arises from his 'mission ... to restore both reason and revelation against the tendency of modern science to deny them both.'[162] Spinoza presented the question of what to
do with the revelatory tradition as it is presented to us.[163] We can, like
him, stand outside that tradition in order to critique it, or we can stand
within it and adapt it to contemporary contingency. Either way, the tradition is weakened or displaced: by standing outside its tradition, revelation is made to speak in alien terms; by standing inside it, reason is.
Early on, at a time when Strauss did not 'read Spinoza literally enough,'
he had understood him as standing outside the tradition. By the time
he wrote the Preface to the new edition of *Spinoza's Critique of Religion*
(1965), he had come to recognize that the reality of the political regime
under which a philosopher writes determines which stance he chooses. Yet, because either stance can be dangerous – the former opening
the possibility of anarchy, the latter, of tyranny – the philosopher must
write always with moderation. Literal reading requires both the previous understanding that reason and revelation are irreconcilable, and
also the recognition that the only realm that is more fundamental than
that of natural law – 'the conviction that there [are] indeed moral truths,
grounded in human nature, and [that] those truths would endure as
long as that nature would endure'[164] – is the political realm.

Because Spinoza is the first proponent of liberalism, which is the
modern condition necessary for Jewish emancipation, he holds a central place in Strauss's thought – indeed, Strauss's first book (mentioned
above) was devoted to Spinoza's thought. The most immediate aspect
of the modern Jewish theologico-political crisis was, for Strauss, on the
one hand, the inherent weakness of the Weimar Republic – more broadly, of liberalism in general, and on the other hand, German-Jewish dependence on the Weimar Republic – more broadly, Jewish dependence
on liberalism.[165] Strauss's concern with the contemporary crisis was
what motivated him to return to early modern and pre-modern sources: the ambiguous situation in which Weimar Jews found themselves

with regard to liberalism is, he argues, merely a particular symptom of the larger crisis in which Western thought found itself.[166] For Strauss, Spinoza's thought is the root of the modern Western intellectual crises: those of liberalism, of revelatory theology, and of rationalism. Strauss concludes, ironically, that Spinoza's attempt to solve the contemporaneous Jewish problem – that problem being exclusion from the political present – had spawned a greater problem: during the Weimar Era, social inequality continued, and Jews, after Spinoza, no longer have a tradition to which to return.

Building on Machiavelli's foundation, Spinoza uses his critique of Judaism as representative of revelatory theology in general.[167] He adopts from Machiavelli the position that what is true is determined by what is effective. Strauss argues that humanitarian ends – his desire to ameliorate the Jewish empirical situation – justify in Spinoza's mind his exceedingly harsh critique of Judaism and the Old Testament. Cohen, Strauss argues, understands Spinoza's critique of Judaism to go beyond even the Christian critique. This severity, according to his reading of Cohen, serves two purposes. First, Spinoza is able to posit an idealized Christianity so as not to offend his audience of potential philosophers who are Christian; and second, Spinoza is able to present his critique of *actual* Christianity in the form of a critique of Judaism. Cohen concludes that Spinoza is a traitor to Jews and to Judaism.[168] Strauss, though he agrees with Cohen that Spinoza appeals to Christian prejudices, disagrees with this assessment.

Spinoza, Strauss discovers, understands his goal of destroying the medieval Church and establishing the modern liberal state as itself a refutation of revelation. No refutation of revelation is actually given in Spinoza. This suggests two things. First, that Spinoza – although adopting the historical sense insofar as he reads the Bible according to the different time periods in which it may have been written – recognizes that revelation cannot be disproved by reason. Even as Spinoza's understanding of revelation is circumscribed by the historical sense, he recognizes that revelation itself may stand outside this sense. But second, Spinoza's determination to read the Bible in the light of natural reason predetermines his conclusion that the Bible itself teaches the truth of natural reason. Strauss discovers that 'Spinoza was not actually interested in Scripture. Rather, the true aim of critical historical method was to subvert the authority of Revelation.'[169] The foundation of modern philosophy is itself therefore not rational. In a point that will become important to Fackenheim, the Jewish project of presenting Judaism for philosophical critique – or, alternatively, of allowing an encounter between revelatory theology and philosophy, which follows Spinoza's critique – is predetermined in favour of philosophy.[170]

Strauss discovers that Spinoza has no desire to refute revelation. His overt teaching, the 'assumptions to which Spinoza appeals,' is that 'the good life simply is the practice of justice and charity, which is impossible without belief in divine justice'[171] – that is, without natural religion. In addition, Spinoza appeals to the belief that 'the Bible insists on the practice of justice and charity combined with the belief in divine justice as the necessary and sufficient condition of salvation.'[172] He recognizes that these teachings will cease to be true once they no longer hold a popular consensus. Recognizing that these latter teachings are merely the means to Spinoza's teaching about the permanent problems, Strauss concludes that Spinoza proposes a return to the classical heritage of philosophical freedom. It is not Spinoza's goal to refute revelation; rather, his goal is to deny the authority of revelatory theology over philosophy.

Strauss's reading of Spinoza exemplifies his approach to texts. In order to understand Spinoza as he understood himself, one must recognize that if an author bases his argument on historical conditions, in order to read the author appropriately, one must try to understand those conditions. In Spinoza's case, the historical conditions were first, the relative tolerance in Amsterdam; second, the fact that the transition to modernity had been accomplished already by Hobbes, Bacon, and Descartes; third, ecclesiastical authority in Christian Europe had been weakened; fourth, a variety of Christian sects had taken hold in some Protestant countries; and fifth and finally, religious persecution had become unpopular. These factors made the time ripe for Spinoza to plea for religious tolerance.[173] Spinoza's ultimate intention was to ameliorate the Jewish empirical situation in Christian Europe.[174]

Strauss begins by identifying in Spinoza's *Treatise* certain contradictions. First, his explicit statements contradict his subject matter. He claims, for instance, that Christianity is universal and spiritual, whereas Judaism is particularistic and carnal; it follows that Christianity can ascend easily to philosophy, whereas Judaism despises philosophy. Yet at the same time, the New Testament is not spoken of as fully as the Old Testament; few if any references are made to Christian commentators; and Spinoza's interpretations are not indebted to Christian sources.[175] Furthermore, Spinoza is indebted to Jewish sources and Jewish commentators for his interpretations. For reasons that will become more apparent below, Strauss rejects the explanation that Spinoza is more versed in the Jewish than in the Christian tradition. The second contradiction in Spinoza's *Treatise* to which Strauss points is that Spinoza's explicitly stated goal is to separate philosophy from revelatory theology, yet he allows that theology – Hobbes's 'fundamental religion,' the Incarnation – to form the basis of his argument for privatizing religion.[176] Third, Strauss identifies in the *Treatise* a contradiction between Spinoza's claim that the Old Testament and the New Testament teach equally the universal divine law, yet only the Old Testament is mercilessly attacked.

The resolutions to these contradictions that Strauss discovers point the way toward identifying Spinoza as an esoteric writer.[177] The resolution to the first contradiction – between Spinoza's explicit statements and his subject matter – Strauss adopts from Cohen: Spinoza 'fights Christian prejudices by appealing to Christian prejudices.'[178] Thus, Christianity can ascend easily to philosophy once it rids itself of its carnal Jewish heritage. This strategy, if correctly identified, would provide Spinoza with multiple benefits. First, he would be able to convert as many Christians as possible to his new, post-religious religion. Furthermore, the preponderance of Jewish subject matter in the *Treatise* enhances Spinoza's status as a teacher of things Christian to Christians. Second, there were in Spinoza's day a considerable number of Christians who were liberal and who reduced religious dogma to a minimum; his appeal to these Christians was timely. It was, of course, less dangerous to attack Judaism than Christianity, but, Strauss discovers, Spinoza's argument against the Old Testament was meant to apply to both the Old *and* New Testaments. Vulgar Christians, careless Christian readers, not understanding him, would not persecute him, while more prudent Christians would understand the implications of his thought. At the same time, Spinoza needed to suggest to these more prudent Christian readers that Jews, giving up the problem of serving two masters – the state's laws and their God's ceremonial laws – can, because the Old Testament too contains the true religion of universal divine law, be equal members of the new liberal state.

Strauss discovers that the resolution to Spinoza's second contradiction – that the Incarnation remains an integral part of his attempt to separate philosophy and revelatory theology – is that the *Treatise* is addressed to potential philosophers among Christians. Even while Spinoza attempts to prevent revelatory theology from informing philosophy, he must maintain a connection with theology, with the Incarnation, in order to address the people whom he wishes to convert. Spinoza's ultimate intention is not simply to separate philosophy from revelatory theology; it is also to eliminate the persecution of philosophy by religion. To this end, he argues that Christianity developed as follows. First, with Jesus, Christianity was purely spiritual. To spread the Word, the apostles appealed to the views of the audience that were accepted at the time. Once religion was adapted to popular opinion through the introduction of human intellectual elements, philosophy was introduced into faith. The result has been that religion, as the authority for philosophy, can persecute or invalidate philosophy. For Spinoza, the sceptic is someone who does not believe in true religion but does not believe in philosophy either.[179] By separating philosophy and revelatory theology, Spinoza can free philosophy from the constraints of religious authority. Equally important is that through this separation, he can return Christianity to its original basis: a basis that teaches universal love. Spinoza grounds his plea for religious tolerance of Jews in the very roots of Christianity.[180]

With these resolutions, and his discovery of Spinoza's esoteric writing, Strauss is able to identify the resolution to the third contradiction – that is, that Spinoza both attacks the Old Testament and also affirms that it contains the universal divine law. Spinoza's real goal, Strauss argues, is to establish a liberal democracy based on the Noachide laws, which are derived from both the Old Testament alone and also from the Old and New Testaments taken together.[181] Jews are capable of being citizens of the new state because their religion, like Christianity, teaches universal love. Both Jews and Christians, by returning to the true religion and by giving up its various interpretations, can be united in the modern liberal state. Christians need only return to a purely spiritual Christianity, the Christianity that preaches love and that should be amenable to Spinoza's plea for toleration.

Ingeniously, Spinoza bases his argument for the separation of philosophy and revelatory theology on the assertion that the Bible itself denies miracles. Strauss spells out the perhaps disingenuous argument[182] that Spinoza uses to dismiss religion as the basis of his modern democracy.[183] He points out that Spinoza is always restrained in his discussions about revelatory theology, except regarding one point, which is 'unambiguously expressed': the impossibility of miracles as supranatural phenomena.[184] Though it clearly contradicts his willingness to presuppose the suprarational teaching of the Incarnation, Spinoza must make this claim in order to separate philosophy from revelatory theology. To preserve philosophy and religion even while separating them, Spinoza must deny both that biblical teaching is equivalent to rational teaching and also that there is no truth in biblical teaching, in which case there would be no religion. He solves the contradiction by arguing, as Strauss frames it, that miracles either are 'implicit' and 'sacred,' and therefore, like belief in the Incarnation, 'obligatory,' or are 'explicit' and 'indifferent from a religious point of view,' in which case miracles are non-obligatory.[185] To put it perhaps too simply, because the Incarnation is, for Spinoza, suprarational but not supranatural, it is not a miracle proper; rather, each human being can be a Christ.[186]

The unevenness with which Spinoza deals with the suprarational and the supranatural is paralleled by the unevenness with which he deals with the universal and the particular. Again, Strauss points to the irrational basis of Spinoza's argument. Spinoza argues that prophecy is a natural phenomenon. Yet Spinoza's argument, to be rational, should begin with this question: What phenomena can possibly be peculiar to a nation? He might then go on to conclude validly that prophecy is both universal and natural. Spinoza presumes the superiority of the universal to the particular, or to a particularism – such as Judaism's concept of election – that builds to, or interacts with, universalism.[187] While it may be correct that Spinoza felt alienated equally by Christianity and Judaism, or that his attack on the Old Testament was meant to represent his attack on both Judaism and Christianity, the suprarationality at the basis of his democracy and the universal basis of his conversion to the new philosophico-religion result in qualifications for citizenship in Spinoza's democracy that are more problematic for Jews than for Christians.

The result of Spinoza's arguments for the superiority of the suprarational and of the natural conception of the universal is the dismissal of Jews as Jews from the liberal state. Jews as Jews can adapt their thought to contemporary necessity, but Spinoza's model for a Jewish secularism, Strauss argues, must be rejected because it breaks with Judaism – that is, it does not develop from Judaism. The assimilationist model that Spinoza offers for modern Jews is not a solution to the permanent problem of Jew hatred, but only a stopgap measure. Not only this, but also, as Strauss notes, the traditional Jewish ascription of suffering to the state of election is no longer an option for modern Jews. Because the state is underwritten with (as Fackenheim calls it) Spinoza's post-Christian religion – a religion that is universal and anthropocentric – for Jews as Jews to adopt the ethic of the state is, Strauss argues, to deprive themselves of self-respect.[188] The fact that social inequality continued to exist in Weimar, and the fact of the modern liberal state's avowed obligation to defend the private realm of its citizens, despite what that private realm might contain, is, Strauss argues, a weakness built into that state. Strauss writes: 'To recognize a private sphere in the sense indicated ["protected by the law but impervious to the law, with the understanding that, above all, religion as particular religion belongs to the private sphere"[189]] means to permit private "discrimination," to protect it, and thus in fact to foster it.'[190] Furthermore, because the private realm of Spinoza's democracy is defined by belief in the suprarational concept of the Incarnation – or, alternatively, Judaism's necessary denial of that concept – the private realm of the citizenry is, seemingly, antithetical to Jewish thought.

The weakness of the modern liberal state is not simply a result of its necessarily protecting the private realms of its citizens. More pointedly, when religion is located within the private realm, revelation is translated into the terms of reason, which thereby diminishes religion's standing. The private realm, as Spinoza defines it, is a construction based on the irrational dismissal of revelation. His liberal state is a reversal of the classical relationship between philosophy and religion; and, because Judaism in Strauss's formulation is primarily revealed Law,[191] Judaism as such is expelled from even the private realm. Because revelation is irrationally seemingly dismissed, neither revelation nor reason can provide a standard for right action. Reason cannot provide a standard because the foundation of the argument on which the modern liberal state is based is not rational; access to the eternal verities is seemingly not an option for its citizens. Yet at the same time, revelation itself has been seemingly invalidated; there is no means to guide moral action politically.

The situation that Spinoza created for modern Jews is one of choicelessness. Even the Zionist alternative, Strauss argues, is but a special case of the assimilationist alternative because it threatens, or even nullifies, the 'spirit of Judaism,' its opposition to war and the 'energy of government,' or more simply, its 'hope for divine redemption.'[192] Jews as Jews cannot be part of a modern liberal state, yet neither can they remain within, or return to, pre-modern Judaism. Spinoza is the single person who accomplishes a break with Judaism. Whether he disapproves of Christianity equally or not, his break with Judaism is defined by his presumption that Jewish specificity is a prejudice. Spinoza understands the idea of prejudice in the light of the modern sanctification of freedom, which, Strauss argues, inverts the medieval polarity of 'faithfulness and rebellion' to one of 'freedom and prejudice.'[193] Inherent in such an inversion is a conception of an imperfect beginning, one of enslavement from which the human being can progressively free himself. The beginnings are inferior, and Judaism's antiquity is in principle a sign of its backwardness.[194]

According to Strauss's reading of Spinoza, esoteric writing teaches readers that the wise person has a duty to keep dangerous things to himself: 'Whereas truth requires that one should not accommodate the words of the Bible to one's own opinions, piety requires that everyone should accommodate the words of the Bible to his own opinions.'[195] While Spinoza rejects exoterically the 'nonevident meaning of the Bible,'[196] Strauss discovers that the evident meaning of something is not always its true meaning: it is in the esoteric that Judaism and philosophy come into contact.[197] Both thinkers agree that the wise person can exist, can be pious, even in a tyranny, as long as he keeps silent about his true opinions. Jews can be part of the modern historical/political world by adapting their speech to contemporary necessity, or alternatively, by formulating their thought with an awareness of the surface of contemporary political circumstances. Fackenheim rejects this conclusion: in the Holocaust, Jews as Jews were denied even the right of self-preservation; for this reason, and others, Jews as Jews cannot be people-in-general. The wise person cannot preserve himself in all tyrannies. Esoteric writing is not, for Fackenheim, a viable means of addressing the Jewish problem.[198]

Strauss on Cohen

Hermann Cohen had an enormous influence on Strauss, and, since his work on Cohen introduced him to Guttmann and provided his entrée into Jewish teaching, one might suggest that Cohen marks the beginning of Strauss's Jewish intellectual career. Strauss, in fact, went to Marburg to study – although it was after Cohen's death – and was by his own account attracted to him 'because he was a passionate philosopher and a Jew passionately devoted to Judaism.'[199] Perhaps most important to Strauss, he took political philosophy seriously.[200] When Strauss wrote the introduction to the English translation of Cohen's *Religion of Reason*, he recognized the latter's importance to modern thought as a political thinker who both began the critique of Spinoza – which would become the major starting point for Strauss's mature independent thought – and who also recognized that reason and revelation, the traditions of Athens and Jerusalem, are distinct teachings.

Strauss admired Cohen and was indebted to him for dismantling the German deification of Spinoza. Even so, Strauss also recognizes in his thought two underlying, and particularly modern, mistakes.[201] First, with regard to his political philosophy, Cohen believed in the possibility of 'redemption through the state.'[202] This position betrays a modern prejudice that the state's connection with religion is not, as Plato had argued, a means of establishing authority as opposed to attaining wisdom, but rather that the state itself, as a construction of the human being's autonomous reason, synthesizes both authority and knowledge. The state, following Hobbes and Spinoza, can be a realm that makes infinite progress toward its own self-fulfilment.[203] Cohen's belief that the state can be a realm of infinite progress toward a necessarily ethical goal accounts for what Strauss identifies as his second mistake: his belief that reason, not obedience, can serve as the basis of Judaism.[204] His belief in reason as the foundation of both the state and also revelatory religion betrays, to Strauss, Cohen's specifically modern attempt at a synthesis between reason and revelation – an attempt that he indicts.[205]

Strauss believes that we owe a great debt to Cohen as a philosopher and as a Jew; even so, he critiques Cohen's thought as 'fundamentally flawed by its historicist outlook.'[206] Cohen attempts to understand Plato and the prophets as the two most fundamental elements of modern culture, but his adoption of historicism, or the idea of history, precludes him from understanding either Plato or the prophets, either Athens or Jerusalem, in its own terms.[207] The result is a naivety revealed through a synthesis of reason and revelation, a naivety that begins in an understanding of the human being that is removed from the most basic and elemental recognition of what it is to be a human being: from the surface of things that is accessible to the human being as human being. Cohen, in a theme that will be picked up by Fackenheim,[208] could not recognize the brute fact of history – the occurrences of actual empirical events – because he understood history already as an *interpretation* of those events.[209] Cohen's 'misunderstanding of man'[210] is also a misunderstanding of man's thought – the thought, specifically, of Plato and of the prophets. He had concluded that the prophets provided the means by which to overcome Plato's elitism, an elitism that made impossible – because philosophers are too few – the establishment of his Republic. Plato provided the science through which suffering can be overcome.[211] Cohen's synthesis, in his own account, provided the means by which human beings can overcome evil and progress through their own efforts toward establishing the kingdom of heaven on earth. In Strauss's account, Cohen's recognition of the distinction between scientific and prophetic knowledge, his recognition of the importance of each Athens and Jerusalem, is to be commended. At the same time, his synthesis of the two reveals to Strauss his failure 'to see that the fundamental quarrel is between the moderns and the ancients and not between Plato and Aristotle or Kant and Hegel.'[212]

According to Strauss, Cohen deserves credit for recognizing that there had not been since the time of Spinoza a serious encounter between philosophy and revelatory theology. Yet his attempt to inform philosophy with revelatory theology is a failure. By adding the third Hegelian category of history, into which both reason and revelation are subsumed, Cohen hopes to synthesize philosophy and revelatory theology. The dynamic of the rationality of the historical process synthesizes Platonism and Judaism. Cohen in effect claims that if one can uncover, in classical Jewish texts, neo-Kantianism as their highest possibility, then Judaism as a living, creative dynamic is dead. His attempt to resolve the conflict between reason and revelation is a failure because he exposes both philosophical thought and Judaism to historicism.

It is through an 'intricate polemic against Cohen' that Strauss returns to the thought of Maimonides.[213] The critique encompasses at least two points. First, Cohen did not sufficiently understand the idea of political authority: by adopting the Kantian categorical imperative as the basis of ethical behaviour, he adopts also the idea of political self-creation, or the understanding of the political community as a product of 'culture.' There develops a certain political naivety: the reality of the meaner aspects of human behaviour is concealed but not eliminated in the idea of human universalism. Not only is the idea that political exigency must provide the authority for thought and the surface of its expression overridden in favour of idealism, but also the need for philosophy is seemingly abolished, as there is no longer a need for philosophical wisdom, the wisdom to contemplate or elaborate on the good. There seems no longer to be the need to ponder the permanent human problems – or rather, no problem seems any longer to be permanent.

Second, Strauss argues, Cohen's adoption of Kantianism leads him to presuppose the impossibility of a return to pre-modern thought. By adopting the Baconian concept of nature, Kant necessitates the introduction of the idea of history as the means by which to separate the human being from his fixed position in the natural hierarchy.[214] The idea of history, or recorded human progress that literally manipulates or alters human consciousness, supplies for Kant the freedom necessary for ethical behaviour. But this freedom is necessary only because Kant has pre-defined human consciousness as separate from Bacon's natural mechanism. Cohen presupposes the impossibility of a return to pre-modern thought only because he presupposes the Kantian natural world: the presupposition of the inability of accounting for historical development in philosophical thought is a consequence of the modern anthropocentric view of reality. By rediscovering a physiocentric and/ or theocentric formulation of reality, it is possible to discover as well a mode of thought that does not presuppose the idea of history.

The thinker to whom Strauss turns, as a corrective to Cohen, toward an understanding of the relationship between reason and revelation, is Maimonides.[215] Strauss's return to Maimonides is predicated both on the need for a fundamental political authority – be it the authority of the human soul or that of the revealed Law – and also on the rediscovery of pre-modern thinking. The redefinition of nature begun in the Enlightenment and concluded in the nineteenth century's reintroduction of Enlightenment thought and beyond – a thought that both incorporates the success of the Enlightenment's exoteric push for atheism and that also synthesizes this success with a return to the orthodox tradition[216] – had served to displace both philosophy and law and to distort revelation: 'since both [the idea of philosophy and the idea of law] took their bearings by nature – philosophy as quest for knowledge of nature and law as necessitated by human nature – both disappeared with the oblivion of nature.'[217]

Strauss on Rosenzweig

By 1925, Strauss recognized that the liberalism of the Weimar Republic was doomed and that so was the status of Jews in Weimar Germany.[218] He characterizes Rosenzweig's thought as a critique of liberalism expressed in an existentialism adapted to a Jewish perspective. Since Germany had fought against liberalism – in the forms of Romanticism, nationalism, and modern antisemitism – Weimar Jews had found themselves in the political position of having to defend the state even while Jewish thought – even Jewish existential thought – recognized its intellectual inadequacy.[219] Strauss argues that Rosenzweig's Jewish existentialism, far from ameliorating the Jewish theologico-political crisis, compounds it: one cannot preserve liberalism's legitimacy while rejecting its intellectual basis. Rosenzweig's existentialism is non-rational, and his intellectual undermining of liberalism, however necessary for Jewish inclusion, makes Jewish existence even more precarious.

Strauss recognizes Rosenzweig's great contribution to Jewish thought – his argument that revelation remains a present possibility[220] – but he is ultimately critical of his new thinking and of neo-Orthodoxy in general. The basis of his critique is Rosenzweig's loss of confidence in reason, his consequent introduction of non-rationalism into reason, and his consequent misconstrual of both traditional revelation and reason. Rather than Rosenzweig, Strauss identifies Spinoza as providing a more appropriate relationship between revelation and reason: Spinoza neither affirms nor refutes revelation; rather, he recognizes – even while arguing for natural reason – the tension between reason and revelation.[221] Rejecting Rosenzweig's neo-Orthodoxy – which, he discovers, is an admixture of reason and non-reason – Strauss asks instead whether an 'unqualified return to Jewish orthodoxy'[222] is possible, since only an unqualified orthodoxy can both provide the terms appropriate to biblical revelation and also preclude the self-destruction of reason initiated by the introduction of the non-rational into rational thought.[223]

In Strauss's formulation, the source of the admixture of reason and non-reason in Rosenzweig's neo-Orthodoxy is the grounding of his thought – despite his return to revelation – in Enlightenment ideals. Because these ideals – those of progress, of autonomy, and of freedom – are at odds with traditional Judaism, which teaches *teshuvah*,[224] and which does not clearly demarcate autonomy from what Kant would call heteronomy, and freedom from authority, one cannot affirm them without drastically idealizing, and altering, Judaism.[225] Strauss's primary critique of Rosenzweig's neo-Orthodoxy is that it fails to recognize adequately Judaism in its own terms; therefore it cannot serve as a means of its perpetuation.

Rosenzweig's misunderstanding of traditional Judaism is evidenced by what Strauss perceives as his attempt to accommodate Judaism to his Christian surroundings. So, for instance, Strauss argues that Rosenzweig seeks to 'identify a starting point for Judaism that corresponds to the role of Jesus as the Christ in Christianity.'[226] When Rosenzweig finds this starting point in the Jewish concept of election, he reverses, without either rational or biblical justification, the traditional relationship between Torah and the Jews: for him, Judaism begins with the Jews.[227] Yet his justification is and remains political. Strauss criticizes him for what may be termed an incorrect contextualization of Judaism, an error that promotes a *literal* misunderstanding of Judaism, eliminates the possibility of ascension – through either philosophy or revelatory theology – to its more esoteric meanings, and inherently cannot succeed in ameliorating the Jewish political situation. The basis of his critique of Rosenzweig on this point is not that he defines his political situation in Jewish terms, but rather that he misdiagnoses that political situation, contextualizing it within Christianity instead of within Judaism.

Second, Rosenzweig's misunderstanding of traditional Judaism is evidenced in his concept of 'absolute empiricism.' Because he reverses the traditional relationship between Torah and the Jews, his 'absolute empiricism' is not empiricism at all, but rather a result of his prior intellectual commitment.[228] Underlying his empiricism is a dogmatic claim. In actuality, Rosenzweig, despite his affirmation that revelation is a present possibility, denies the possibility of a direct encounter with the God of the Torah. Strauss rejects his new thinking as a concession to a presumed superior philosophy. Despite rejecting Spinoza's 'old thinking,' Rosenzweig allows just enough rationalism – in the forms of his Enlightenment ideals and of the underlying dogmatism of his 'absolute empiricism' – to inform his new thinking to make impossible both the adoption of an unqualified return to Jewish orthodoxy and also a direct, empirical, encounter with God.

Notwithstanding Rosenzweig's argument, commended by Strauss, that revelation can be a present possibility, his neo-Orthodoxy perpetuates the break with traditional biblical revelation. Especially problematic for Strauss is the resultant impossibility of belief in traditional revelation: Rosenzweig is blind to the surface of the biblical text, and he rejects 'the immutability of the law'[229] – an immutability that, on a political level, is necessary for stability and peace. Strauss critiques him for reading Torah in a way that is inconsistent with the authors' intention – an inconsistency that by definition deprives law of its authority. The law, for Rosenzweig, becomes solely a means to connect God and human beings. This inconsistency – his willingness to reverse the traditional relationship between God and the Jews, and the consequence of his loosening the law's constraints – is based in his optimism (or idealism) with regard to human nature.[230] Strauss argues against this idealism: if law is not understood as constraint imposed on human beings by God, and if human beings are viewed as naturally good, then human beings become the originators of their own laws. These laws can result in a Hobbesian state of nature, or in a Germany that builds death camps.

In the sense that Rosenzweig reads the Torah in a way that is inconsistent with the authors' intent, the Bible's 'literary character' is ignored. Without recognition of its surface, a reader cannot ascertain a text's more esoteric meaning.[231] Furthermore, such a reading presupposes the superiority of the reader's historical context and is irrational at its very root: it results merely in self-congratulatory and self-perpetuating understanding (what the New Critics call the affective fallacy).[232]

Rosenzweig's accommodation of Judaism to the Christian political context perpetuates the break with traditional Judaism; at the same time, his new thinking perpetuates the break with classical and medieval philosophy. The grounding of his Jewish theological thought in Enlightenment ideals accommodates Jewish revelation to reason and perpetuates the self-destruction of rationalism. Rosenzweig, through his misdiagnosis of his political situation and his blindness to the surface of the text, perpetuates the modern belief in progress and the superiority of the reader's historical context. And so, he perpetuates as well a form of modern historicism: his new thinking, although it includes within rationality revelation's personal standpoint, is, by definition, incapable of refuting the rationality that it presumes. At the same time, because he uses the 'old thinking' – Spinoza's thinking – to defend revelation, he misunderstands or misrepresents revelation in its own terms. His failure is 'mainly as the result of his inconsistent application of his own principles.'[233] His abandonment of faith in reason and his creating a sort of irrationalism built on the foundation of rationalism, perpetuate – despite his attempt to put Judaism on an equal political footing with Christianity – the losing exposure of Judaism to philosophy, and, indeed, of Jews in the political realm.

Strauss concludes that Rosenzweig's neo-Orthodoxy is not an unqualified return to orthodoxy. What is more, he faults Rosenzweig for never attempting a philosophical defence of an unqualified return to orthodoxy. Strauss's critique of his neo-Orthodoxy in favour of an orthodoxy uninformed by historicism emerges from his discovery of nature, or natural law, as the surface of things. Strauss's adoption, and subsequent rejection, of neo-Orthodoxy as a viable option for resolving the theologico-political problem is a result of his return to Spinoza and Maimonides, in whose work he had discovered how pre-modern thinkers may have understood themselves. Ultimately, he agrees with Maimonides's 'expression of a theistic rationalism ... departing from Rosenzweig's more mystical position, which was at the basis of the book he had then written on Spinoza.'[234] Strauss discovers natural law, which, although it implies the question of what is God, does so by affirming that God is an objective measure of human duties. Rosenzweig's neo-Orthodoxy blurs the delineation between revelation from God and human activity. Strauss rejects this blurring as informed by Enlightenment idealism – as dismissing without refutation the traditional transcendent realm of revelation.[235]

Conclusion

For Strauss, philosophy in its original sense and revelatory theology are equally irrefutable.[236] Because it has never created a completed system – a whole from which to understand all the parts – reason has never succeeded in refuting revelation. The fundamental difference between revelatory theology and philosophy in its original sense is that revelatory theology solves the problem of varying cultures by claiming the truth of one particular culture and creates a transcendent, omnipotent, covenantal God. Philosophy solves the same problem by claiming that the truth underlies all the various cultures and can be found in the first principles of the nature of things. There can be no philosophical knowledge of the transcendent God, nor can philosophy verify its own truth. Informing philosophy with revelatory theology is in principle a failure because, in any synthesis, either philosophy or revelatory theology must work in the terms of the other and thus assume the position of inferiority.

Strauss argues that the theologian uses knowledge for the sake of understanding – or, more broadly, serving – God, in keeping with the biblical injunction of loving God with all one's mind. The philosopher, by contrast, uses knowledge for the sake of knowing what he can know, his place in the world, and his prejudices. For Greek philosophical thinkers, defining religious experience or connection with God as the means of understanding one's own soul is a prejudice. For biblical thought, the Greek ideal of contemplation is heresy: God's omnipotence is challenged when thought seeks first principles in nature.

The Bible and philosophy can seem to be synthesized in modern thought; this seems to be theoretically possible if one idealizes one's thought – if one grounds revelation in (exoteric) Enlightenment ideals. Strauss argues against such a synthesis because it ignores the most primary level of thought and its most important aspect: things as they appear to us. The failure of the modern synthetic project of the Bible and philosophy is based on a fundamental blindness to the practical aspects of thought: philosophy is not an instrument to be used to dismantle previous thought, both philosophical and theological. Rather, philosophy is a way of life.[237] In its original sense, philosophy is both open, in the sense that all solutions are questionable, and closed, in the sense that, because ignorance of the most important thing is the starting point, philosophy defines the most important thing as the *quest* for the most important thing. Paradoxically, the philosopher rejects revelation without sufficient proof, defying philosophy, even as his rejection is the basis of his continual allegiance to the quest of philosophy. The Bible, on the other hand, begins, not in wonder, but in wisdom, in revelation of the most important thing. Strauss, then, affirms the practical necessity of making a choice: 'No one can be both a philosopher and a theologian, or, for that matter, some possibility which transcends the conflict between philosophy and theology, or pretends to be a synthesis of both.'[238]

Strauss's recognition that each philosophy and the Bible must be understood fundamentally as a way of life provides the methodology for his reading. A reader must recognize and remain with the surface of the text. Because the modern idea of history has introduced, through the work of Machiavelli, Bacon, Hobbes, and Spinoza, the possibility of emptying the revelatory tradition of content, and then – through, for instance, the work of Cohen and Rosenzweig – the possibility of reintroducing (in a historicized formulation) belief in that tradition, the modern idea of history has also made possible the choice of whether to stand inside or outside the revelatory tradition in thought. To understand a text, modern readers either must recognize which stance an author takes, or must assess whether an author, such as Cohen or Rosenzweig, makes a choice appropriate to the literal level, to the surface of things, in his attempt to make a theoretical synthesis between reason and revelation. Without such a recognition, knowledge, for both the writer and the reader, remains elusive because reason and revelation lose their respective authorities and become idealized.

Strauss proposes an exploration of the possibility of an unqualified return to Jewish orthodoxy or to classical philosophical thinking. He recognizes the near impossibility of such a task. Indeed, he recognizes a temporary need for the study of the history of philosophy as a tool by which we might extricate ourselves from historicism in order to return ourselves to the appropriate cave.[239] From that cave, he discovers that there is a theoretic openness of philosophical thought to the possibility of revelation, just as a theoretic openness exists from the side of revelation to reason. The question arises: Does Strauss choose Jerusalem or Athens?[240]

3 Fackenheim's Formulation of the Relationship between Philosophy and Revelatory Theology in Modern Thought

Introduction

This chapter explores Fackenheim's formulation of the crisis of modernity – the loss of faith in both reason and revelation – as well as his attempt to construct a new thinking that is at once both philosophical and Jewish. As we saw in the last chapter, Strauss had articulated the development of the crisis as the loss of the art of esoteric writing, which had led to confusion between the critique of the external and internal truths of religion, which in turn had led to the attempt to reintroduce revelation into reason, or to synthesize it with reason. Fackenheim, working as a philosopher primarily within the German Idealist tradition, traces the crisis to the human internalization of God. This internalization led to the belief in human self-creation as well as to an idolatrous stance that is the source of the specifically anti-Jewish animus in modern philosophical thought. Fackenheim rejects a return to esoteric writing because to emphasize the esoteric meaning of a work precludes the definition of existence as an ontological category. He understands existence as the surface of the thing from which ontological categories arise or are derived. The emphasis on esoteric meaning ignores how a text's exoteric meaning actually played out in history. So, for instance, Spinoza asks that he be read historically. The fact that historical events have proved the impossibility of Spinoza's state coming into existence renders moot Spinoza's esoteric meaning.

This chapter begins with Fackenheim's work in Western philosophy, including Kant, Hegel, Schelling, and Heidegger. He seeks to encounter, and through these encounters to refute, the human internalization of God, the incorporation of revelation into reason, and the radical historicism to which the internalization led. By reaffirming – or rediscovering – revelation as the incursion of an Absolute Other into history, he attempts to undo the synthesis of reason and revelation. He takes history seriously as a category of thought: history is the only locus in which the human being can encounter God. In Fackenheim's understanding, the work of Kant, Hegel, Schelling, and Heidegger has 'entered into' human history, and therefore it has entered into human consciousness. This in turn has changed human self-consciousness. This position is the source of Fackenheim's acceptance of a quasi-historicism (discussed in chapters 4 and 5) and would seem to indicate that more pressing to him than the philosophical question 'What can the human being know?' is the question of how the contemporary Jew is to formulate a narrative that at once leads to holiness,[1] connects to the Jewish past, and is believable. Fackenheim seeks not to return to pre-modern thought, since any attempt to do so would be too 'grim' – because it would deny the possibility of God's incursion into contemporary, secular history – as well as not 'grim' enough – because it would amount to escaping the historical realities of secularism and of evil, and of the Holocaust in particular.[2] Rather, he seeks to encounter and reformulate modern thought.

Fackenheim traces the origin of the human internalization of God to Kant's anthropocentric understanding of religion: religion within the bounds of reason alone. Yet in Fackenheim's reading, Kant did not discount the possibility of a non-anthropocentrically based revelatory religion. For this reason, Kant's thought remains fruitful for him, as it provides for him a key element for his 'new thinking': through an encounter with Kant, Fackenheim may establish evil as an ontological category.

Hegel dismissed altogether the possibility of a non-anthropocentrically based religion by formulating revelation as the gradual unfolding of God within historical experience. Yet Hegel will provide for Fackenheim his most fruitful encounter: by returning to Hegel, he returns to the source of the battle between philosophy and history, to the source of what later became historicism. Hegel himself, according to Fackenheim, was not a historicist: although Hegel the philosopher precludes Judaism ontologically, Hegel the historian recognizes the continued existence of Jews and Judaism. His return to Hegel's thought as a foundation for future Jewish thought is therefore not philosophically precluded. Furthermore, his return to Hegel's synthesis of the religious concern for history and philosophy's concern for the eternal enables him to ground his attempt to make existence an ontological category, even as he avoids the radical historicism of the later Heidegger.

The 'pointing' of Schelling's positive philosophy provides for Fackenheim the basis for a philosophy that is open both to the possibility of revelation and also to the varieties of human experience. This philosophy will become one basis of his attempt to establish a doctrine of a qualified historicism – a 'new thinking' based in both metaphysics and human being – emerging from what he calls the meontological tradition of metaphysics.[3] The philosophy is – to the extent that history is fundamentally different for us than it was for pre-modern thinkers – historicist, but Fackenheim's historicism is qualified by the rational necessity of leaving open the possibility of God as an Absolute Other – qualified, in other words, by the facticity of the given. His rejection of Heidegger demonstrates that Fackenheim's open philosophy remains philosophical: it is not open to all forms of self-conscious thought.

Fackenheim's effort to open philosophy to revelatory thought, and the difficulties for traditional metaphysics that arise as a result,[4] are met equally in his efforts to open revelatory theology to philosophy. The second part of this chapter examines Fackenheim's work on Jewish thought, including the Bible, Spinoza, Cohen, Rosenzweig, and Buber. In his work on Jewish thinkers, he returns to Strauss's question: Is the revelatory tradition reliable? Unlike Strauss, however, he seeks to encounter their thought with the claims of metaphysics. Only by informing Jewish revelatory thought with philosophy can Judaism provide meaning for we who live in a secular context, as well as hope (as distinct from idealism) that the secular context in which we live may be the locus of divine action. It was Cohen who began the process of encounter between Jewish and metaphysical thought in the modern world. Fackenheim, however, finds that Cohen, while deeply committed to Judaism, was too deeply influenced by German Idealism to retain Judaism's affirmation of a loving and awesome relationship with the Sinaitic God. Fackenheim returns to the Bible in order to define a basis – organically Jewish, yet open to the claims of both metaphysics and the existential context of contemporary Jews – from which a contemporary Judaism might grow. Unlike Spinoza, he takes the Bible seriously on its own terms instead of dismissing its message as incoherent. Rosenzweig and Buber too had returned to the Bible with a contemporary seriousness; but Fackenheim deviates from these thinkers insofar as he affirms the possibility of defining a philosophically informed, Jewish, and historically relevant way of thinking. Just as he rejects what he understands – perhaps somewhat partially – to be Strauss's return to Greek thought as a means of rediscovering the authority of reason,[5] so too he rejects Buber's revelatory thought as a means of reaffirming the authority of revelation: Buber's reaffirmation of the boundaries of revelation and revelatory theology does not take seriously enough either radical evil or the possibility of God's intervention in secular history.

The third part of this chapter examines Fackenheim's attempt at re-synthesizing reason and revelation in a way that makes both viable for future Jewish thought. He suggests the possibility of a way of thinking that is at once committed to philosophical objectivity – a commitment, derived from Strauss, that precludes the idealism implicit in a whole-hearted ascription to the doctrine of historicism – and to Judaism, or at any rate, to an ongoing covenantal relationship to the Sinaitic God.

I remind the reader of Fackenheim's methodology, which I follow, in an attempt to understand his thought as far as possible as he himself understood it. Fackenheim suggests that 'the present must reach out for the past,'[6] that his readings of past thinkers are informed by present historical need. In some cases this methodology leads to what may be misapprehensions regarding the thought – misapprehensions that, as we shall see more pointedly in chapters 4 and 5, result from this historicist, or quasi-historicist, reading methodology. Fackenheim's arguments with the thinkers represented in this chapter have as much to do with their particular syntheses of reason and revelation as with their overall project of synthesizing them. It is a question of whether his reformulating the project of synthesis as one in which reason and revelation are in dialectical, or fragmented, relationship – as they are in Fackenheim's understanding of 'Judaism' – is sustainable.

Fackenheim on Kant

The decisive break between pre-modern (indeed, all the moderns preceding him) and modern understandings of the relationship between revealed morality and philosophy came, according to Fackenheim, with Kant.[7] In the pre-modern period, revealed morality and reason could coexist as long as the foundations of each retained their integrity: philosophical morality required that morality be universal and that it issue from a source independent of revelation; revealed morality could concede a distinction between rational and ceremonial laws, with rational laws satisfying the foundational requirements of philosophical morality and ceremonial laws satisfying Judaism's fundamental belief in revelation and its concomitant belief in the concept of chosenness. Just as Judaism need not object in principle to the requirements of philosophical morality, so too philosophical morality, in the pre-modern world, need not object in principle to Judaism's positing of ceremonial laws. The disagreement between philosophical and Jewish ethics related to the content of morality, not its foundations.[8] Kant posed these questions: If law cannot obligate one unless the law 'spring[s] from [one's] own will,'[9] is revealed morality a contradiction in terms? Is revelation alone insufficient for morality since morality requires an act of self-obligation? And if morality is utterly separate from an immediate experience with God, are the ceremonial laws either a human invention, or irrelevant to morality, or both?

By raising these questions, Kant not only challenged the validity of revelation, but also, and more important, undermined the medieval model of the mutual toleration of reason and revelation. It now seemed that revelation had been rendered irrelevant because it required the mediation of morality. Fackenheim, in response, attempts in *Encounters* to remedy the distortion of revelation even while he takes seriously Kant's challenge. By reaffirming the 'pristine Commanding Presence' of God, Fackenheim attempts to bring back to human life – insofar as the life is lived in accordance with the commandments – its direct relation to revelation.[10] He reaffirms the integrity of revelation distinct from philosophical foundations; but at the same time, by discovering God as the source of both autonomy (insofar as He commands) and heteronomy (insofar as His Presence, transcending human standards, presents to human beings the choice of whether to accept or reject Him), Fackenheim attempts a philosophical justification of the claims of Judaism. This is very much like Kant's affirmation of human autonomy; and indeed, elsewhere Fackenheim would concede that the theme of Kant and Judaism may be 'inexhaustible' because the two share a 'common core': 'the categorically commanding voice of Kant's moral reason, and the no less categorically commanding voice of the God of Judaism.'[11] The 'encounter' between Kant and Judaism here is (almost) as if Fackenheim is modelling the Jew's acceptance of the Divine Presence on Kant's model of how the moral human being accepts the moral law: Torah serves as the bridge connecting the Commanding Presence and the free appropriation of the Divine Will as one's own.

But, like Fackenheim, Kant also recognizes the problem of how to relate revealed and rational law, and Fackenheim detects in him a certain hesitancy regarding the revolutionary implications for revealed morality of his theory of autonomy: 'this is a theme to which he kept returning, as if unable to leave it alone.'[12] Kant is unable to discard what Fackenheim identifies as his reality principle, whereby realism is conjoined with idealism;[13] because, in Fackenheim's reading, he remains cognizant that human existence includes irrational aspects, Kant is unable to deny the existence either of evil or of the possibility of revelation. The reality principle includes the personal, the historical, and the religious realms. In the personal realm, Kant is aware – despite his suggestion that duty alone determines morality – that human inclinations matter deeply to us. Accordingly, he does not claim that inclinations are evil – only that they are irrelevant to moral action. In *Metaphysics of Morals* he goes even further by arguing that certain duties follow certain feelings. In the historical realm, Kant, while pursuing 'perpetual peace,' recognizes the need for the 'grim political necessity' that will compel bad people to right action.[14] Religiously, Kant includes as a property in his kingdom of ends a 'deserved happiness … such as can only be the gift of God.'[15] His motivation is to provide context for pure reason; so, for instance, life after death establishes the reality of a realm separate from the empirical. His moral theology implicates the transcendent God even as this God is articulated as an idea of pure practical reason: if He does not exist, eschatological hope is not warranted. While the 'God-Idea suffices to inspire moral action … only an *existing* God can warrant an eschatological hope.'[16] Kant, in Fackenheim's reading, unlike his followers, retains the possibilities of a transcendent God and of revelation.

Kant's goal is to create a new metaphysics, one that is based not on speculation but on moral consciousness.[17] Accordingly, he seeks to prove that belief in a transcendent God and immortality is implicit in moral consciousness. He highlights the human condition as one of internal contradiction: we are not animals seeking happiness and presuming that virtue is its by-product, but neither are we gods seeking virtue and presuming that we have no share in the natural world. Human beings are finite moral agents seeking infinite or absolute morality. Kant resolves this contradiction by positing God as the common author of the natural and moral worlds; God must be transcendent if He is to reconcile the inherent contradiction of the finite moral standpoint.

Yet Kant, by recognizing that human theoretical and moral standpoints are finite, gives rise to the notion of the absolute standpoint. With the absolute standpoint, the early Schelling and Hegel are able to posit what Fackenheim refers to as 'the God within' and to bring closer to fruition the project that, in its attempt to synthesize revelatory theology and philosophy, identifies God with the human absolute standpoint. But Kant escapes this conclusion by suggesting that morality give way to religion. When we heed the human ability to recognize and thus enact the transcendent moral law, the search for a pure, *a priori* source of certain knowledge can lead us to uncover principles of morality, God, and immortality – principles that are implicit in moral consciousness.

According to Kant, the metaphysics that has moral consciousness as its grounding is but a partial representation of human knowledge. Morality, because it is the highest sphere of rationally accessible truth, is autonomous, but this autonomy in no way suggests that the human being is autonomous with regard to revelatory truths. God and human immortality are concepts implicit in the rational constitution of the human being and must lead the moral consciousness to religion. These concepts are not certain as *noumena:* they may or may not really exist, but they certainly exist as concepts necessary for all human understanding.

Since in Kant's formulation, reason requires God as the ultimate unconditioned being, reason articulates God as only a 'symbolic anthropomorphism.'[18] Kant's God is, apparently, only a representation of the unity of the finite and the infinite that exists as human reason, which is then projected by human reason outside itself. The transcendence that is necessary for the perpetuation of finite reason's thinking outside finiteness is, in these apparent terms, a self-projection of reason. But in Fackenheim's reading, while for Kant 'morality is the highest sphere of rationally accessible truth ... [and] must also be autonomous, i.e., unlimited in scope and authority by a sphere beyond it,' he also asserts 'the necessity of a "transition" from "morality" to "religion."'[19] The decisive question is whether he can justify the necessity of this transition because without such justification, Kant's new metaphysics is a failure of philosophy and of religion. It would fail philosophically because Kant's God representation would be derived only from the supposition of first and final causes, which Bacon – whose *New Organon* is excerpted by Kant in a long epigraph to his *Critique of Pure Reason* – had understood as at least beyond human comprehension and more specifically as an 'idol of the mind.'[20] The rational projection of God as only a symbolic anthropomorphism would fail religiously as well because it focuses on religion as a means of achieving moral stature. Kant's religious philosophy aims at clarifying what we may (rationally) hope for; in the absence of knowledge, it clarifies what we are obliged to believe in order to strengthen our capacity to obey the moral law. Kant, then, reformulates the religious dimension of morality – from the priority of God who reveals the moral law to the priority of the moral law that may reveal God. In authentic religion, according to Fackenheim, we accept the contradiction that is inherent in moral finiteness: the human inability to know through the apparatus of our own thinking if we fulfil any aspect of transcendence. It is faith that both teaches that the contradiction in the human condition between finiteness and transcendence (i.e., access to God) is not ultimate and also enables human beings to continue to strive for moral integrity. Without Kant's 'transition' there can be no room for revelatory religion; indeed, in Fackenheim's formulation, this failure initiated the project of the human internalizing of God.

Fackenheim concludes that the necessity of the transition from the realm of morality to that of religion for which Kant argues – the connection between what ought to be and what is – cannot be sustained; and that for his successors, the moral theology of Kant speaks, as it were, for revelatory theology. And while Kant recognizes the existence of evil, he denies that evil has any independent (ontological) existence; it becomes simply a 'perversion of the order of maxims.'[21] Fackenheim's argument with Kant, then, is based primarily on Kant's belief that the moral law is implicit in human consciousness – a belief that precludes him from recognizing the ontological reality of evil: by understanding evil as simply a perversion of the order of maxims, Kant understands evil as something that is not permanent in human nature. In his view, human beings have the ability, within their permanent rational constitutions, to fulfil their own morality, or to self-convert. Kant here creates a moral parallelism between good and evil, a parallelism that he presumes will issue in the good because of his belief that the moral law, unlike evil, is a permanent part of human consciousness. But because he rejects the possibility that evil might in fact be chosen as a 'duty,' and even 'respected,'[22] Kantian morality precludes the possibility that evil has independent existence. Without the existence of evil as an actual entity, Kant has no need to provide an ultimate rational grounding for the choosing of good over evil because the choice is, as it were, a choice of necessity. He does not provide for moral consciousness a standard by which to judge itself and in accordance with which to self-convert. Kant's 'evil,' in Fackenheim's formulation, is not 'radical'; it does not recognize that evil must be understood as a transcendent (ontological) principle equal in reality to good.[23]

For Fackenheim, the Holocaust has demonstrated that the moral law is not implicit in human moral consciousness, that the human being cannot transcend his finite moral standpoint and that he is capable – in the Kantian spirit – of choosing either good, as in the case of Kurt Huber, or evil, as in the case of Eichmann.[24] Kant's 'divine spark within' the moral consciousness – that spark which is a permanent part of the constitution of rational nature that so constitutes human rationality according to principles of 'duty' and 'respect' – can be destroyed by the human being who chooses evil. In Fackenheim's formulation, so unsubstantiated is the grounding of Kantian morality that the Nazis were able to adopt it with an alternative grounding principle: there is no divine spark in human consciousness. Kantian morality lends itself to the establishment of what Fackenheim calls – in allusion to Alexander Donat,[25] and in contradistinction to Kant's 'kingdom of ends,' wherein a state or commonwealth is a harmonious constitution of the ends of the universal moral law and of each citizen – the 'Holocaust Kingdom.'[26] So too in Auschwitz, the commonwealth was a 'systematic union ... through common laws'[27] between the ends of the perpetrators and those of the victims: the Nazis, through the autonomy of their consciousness, denied the divine spark in the human being, and through this denial, the divine spark in both perpetrators and victims was denied existence.[28] Kant's explanation for the necessity of the transition from morality to religion pales next to the historical reality of its lack.[29]

As a corrective to Kant – in order to recognize the historical reality of radical evil in the advent of the Nazis, and in order to propose a means of reinvesting the world with good – Fackenheim seeks a standard by which to recognize evil as transcendent, and good as qualified by its ability to 'mend the world.' The standard must articulate the existence of transcendence separate from human autonomy – as a means of recognizing and judging evil – and must also establish good as a product of human choice – as a means of bringing into empirical history the divine spark. As has been mentioned, Fackenheim in his earlier work *Encounters*, following Kant's model, disavows a duality between autonomy and heteronomy in order to allow room for revelatory religion within the construct of human autonomy. He suggests that the autonomous be identified with the heteronomous because divine love is in the commandments, not subsequent to them.[30] Since God made human appropriation of the commandments possible, fulfilment of the commandments enacts God's love. Because it is human choice to fulfil the commandments, there is no duality between autonomy and heteronomy: God adapts His will to human will. Kant's moral imperative is translated by Fackenheim into *teshuvah*, the theological turn from evil to God – not from the idea of evil but from the event of evil that even God's grace cannot overcome.[31] Evil is recognized as a 'radical' principle; good is recognized as being qualified by human choice.

But Fackenheim's earlier formulation of evil as a transcendent principle – and he himself comes to see this – fails to recognize that, since morality is defined as the means through which one comes to God, his formulation continues to rely on Kant's belief in the necessity of the transition from morality to religion. Kant left room within reason for revelation by trying to establish as its ultimate principle the implicitness of moral consciousness within the human being; so too, Fackenheim's earlier attempt to adapt Kantian morality – through the equation of God's will and human beings's will – simply translates Kant's innate divine spark into the motivation for Jewish observance of the commandments. Finding divine love in the commandments, according to the later Fackenheim, 'seems more a sublimation of divine love to the moral than a "coeval" existence.'[32] To resolve this difficulty, in *To Mend the World* he reframes his position to argue that the moral dimension is situated within God. His position undergoes a reversal of the relationship between the moral and the religious: the commandments become the human means of approaching God since they 'find [their] way *into* God.'[33] At the same time, the reversal of his position indicates his recognition of the impossibility of an encounter between philosophy and revelatory theology based solely in the realm of reason.

Kant, for Fackenheim, begins the modern project of internalizing God by redefining God as the principle of autonomy through which the human being transcends his finite standpoint; however, Kant fails in his attempt to retain the tension between reason and revelatory theology. His argument against continuing to consider the metaphysics of morals a branch of natural theology – the theology that claims that the moral law is of one's very being – in favour of considering it a branch of moral theology leaves room within reason for revelation: the theology makes of revelation a projection of the mind with the possibility of a *noumenon* behind the phenomenon. But Kant's delicate balance between reason and revelation cannot be philosophically or empirically validated. This inability provokes later thinkers to drive toward establishing a synthesis between philosophy and revelatory theology, a drive that culminates in the redefinition of revelatory theology as the autonomous uncovering of 'the God within.' Philosophy, meanwhile,

while retaining the semblance of its dependence on revelatory theology, loses recognition of its partiality.

Fackenheim on Hegel

The need for a new encounter with Hegel, after the encounters (not wholly successful) with Rosenzweig and Buber,[34] is twofold: to dissolve – following Rosenzweig – the division of nineteenth-century Jews between those who promoted Jews and Judaism as missionary, such as Hermann Cohen,[35] and those who espoused secular Zionism; and to provide Jewish witness against 'Constantinian' thought.[36] These two motives guide Fackenheim's thought on Hegel in two directions. First, he understands the Holocaust as having in some sense reinforced the theological concept of election insofar as Jews were singled out not simply by their beliefs or practices but by their blood.[37] He believes that an encounter between Judaism and Hegel's religio-secular thought provides the means by which to unite Jews, both religious and secular, who are united already within the realm of empirical fact, within the realm of thought as well.[38] Second, while he recognizes along with Hegel that historical experience is essentially religious, Hegel's thought uses the concept of the identity between the divine perspective and the infinite human one. As a consequence, Hegel gives primacy to thought over being. To correct this Christian bias – that revelation is primarily Credo without Law – Fackenheim suggests that we not allow the identity to inform philosophical thought. Jews and Judaism will be able to witness against Hegel's Constantinianism – his belief that the Christian revealed truth is both complete and essentially political; and this in turn will disable modern thought from continuing its initial assumption that Judaism is inadequate to inform modern thought and its resultant hatred of Jews as the bar to cultural salvation.

According to Fackenheim, Hegel claims to synthesize not all things, but specifically Aristotle's concern with eternity and the Judeo-Christian concern with history.[39] His claim to comprehensiveness forces Jews to confront his thought with total self-exposure instead of, for instance, relying on either the ancient model of flight from empirical reality (as the Orthodox have done) or the medieval model of (apparently) harmonizing only those parts of Judaism that are already compatible with non-Jewish thought. The Liberals, by defining Judaism as merely one of many contributors to modern culture, have in this sense adopted the medieval model.[40] In Jewish self-understanding, Judaism, like Hegelianism, is comprehensive. Judaism is historical; it understands its existence as between Creation and the Messiah.[41] Judaism is also world-historical: 'the beginning and end of history are universal, and Jewish existence between these extremes is that of a *witness* in which the abstractions "particular" and "universal" are concretely intertwined.'[42] Third and decisively, Judaism understands that in order to inform world-historical experience, it must 'relate itself not only to non-Jewish world history but also to non-Jewish ways of understanding it.'[43] It is this third point that forces Judaism and Jewish thought to confront head-on Hegelian thought, which in its comprehensiveness claims to mediate all particular points of view from its world-historical point of view.

Although Hegel's claim to comprehensiveness is antithetical to Judaism's, Fackenheim is drawn to him because, in his thought, God is operative in history. Like Fackenheim, Hegel understands human existence to be essentially religious. Because philosophy, too, is rooted in human existence, both thinkers attempt to interconnect philosophy and religion within human experience.[44] Hegel attempts to synthesize philosophy and religion: his synthesis, more specifically, connects modern secular self-confidence with religious confidence in a redeemed world.[45] In the sense that Hegel includes confidence in redemption within philosophy and secular self-confidence within religion, his philosophy, like Fackenheim's, recognizes that the terms for an appropriate encounter with Spinoza, or with modernity in general, include both secularism and religion.[46] Hegel attempts a reaffirmation of the God of revelation; but because his religion is transfigured into philosophy, his religion also defines God ultimately as solely immanent. Even so, he recognizes that, while modern religion needs secular experience so as to avoid a lapse into worldless pietism, modern secularity needs religious inspiration in order to avoid either 'spiritual chaos or spiritless fragmentation.'[47] This recognition, according to Fackenheim, will aid Jews in their endeavour to define an adequate post-Holocaust Judaism, a Judaism that reflects in its theology the reality of the indiscriminate murder of religious and secular Jews alike in the Holocaust.

Hegel recognizes that, in order to affirm the synthesis within human existence of secularism and religion, he must redefine philosophy and revelation. Unlike the philosophy of, for instance, Plato, his philosophy must remain bound to the contingent. Hegel's philosophy, like Plato's, understands itself as justified in its ability to distinguish between what is real and what is appearance, but in Fackenheim's reading, Hegel goes a step further. Even as his philosophy makes intelligible what is real in the human realm, its conclusions are not eternally true: Hegel's philosophy remains bound to the contingent and can determine only what is known to have existed already.

At the same time, Hegel's religion is both Christian and secular: Christian, because the model for the supersessionist God manifestation in history (which appears to philosophy) is the Christian synthesis of God and the human being in Christ; and secular, because history itself is the process by which God is made manifest. Insofar as God's activity is identified with human activity, Hegel's religion can no longer allow for new incursions into the world by an Absolute Other. Although Christianity serves as the culmination of the human quest for self-activation in history – the reaching for the divine synthesized with God's activity of reaching toward the human – Christianity itself has been superseded by a secularist's realism with regard to empirical history. Since philosophy has superseded religion, Hegel's is a Christianity informed by empirical history. His synthesis of philosophy and religion results, Hegel believes, in a system of thought that is both secular and religious: it both unveils the real and is contingent; it recognizes both the Otherness and the immanence of God.

When Fackenheim wrote *The Religious Dimension in Hegel's Thought*, his main goal was to 'refute and discredit' the interpretation of Hegel's thought that suggests it is not grounded in human existence.[48] At the time, he understood this interpretation of Hegel to be 'right wing' Hegelianism – a position that interprets Hegel's thought as oblivious to empirical history, as totally committed to a metaphysical principle,[49] and as a philosophy that exists only 'in the realm of mere shadows.'[50] But Fackenheim also did not promote the 'left wing' interpretation of Hegel, which suggests that self-fulfilment is possible without God, or without the aspiration toward God. In left-wing Hegelianism, Hegel's philosophy is limited to the contingent, and because it cannot achieve 'transhistorical absoluteness,'[51] it is thrust back onto history, which paves the way for radical historicism,[52] which, too, exists only in the realm of mere shadows. Yet in both positions, religious immediacy – because in its right-wing form it is removed from historical experience, and in its left-wing form it is recognized as historically situated – must prove its relevance in the secular world.[53] According to Fackenheim, Hegel's position inhabits the middle of these extremes: philosophy, although contingent, can achieve transhistorical absoluteness; whereas religion remains pertinent as the means by which secular experience is informed with confidence in redemption. Because Hegel's synthesis of secularism and religious redemption is grounded in human existence – so Fackenheim reads him – his thought remains open to contemporary circumstance and simultaneously connected to the transhistorical confidence in redemption. Hegel's empirical basis distinguishes his philosophy from ancient thought's flight from the world; his synthesis is the redemption of the world.[54]

The difficulty inherent in Hegel's attempt at synthesizing religion and philosophy is recognized by both right- and left-wing Hegelianism: Hegel's thought, by recognizing an interconnection between absolute transhistorical truth and the contingent, is, apparently, contradictory. In 'Hegel on the Actuality of the Rational and the Rationality of the Actual,'[55] Fackenheim spells out Hegel's conception of the process by which absolute transhistorical truth can be known without the contingent being superseded. This process is what Hegel calls history. To Hegel, historical experience includes both a religious dimension and what he refers to as the merely existent – that is, that which exists in the world that is untouched by the divine.[56] It is the task of the secular world to separate the merely existent from worldly events that manifest God – that is, from what Hegel refers to as the 'actual.' The knowledge that the merely existent requires separation is accomplished by Hegel's secular optimism, which renders apparent the contingent sources of absolute transhistorical truth. At the same time, the separating itself is accomplished within the worldly context of continual human action. Hegel includes the transhistorical truth of religion – the actual – within the grasp of philosophy. Historical experience grounds both religion and philosophy. While it is true that Hegel's philosophy is led toward the conquest of contingency, at the same time, in Fackenheim's reading, Hegel affirms that contingency must be and must remain real if philosophy is to be real.

Since the merely existent must be separated from the actual, not all that is contingent, according to Hegel, is real. Hegel's famous statement in his *Philosophy of Right*, and then repeated in his *Encyclopedia*, that 'what is rational is actual and what is actual is rational,'[57] refers, according to Fackenheim, only to the religious dimension of existence, not to the merely existent. Hegel affirms that what exists as actual is, like God's plan, rational. Hegel can make this assertion through his use of the Christian theological concept that the human being has been united with God:[58] the connection between the actual and the rational is, in Hegel's vision, the manifestation of the external God in historical experience. The rational is not primordially in the human being. Fackenheim compares Hegel's rationality with Plato's idealism: in both concepts, the data of thought exist as entities external to the human being.[59] Yet unlike Plato, Hegel, by dividing his sentence into two phrases, distinguishes between the actual and the rational: 'the world is not identified with or dissipated into God even though God is its Creator and Redeemer.'[60] The actual must be separated from the merely existent; it must also be separated from the rational. The separation of the actual and the rational both enables Hegel to remain aware of historical experience as the means of informing thought and also separates God from historical experience. While Hegel's thought connects the contingent with absolute transhistorical truth, also it maintains a distinction between them – that is, the distinction between the historical human being and the extra-historical God. As a consequence of the distinction between the historical human being and the extra-historical God, Hegel is able to affirm that the contingent persists even as it itself becomes absolute transhistorical truth.

In order for Hegel to affirm that God represents Himself in historical experience, and that at no point does this representation dissipate God into historical experience, there must exist a religion that is absolutely Other than historical experience. In order to maintain the distinction between the rational and the actual, and the consequent separation of God from historical experience, Hegel recognizes the existence of pre-philosophical religion.[61] Put another way, for Hegel to be able to synthesize religion and philosophy within historical experience without dissolving the one into the other, there must exist a realm external to either the religion or the philosophy that is being synthesized, and for Hegel, that realm is essentially religious.

The duality of the divine nature and the human one at the core of human existence suggests to Hegel that, before one can validly transfigure religion into philosophy – that is, synthesize it with philosophy – religion must be understood on its own terms, as promoting God, at least partially, as an Absolute Other.[62] So, for instance, in Fackenheim's reading, the bases of Kant's argument for the necessity of philosophically acceptable anthropomorphisms are misguided.[63] Kant seems to argue that they are necessary, first, because philosophy cannot attain a higher conceptual form of truth, and second, because human beings need symbolic anthropomorphisms in order to be complete. Yet because these anthropomorphisms, within these rationalist terms, are true only symbolically, Kant, while allowing the symbolic affirmation of God, denies in this argument the possibility of a divine–human relationship.[64] Hegel, in contrast, recognizes that the ground for Kant's denial is his elevation of human moral autonomy. According to Hegel, in order for religion to be transfigured into philosophy, religion must first be understood as including an acknowledgment of the existence of the infinite, or an Absolute Other.[65]

To correct what he sees as Kant's misguided attempt at demythologizing religion, Hegel, like Kant, recognizes first that philosophy must acknowledge that human beings continue to live as human beings, in need of the infinite. To Hegel, this recognition, unlike Kant's affirmation of the human need for symbolic anthropomorphisms, suggests that religion cannot be validly defined from the perspective of moral autonomy; rather, the root of religion is inherent in the human being himself. By initially removing philosophical considerations from religious understanding, Hegel enables the appropriate demythologizing of religion.[66] Once religion is appropriately demythologized, according to Hegel, it may be remythologized; it may again be understood as including an acknowledgment of an Absolute Other.

Hegel's goal is the transmythologizing of religion, the transfiguring of the form of religious experience into philosophy. This requires – in order to acknowledge the involvement of both the finite and the infinite in religion – that thought become at once human and divine. To this end, Hegel affirms that myth and symbol are not superstition but rather representations of religious truths. While it may be impossible to transmythologize religion, Hegel maintains that the demythologizing of religion in its own terms would make possible the valid remythologizing of religion, which would not preclude the possibility of the divine–human encounter.[67]

Hegel suggests that in order to leave open in his religio-secular thought the possibility of the divine–human encounter, religion must first be understood on its own terms. On its own terms, religion requires that both the infinite divine and the finite human participate. The problem in establishing an adequately representational religion for his synthesis of philosophy and religion – or, one might say, a representation of pre-philosophical religion adequate to being transfigured into philosophy – is defining how the human being is to recognize Absolute Otherness from within the realm of the finite. The effort to transfigure religion into thought is hampered by the limitations placed on the human being by his contingency as well as by the necessity – in order to allow the possibility of an encounter with God – for him of retaining his contingency. The human being, because he has only a finite standpoint, has no means by which to assume God's activity: human activities, while they have contact with the infinite, can achieve only partial truths.[68] Yet Hegel, referring to the Christian affirmation of the identity between the divine and human infinite perspectives, suggests that the human being, by recognizing the Absolute Other as both within and also outside himself, is able to recognize human finite experience through an infinite perspective, even as he recognizes himself as distinct – insofar as he resides in the finite realm – from the infinite. Because God is present within the human being, Hegel's philosophy is capable of understanding absolutely certain aspects of human existence; because God is present outside the human being, philosophy's absolute understanding is bound to the contingency of human existence. By invoking the identity between God and the human divine perspective, Hegel is able to preserve the ability of absolute transhistorical truth to inform his thought, and also he is able to affirm the possibility that pre-philosophical religion can be transfigured into philosophy: because the human being is capable of achieving an infinite perspective even as he remains finite, also he is capable of differentiating God's Otherness from God's immanence.

Hegel suggests that, in order to achieve an infinite standpoint, the human being cannot rely simply on finite reflection on finite experience – which reliance would issue only in contingent knowledge. Rather, in order to achieve an infinite standpoint even while remaining bound to the finite, the human being must reenact finite experience. Through the union of the infinite (i.e., the divine perspective in the human being that is capable of reflecting on reenactment) with the discordance between the human and the divine in the human being (i.e., the aspect of the human being that experiences, re-experiences, and reflects on his experience), the human being can recognize his experience as idea, and translate his experience into idea. The human being's recognition of his ability to recognize the infinite – accomplished by his divine nature through the reenactment of finite experience – is simultaneous with his recognition of the infinite – accomplished by the duality of the divine and human nature in the human being. Through the 'union of union and nonunion,' the absolute appears in the world.[69] Finite experience is transfigured into infinite thought, even while thought itself is transferred into the realm of experience.

For Hegel, there exists a dialectic between the infinite and finite aspects of the human being.[70] Each both seeks and flees the other.[71] The infinite, or the human being's recognition of his own divine perspective, seeks the finite in order to find grounding, yet flees the finite to find absolute truth. The absolute transhistorical truth of human existence requires the input of contingent, actual existence, even as it must separate itself from the contingent in order to establish itself as absolute, rational truth. The finite, or the human being's distinction from Absolute Otherness, seeks the infinite to find truth, or to escape fragmentation, yet flees the infinite in order to find humanity: contingency, to be understood, must be measured against the rationality of absolute transhistorical truth, even while it must remain actual or contingent in order for its truths to be pertinent to human existence. Thought, Hegel concludes, both flees and needs being: the human being can achieve absolute transhistorical knowledge and also is limited to knowledge by his contingency. There exists in the human being both an inherent ability to overreach the limitation of his contingency and an absolute limitation to human knowledge. Hegel's thought, by continuing to recognize the reality of contingency, limits the human ability to overreach his empirical existence.[72]

The human being can, according to Hegel, achieve an infinite standpoint and at the same time retain his finite perspective. The duality of human nature suggests to Hegel that the terms of religion, though they are not superstition, are ultimately representational: religion, as the human being experiences it in finite, empirical history, is in reality a representation of the absolute truth of pre-philosophical religion. In Hegel's understanding, this representational religion has three aspects. First, it is feeling, which is an aspect of internal involvement of the adherent. Second, there is an aspect of representation, which has a specific yet inadequate content.[73] The content is specific because, in its representation, religion points to the infinite; it is inadequate because the human being cannot comprehend the divine. In this sense, the representational aspect of religion is symbolic. Third, a religion produces a cult comprised of its adherents, and this cult, insofar as it 'acts out the difference of the divine–human nonunion which is yet a union, and so transfigures that relation ... produce[s] ... a kind of actual union.'[74] 'Every genuine religion,' according to Hegel, 'is a totality of existence in which inwardness of feeling is united with outward action and external occurrence, through a representational meaning that permeates both.'[75]

Not surprisingly, because Hegel's synthesis of philosophy and religion begins with a pre-philosophical tenet of Christianity – the identification of the divine principle and the human infinite principle – Hegel concludes that Christianity is the absolute religion. The pre-philosophical religion that is capable of being transfigured into philosophy must be a religion that has as its form the representation of the possibility of religious experience as a result of human self-transformation. In addition, the religion appropriate for this transfiguration must represent that the means by which to guide human self-transformation is human recognition of an Absolute Other. Christianity represents religious experience from the perspectives of both the human finite standpoint – insofar as the human being requires God as an Absolute Other in order to achieve religious experience – and the human infinite standpoint – insofar as the recognition of this need enables human self-transformation.

To put this in Hegel's terms, Christianity is the absolute religion because it is doubly representational. Even as the human reaches toward the divine – human practice represents the God-given law of life – the divine reaches toward the human, insofar as that life accords with God's will.[76] Furthermore, Christianity fulfils Hegel's other requirements for genuine religion – feeling, representation and cult – as each a double representation. First, there is in Christianity a double feeling: the adherent is gripped by the divine and also encounters the divine as a free commitment. Next, in its representation, Christianity has a double aspect: the infinite divine is involved with the human being, and the finite human being is an active partner in the divine–human relationship. The cult aspect of Christianity also is double: both God and the human being are at work and are known to be at work.[77] But Christianity is the absolute religion, according to Hegel, because, since in Christianity the divine principle is identified with the human infinite principle, the double-representation of Christian faith is really one activity.[78] Christianity represents the highest aspiration of religion because it seeks to achieve the unity of the duality of the human being's divine and human natures. To verify this assertion, Hegel looks to empirical evidence: because it is Christian, already the modern world is doubly overreached; the human being has both retained and gone beyond his contingency, while God has been transfigured into immanent historical experience and also has retained his Absolute Otherness. God is manifest in the modern world in the human being both to preserve and to raise him above his finiteness.[79]

Hegel is able to synthesize philosophy and religion because he presumes that religion is the self-transformation of finite into infinite spirit. This presumption, according to Fackenheim, leads Hegel to two erroneous conclusions. First, his synthesis of philosophy and religion is possible only because it takes place, ultimately, not in empirical historical experience but rather in the realm of philosophy. Hegel, using Schelling's identification of reality and experience,[80] recognizes God Himself as religious experience. Because for Hegel the philosophical is experiential, he concludes that his synthesis of philosophy and religion is based in historical experience. Hegel's failure is that he posits religion-in-general in order to inform historical experience, rather than using historical experience as the foundation for religion-in-particular. For Fackenheim, this mistake leads to his confusion about the relationship between philosophy and empirical existence. Second, because he presumes that religion is the self-transformation of finite into infinite spirit, Hegel's highest form of human self-constitution disavows any aspect of Otherness. According to Hegel's concepts, art, religion, and philosophy are disciplines in which what is beyond human knowledge – what 'transcends selfhood itself' – is internalized and thus made immanent.[81]

Despite its Christian character, Hegel's system is challenging for Judaism. According to Fackenheim, 'the ultimate reason why the Jewish witness to the otherness of God ... is genuinely challenged' is that Hegel preserves 'divine otherness' through his definition of the activity of grasping the 'otherness of the Divine' through a 'divine self-othering in the human.'[82] The activity of grasping is itself more than human. Because he understands the primacy of the dialectic of the human and the divine in all human endeavour, Hegel entices the Jewish thinker and comes closest of all German Idealist philosophers to understanding Judaism. Yet, even though the activity of grasping is more than human, the precedence that Hegel gives to philosophy over empirical history, and the priority of human action over God's action, together preclude Absolute Otherness from informing his philosophy. Jewish witness is disregarded as a valid source of religious knowledge.

Hegel, for his part, because his goal is to establish comprehensive, or infinite, knowledge, attempts to understand Judaism on its own terms: 'Hegel himself (unlike Kant and similar critics of "Jewish legalism") understands the law of Moses ... not as a bar between divine Giver and human recipient, but rather as a bridge.'[83] Because Hegel rejects historical data as abstraction, he proposes, against the unofficial motto of post-Revolution France,[84] to give to Jews as Jews everything; yet for Jews to receive everything, they must free themselves from their 'unfree' past[85] – a past that in Hegelian terms allows for no human free will and that cannot therefore be transfigured into philosophy. 'But,' Fackenheim asks, 'what will be the Jewish people once it has superseded its "unfree" religious past?'[86] With this unanswered question, Hegelian thought on Judaism ends.[87] Yet, Fackenheim notes, Hegel – despite the philosophical necessity to do so – never discards Judaism entirely because Jews continue to exist in empirical history.

Because he posits religion-in-general in order to inform historical experience, rather than using historical experience as the foundation for religion-in-particular, Hegel's failure is a philosopher's but not a historian's, failure. Because Hegel continues in some sense to be open to historical experience,[88] Fackenheim suggests that post-Hegelian thought may evolve in contradiction even to positions first laid out by Hegel. It is this possibility that attracts Fackenheim to Hegelian thought and that convinces him that his thought may have at its core an eternal albeit fragmented truth.[89] Although, for instance, he recognizes that Hegel's criteria for distinguishing the actual from the merely existent may not be defensible,[90] the possibility of openness to a more comprehensive human experience remains. This possibility of openness remains for two reasons. First, God remains separate from historical experience as Hegel conceives it; and second, the secular realm informs Hegel's thought in the sense that one must recognize the actual from within all human historical experience.

Fackenheim's return to Hegel as he might be today, with a continued openness both to empirical historical events and to the possibility of God's operation in history, is warranted for three reasons. First, as stated above, Hegel's thought, despite its image of Judaism as having been superseded, never dispenses entirely with Judaism. Despite the philosophical necessity to do so, Hegel can never quite discard Judaism as having been superseded: knowing the importance of empirical history to thought, Hegel cannot deny the continued existence of Jews and Judaism.[91] Second, Hegel's thought recognizes the interdependence of philosophical and historical thought – that empirical history continually and necessarily informs thought. Because Hegel understands the conclusions of pre-ultimate human thought as not eternal, and even more, because he remains open to the empirical data of history, Fackenheim concludes that Hegel, like him, would recognize both that it is impossible – as history has confirmed through the construction of the secular state – to return to the naive belief that authority is the source of faith,[92] and also that the Holocaust has destroyed utterly Hegel's conception of history as the actual, as distinct from the merely existent. Fackenheim concludes, in other words, that Hegel 'would not [today] be an Hegelian.'[93] Third, Fackenheim may use Hegel's thought as a model for his own because, although Hegel recognizes the inter-dependence of philosophical and historical thought, he does not fall prey to radical historicism. Like Schelling, Hegel recognizes that self-making is limited by, in Schelling's case, the choices with which one is presented, and in Hegel's case, the contingent, or the moment within the progression of God's revelation in which one lives.[94] Rediscovering God as Absolute Other remains a possibility in Hegel's thought.

According to Fackenheim, the residual openness of Hegel's thought to Jewish experience, to historical events and/or radical evil, and to the actuality of God as an Absolute Other, enables him (Fackenheim) to eliminate from Hegel's thought its post-Christian bias. First, Judaism cannot be a term in a Hegelian synthetic operation. To claim that Judaism can be assimilated, or has been assimilated, is to ignore the post-Christian bias of modern philosophy, its *a priori* dismissal of Judaism as exclusively heteronomous – or, in Hegelian terms, as unfree. Against Hegel, Fackenheim suggests that Christianity, with its unifying of the human being and God as its highest form, is not the absolute religion. Hegel fails to recognize that Judaism, too, in Hegel's terms, is doubly representational. The Jew recognizes both his contingency and his ability to overreach that contingency, while recognizing as well the ability of God to be both immanent in and Absolutely Other than human historical experience. This recognition occurs in Judaism in the concept of the covenant: Jews are free to accept or reject the Law, while God both enters and remains distinct from historical experience in order to give the Law. The distinction between the Sinaitic revelation and the Incarnation, according to Fackenheim, is that the Sinaitic revelation, or its interpretations, refuse even in their ultimate manifestations to dissolve the activities of God and the human being into a unity. Furthermore, while Hegel recognizes the Law as a bridge between Jews and God, he does not recognize its similarity to Christianity's antinomy of Grace: while God gives Grace, the human being must receive it by his free act.[95] Fackenheim suggests that, by recognizing Judaism's concept of covenant as representationally comparable to Christianity's Grace, post-Hegelian thought may reject Hegel's identification of the divine and human nature and replace it with Judaism's or Christianity's enduring interconnection and tension between them.

Second, because Hegel cannot be philosophically open to Judaism, or to a religion that cannot and does not distinguish between the actual and the merely existent, also he is unable to recognize the empirical historical reality of radical evil. Because, in Hegel's conception of history, only God is actual, what exists in historical experience as appearance, or as the merely existent – and this would include all events unconnected to Hegel's posited pre-philosophical religious dimension – does not merit philosophical (and more pointedly, religious) reflection. Just as Judaism cannot be assimilated in a Hegelian synthetic operation, neither can the Holocaust. Hegel's conception of history as a slaughter bench belittles evil by justifying it 'as a means to some supposedly higher end.'[96] His radical incorporation of secular idealism in his distinction between the actual and the merely existent, made possible by a philosophical transfiguration of Christ, or the internalization of God, for instance, and his consequent characterization of evil as un-rational and therefore un-actual, renders impossible any attempt to address evil as an actuality, either philosophically or theologically. To claim that the Holocaust can be assimilated to historical progress is, to Fackenheim, nothing short of an unpardonable sin.

The replacement of the attempt at the synthesis of philosophy and religion with an attempt at an interconnection between the two would according to Fackenheim eliminate the problem of Hegel's residual Constantinianism – Hegel's concept, adapted from a theo-political conception of revealed Christianity,[97] of the progress of historical evolution and the irrelevance of aspects of human existence that do not fit into his progressive schema. Fackenheim recognizes Hegel's Constantinianism as taking two forms: supersessionism – that as history proceeds, it diminishes the relevance of the past; and triumphalism – as though history actually and simply proceeds. Fackenheim promotes, for post-Hegelian thought, what he perceives to be the position of Hegel as historical thinker: 'neither flight from the empirical world, nor reductionist embrace of it.'[98] Relying on Hegel's openness to empirical history, Fackenheim suggests, against Hegel as philosopher, the preservation of the absolute distinction between thought and life: by keeping in tension the limits of human existence with the possibility of human overreaching, historical experience will at every moment have priority over thought. History cannot be presumed to be the means by which the present supersedes the past, nor can it be presumed to be proceeding. Without these presumptions, evil cannot be ignored as unactual, unreal, or irrelevant.

Third, Hegel's thought may be corrected by Fackenheim through a reinstatement of God as Absolute Other. In empirical history, Hitler has destroyed Hegel's identity between the divine and human natures and with it the possibility of the progression of Hegel's World Spirit through the secular world.[99] By distinguishing absolutely between thought and experience, between the divine and the human, Fackenheim's post-Hegelian thought would not synthesize, in empirical history, the extremes of a transhistorical relationship with God or Idea, and a worldly or exclusively autonomous human activity.[100] Rather, each moment would be understood as a discrete opportunity to encounter, as a finite human being, the divine Other; or alternatively, as an opportunity for the human activity of radical evil. By acknowledging both human limits and the possibility of human overreaching, Fackenheim affirms that in the secular realm, history can be but need not inevitably be progressive, even while each moment, because it is discrete, can never be overreached. Human activity can reach toward the infinite, even while the human being remains open to an encounter with an Absolute Other.[101] By recognizing that Judaism was disregarded without philosophical refutation, that the Holocaust has ruptured Hegel's conception of historical continuity, and that God is Absolutely Other at every moment of historical experience, post-Hegelian thought would both open itself to Jewish historical experience and also discard its Constantinianism.

Furthermore, Hegel's post-Christian bias may be eliminated from, even while preserving, his conception of the interconnection of the religious and the secular. Fackenheim agrees with Hegel that the religious and the secular must be combined in thought: since Hitler, Jews, according to Fackenheim, can longer be separated between the religious and the secular:

> The Holocaust Kingdom murdered religious and secularist Jews alike. The decision [to remain Jewish after Auschwitz] requires philosophical thought to restructure the categories of religiosity and secularity. Only by virtue of a radical 'secular' self-reliance that acts as though the God who once saved could save no more can even the most 'religious' survivor hold fast either to the Sinaitic past or to the Messianic future. And only by virtue of a radical 'religious' memory and hope can even the most 'secularist' survivor rally either the courage or the motivation to decide to remain a Jew, when every natural impulse tempts him to seek forgetfulness and even bare safety elsewhere.[102]

As in the empirical realm, there can be no Jewish distinction between the religious and the secular in the philosophical realm. On the one hand, the complete (in Fackenheim's formulation) unintelligibility of the Holocaust breaks down Hegel's synthesis of the secular and the religious in thought, because philosophy cannot ground itself in empirical reality.[103] On the other hand, the empirical reality of the Holocaust confirms that secular optimism, and confidence in redemption as completed, are no longer warranted.

Hegel's radical secular self-confidence reveals his post-Christian bias with regard to the relation between the religious and the secular: because in Judaism there is an absolute distinction between thought and being, or between religio-philosophical speculation and empirical history,[104] historical events that involve Jews or Judaism, and that ostensibly have no religious significance, have for Jews religious significance. Hegel's error of positing religion-in-general – or Protestant Christianity as religion-in-general – or of ultimately assigning primacy to philosophy over empirical history, results in an error with regard to the means by which secularism and religion meet in empirical history in Judaism. Hegel's failure with regard to Judaism includes an inability to be open to Jewish religio-secular historical experience. Hegel properly recognizes that philosophy cannot remythologize religion if religion itself is no longer extant, but he does not understand that for Jews, 'political events have ... an immediate religious significance.'[105] So, for instance, Hegel, as a means of reinvesting philosophy with religious form, refutes the philosophical position that myth and symbol are superstition; but because he does not recognize that, for Jews, the secular, as pure being, may be the religious, he does not and cannot refute that they are dead. This is something that Fackenheim, in both secular political and also religious terms, can refute. The mythmaker in Judaism, the midrashist,[106] is, according to Fackenheim, doubly representational: he knows both the need to create a myth and also its inadequacy, the need for human action and also the need for divine (as Other) action. The fact that midrash continues to be written contests Hegel's claim that the modern world is demythologized, that religious life has vanished.[107] In addition, in secular, empirical terms, there is a crisis in Judaism that bears little resemblance to the crisis in Liberal Protestant Christianity: 'the end of the state of Israel would equal the end of the Jewish people.'[108] For Jews, remythologizing remains possible for as long as Jews survive, and Hegel's model of connecting the secular and the religious is sound, provided that the connection can at the same time be based, not in philosophical hope, but in empirical reality.

The refutation of Judaism as dead is crucial for Fackenheim and is the source of his oft-quoted 614th commandment.[109] Jews after Auschwitz both require Hegel's thought in order to redefine a Judaism that is adequate to the needs of their religious and secular existence, and also become those who might best reinform the secular world of the necessity of its religious dimension, through a reconstruction of Hegelian thought accomplished through its encounter with Judaism. Hegel's post-Christian secularism becomes for Fackenheim the model for formulating a fragmented religio-secular Judaism. Because Hegel's dialectic of actuality and rationality, though dismissive of certain aspects of human existence, builds within itself a historical basis that is theological, Fackenheim's adoption of Hegel's model of the interconnection of the religious and the secular provides a unified basis for the religious and the secular. At the same time, in translating Hegel's claim of the identity of the religious and the secular into an interconnected tension between the two, Fackenheim need not dissolve the two into one entity. Like all philosophical and religious thought, ultimate unity is elusive throughout historical experience. Fackenheim's interconnection between the religious and the secular enables the philosophical resolution of the nineteenth-century division of Jews, who in the twentieth century were united *in actu*.

Fackenheim concludes that Hegel's synthesis of philosophy and religion can no longer be sustained, yet he also believes that the ability to break down Hegel's synthesis is available from within Hegel's philosophy.[110] This breakdown, which entails in some sense a dissolution, entails as well a translation of the synthesis of philosophy and religion into a tension between them. It is the tension without synthesis that distinguishes both Fackenheim from Hegel's thought, and Jewish covenant or midrash from Christian Incarnation or myth. The tension, just as the synthesis, is comprehensive still; but the comprehensiveness is not of a union or absoluteness, but rather of a fragmentation. The fragmentation contains both ultimacy and incompleteness, or an eternal core of truth, which core, because it exists within human temporal experience, can never be frozen or stilled. Because Fackenheim's conception of truth is one that cannot be stilled, transcendence must be understood, not as a metaphysical principle that may or may not be bound to historical experience, but rather as a witnessing or involvement against absolute evil. His conception of truth is eternally available for Jews to return to. What is more, because Jews were transformed into the 'living dead' in Auschwitz, and because the Jewish covenant with God lives within history, Jews are particularly apt to witness to, or create in the world, the divine spark in the human being.[111]

Fackenheim on Schelling

Fackenheim devotes four essays to Schelling,[112] indicating an interest that, although he recognizes Schelling's ultimate inadequacy, remains an influence on his thought. His interest in Schelling stems from two considerations. First, Schelling's thought develops one stage to the next, and the fact of this development suggests to him – in what will become a persistent aspect of his thought – that knowledge is indispensably historical.[113] Second, at the same time, in Schelling's later thought, historical events occur in a context that is extra-human. The self requires a background other than itself for self-making. Not only does the positing of this background prevent Schelling's thought from falling prey to radical historicism,[114] but also, since this background establishes a transcendence beyond the self, Schelling's later thought is a philosophical attempt to rediscover an Absolute Other from the authority of the given.[115]

Fackenheim divides Schelling's career into three phases, each of which springs from problems in the previous one. In his first phase, transcendental idealism, Schelling asserts that through art, the internalized God is disclosed; in the second phase, philosophy of religion, Schelling posits an identity between experience and reality. In his second stage, he understands reality as those things that can be rationally explicated. Since religious experience cannot be interpreted by reason, Schelling concludes during this stage of his thought that religious experience does not exist; he does away with supernatural revelation.[116] In the third phase, his positive philosophy, Schelling attempts the reinstatement of revelation.[117] His position that the self requires an other-than-self context in which to self-make suggests also the need for revelation as part of any thought that attempts to represent reality. Although his positive philosophy met, at the time, with little success,[118] his debate with Hegel as to whether to recover or to internalize the God of revelation begins the philosophical attempt to reaffirm the transcendence of God. This starts Fackenheim on his project of attempting to understand revelation as able to break through human defences.[119]

Schelling begins his positive philosophy with the question: 'Why is there something rather than nothing?' The question does not ask whether anything exists, but rather, what is the meaning of existence.[120] Implicit in the question is the presumption that thought must base itself on pre-existent fact. Schelling's initial recognition is that the issue is not the systematizing of the existent, but rather the gap between what exists and human thinking: he was struck with facticity, by which he recognized that reality cannot be represented by thought or system exclusively. Schelling is led, according to Fackenheim, to his second question: 'Why is what exists in discrepancy with what it ideally ought to be?'[121] Since there is a discrepancy between reason's conclusion of what ideally ought to be and what is, there must be meaning in facticity. Even the meaninglessness of fact itself is not ultimately meaningless: both the meaningful and the meaningless constitute reality.[122]

The error of Hegel's idealism, according to the later Schelling, is its making absolute the dialectic between reason, or essence, and experience. Because, for instance, Hegel's Absolute Idealism is unable to assimilate the facts of freedom and existence,[123] his philosophy of religion is inadequate. His dialectic does not recognize that there is a fundamental incommensurability between the dialectic and the unassimilable particulars that comprise its data.[124] Yet Schelling concludes that is Hegel's Idealism itself, by omitting facticity in its dialectic, that reveals the import of its omission. Hegel's philosophy, although not comprehensive, is necessary because it reveals the limitation to essence of Idealist philosophy. Schelling's later philosophy uses as its foundation the limit of Hegel's philosophy, even while it builds from it, in contrast, a philosophy of human existence. In Schelling's judgment, Hegel's philosophy is a '"negative" philosophy of mere "Essence,"'[125] whereas his own philosophy of existence is a positive philosophy: in order to negate the Absolute as an idea and to recognize the Absolute's share in existence, philosophy must negate itself. It must point beyond itself toward existence beyond essence. For Schelling, this pointing beyond points to a redefinition of the realm of God's existence as transcendent to both human thought and human existence.

Schelling concludes that the *a priori*, as revealed by Idealist philosophy, is meaningful but also limited by its inability to reveal all meaning and that fact is meaningful, yet its meaning cannot be revealed in thought. Schelling's positive philosophy, in building on Hegel's negative philosophy, attempts to 'combine a dialectic of essence and necessity with an undialectical doctrine of existence and freedom.'[126] The combination results in the first principle of reality as an absolute fact that is above human knowledge.[127] This absolute fact is by definition an existent; that it is above human knowledge suggests an essence that is absolutely Other. The first principle of Schelling's positive philosophy is the realm of God's existence. What is required, in order to build a philosophy of human existence, is a 'leap to fact'[128]: one accepts God as prior to both thought and experience in order to unify idea and existence. The priority of God reaffirms God's existence as outside human self-making. In the sense that Fackenheim's Schelling attempts to transform God from an idea through which the human being gains autonomy over his self-creation, Fackenheim sees him as the originator of existentialism: Schelling's thought supersedes idealism insofar as it is a 'post-idealistic "return" to the "divine Other" of revealed religion.'[129]

Schelling's proposed leap involves a paradox: reason must negate itself in order to affirm existence, but it cannot do this on its own resources. Because reason begins as an abstraction from existence, it can never make the required leap to fact. Reason points beyond itself to a pure Existent beyond all essence, but it can never achieve this knowledge because reason's own beginning was an abstraction from existence.[130] To resolve the paradox of reason, Schelling suggests that the synthesis of thought and existence can be achieved only by the will. He argues that the will shall choose to make the synthesis between thought and existence because the existential setting of the philosopher, when he begins his abstractions, is the search for God.[131] The decision to accept God as prior to reason and existence unifies reason and existence and, one might say, restores to the philosopher the integrity of his thinking and his being. The contentlessness of the act of leaping, Schelling argues, provides the grounding for reason:[132] by virtue of one's leaping, one has actually willed the world into existence. One can anticipate the results of free action since all existence is, in effect, governed by will, which in turn is the ground of essence. Yet, although the decision is a free act – one can choose whether or not to accept God as the grounding principle of essence and existence – the freedom is limited by facticity: one cannot create a specificity simply by willing it.[133] While the self is free to self-create, it can self-create only within the context of a background other than the self.

We return to Schelling's attempt to combine the dialectic of essence and necessity with the undialectical doctrine of existence and freedom. While it is true, according to Schelling, that absolute essence is the ground of all dialectical necessity, this essence is itself existentially grounded in an act of will, a will that is free and that informs absolute essence with indeterminancy.[134] Once essence is in existence, it is no longer dialectically necessary at all times. While absolute essence grounds determinately Schelling's combination of the dialectic of reason and necessity with the undialectical doctrine of freedom and existence, the essence that is accessible within human existence is indeterminate and allows room for free acts of will. Philosophy can discover only *a posteriori* which alternatives among the many possibilities within existence become fact.

Although Fackenheim finds in Schelling's positive philosophy a foundation of facticity with which to inform his own philosophy, he critiques Schelling's idea of the existent. In his reading, Schelling suggests that existence is only relatively, and not absolutely, other than reason, or that existence is inevitably rational. Schelling reinvokes 'the "divine Other" of revealed religion,' but only insofar as his thought connects the essence revealed by Idealism with the facticity of existence.[135] One must go through Hegel's negative philosophy of essence to arrive at Schelling's positive philosophy of existence. The question of whether the God of revelation exists is external to Schelling's combination of the dialectic and the non-dialectical; but if God exists, in order for Him to be a suitable unifier of idea and existence, He exists necessarily and moves through existence necessarily.[136] And Schelling must make this concession to philosophy: without the presumption that the Absolute must express itself in rationality, he would have to relinquish all *a priori* constructions of reason. Schelling posits the leap from existence to essence within the power of reason, as if the Absolute existent 'will instantiate principles of reason, what can be called the absolute Essence,' if it acts.[137] The leap is necessary; but Schelling fails to recognize that the leap must be a leap totally outside the bounds of reason and that this leap would negate any connection between reason and existence.[138] While, on the one hand, reason's dialectic concludes that there must be an Absolute beyond itself, there is no means by which reason can either cognize the Absolute or validly ground itself.[139] On the other hand, since the individual existent has no absolute essence, reason cannot be defined as having its basis in absolute essence. Reason can justify only its own systems; yet Schelling's later conception of reason cannot justify his positive philosophy. In addition, because for Schelling reason must combine with existential facts in order to reveal ultimate meaning, there can be no universal reason from which to define reality. There is no means by which Schelling can make the transition from the absolute individual will to the universal category of free will.[140] The first principle of Schelling's positive philosophy is not universal reason, but rather the individual existent, and despite his assertion of the unifying capacity of the Absolute, there is no means by which to connect the two.

The failure of Schelling's positive philosophy, in Fackenheim's reading, is especially prominent after the Holocaust: it denies evil because it cannot assimilate it.[141] After the Holocaust, the individual Jewish situation is existentially unique. It is not universal, nor can it be universalized into an absolute existent. Schelling's positive philosophy cannot reveal the meaning of the Holocaust because the occurrence of the Holocaust is not, and cannot be understood appropriately as, a general human condition.[142] For Fackenheim, philosophy must be a balance of the human historical freedom to structure the world and God's freedom to do what He wills.[143] Schelling's God, in contrast, can will only the rational, and therefore human historical freedom is limited to rational possibility. This is not the existential post-Holocaust Jewish situation.

Although it is a failure, Schelling's positive philosophy is compelling for Fackenheim: it teaches that reason cannot mediate the first principles of existence. Existence must be accepted on its own terms. Fackenheim understands that the meaning of reality can be uncovered only through an interconnection between reason and existence. At the same time, he recognizes the limitations – in terms of their providing meaning – of each reason and existence.[144] Schelling teaches Fackenheim that philosophy and God may not be collapsed into a unity that is beyond philosophy itself, nor can existence be rationalized so as to demonstrate the existence of a transcendent God.

Fackenheim on Heidegger

Fackenheim's relationship to Heidegger's thought is rather complicated.[145] On the one hand, he squarely rejects Heidegger's concept of historically bound transcendence and the latter's pagan or anti-Christian impetus. On the other, like Heidegger, he builds his thought on the Hegelian model of the interdependence of thought and being, and the consequent historicization – or in Fackenheim's case, qualified historicization – of thought. And like Heidegger, Fackenheim attempts to correct the post-Christian bias of Hegelian thought. But unlike Heidegger's correction, which paganizes Hegel or removes all traces of Christian thought from him, Fackenheim's correction Judaizes Hegel, in the sense of dissolving Hegel's identity of the divine nature and human, even while it retains God as an Absolute Other in relation to the human being.[146] While Fackenheim approves of Heidegger's recognition that thought must be based in experience, and that thought must transcend experience from within experience, he rejects Heidegger's rejection of the possibility of one transcendent standard by which to judge experience. Fackenheim concludes that philosophy must root itself not in eternity but in history;[147] but to combat the destruction of all standards, he affirms that there can be universals without a universal realm. For Fackenheim, Heidegger's radical openness to all standards makes it impossible for him to identify a false, or irrational, standard – that is, makes possible modern idolatry.[148]

Early in his career (1961), Fackenheim attempted to refute Heidegger in the lecture 'Metaphysics and Historicity.'[149] Historicism involves the belief that changes in human thinking literally change the object of thought.[150] In the lecture, Fackenheim argues that, because historicism denies the universality of its claim to truth, even as it binds all truth to specific historical situations, there is no philosophical means of escaping the doctrine once it is entered into.[151] Strauss, on reading Fackenheim's lecture, suggested that it does not refute Heidegger because, just as Heidegger does not rely solely on ideas, so too his critic cannot argue against him using solely ideas.[152] Although Fackenheim later recognizes the lecture's inadequacy, and in response to Strauss's critique writes 'The Historicity and Transcendence of Philosophical Truth,'[153] the lecture provides clues to understanding Fackenheim's complex relationship to Heidegger's thought.

Fackenheim begins the earlier lecture with a summary of Gerhard Krueger's brief description – with which he agrees only as a broad sketch – of the development of the awareness of the modern predicament with regard to history. According to the description, there are three possible outcomes resulting from the modern recognition of the paradox that not only our actions, but also our thinking is a part of history. The Enlightenment uses the idea of progress to affirm the continued existence of timeless truths; Romanticism and Idealism try to resolve the paradox by rising above history into timelessness. This resolution, according to Fackenheim, is no longer possible in the modern period, when mutually incompatible standpoints and historicity have been widely acknowledged.[154] The modern results are either (1) 'skeptical paralysis,' in which one cannot commit to a faith and therefore cannot act; (2) 'pragmatic make-believe,' where one simply pretends to believe something (and yet, because it makes truth subjective, pragmatic make-believe ends in self-contradiction); or (3) 'ideological fanaticism,' which results when one adopts a faith that he knows is but one specific product of history.[155] Traditional faith does not become fanatical because it is certain of being true. Ideology, on the other hand, must become fanatical because it must make itself true by re-creating history in its own image. All three of these results are unacceptable.

Fackenheim attempts to reassess the concept of historicity in order to achieve different results.

Fackenheim's first important insight is that history does not prove that a person's very being is subject to historical change. One cannot look to empirical reality to learn that human nature is not permanent.[156] He concludes that the doctrine of historicity is not an empirical generalization, but rather a metaphysical thesis, and as such, the doctrine does not surrender its reliance on the idea of eternal truths. Historicity requires its adherents to posit an exception to make its doctrine coherent: the act by which self-making recognizes itself as self-making and as historically situated is itself situated extra-historically.[157] To this refutation, Fackenheim adds two more. First, historicism is false because it must either renounce all philosophical assumptions, thus becoming simply history, or insist that philosophical questions are superseded by historical questions, thus contradicting its above-mentioned philosophical premise. Fackenheim concludes by suggesting that the statement 'all truth is relative' differs in logical type from the statement 'all truth is relative is true' and that historicism must base itself on the second metaphysical statement.[158]

Yet Fackenheim cannot leave Heidegger's thought at that. He refers to *Being and Time* as 'the deepest and most compelling account of the human condition offered by a 20th century existential philosopher.'[159] Its depth comes from its uniting the 'most relentless rejection of any … escape into "eternity" with the most radical emphasis on human "temporality."'[160] So, too, Fackenheim considers the philosophy of the eternal to be 'escapism-into-universalism.'[161] And so, too, he emphasizes the temporal aspect of human existence as a means to knowledge. Yet Fackenheim rejects what he understands as Heidegger's unqualified historicism as inadequate to the demands both of philosophy – an inadequacy that reveals itself in circular thinking – and of religion and secularism – an inadequacy that results in modern idolatry, or alternatively, in Heidegger's affiliation with Nazism. Just as Hegel's Constantinianism is revealed by his synthesizing into a unity religion and secularism, so too Heidegger's specifically post-Christian bias is revealed by his refusal to allow religion to remain in tension with secularism; Heidegger refuses to be open to alternative understandings of the human condition.

Fackenheim, in 'The Historicity and Transcendence of Philosophical Truth,' begins with a brief summary of the means by which Kant, through his affirmation of the primacy of practical reason, establishes knowledge that is both certain and objective even as it authenticates knowledge that exists in the *Lebenswelt*. The *Lebenswelt* is the *Sitz im Leben* of Kant's moral knowledge that one is morally obligated to the categorical imperative. At the same time, this moral knowledge is the *Sitz im Leben* of Kant's philosophical knowledge that, in order for one's moral obligation to be a true belief, freedom must be actual. Kant establishes a philosophical truth, the actuality of freedom, which is grounded ultimately in the *Lebenswelt*. In *Being and Time*, according to Fackenheim, Heidegger follows the same model. The *Lebenswelt*, or historical situatedness, is the ground for his *existenziell* understanding, *Dasein*'s understanding and self-understanding that being is historical, even while this *existenziell* understanding is the ground for Heidegger's *existenzial* understanding, transcendent understanding of *Dasein*'s historical structure. Like Kant, Heidegger grounds philosophical knowledge in life, but Heidegger's model is 'more radically historical': while Kant's categorical imperative merely authenticates the philosophical insight of the actuality of freedom, Heidegger's 'thrown individuation' extends the knowledge of moral obligation by making transcendent truth manifest within history.[162]

Heidegger bases his claim for what Fackenheim terms radical historicism on the assertion that his quest for Being is the first new thing in philosophy from Plato to Nietzsche and that there is no rational argument through history or metaphysical standard in which to ground a transhistorical rational argument. Yet Fackenheim claims that Heidegger's thought in fact comes out of Kant's practical reason, insofar as Heidegger translates Kant's categorical imperative into a metaphysical standard by which thought can supersede previous thought. If it is the case that Heidegger comes out of Kant, and that he is in fact conducting a transhistorical rational argument, there is, within ontic reality, a standard for rational argument that claims for itself absolute historical transcendence and universality. Despite his claim to the contrary, Fackenheim argues, there exists a metaphysical standard for Heidegger's 'recall thinking.'

Ironically, Heidegger, while insisting on originality as a means of denying the transhistorical rational argument, participates in that argument. In Fackenheim's estimation, Heidegger's means of solving the problem of connecting philosophical truth to the *Lebenswelt*, even while the truth remains eternal, is less adequate than, for instance, either Hegel's or Schelling's solution to the problem. Hegel's self-elevation of finite thought to the infinite or Schelling's positing of finite thought's self-recognition of its finiteness, which recognition points to the infinite, more validly serves to provide a means of achieving a transcendent grasp of the historical world.[163]

Heidegger's solution to the problem of connecting philosophical truth to the *Lebenswelt*, according to Fackenheim, reveals the inadequacy of his philosophical thinking because it involves a circle: one needs the *Lebenswelt* to provide a *Sitz* for both historically situated world views and also for the philosophical insight into the historicity of these world views. As Fackenheim had concluded in 'Metaphysics and Historicity,' historicism is a world view that provides insight into knowledge that all world views are historically situated.[164] Heidegger might respond to this charge, according to Fackenheim, by claiming that in 'authentic' moments, *Dasein* can grasp the whole of its condition, that philosophy can be rooted in life or history yet still reach transcendent truth. Yet Heidegger, by framing the problem as a 'war between life and philosophy,' insofar as he seeks to destroy eternal verities utterly, sets up the inevitable conclusion: because the philosopher lives in history, life must win.[165]

Heidegger, reacting against the Kantian contradiction that the categorical imperative is both connected to the *Lebenswelt* and also eternal, and against the Hegelian solution of informing the historical, or the secular, with divine Otherness, concludes that the human being, although he can in some sense self-transcend, cannot rise above his situatedness in finitude. Even within his finitude, the human being can achieve transcendence through the endurance of the finitude – or rather, through the self-supersession of finitude. Heidegger removes revelatory theology from philosophical thought, but only after philosophy has absorbed revelatory theology through Hegel's thought. While ignoring the limitations imposed by one particular, eternal, divine nature, Heidegger presumes as justified Hegel's concept of 'overreaching,'[166] a concept built on the foundations of an identity between the divine and human natures. This absorption is a mark, Fackenheim argues, of Heidegger's specifically post-Christian bias.

Fackenheim identifies the 'hostility and obtuseness' in Heidegger's few references to biblical sources, but more interesting is his assessment of Heidegger's attraction to Christians. After all, as Fackenheim puts it, citing Hans Jonas, 'Heidegger's primal thinking ... is a pagan rival' to Christianity, because, while in the 'Judeo-Christian tradition God is other than the world ... Heidegger's Being is in and of the world *only*.'[167] Christians may seek Heidegger's absolute insecurity toward the future God 'in reaction to a spurious Christianity that, secure in its salvation, escapes the risks of worldly existence.'[168] Heidegger's paganism may provide for post-Christians absolute insecurity 'because the future is wholly open to all possible gods.'

Heidegger's thought hinges on its ability to identify the authentic, insofar as authentic moments bring into time, so to speak, the necessary 'transcendence' to affirm the existence of the universal human condition and to grasp the whole of it. Heidegger understands himself as refuting historicism, 'the doctrine that human existence has historical limitations so radical that philosophy itself can only reflect and not transcend them.'[169] Whether Heidegger in fact succeeds is based on whether he can find an adequate means by which to distinguish the 'authentic' from the 'unauthentic' without recourse to a metaphysical principle. On this point, Heidegger, Fackenheim argues, falls into a sort of metaphysical quagmire: according to the later Fackenheim, one can describe 'only *one particular* human condition.'[170] What Heidegger diagnoses as the human condition is the post-Christian condition. Heidegger's attempt to base the distinction between authentic and unauthentic on an ontology that remains bound to the ontic does not render certain its conclusions about any possible absolute human condition. Fackenheim points to the circularity of the interaction of Heidegger's ontic and ontological categories. Ontic understanding, when it is authentic, provides the basis for ontological understanding, while the ontological provides the criteria for the distinction between ontic authenticity and unauthenticity. Since Heidegger's ontology rests ultimately on an authentic ontic possibility, it is possible that Heidegger describes as ontic, not 'the' human condition, but rather 'at best only one human condition among others.'[171] What is more, Heidegger defines this authentic human condition as resting on the ontic understanding of being-toward-death. When Fackenheim explores further, he finds that this one human condition is a specifically 'post-Christian condition': it is not the Stoic human condition because the Stoic suicide is ruled out as an authentic escape from life; it is not the Jewish human condition because Abraham's concern for Isaac – or more broadly, post-Holocaust Jewry's concern for others – is ruled out.[172] While Abraham 'faces his own death authentically because he stands in an authentic relation to Isaac,' Paul's 'authentic man *is* authentic toward others because he faces authentically his own death.'[173] Yet Heidegger's description of 'the' human condition is not Christian because in his version there is no access to God.

Heidegger's paganism, while it threatens the traditional Christian God, is open to the post-Christian human condition. Ironically, the thinker who stands so firm in his assertion that Being is of the world only, and who, accordingly, so sensitively diagnoses the post-Christian condition, is, Fackenheim finds, wholly unopen to the Jewish condition.

To demonstrate Heidegger's glaring omission of Jews, Judaism, and the Jewish condition, Fackenheim refers to Buber,[174] who distinguishes between the insecurities provided by Heidegger and by prophetic Judaism. Heidegger's insecurity stems from the absence of a guarantee of salvation, whereas insecurity in Judaism, or prophetic Judaism, stems from the possibility of mistaking false gods for the true God.[175] Fackenheim argues that Heidegger's later thought, had it been exposed to Judaism – to Judaism's witnessing *in actu* to the true God – would be thrown into question.[176] There are, for instance, four areas in which an encounter with Judaism would have informed Heidegger's thought: the meaning or dimension of speech, human existence, history and the gods or God.

For Heidegger, the 'poet names the gods,' while in Genesis, 'he does not name God.'[177] For Heidegger, there is no distinction between false gods and the true God. In addition, for him human existence is based on the poet's speech. For Jews, human existence is not based solely on speech, nor (even more so) is it based on human speech.[178] Because for Heidegger the poet provides the foundation for human existence, 'poetry is the primitive language of a historical people'; for Jews, because they do not name God, poetry is not their primitive language. By Heidegger's definition, Jews are not a historical people.[179] Because he denies, first, that there is a distinction between the gods the poet names and the one God whom the poet cannot name, and second, that the Jews, who witness to the true God's speech in history, are a historical people, Heidegger eliminates *a priori* both the Judeo-Christian God and also the possibility of an open present moment in which to encounter God. As Fackenheim points out, the flip side of Heidegger's conclusion can render terrible results: Heidegger, both early and late, is incapable of defying idolatry as understood within Judaism and Christianity. And because there is no means by which to encounter an Absolute Other, or a metaphysical standard, within a historical moment, Heidegger's thought is incapable also of 'recognizing radical evil.'[180]

Heidegger, despite his avowed existentialism, was 'deaf to epoch-making events in the Jewish community.'[181] In April 1933, Buber had written that 'the Jew was the most exposed man of the age, that in testing him the tensions of the age were testing all humanity, and that, though well-nigh torn asunder, the authentic Jew was he who would overcome.'[182] Had Heidegger been open to Jewish experience and its reportage by Jews of the stature of Buber, he could not, Fackenheim asserts, have become a Nazi and promoted Nazism.[183] More to the point of his intellectual endeavour, had Heidegger recognized the Jewish situation in Germany in the 1930s, it would have taught him 'that some gods – past, present or future – are absolutely false.'[184] Fackenheim argues that this 'lapse' in Heidegger's 'philosophical rigor ... proved ... to be of catastrophic consequence':[185] because Heidegger, without examination, posits 'the' human condition as the post-Christian human condition, he invalidly identifies the authentic community as the *Volk*.

A community, according to Heidegger, is defined by an authentic historicity. In order to recover this authentic heritage, one must define in the concrete a 'shared anticipated future and a shared past.'[186] The community, for Heidegger, does not have the 'capacity for variety,' and since Heidegger does not define what he means by *Volk*, 'it is prey to all the perversions that had been common among Heidegger's countrymen long before Nazism ever came into power.'[187] Because it is unclear whether Heidegger establishes a validity for philosophy to transcend itself, Fackenheim tentatively adds that, because Jews define their community between 70 C.E. and 1948 without a common language or geography, the Jewish is 'ruled out in principle' as an authentic community.[188] Also ruled out is the community created by the German resistance to Hitler, whose only common geography was a 'concentration camp and the world outside Germany.'[189] *Being and Time*, if successful in fulfilling its project, 'produced philosophical surrender when the shout reverberated throughout Germany: *Ein Volk, ein Reich, ein Fuhrer.*'[190]

In the sense that Heidegger's Nazi affiliation reflects an affiliation to the limited scope of his *a priori* definition of history, this affiliation points to Heidegger's actual complete removal from the historical world of fact. Just as his *Lebenswelt* remains ungrounded insofar as it provides a *Sitz* for both historically situated world views and for the philosophical insight into the historicity of these world views, so too Heidegger could not remove himself from his circular argument in order to see the radical evil of the Nazi *Lebenswelt* around him. As a being-toward-death, Heidegger's human being is required to make decisions, but as a purely historicized being, he is unable to establish standards by which to decide. The gross disparity between what was happening and what was said about 'truth' suggests to Fackenheim the ultimate failure of the Heideggerian position: a world in which truth can mean senseless radical destruction points to a misunderstanding of the concept of truth. Heidegger's 'history of Being' excludes Jewish experience; therefore it is, quite simply, unauthentic.[191] The link between philosophy and action that Heidegger insists on ironically reveals Heidegger's failure.[192]

Fackenheim does not propose simply the wholesale rejection of historicism. Although the doctrine of self-making does in fact limit one by both one's past actions and the actions of others, the doctrine of self-making augments human possibility: the making of a human tradition that can, through human effort alone, move toward mending the world. Fackenheim suggests – reminiscent of the later Schelling – that historicism be modified to refer not to human self-making but to human self-choosing. The human being is, as part of his essence, a chooser from among pre-existing ontologies. What situates the human being is not produced by the human being; rather, it is the condition of all human choosing. And the self that chooses originates in its act of choosing. Fackenheim's existentialism originates in the recognition of the human situation as a dialectical mystery and points to an ultimate Other who situates human beings humanly. Pointing to the Other is the last achievement of unaided philosophical thought.[193] Action in accordance with this Other 'proves' the existence of transcendence in time and grounds both the eternal verities of philosophy – most specifically, the Good – and the revelation of theology, or more generally, *Halakha* (Law).

Fackenheim adopts Heidegger's concept of transcendence as self-reflection on one's personal death as one basis of future Jewish thought. The concept enables him to claim that defiant actions in the Holocaust's death camps enable the continuity both of Jewish faith – in the form of *teshuvah* or *tikkun* – and of philosophical thought.[194] Surely the category of *tikkun* undergoes a great shift; indeed, philosophical thought has been ruptured by the Holocaust. But just as Heidegger's transcendence affirms the grounding of thought in Being, so too the Holocaust's uniqueness reaffirms the existence of truth as beyond human rationality. Fackenheim has been criticized for not exploring more deeply his concept of 'uniqueness' and his assertion that the Holocaust is unique,[195] yet his adoption of Heideggerian transcendence precludes the need for such an explanation. Fackenheim does not need to prove the uniqueness of the Holocaust because the old philosophical categories no longer hold: the Holocaust cannot be reduced to an idea. It is 'proved' unique when the particular post-Holocaust human being opens himself to feel and experience the full extent of the horror and knows its uniqueness and the reality of its having ruptured the continuity of ideas. While Fackenheim seeks transcendence from within existence, also he recognizes that this transcendence requires witness, not reason: Jews must relearn hope in the world, and in God, and must forget Hitler's name.[196] And the resources for this re-education exist already within Judaism: the midrashic framework, Fackenheim suggests, is open to historical modification. Following Heidegger, Fackenheim understands the resistance to the Holocaust as an ontic reality; consequently, thought can understand such resistance as an ontological reality.[197]

On the point of the adoption of some aspects of Heidegger's thought, Fackenheim shows a marked divergence from Strauss, who rejects as far as possible the doctrine of historicism.[198] By adopting Heideggerian 'transcendence' in place of either traditional philosophical or theological transcendence, Fackenheim threatens the existence of an external standard by which to prove anything and opens himself to the charge of historicism. Yet he argues for the possibility of disengaging Heidegger's notion of transcendence from his 'moral degeneracy'[199] and avoiding a radical historicism. Fackenheim's refusal to divorce idea from action, his insistence rather on their identity, provides for his future thought an ethical standard. Because Heidegger, who also insists on this link, bases his philosophy on the concept of a single, universal human condition that, in the realm of action, in history, cannot be sustained, neither can the link be sustained.[200] An ethical standard for the variety of human conditions, and specifically for 'the religious, philosophical and moral riddles of contemporary Jewish existence,'[201] is wholly absent in Heidegger. Fackenheim's marriage of idea and action, in contrast, by positing itself as only quasi-historical – as based ultimately on a transcendent standard – opens up thought to all the varieties of human existence, even while preserving the ability to bear witness against idolatry.[202]

Fackenheim writes: because Heidegger 'refuse[s] to say no to Apollo, his thought has rendered itself impotent to say no to Baal, including and above all the modern Baal who devoured the souls of his countrymen and to whom these countrymen sacrificed the bodies of one-third of the world's Jewish population.'[203]

PART II. FACKENHEIM ON JEWISH PHILOSOPHY

Fackenheim on the Bible

Fackenheim writes:

> More than thirty years ago [i.e., before 1940], largely under the influence of Martin Buber and Franz Rosenzweig, I had responded to the demonic fact of Nazism by turning my back on my nineteenth century liberal Jewish heritage and embracing what may broadly be called a neoorthodox faith and theology. I had rejected the dissipation of the distinction between the Word of God and the word of man, between the divine covenant with Israel and the random events of history – above all, an ideology that had confused the messianic days with the achievements and promises of the modern world. To this day I remain largely within this neoorthodox stance.[204]

Fackenheim goes on to write that he had at the time erroneously omitted the fact of the Holocaust's uniqueness. The omission allowed him to remain within his predecessors' neo-orthodox tradition, which he holds to mean, first, a reaffirmation of the utter distinction between God and the human being, and second, that the human condition is the foundation for arguments regarding the necessity of faith.[205] Once Fackenheim faces the uniqueness of the Holocaust, he is able both to develop further Rosenzweig and Buber's position and also to suggest that the Holocaust has 'radical religious significance': like the events at Sinai, the Holocaust informs the Jewish understanding of being singled out as Jews 'by God as a people in history.'[206]

While in his earlier work, Fackenheim affirms God's relevance within the secular world, in his later work he expands that relevance to include not simply the possibility of God's incursion into the present, but also the possibility of God's action in the secular world.[207] After 1957 he elevated the concept of election and translated it from God's election of the Israelites to the singling out of the Jews by both God and other human beings.[208] The elevation of this concept allows God's revelation both to act in present history, in particular communities, and to evoke radical surprise. Later, using this stance, Fackenheim is able to go beyond Rosenzweig and Buber's affirmation of the human condition as the foundation for religious authenticity: by reinvesting religious thought with the particularity of both the history of one's community and the community itself, Fackenheim makes room not only for God's incursion into the secular world, but also for God's present activity in empirical history. On the one hand, God's activity is present – not, as in Rosenzweig, an echo from the sacred past. On the other hand, God's activity is not limited to the Buberian discoveries of His presence; God's present activity in the secular world defines an evolving history. At the same time, by affirming the priority of one's particular human condition, Fackenheim is able to discover that the Voice that speaks in the secular world is the Voice that spoke at Sinai. He combines Buber's equalizing of the possibility of contemporary dialogue with God and the Sinaitic revelation[209] with Rosenzweig's elevation of the Sinaitic Voice, which, although one can hear it still, no longer 'speaks' in the present.[210] The result is the affirmation of the possibility of God's continued speaking: the continuation in the present of a dialogue that began at Sinai.

In the earlier work, before positing a God in history – a God who is active and whose activity with human beings defines an evolving history for human beings – Fackenheim turns to the Bible and midrash. He uses these sources to demonstrate the ability of Jewish sources to stand up to the test that modernity has posed. This includes their ability to encounter Hegel's idea that the divine and human unite in history, 'even as they bear a critical witness against those optimistic and idealistic strands in Hegel, stemming from his Christianity, that render his philosophy incredible'[211] – or, more generally, the ability of Jewish texts to remain valid in the modern, secular world. Fackenheim seeks neither to flee into the ancient texts nor to adopt the optimistic premises of the modern world. Rather, he seeks to rediscover God as Absolute Other,[212] even within the living context of secularism.

The modern secular world posits the primacy of criticism over the primacy of authority. The first step in modernity's development toward the primacy of criticism is the assertion that God is not in history, but rather has providence over it, that God uses nature and human beings in history for His will.[213] Since God is no longer in history, the human being has growing authority over himself and over the unfolding of historical events. Modernity's next step, because it is forced to respond to the challenge raised to the concept of human free will by positing the human being as God's tool, is to propose that divine providence is immanent in human freedom as what is progressively realized.[214] As Hegel proposes, the forward direction of history reveals its meaning, while 'human freedom raises itself ever higher toward Divinity.'[215]

These two steps, according to Fackenheim, have specific consequences for Judaism.[216] First, when the primacy of authority is abandoned in favour of the primacy of criticism, the authority of classic Jewish texts is threatened and their relevance is limited: 'Modern historiography understands itself as critically reconstructing the past rather than passively receiving it from past authorities. Once this step is taken no distinction is possible either between secular and sacred facts, or between the sources through which the facts are to be reconstructed.'[217] Because the Bible becomes in modern thought one contributor among many to the reconstruction of the past, rather than the authority on which the understanding of the past is based, the distinction between Israel's covenant and more mundane human empirical history – indeed, the comprehensiveness of Judaism's world view – is threatened.[218]

Second, Fackenheim argues, modernity threatens not only Judaism's comprehensiveness but also its specific religious understanding. By translating the human being, God, and nature into ideas, modern thought introduces an unwarranted optimism into religious thought and abandons the primacy in Judaism of being, or of witnessing, over thought. Modernity posits God as both an idea and, optimistically, a human goal to be progressively realized. Because the source of this understanding of God has its foundation in the human being himself, the transcendent God is at best irrelevant. The God of modernity is internal and immanent. Judaism's God, while He may become immanent, cannot at any moment be non-transcendent. The Jewish God cannot be an idea; He cannot be abstracted out of His particular relationship with the people Israel. Without God's directive, Jewish activity cannot progress toward perfecting its imitation of the holy. By translating the human being and nature into ideas, modernity dissolves Judaism's concept of the people Israel, with regard to both its collectivity – its communal aspect – and its particularity from among the nations. Because God, human beings and nature are abstractions in modern thought, Judaism's foundation in a moment of encounter at Sinai is dissolved. Jewish witness to God's Absolute Otherness stands in antithesis to the modern world; so too does Israel's relationship with its God.

The modern view is that the Bible is of human invention and thus subject to historical influences. Therefore 'the meaning of God and of life with God as reflected in biblical and rabbinic tradition ... modernity has unconsciously tended to misinterpret ... in accordance with its own very different ideas.'[219] This misinterpretation takes the form of the 'naturalization of Biblical history.'[220] Nature is presumed by the

Bible to be 'evidence of a God who guides it'; history is presumed to 'prove divine retribution'; and personal experience is presumed to be certain.[221] Modernity, through what it considers to be critical examination of the biblical text, finds little evidence to support the text's claim that it is 'impossible to doubt or deny the existence of God.'[222] Fackenheim argues against modernity's refutations of the biblical account. Ultimately, he ascribes these refutations to the modern prejudice that 'all religious life is an evolution of religious *feelings* or *ideas*.'[223] Modern criticism, because it interprets ultimately revelation as experience-of-revelation, ends in a 'dissolution into humanism,'[224] a dissolution that, at the very least, acknowledges that the existence of God cannot be refuted. Faith begins with the decision that 'God is inescapable.'[225] In the biblical and rabbinic views, the failure of the evidence for the Sinaitic revelation proves not that God does not exist, but only that we cannot understand God.

In his earlier work, Fackenheim challenges the translation of religion into thought and the abstracting of (1) God into an idea of human freedom, (2) the human being into an instrument of God's Will – or alternatively, into a paler version of God,[226] (3) nature into the empirical data of modern criticism, and (4) history into the realm of exclusively human, or of human-as-divine, action. Against modernity's abstractions, he posits the brute fact of the experiences at Sinai: human beings may not know what happened at Sinai, but they do know that something happened. While his distinction between the fact of revelation and its content is problematic, perhaps even arbitrary – after all, how do we know that something happened any more than we know what happened? – he bases the distinction in Strauss's argument against idealism. For Strauss, in order to eliminate the idealism that is implicit in modern thought, modern thinkers must return to the authority of the surface of things. Fackenheim follows Strauss in this matter because the only way to salvage the content of the Sinaitic revelation within the context of secularist history – or to return authority to God – is to begin outside all human ideas.[227] Although, for instance, one may doubt the content of the Sinaitic revelation, 'it is not possible to doubt that the Biblical account of Jewish origins, however mythological, reflects something which did take place … a succession of overwhelming religious experiences. The presence of the Nameless was felt in experiences which were themselves nameless.'[228] For Fackenheim, combining the acceptance of revelation in general with modernity's abandonment of the Bible's account of a specific revelation provides the means by which to invest the Bible with continued validity and 'sets the agenda for modern Jewish thought.'[229] This agenda begins with the insight that Sinai teaches that empirical history must remain open to God's incursions. In order to facilitate this openness, Fackenheim suggests that, because empirical history becomes the place in which God is experienced, the Bible must open itself to reinterpretation in every generation, according to the needs of each generation.[230] To a certain extent, the Bible is historicized; yet in order for Fackenheim to create a space within secularity for a relationship with God, the people Israel must become the source from which Judaism is defined.[231]

Fackenheim seeks a move beyond modernity's humanism to modern supernaturalism. In an earlier essay he argues that all 'customs, ceremonies and folklore, [including those in the Bible], are mere human self-expression.'[232] But he does not leave it at that: although his strategy is to build a new theology from the bottom up, so to speak, rather than the top down,[233] Fackenheim, following (or expanding) Schelling's 'ecstasy,' suggests a leap of faith to God as fact. The leap, by bringing with it God's command to fulfil *Halakha* (Law), mediates between Jewish life and Jewish faith. By fulfilling *Halakha*, the Jew is able to reenact the Sinaitic relationship with God. He becomes a member of Israel, and according to the earlier Fackenheim, he is thereby able to reflect on the Bible anew in order to encounter a real God.[234] The Bible, accordingly, is the 'human reflection' of 'actual events' of divine 'incursions into human history.'[235] And revelation is a moment when 'the Divine meets the human ... [by] enter[ing] into the human situation ... [without] forc[ing] the human into a mystic surrender of its finitude.'[236]

Like Rosenzweig, Fackenheim, at this point in his theological development, reaffirms the recognition that revelation means itself only; the content of revelation may be challenged, disproved or even modified, but the event of revelation cannot by definition reveal any content:[237] 'Revelation, in short, has a built-in content if only because it is revelation – because it is not an ineffable Presence in man which dissolves him, but rather a Presence speaking to man which singles him out for response.'[238] The minute that 'God spoke,' He highlighted the human being's separation, his finiteness; by interpreting revelation, by giving to it content, one creates a religion, which may be more or less valid but which cannot be identified with revelation itself. The interpretation of the experience of revelation 'distinguishes forms of religious life,' that is, distinguishes one religion from another.[239] According to Fackenheim, 'Orthodoxy identifies the human – if ancient – interpretation of the revelation with the revelation itself ... Modernism ... identifies divine revelation and human interpretation, but commits the opposite error: instead of making the interpretation divine, it makes of revelation a purely human "creation."'[240] In order to reaffirm the pertinence of the Bible even while allowing for modernity's assertion of human autonomy, Fackenheim must disentangle revelation from its interpretation, and the divine from the human.

The Jewish interpretation of God's revelation to human beings at Sinai, as recounted in the Bible, is, Fackenheim argues, comprised of three elements. First, the experience is interpreted 'as a call to action.'[241] Because it was a call, there was both God's speaking and human hearing; because it involved two partners, One challenging the other, it was also the establishment of a covenant. Second, it was a collective experience; the challenge was issued to the group. Third, 'it was an experience so profound as to persist even after its universal implications had become manifest.'[242] The structure of Jewish experience,[243] which has persisted despite the evil and meaninglessness in history, is the refusal to separate God from history: God was present, as Absolute Other, in history.[244] It is these three elements that, for Fackenheim, define Judaism because even in the prophets we see their persistence. For Fackenheim, the prophets, while addressing the commandments now to each person, neither translate the divine call into a generality, nor remove the divine challenge from the here and now, nor interrupt God's commanding.[245] Although prophetic religion is addressed to each person, Israel, remembering its covenant, does not interpret the challenges now made to other peoples.

Fackenheim recognizes that if it is to persist, Judaism must reaffirm the perpetuation of the experience at Sinai as its foundation. Even as he rejects the nineteenth-century liberal compromises with modernity, he rejects as well what he considers to be the Orthodox flight from the world. On the one hand, the form of revelation must be retained in its initial interpretation; on the other, revelation must be interpreted so as to be accessible: 'Orthodoxy errs in its belief that a revelation could be possessed in the form of a body of truths and laws unaffected by human contingencies and unchanging in validity.'[246] The solution to what is ostensibly a contradiction – that the religious should be combined with the secular – is, in Fackenheim's view, as the midrash teaches: Torah is given at the moment one receives it.[247] But in an important sense his version deviates from what he conceives to be traditional religious understanding:[248] he argues against 'the importance of the

Jew's openness to God's voice as it was manifested in past events ... because it turned faith into a static thing by closing off the possibility of God's voice in the [modern, secular] present.'[249] Fackenheim, following Rosenzweig,[250] understands that Judaism no longer 'rest[s] on the divine promise at Sinai ... [but] rather on an *experience*, forever renewed and rejuvenated, the structure of which includes a *human commitment* to a divine promise.'[251]

Because the secular world is the realm in which Jews do and must live, the continuity between the past and the present that is presupposed by rabbinic hermeneutics can no longer be sustained. While each generation, as of old, must reinterpret the Bible, the generations of the modern world know themselves to be the source of authority from which the interpretation of the experience of revelation is hewn. Each modern generation's interpretation begins with the knowledge of the discontinuity of its empirical secular existence and the wholly religious context of the Bible. More pressingly, as Fackenheim comes to understand in 1967, the Holocaust has ruptured historical continuity even in the context of the eternal divine promise, or the permanent structure of Jewish experience: God was, in Buber's phrase, 'in eclipse'[252] – a situation that negated the possibility of covenant and that threatened the perpetuation of the people Israel both as the people Israel and as individual Jews.

In his earlier thought, up through 1967 – before he recognizes the enormous challenge posed to Jews by the Holocaust – Fackenheim attempts simply to create within secularism room for the incursion of an Absolute Other. The earlier work, up through and including *Quest for Past and Future*, following Rosenzweig and Buber, attempts to bear witness to God as Absolute Other within a secular context by conceding to modernity the beginning of religious thought as the human condition.[253] After confronting the Holocaust, Fackenheim recognizes the inadequacy of this earlier response and attempts to find room in the secular world not only for God's incursion, but also for a particular incursion of God, at a particular historical moment, to a particular historical person, within a particular historical community. He recognizes the necessity of making thought vulnerable to empirical history or to God's activity within the secular realm. As a consequence of this insight, he argues that if Judaism is to persist, the Holocaust must inform Jewish religious understanding. One might understand Fackenheim not so much as a rabbinic interpreter of the Bible, but more 'as a thinker in the tradition of Deutero-Isaiah ... who unforgettably endowed historical catastrophe with religious meaning, offered consolation for the devastating burden of sin and defeat, and found hope of redemption in a return to Zion.'[254]

Fackenheim believes that a theological response to the Holocaust is necessary for three reasons. First, the people Israel has been responding already. Jews have recognized that theology must begin with experience. Second, there is a sacred obligation to remember and to witness. Third, Jews must, in order to keep God in the present, 'refuse to disconnect God from the holocaust [sic].'[255] Only if God acts in the present is it possible to be open to God's incursion into human experience – and indeed, to be capable of validating a living theology. The modern Jew, without the ancient rabbis, must confront 'the naked text'[256] in an effort to reframe the root experiences of Judaism, the permanent structure of Jewish experience, and the divine promise, in the light of the Holocaust.[257]

The Holocaust, in light of God's absence, has ruptured the continuity of Judaism. At the same time, because Jews were singled out, Fackenheim understands that the Holocaust reinforms the biblical affirmation that all Israel stood and stands at Sinai:[258] the Holocaust informs the theological concept of election insofar as all Jews, religious and secular, rich and poor, old and young, male and female, were singled out.[259] The basis of the singling out was, as in the Sinaitic revelation, an empiricism stripped of intra-Jewish particularity. In an effort to reframe appropriately Judaism's root experiences, one may look to the prophets. The prophets do not make religion abstract, nor do they imagine the Voice as addressed to humankind rather than to human beings: such an abstraction or imagining is to flee 'from commitment and the divine challenge.'[260] So too, for Fackenheim, to translate the primeval Jewish interpretation of revelation – as a covenantal call to action, as collective, as particular – into abstractions fostered by such movements as humanism and relativism[261] is to flee God's challenge to Israel. One sees, for instance, that because for Jews God was present in history at Sinai only to particular people, people do not rise above their situations – do not become, as modernity would posit, abstract representatives of the human condition – but rather become witnesses as a result of their particularity. Neither the dissolution of being into thought nor of particularity into abstraction can respond to God's challenge to the Israelites at Sinai. So too, these dissolutions cannot respond to the Holocaust.

Paradoxically, Fackenheim understands the Holocaust as a demonstration of God's action (or anti-action) in history, even as the event serves to throw into question the relationship between Jews and God. He can argue that there is religious meaning in the Holocaust because it meets the three necessary criteria for the permanent structure of Jewish experience. It is a call to action; it was addressed to all Jews collectively; and it singled out Jews, not as individuals, but as a particular people. At the same time, the Holocaust has transformed Jewish consciousness. While in Fackenheim's view, the Bible remains the source of Jewish identity, 'Jewish theology [after the Holocaust] is possible only after the commitment to Jewish existence.'[262] Fackenheim proposes adding to this structure an additional, 614th, commandment: be committed to Jewish survival and Jewish unity, witness to the event, hope in the future.[263] A Jew, to authentically believe, must 'expos[e] himself *both* to the fact that the image of God was destroyed, *and* to the fact that the unsurpassable attempt to destroy it was successfully resisted ... by the survivor. *Hence the wish to bear witness turns into a commandment, the commandment to restore the divine image to the limits of his power.* The Jew witnesses through living and being human.'[264]

Fackenheim on Spinoza

Fackenheim writes:

> Biblical criticism ... it is sometimes supposed, constitutes a refutation of the claim that the Scriptures are the revealed word of God. But in fact Biblical criticism either presupposes what it imagines itself to be proving, or else it leaves the issue open. For if the critic declares that what the Bible itself regards as the reflection of human dialogues with God is nothing more than an expression of the evolution of religious feelings and ideas, it is he who has brought such categories to the Bible ... His criticism, in other words, already assumes a position of subjectivist reductionism.[265]

Subjectivist reductionism, according to Fackenheim, has reduced knowledge to one of two things: either empirical evidence of an objective event, or subjective feelings of a divine Presence. The former cannot disprove revelation because, according to the principles of empiricism, what is inconsistent with natural law is not accepted as a ground of knowledge. Revelation – which by reenacting a natural-historical event, reenacts also an abiding astonishment – is at odds with an empiricism that has as its goal the dissolution of astonishment.[266] Reducing revelation to subjective feelings of a divine Presence discounts revelation, and does so without refutation, because the objective actuality of revelation cannot be inferred from what are predefined as feelings.[267] Spinoza does not prove that the revelation of Scripture is inauthentic,[268] but he does make clear to Fackenheim that, in order to recognize biblical revelation as valid, and to continue to hear God's voice, it is necessary to begin with the standpoint of a 'believing openness.'[269]

The premise of Spinoza's biblical criticism is paradoxical: philosophy claims comprehensive authority without philosophically authorizing its claim. Despite this invalidity, Spinoza has disproved *in actu* biblical revelation: on the foundation of Spinoza's philosophy is built the modern secular state – which Fackenheim defines as one governed by the philosophical principle of human autonomy.[270] For Fackenheim, regardless of whether the foundation is philosophically valid, the foundation, because it has informed the events of modern empirical history, is in some sense true. What happens in the world – the contingent, the arbitrary, the evil – is as much a part of truth as hermetic systems, regardless of how thoughtfully, conscientiously, or consistently those systems are argued.[271] To remain vital, meaningful, and strong, Jewish thought – which is based on the belief that God appears from Absolute Otherness into historical particularity – must be vulnerable to epoch-making events.[272] Although, like Strauss, he understands that Spinoza discards revelation without disproving it – and even, perhaps, that this discarding is only apparent or exoteric – for Fackenheim, Spinozistic thought has entered empirical history in a real way; and if God is the God of history, he must be the God of contemporary history as well. Despite the mutual irrefutability of faith and secularity, religious thought must confront God within the context of the secular world.[273]

Spinoza apparently discards revelation in order to make philosophy 'free' in the modern world.[274] The modern world newly understands the tension between philosophy and revelatory theology as constituting one reality; thus, by abandoning revelation, Spinoza abandons also the restraints on philosophy. Philosophy is constructed as 'self-productive subjectivity'; Spinoza espouses an absolute hostility to religion as non-self-productive, or as receptive.[275] His God – God as Substance – displaces the beginning of religious wisdom – fear of the Lord – in order to promote the beginning of thought as philosophical wisdom.[276] This displacement will have an extraordinary influence on modern idealistic thought through its culmination in Hegel and beyond, and – as rejection – into the early period of existentialism.[277]

Spinoza, for perhaps only political reasons, does not want to choose between Judaism and Christianity.[278] As a consequence, reason, as it must, identifies the contents of the revelations of the Old and New Testaments insofar as each is able to claim validity. Spinoza's rejection of revelation fails to distinguish between the Jewish and Christian revelations;[279] yet at the same time, the aspect that is different between them – Judaism's traditional marriage of belief and action, as opposed to Paul's separation of them or Augustine's distinction between the sacred and secular realms – defines the public realm of reason as specifically post-Christian.[280] While privately there is a diminishing of the validity of the practice of religion, publicly, reason is operative in a secular realm that had been, early on, carved out exclusively in Christianity.

While it is true that Spinoza frees God 'from His premodern otherness,'[281] this freedom was at a great cost. First, his system lacks particularity: all is abstracted or universalized; and second, there is a loss of life, of empirical reality, in favour of pure thought.[282] As a result of these two things, the particular person becomes a human-being-in-general, and in addition – because in Judaism, the universal is intertwined already with the particular,[283] and revelatory theology is tied already with existence – also the Jew in particular becomes divided against himself. He is both human-being-in-general and Jew-in-particular, both citizen of the liberal state and member of Israel. Jews cannot 'dissipate [themselves] into bloodless Spinozistic thought;'[284] therefore, Spinoza sets up the problem in modern thought of defining in what way Jews and Judaism share, for instance, in Kant's idea of humanity, or in Hegel's philosophical account of Jewish existence as empirical fact.[285]

As the first human-being-in-general, Spinoza begins the process that will end in Rosenzweig's return to Judaism. His affirmation of humanity-in-general or religion-in-general precludes Jews and Judaism from participation in the conceived universal human experience. Both he and – as we shall see – Rosenzweig,[286] Fackenheim argues, merely guide one to the point where each spurns history, where each conceives of truth as somehow outside the scope of empirical reality. Rosenzweig argues for Galut as a metaphysical principle;[287] for Spinoza, one achieves blessedness neither through revelation nor through experience, but rather through a science of human nature.[288] Rosenzweig, against Spinoza, attempts to reinvoke both the God of revelation and His ability to enter into empirical reality; but because Spinoza's starting point, the 'old thinking,' is non-historical in the sense of being closed to both God as Other and the particularity of empirical experience, Rosenzweig can invoke only the idea, the metahistorical reality, of the Jewish God and His covenant. He cannot rediscover the existential reality of the Jewish covenant with the God of Moses. Rosenzweig may succeed in his attempt to inform thought with empirical experience, but he is able to do so only insofar as that experience is defined as absolute. Jews remain, in Rosenzweig's thought – as they did once in Spinoza's liberal state – outside of political or historical reality.

Fackenheim does not propose the wholesale rejection of the tradition from Spinoza to Rosenzweig. Instead he begins his thinking about Spinoza with Hegel, for whom, Fackenheim discovers, the mediation of Judaism and Spinoza is 'central to [his] philosophy as a whole.'[289] Hegel recognizes that in order to translate Christianity into philosophy, he must begin with Spinoza's rejection of Judaism as a basis for modern philosophy.

On the philosophical level, Hegel looks to Spinoza because he, like Fackenheim, considers Spinoza – insofar as Substance is the truth of human existence – to be the beginning of modern philosophical wisdom. According to Hegel, because Spinoza surrenders the world and the self, he is only the beginning. The union with God must be real, and must exist not merely in thought, in order to 'avoid a devastating protest from life'[290] – the hypocrisy of serving God without sensing any connection to Him. Hegel cannot adopt Spinozism as the whole of truth: he needs to consider the insights of what he understands as rabbinic Judaism because Christianity requires Jewish Otherness in order to avoid paganism. At the same time, he requires Spinozistic thought because, in the realm of philosophy, the subject must keep the principle of Substance, the One, in order to avoid fragmentation.[291] Through a process of mediation, Hegel seeks to produce a synthesis that is neither anti-Spinozistic nor anti-rabbinic, but rather post-rabbinic and post-Spinozistic: a truth higher than either alone.

On the historical level, also, Hegel must mediate between Spinoza and the rabbis. For Hegel, the rabbis affirm the notion, in Hegelian terms, of the renunciation of the renunciation, the belief that after the 'surrender of the human servant to the divine Lord ... the finite human is restored in his finitude.'[292] This understanding of the rabbinic position reaffirms not only the reality of religious transcendence but also the primacy of historical experience. Yet Hegel must look to Spinoza as well because the modern state has been successfully operative in history. Spinoza creates the philosophical necessity to 'reconcile the most radical (i.e., orthodox) claim on behalf of the God of scriptural revelation with the most radical (i.e., autonomous) claim on behalf of modern reason.'[293] Hegel must therefore complete the dialectic between Judaism and Spinoza, between 'religious Jewish affirmation of revelation and its secularist Jewish denial.'[294]

Hegel, like Fackenheim – and indeed, like the modern state itself – distinguishes himself from Spinoza's Neo-Platonism by his ability to stay with the world.[295] And ironically, Hegel begins the process of returning Jews to history: by mediating between Spinoza's Neo-Platonism and the rabbis's 'renunciation of renunciation,' Hegel is able to affirm that Jews persist in history, in the histories of both philosophy and the modern state within the context of their relationship with God. The legacy of Hegel's reading and interpretation of Spinoza profoundly affects Fackenheim: Hegel's success in mediating between Spinoza and revelatory Judaism proves for Fackenheim that revelation need not be a stumbling block for Jewish modernity. Just as Hegel recognizes that modern Christianity must be informed by both revelation and Spinozistic thought, so too Fackenheim recognizes that, in order to affirm a new modern Jewish theology, he must begin in dialogue with Spinoza.[296] Since Hegel affirms that this mediation must be continually reenacted philosophically, and that this reenactment must take place within the understanding that life cannot be reduced to thought, Fackenheim's post-Holocaust mediation is religiously, philosophically, and historically valid.

Fackenheim on Rosenzweig

Fackenheim writes: 'Without the inspiration and the pioneering accomplishments of Martin Buber and Franz Rosenzweig [*Encounters*] could not have been written.'[297] Rosenzweig begins for Fackenheim the process of making 'the significance of revelation come alive for modern man.'[298] Rosenzweig recognizes that 'if "no conclusions" can be derived from the "belief ... in the revealed status of the Torah" concerning "the literary origin and philological value" of the present biblical text, then the reverse is true as well: The belief in the revealed status of the Torah does not depend on the Wellhausens of this world and their theories.'[299] While faith can make 'no objections in principle ... to biblical criticism,'[300] so too, biblical criticism cannot assail the validity of faith. In addition to affirming the possibility of faith,[301] Rosenzweig brings revelation alive to the modern Jew by recognizing that the Law is not a 'static block' of 613 commandments:[302] the Law's relationship to the individual Jew changes as the individual Jew takes 'the opportunity ... to live out [his] response to these commands.'[303] It is possible to find room for revelation within the realm of 'reverent criticism'[304] – criticism that recognizes its inability to impeach the validity of faith. According to Rosenzweig, the means by which one is fully in the world is a combination of the philosophical and religious ways of life.[305]

Rosenzweig's thought is not simply a denial of the insights of modernity arrived at through the 'old thinking'[306] – specifically, Spinoza's apparent disproof of biblical revelation – but rather a response to them. His categorization of the history of philosophy as first physiocentric, then theocentric, then anthropocentric, indicates that philosophy has exhausted all of its possibilities. Philosophy must now turn to a new methodology, found in theology, in order to continue. Both Rosenzweig and Fackenheim suggest that theology can inform philosophy through an existential 'leap to life,' but they disagree as to whether this leap appears in Jewish thought with Cohen, or only with Rosenzweig. According to Fackenheim, it is Rosenzweig who, in his 'new thinking' introduces the personal standpoint into philosophy, an introduction that gives voice to the possibility of revelation.

The 'new thinking' changes the categories of thought. Despite this change, Fackenheim understands Rosenzweig as being markedly influenced by Schelling[307] – and by German Idealism in general – 'in his problems, method and even his language.'[308] Rosenzweig uses philosophy to answer not technical philosophical questions, but rather existential ones. Just as Schelling attempts a leap from the end of thought to existence, so too Rosenzweig uses philosophy as a means to arrive at his goal of 'living as a Jew before God, and "learning" in the traditional Jewish sense – that is to say, learning in the sight of God.'[309] In his encounter with Hegel, Rosenzweig learns the necessity of making the personal standpoint compatible with the objective standpoint of philosophy's 'old thinking.' In Hegel, 'the standpoint of objective thought is regarded not only as different from, but also as superior to, the personal commitment of the believer, and if this is true, then the authenticity of the God-man-relation has disappeared.'[310] Through what Fackenheim describes as an 'inversion' of Hegel,[311] Rosenzweig posits the possibility that objective thought might deem that 'the personal standpoint of faith ... is authentic and true.'[312] If such were the case, only through the personal standpoint would one be able to hear God's voice, and one would conclude that objective thought is inferior to the actual relationship with God.

Rosenzweig goes a step further, a step that goes beyond Buber's mere assertion of the possibility of the standpoint of faith:[313] Rosenzweig's 'new thinking' is a philosophy because it 'seeks to justify the principle of revelation.'[314] Insofar as Fackenheim understands him as philosophically justifying Judaism's covenant as a possibility of thought, Rosenzweig is the most influential modern Jewish thinker for Fackenheim. Perhaps more important, by confronting the existential differences between Christians (or post-Christians) and Jews, Rosenzweig's thought offers the 'beginnings of a liberated modern Jewish philosophy.'[315] In 'Franz Rosenzweig and the New Thinking,' Fackenheim has two goals: first, to demonstrate that the 'new thinking' is thinking; and second, to demonstrate that it is new insofar as it adds a third possibility – the possibility of covenant – to the already existing categories of the means by which the human being may be related to God. Because Fackenheim seeks to create a Jewish philosophy that positively affirms the possibility of God's action in history, Rosenzweig, as both thinker and Jew, becomes, as Fackenheim writes, perhaps 'the most important Jewish thinker of our time.'[316]

To establish the 'new thinking' as thinking, first, Rosenzweig recognizes that there is a distinction between the principle of revelation – which can be recognized only as a philosophical category – and a particular experience of revelation.[317] It is the category of revelation, revelation-in-general, that he philosophically validates. Second, he recognizes that philosophy is needed to argue 'the real separateness of God, man, world … the conception of history as a developing God-man-encounter (rather than the mere evolution of religious experience) – and many other [metaphysical presuppositions of the man-God relationship].'[318] Having established the philosophical possibility of the personal standpoint, Rosenzweig argues that there can be objective, philosophical validity to the line of thought that develops from faith as a first principle. Fackenheim concludes that Rosenzweig's 'new thinking' is in fact thinking.

Next, Fackenheim attempts to show not only that Rosenzweig's 'new thinking' is thinking, but also that it is new. The categories by which philosophy, up to Rosenzweig's time, understands the human being–God relationship take one of two forms. It may be the God–idea – the universal, abstract thought of the religion of philosophy – which understands absolute truth as outside of experience, in pure thought alone. Or it may be the individual thought of personal commitment, which is affirmed by existentialism. This latter category places thought within experience and saves God as actual, but it may fail to maintain the universal categories of thought[319] or to enable interhuman relationships. To these universal categories, Rosenzweig adds a third: the possibility of a God relationship with human beings as a 'flesh and blood community.'[320] While the first two alternatives, idealist and existentialist philosophy, allow for universalist and individualist standpoints respectively, neither alternative incorporates into its categories history as the locus of the human being–God relationship. Rosenzweig affirms that Jews as a people have believed in an ongoing covenant between themselves and God. The human-being-within-community-God relationship implicates both universal abstract thought (it is a fact that Jews as a people believe that a covenant between themselves and God exists) and the individual thought of personal commitment. Rosenzweig's empirical history 'already presupposes metaphysical categories, which ... have established history, not as human, but as human-divine (Schelling's term); an infinitely free God, and a finitely free man, whose essential historicity lies in his relation to God ... [Rosenzweig's] ... Jewish history [is] one of the three possibilities by which man may be related to God.'[321] Rosenzweig's argument is both universal and individual, both abstract and committed; and like Schelling's, it is *a posteriori*: Rosenzweig argues from what thought beyond itself points to.

The 'new thinking' recognizes its reliance on historical moment – on its fixedness in the flow of the philosophical tradition – to define and limit its insights. Rosenzweig argues that this reliance enables experience to be absolute. With these new categories of absolute yet experiential thought – of thought as implicitly bound to being-in-time – Rosenzweig is able to affirm that the three foundations on which he builds his system – Man, God, and World – are in fact empirical data.[322] In a move that, according to Strauss and adopted by Fackenheim, matches the intellectual achievement of Heidegger,[323] Rosenzweig is able to create a universal system that retains particularity, and equally important, that enables post-Christian dialogue with Jews by putting 'the divine-Jewish covenant as central in all its stark particularity.'[324]

Rosenzweig adopts from Hegel the latter's belief in the unfolding of God or Spirit through history, even while he offers a Jewish critique of Hegel's thought. In this sense, Fackenheim recognizes Rosenzweig's thought as a 'radical response to Hegel.'[325] By using the 'new thinking,' Rosenzweig is able not simply to deny but rather to intellectually refute Hegel's consideration of the God of Moses as anachronistic.[326] By reaffirming the transcendent God of Judaism, Rosenzweig allows for the creation of a 'new thinking,' which, having 'passed through [Hegel's identity of the divine and the human], exposed it as a false abstraction of mere thought, and only after having done so reaffirms the present otherness of the God of Sinai.'[327] Although Rosenzweig's thought borders on historicism, the historicism of human beings is bounded by the reality of an infinite God.

Rosenzweig's reaffirmation of the Jewish God, without the disavowal of the modern principles of biblical criticism, begins the process of historicizing traditional Jewish beliefs. He, following Cohen's insistence on foundations for modern philosophy, 'which were originally, if no longer exclusively, Jewish in character,'[328] suggests that Cohen's God-Idea may be translated into the God of Moses. This development, this historicization, becomes crucial for Fackenheim's thought on two levels. First, by allowing empirical history to inform thought, Rosenzweig (following Cohen) is able to offer a critique of the 'self-interpretation of Hegel's Europe';[329] and the results of that critique show a world far from the progress toward a God-infused world that Hegel had predicted.[330] One such circular argument for the godliness of Germany is that, since empirical history is essentially religious, the religious rectitude of Christianity has been demonstrated in the fact of the emergence of the Christian state.[331] The difficulty associated with abandoning Hegel is that his ideas – specifically, his description of life as essentially religious and as containing within it the fundamental elements of thought – continue to be potent, even while empirical reality testifies against them. The consequence of this unsubstantiated description is a discontinuity between the real struggles of the economic and social classes, and of nations and races, and the ideal political structures that were in place. Jews were considered a separate nation, and their emancipation was of only 'secondary importance.'[332] Rosenzweig's *Star of Redemption* defies the exclusion of the testimony of empirical existence, and, by recognizing the Jewish divine–human encounter as central, provides a 'new orientation in the world'[333] and establishes the equal importance of Jewish experience.

In another sense, by allowing empirical history to inform thought, Rosenzweig is able to address the division of nineteenth-century Jews between those, such as Hermann Cohen, who conceive of Jews and Judaism as missionaries to humankind, and secular Zionists, who reduce Judaism to Jewish culture. Jewish existence becomes, in his thought, the grounding for a unified Jewish thought. His attempt to dissolve the division is of utmost importance for Fackenheim's thought: the Nazis aimed to destroy both Jews and Jewish faith, and therefore there can be no longer a dichotomy of the secular and the religious.[334]

Second, the historicization of Jewish thought is crucial for Fackenheim because it allows Judaism to inform politically the secular world. Rosenzweig's 'new thinking,' because it is bound in some sense to empirical history, begins with the knowledge that it is no longer possible to submit to pre-modern authorities. Rosenzweig is aware that he himself is a product of Spinoza's legacy of the liberal state and that he is, therefore, in Fackenheim's terms not anti-Spinozistic, but rather post-Spinozistic.[335] Yet at the same time, Rosenzweig's unwillingness to return to pre-modern thought enables him to enter into dialogue with the post-Christian secular world: because the secular world is for Fackenheim defined by the specifically post-Christian internalization of the transcendent God, the possibility of dialogue between post-Christian and Jewish thought allows, in a very real way, both the entry of Jews into political history (in its broadest sense) and the exposure of the anti-Jewish presuppositions of modern thought.

Despite Rosenzweig's desire to tie thought to being, he fails in one crucial sense. Because he has adopted Hegel's idea of historical progress, his thought is unable to address or incorporate post-biblical Jewish experiential history.[336] Oppenheim writes that 'Fackenheim once summarized Rosenzweig's position in the *Star* by saying that Jewish history is circumscribed by two poles. One marks the shofar that was blown at Sinai and the other is represented by the sound of the shofar that will signify the eschatological end of time. Fackenheim concluded that for Rosenzweig "nothing decisive has happened or can happen between these two poles."'[337] Rosenzweig succeeds in defying Hegel's idea that the God of Moses has been superseded; yet he cannot, having adopted Hegel's parameters for historical development, find room for the God of Moses, and His covenant with Israel, to inform empirical history. Like Heidegger, Rosenzweig, according to the later Fackenheim, errs by beginning with the human condition, rather than with a particular human situation, as the foundation of the leap to religion.[338] His later critique of Rosenzweig's position is that 'the historical and communal dimensions of God's revelation were either minimized or ignored.'[339] Rosenzweig restores the divine–Jewish covenant; but because the covenant, having happened in the past, is superseded, the covenant remains unhistorical.[340] While Christianity to Rosenzweig is '*of* history,' Judaism is 'merely *in* it, unmoved between Sinai and the Messianic days.'[341] Rosenzweig's insistence on informing modern thought with historical data is, since the Holocaust, dated, a 'datedness [that] lies in a one-sided crypto-Protestant fideism alien to Jewish existence, always rightly opposed by an equally onesided [sic] "national" or "Zionist" secularism, and now wholly anachronistic.'[342] This 'Protestant fideism' lurks in Rosenzweig's adoption of philosophical principles – such as Kant's artificial apparent dichotomy of autonomy and heteronomy or Hegel's affirmation of cultural or religious progress toward an ultimate identity of the human and the divine – that precluded Judaism from informing modern thought. While Rosenzweig is the first thinker since Spinoza to point to an alternative to Judaism as the religion of humankind, he is unable to bring the particularities of this religion into the realm of empirical reality.

Though in some senses Rosenzweig is unable to include Jewish experience in his philosophical system, his work provides for Fackenheim a foundation on which to build his religious existentialism.[343] Because Rosenzweig in his 'new thinking' recognizes that history is meaningful – that the 'new thinking' came into being as a historical development from the 'old thinking' – so too his 'absolute empiricism'[344] can be overwhelmed by what comes after. Fackenheim argues, in the spirit of Rosenzweig, that he understands Rosenzweig better than he understood himself;[345] and it is Rosenzweig's misunderstanding that experience can be absolute. For Fackenheim, experience cannot be absolute because it cannot be self-authenticating.[346] Experience can be transcended through the incursion of an Absolute Other. The Holocaust, according to Fackenheim, has returned Jews – in every concrete, empirical way – to history and has in fact put Jews in the centre of history.[347] Now Rosenzweig's thought must, Fackenheim argues, be made 'to absorb the overwhelming fact that, having been for two millennia merely of history, the Jewish people is suddenly, once again, in history, with consequences unforeseeable for the destiny of the people and the faith alike.'[348]

According to Fackenheim, Rosenzweig offers two important elements to the modern project of synthesizing philosophy and revelatory theology. First, he establishes that revelation as a general principle is rationally defensible. Second, he introduces the personal standpoint into philosophy. Two results follow from this: the first point recognizes that philosophy can be both systematic and universal; the second point establishes the witnessing of Torah as primary to Torah itself. Rosenzweig succeeds in creating a philosophy that is universal, even while existence between Christians and Jews is differentiated.[349] In what is a crucial point for Fackenheim, Rosenzweig establishes the knowledge that we need transcendence, 'eternity-in-time,' in order to confront history.[350] Philosophy and revelatory theology coexist as the philosophical interplay of the individual standpoint of one's knowledge of the possibility of revelation as a general principle and the universality of rationality. It is up to Fackenheim now, using the 'new thinking,' to bring Rosenzweig's insights to their fruition, to bear on and inform empirical Jewish experience, and to enable the 'Jewish return into history.'

Fackenheim on Buber

> Certainty of faith is not accessible to the Man of Today, nor can it be made accessible to him ... But he is not denied the possibility of holding himself open to faith ... He too may open himself to this book and let its rays strike him where they will.[351]

Not long after Fackenheim arrived as a student at the *Hochschule* (1935), he read Buber's 'The Man of Today and the Jewish Bible.' This essay 'changed [his] life.'[352] Fackenheim would return to the essay over the course of years, seeking to ascertain whether it had withstood 'the test of time.'[353] In one respect, he affirms that it had; but the essay was written in 1926, before the epoch-making event of the Holocaust. The 'man of today' referenced by Buber, the European intellectual disillusioned with modernity, of which a Jew was but one example, no longer existed. Europe could no longer be considered the heart of civilization; and, it had become increasingly clear, the contemporary 'savage fanatics'[354] were a product not of the vestigial attachment to the Dark Ages, but of modernity itself. Still, Buber's attempt to find an intellectually honest way back to the ancestral faith gave Fackenheim 'the first glimpse of what [he] was looking for.'[355]

Fackenheim, like Buber, was looking for a way back to the ancestral religion. Buber's essay for him zeroed in on the 'crucial issue – "the encounter between a group of people and the Nameless One."'[356] Buber recognized that it does not matter whether the encounters actually took place, only that the biblical authors believed them to have taken place. Furthermore, these encounters were distinct from those with the gods of the Greeks: the Jewish God is 'beyond the world (hence nameless) who yet entered into the world.'[357] The core of biblical faith is defined by that very thing: an openness to the Nameless One's incursion into the world. Most important, 'that core was stubbornly held fast to – both by the biblical writers and by Jewish readers of their writings – even in times when no such incursion took place, when the "Nameless One" was said to "hide His Face," to "have abandoned," to "hear not" (e.g., Ps. 22:2, 44:24, 88:28).'[358]

Just because the biblical writers and their readers held fast to the belief that encounters between the Nameless One and a group of people take place does not mean that we moderns can claim the same belief. Can we with good intellectual conscience view the world as anything but 'closed to incursions of divinity into it'?[359] This question, and Buber's answer to it, 'occupied [Fackenheim] for a lifetime.'[360] Like Buber, he 'conclude[s] that nothing in science, history, psychology, philosophy, or any other relevant discipline demonstrates that the world of man is closed to the incursion of the Divine; as well as that nothing in theology, philosophy, or any other relevant discipline demonstrates that it is open.'[361] But what we can do, no less than Buber's 'man of today,' is, as 'Jew of today,' adopt a stance, critical yet open to the possibility of divine incursion into the world.

Buber begins for Fackenheim the process of opening up philosophy to revelatory theology, or thought to dialogue, in a way that brings revelation into the modern secular world. According to Fackenheim, 'Buber ... offer[s] a doctrine of revelation intended, among other things, to meet the modern critique of revelation.'[362] He learns from Buber – especially from his encounter with Hegel and Hegel's affirmation of the interdependence of secularism and religion – to confront the secular world with total self-exposure, and to continue to listen to God even if one does not hear Him. From Schelling, Buber learns that, if the human being engages in the world with a personal commitment rather than making the world into an object of study, the human understanding of the world can transcend the phenomenal.[363]

Modern thought argues, through what Fackenheim labels subjectivist reductionism,[364] that since faith is only an inference from the believer's feelings, the God-hypothesis must be discarded. Buber suggests that religion that is solely feeling is not genuine and should be discarded. However, he does not agree with the proposition that religion is solely feeling. For Buber, it is possible to affirm the possibility of a genuine religion in which God exists, exists in relation to the human being, and exists in immediate relation with the human being. Against the modern claim that all religion is religion as feeling, Buber recognizes that the 'God is dead' theologies result from the lack of recognition that one does not, by discarding the God-hypothesis, thereby dispose of the God of revelation.[365] Against these theologies, through which God is by definition absent, Buber attempts to make God present in the world. He argues that the important knowledge comes not from the laws and causes uncovered through the objectifying of the world, but rather from a direct encounter with the Divine in the world. This encounter is to be distinguished from an illusion by recognizing (or at least beginning with a definition of) God as distinct from one's subjective feelings about God. Buber is willing to concede to modern secularism that feelings and images about God are in fact created by the believer. However, he proposes that the moment of encounter exists, but exists outside human categories. The only way for Buber to address the modern critique of revelation is with 'a doctrine which argues ... that the category of revelation in terms of which the religious standpoint understands itself is the category in terms of which it must be understood.'[366]

The primary term of the category of revelation, according to Buber, is the immediacy of the experience of encounter.[367] Buber recognizes that the 'core of revelation is not the communication of content but the event of God's presence.'[368] Although under the guise of philosophy, revelation is discounted as a valid criterion of knowledge, actually, since it does not prove the impossibility of revelation in general, ascription to modern philosophy's synthesis of reason and revelatory theology is itself based on faith – the faith that accepts the terms of modernity's categories over those of revelation. Modernity's disavowal without refutation of revelation opposes one faith to another.[369]

Against this modern faith, Buber suggests that, because human nature is twofold, the human being, even while he recognizes the secular context of his existence, requires also a relationship to the God of revelation. Buber reformulates the 'God is dead' theologies to claim that God is in eclipse.[370] The eclipse is the result of the lack of recognition that modern rationalism is itself based on faith and the human reduction of God to a delusional projection.[371] God's eclipse is self-imposed by human beings. Yet Buber suggests the image of an eclipse because eclipses are temporary: God's absence in modernity – especially at Auschwitz – does not entail a break in the tradition of the human being–God relationship. Furthermore, the human being–God relationship has always been beyond rational categories; human beings cannot know whether God is ultimately absent or not. Modern human beings do not hear God because they are not open to hearing Him.

Although Buber refers back to the traditional Jewish image of the Hiding of God's face, his image of God's eclipse differs from the biblical one. For Buber, the eclipse of God is 'concerned not with "belief in

God" or "explaining" His ways, but rather with the possibility of divine–human speech.'[372] After Auschwitz, he calls into question the significance of speech; but at the same time, he allows that future speech may be significant.[373] His teaching has a 'religious center': 'the divine-human speech that confers meaning on all speech.'[374] Most important, Buber upholds the one principle that is beyond a doubt revealed by all speech: idolatry, in both its ancient and modern forms, is false. He witnesses against this idolatry in terms that, although they may not be exclusively Jewish, are not alien to Judaism, its conception of prophecy and its denial of past salvation.

The great importance of Buber's work for Fackenheim, beyond its making room within the secular world for a divine incursion, is its use in diagnosing modern idolatry. Modern idolatry is, as Fackenheim argues, the deification of secularism[375] and is the motivating force behind Nazism. It is the result of modern thought's internalization of God, of God's immanence replacing his transcendence, and more generally, of the rash and misguided syntheses of philosophy and revelatory theology in modern thought. Philosophy, following Hegel, had reduced God's word to human beings's, which word is itself a product of culture. Human beings's word is understood to be itself divine. On the other side, the private realm of conscience – on which Kant, because of its apparent identity with the categorical imperative, had insisted – was destroyed. Absolute conformity to the public realm became the means of manifesting ethical consciousness. Likewise in Nazism, ethical consciousness takes the form of the simultaneous deification of human beings's word and the destruction of the private realm.

Buber's prophetic Judaism, in Fackenheim's understanding, witnesses against idolatry in general and modern idolatry in particular. The prophets in Judaism, according to Buber, teach the insecurity that is necessary to be able to recognize false gods, or at least they teach us to be diligent in our scepticism. By remaining in some sense totally insecure in the historical world, the prophets teach that to know the true God in relation is to shatter all security for the historical human being.[376] At the same time, this insecurity is augmented by knowledge of the fact that one might 'mistake false gods for the true God.'[377] Judaism, according to Buber, knows that 'some gods will always be false.'[378] Security for the individual Jew remains in two areas: first, the structure that comes from the recognition that idolatry is false always; and second, a related point, the possibility that comes from one's openness to an encounter with the true God.

Buber attempts to respond to idolatry in its modern form. Heidegger, for instance, understands the insecurity of the prophets as teaching precisely the opposite lesson: because there is no security, there is no means by which to know the true God from false gods.[379] In order to witness against this thinking, rather than to simply argue against it, Buber accepts the modern principle of rational inquiry. Yet he does not concede that this principle reveals all of reality. Buber 'pointed out the vast difference between a radically open Christian or Jewish encounter with the world, and a [total] surrender to the world' because not to make this distinction presupposes the truth of modern rationalism.[380] And the difference of this self-exposure is that 'it bears witness to the "confronting" God while, self-exposed to a secularism that would "explain" away belief in this God, walking on the narrow ridge of risk.'[381] Because Buber accepts both the security derived from the knowledge that there is one true God Who confronts and also the insecurity derived from the modern principle of rational inquiry, his thought is able to address, and to counter, the modern critique of revelation. Because he limits the applicability of the modern principle of rational inquiry, he is able to promote an alternative line of thinking.

Fackenheim eloquently describes the limitation that Buber places on the principle of rational inquiry and Buber's implicit critique of it. 'Buber limits the sphere to which the principle of rational inquiry applies ... This sphere is transcended not when the *I* comes upon an *It* supposedly escaping rational inquiry, but when the *I* abandons the detachment of the *I-It* relation for the engagement of the *I-Thou* relation. If the *Thou* escapes rational inquiry, it is not because the latter is rational but because it presupposes detachment.'[382] The basis of Buber's counterattack is 'first, [Buber's doctrine] implies complete acceptance of the modern principle of rational inquiry; secondly, it yet limits the sphere to which that principle applies; thirdly, it points beyond this sphere to quite another sphere in which it is at least not impossible that revelation could be found.'[383]

Fackenheim argues that Buber's acceptance of I-It knowledge – knowledge that results through the principle of rational inquiry – as at least part of reality, establishes his thought as a thought that makes metaphysical and epistemological judgments. His thought is, according to Fackenheim, a doctrine.[384] Fackenheim is not unaware of the arguments against recognizing Buber's thought as a form of knowing, but ultimately he argues for inclusion of Buber's categories into epistemological thought despite, for instance, Bertrand Russell's assertion that one can know only another's affirmation of being in relation, but not whether his relation is a fact.[385] Fackenheim's argument:

> I am persuaded that, while this line of reasoning [Russell's, and other subjectivist reductionists'] has some value in bringing to light certain specific philosophical issues, it is altogether misguided. A self is primordially open to other selves; and unless it were thus open it would never become a self at all. A child becomes an 'I' in a relation of openness to a 'Thou'; indeed, he knows the meaning of 'Thou' before he knows the meaning of 'I.' There is, to be sure, a problem involved in knowing other selves. But the problem is not whether they exist; it is who they are. And it arises, not because the self is to begin with in a subjectivist prison from which it must subsequently try to escape; it arises because, born free of prisons of this kind, the self is subsequently cast into them by the breakdown of communication. And when the breakdown is complete there is mental disease.[386]

Buber's thought is a form of knowing because the relational aspect of human being is a primordial fact. Knowledge in Genesis, for instance, is understood as intimacy or relationship. By restoring the channels of dialogue – speech itself – Buber returns us to a most basic aspect of human knowing, even while he limits the sphere of that knowing to existence only. To Buber, 'the shortcomings of rational inquiry are epistemological and metaphysical only because the engaged *I-Thou* dialogue is itself a form of knowledge; indeed it is the form of knowledge in which the fullness of reality is encountered.'[387] Because Buber judges that I-Thou knowledge is superior to I-It knowledge, his thought is, Fackenheim agrues, not simply homily for spiritual guidance. Rather, in what Fackenheim considers to be a real encounter with secularism, Buber's thought contributes to the beginnings of modern Jewish philosophy.

For Fackenheim, Buber dramatizes in life his commitment to I-Thou dialogue,[388] but because he does not validate the reality of the dialogue, he does not succeed in creating a philosophy. According to Buber, revelation must be open-ended or inexhaustible.[389] Any system of theology is misguided: one must be open to an immediate encounter with the divine. I-It knowledge is always knowledge of the past and can never issue in knowledge of the present. In Fackenheim's understanding, the dialogue that Buber creates does not recognize its potential as a means to use all the powers within human reach to lift up the world through a corrected synthesis of philosophy and revelatory religion. Fackenheim builds on Buber's establishment of the room for divine incursion in the secular world; but because Buber insists on the presentness of revelation, he is unable, or unwilling, to establish a system from his doctrine of encounter. Fackenheim critiques this position for three reasons. First, by making room for an encounter with God solely in the present – that is, by refusing to develop or establish a Jewish theology – Buber diminishes the relevance of the Voice at Sinai for the present: 'Buber does not believe that any revelations in the past, including Sinai, stand as supremely important moments in the divine-human dialogue.'[390] This diminishment, in Fackenheim's thought, threatens the continuity of Judaism. Second, relatedly, by diminishing the importance of any particular revelation, Buber diminishes the importance of the cultural and historical context in which revelation occurs. Because 'in crisis the religious center of Buber's teachings ... remained undamaged,'[391] even after the Holocaust, Buber's teaching with regard to God's eclipse shows itself to be inadequate to the present need.[392] For Fackenheim, by minimizing the context of revelation, Buber, while allowing room for God to reveal Himself in the present, allows no room for God's action in the present.[393] Finally, Buber, in effect, by focusing solely on the present, replaces the Jewish condition with the human condition.[394] The ongoing covenantal relationship between God and the Jews is thus downplayed or eliminated.

Fackenheim argues that Buber's insistence on the priority of the present has a further result: 'By itself this insistence [that the Bible be understood in Biblical categories] only means that Buber has understood the Biblical belief in revelation; it does not mean that he has justified his own acceptance of it.'[395] Buber's doctrine must ultimately be accepted on faith, even if – because its religious centre remains, after the Holocaust, unchanged – it is the faith of the ancient rabbis. The problem with his doctrine is that he must presume the reality of the dialogue in order to justify his thought: after one commits to the reality of revelation, then one can apply Buber's thought cohesively and comprehensively; but without the commitment to begin with, there is nothing to sway one to his doctrine as opposed to the rational principles of modern thought.[396] Buber's I-Thou doctrine argues only against modernity's simple disavowal of the reality of revelation, but it does not by itself 'justif[y] ... the positive assertion of the possibility of revelation.'[397] Fackenheim recognizes himself as he who must make this positive assertion, that is, make room for the true God to speak, as He did at Sinai, in the present, even while the revelation-as-content may differ from what it was in the past. While Buber implies that I-Thou and I-It exhaust the categories of knowledge, Fackenheim argues for a third alternative: 'Conceivably there could be a third kind of knowledge which is unlike I-It knowledge in that it understands, and at least to that extent transcends, the limitations of I-It knowledge; but which is unlike I-Thou knowledge in that it is detached rather than committed. Such a knowledge would have to be classified as philosophical.'[398] This third kind of knowledge would involve, paradoxically, a detached form of self-consciousness: the 'I' would persist, but because it would recognize itself and hence what is beyond itself – what its limitations are – it would at the same time, without the involvement of the 'I,' point beyond itself.[399] While Buber considers philosophical knowledge to be I-It knowledge, Fackenheim argues that, because philosophy can recognize the limitations of I-It knowledge, it can transcend it and even point to I-Thou knowledge. Accordingly, I-Thou and I-It knowledge are not exhaustive because philosophy is not I-It knowledge, but rather a dialectic with this sort of knowledge.[400] Through a sort of covenantal dialectic that plays out in the empirical world, philosophy can in fact open itself up to revelatory theology, and there can in fact exist the category of Jewish philosophy.[401]

Buber's strength, according to Fackenheim, is clear in *Eclipse of God*: one must continue to listen for God, even if there is no hearing.[402] Buber's weakness, as Fackenheim sees it in *I and Thou*, is that – since for Buber, God speaks constantly – human hearing is a purely human response.[403] For Fackenheim, this position was not sustainable in biblical times, and 'in the modern-secular world it is intolerable.'[404] Ultimately, he critiques what he perceives to be Buber's overemphasis on the present at the expense of cultural and historical continuity[405] and his consequent use of the human condition, instead of a particular human condition.[406] While it is true that Buber suggests that, during an encounter, 'the response called for [from human beings] is not some universal response, but the unique response appropriate to the situation,'[407] the uniqueness of the response is limited to the present. Buber does not allow for the uniqueness of cultural or historical context. But Fackenheim's is not simply a critique of Buber's aspiration toward a possibility for all human beings to be in relationship with a living God; even more so, Fackenheim notes that Buber as Jew is at times excluded from the post-Christian struggle for authenticity that bases itself on the human condition.[408] In addition, from Fackenheim's point of view, Buber's use of the human condition as the basis for encounter with the divine precludes him from facing authentically the reality of the Holocaust.

In *To Mend the World*, Fackenheim argues that Buber's overemphasis on the present precludes his thought from adequately facing the reality of empirical history, specifically the Holocaust. For Fackenheim, the Holocaust must change not only the way in which biblical categories, such as the 'hiding of His Face,' are applied, but more so, the very core of Jewish religious teachings. He writes: 'Buber had a lifelong difficulty with the recognition of evil. Religiously, he was predisposed to hold "no one to be absolutely unredeemable." Philosophically, his basic framework, the celebrated "I-Thou/I-It," leaves room for decay and dehumanization, but not for an evil that is truly radical.'[409] The possibility of revelation must be positively affirmed, and in order to do this, one must go beyond Buber's assertion of the possibility of divine–human dialogue to establish the possibility of God's action, the eternal God's making actual a change for the future of the divine–human relationship. Only through recognizing the need for God's action in history can one adequately face both the present and the reality of the radical evil in that present.

PART III. FACKENHEIM'S SYNTHESIS

Fackenheim's Synthesis of Revelatory Religion and Philosophy

Fackenheim claims that German Idealism speaks indirectly today through the 'mediation of existentialism.'[410] In order to salvage the contributions of German Idealism to human thought – for instance, its belief in God's being operative in history – contemporary thought must begin in existentialism. While in *Encounters*, Fackenheim had used as his methodology the confrontation between modern philosophy and Jewish thought as the means by which to expose the partiality of modern philosophy, in *To Mend the World*, his approach is what he calls a 'historical dialectical approach': one must seek out the relevant first-rate thinkers in order to confront their thought with events.[411] Because events happen to, and are understood by, only the particular, his existentialism must seek universal truth from its standpoint, from the particularity of one's personal existence.[412] Just as all universal truth must be sought from one's particularity, so too universal claims – made in the name of modern philosophy – must be tested in light of Jewish particularity. An idea, according to Fackenheim's existentialism, must reflect and affect events in empirical history in order to be valid. Also, it must begin and remain in the particular.

Fackenheim's existentialism issues from what he conceives to be the failure of ideas when divorced from empirical reality. The Holocaust, in its uniqueness, has ruptured the continuity of both ideas and experience. The making of genocide into an idea or ideal is inaccessible to reason, while its experience threatens the continuation of Jewish faith. Because it is unassimilable to thought and to all previous and subsequent human experience, the Holocaust becomes for Fackenheim, in effect, a revelatory (or anti-revelatory) event; it is necessary that it inform future Jewish thought. He recognizes the Holocaust as a reminder of the Jewish singled-out condition. Because the covenant is established by God, so too the Holocaust involves the Jewish relationship with God. Ironically, in order to keep God alive to Jews – to keep God in the present and therefore accessible to thought – Jews must recognize a connection between the Holocaust and God.[413]

The response to the Holocaust adopts as its basis the existential experience of the Jewish singled-out condition; the response must begin in the realm of existence, specifically in the commitment to Jewish survival. Yet at the same time, the response must include the possibility of transcendence; it is not simply survival of Jews that is at stake, but also survival of Judaism, of the belief in a covenantal relationship with a Commanding Presence. The synthesis is to occur in 'action-concepts,'[414] concepts that are at once experience and ideas. These action-concepts begin in experience and rise to ideas. Fackenheim's synthesis does not parallel the post-Christian synthesis because it does not prioritize thought over being. What is more, Fackenheim finds in Jewish theology, in the concepts of *teshuvah*[415] and *tikkun*,[416] action-concepts that are suitable for addressing and confronting the Holocaust. Although he adopts the modern disproof of biblical revelation and the consequent disbelief in God's authority as the source of faith, Fackenheim maintains that religious ascription and Jewish faith can continue despite this new revelation, this new incursion of Absolute Otherness in empirical history. 'Faith,' he writes, 'is a "subjective attitude"; but because it is a *believing* attitude, it takes itself as receptive of an objective truth accessible only in the believing attitude and inaccessible otherwise.'[417]

Somewhat surprisingly, then, in order to confront the reality of the Holocaust, Fackenheim proposes a synthesis between revelatory theology and philosophy. The synthesis is necessary because, although God was present in the sense that Jews were singled out, also God, in a more obvious sense, was absent. There is no religious meaning in the Holocaust, yet it is necessary to respond religiously.[418] The first principle, so to speak, of Fackenheim's synthesis is that the only valid philosophical universalizing is one that produces wonder, that is, one that ends with 'a problem, a riddle, an enigma ... [Otherwise] it is simply "escapism-into-universalism."'[419]

Whereas Rosenzweig-Buber (as Fackenheim referred to this position[420]), by reintroducing the personal standpoint or the particular into thought, start the process of bringing philosophy into theology, Hegel brings revelatory theology into philosophy by insisting on the speculative durability of the particular within the universal. The interconnection, or ultimate unsustainability, of these two positions defines Fackenheim's position with regard to the relationship between revelatory theology and philosophy. Because he understands Hegel's universalizing as beginning in contingent historical experience, he turns to his thought in order to construct his new theology. Hegel, in his attempt to synthesize eternity with history, attempts also the synthesis of the universal with the particular. Implicit in this attempt is Hegel's recognition of the distinction between these two realms, a recognition that is crucial for Fackenheim in his attempt to confront the reality of the Holocaust even as he perpetuates the philosophical and theological traditions. The Holocaust has shown that thought can destroy empirical reality. Since the destruction is possible, one must make a commitment, but not on the side of thought – this would be Heideggerian philosophy – and not on the side of empirical reality – this would be empiricism or, in Fackenheim's analysis, despair.[421] Rather, one must make a commitment on the side of a new theology, a theology committed not only to thinking about the transcendent, but also to preserving the present. This commitment Fackenheim recognizes in Hegel, although not, alas, in the latter's optimistic analysis of historical development – since he had no knowledge of the Holocaust, nor could he have – but in the latter's thought. Hegel is able to recover the past, to both heal from it and bring it to its completion in thought. But Fackenheim insists that, had Hegel witnessed the Holocaust, he would have recognized – and more important, his philosophy would have been able to recognize – that history cannot be translated into eternity, that the particular cannot be translated into the universal. Jews may indeed be able to 'mend the world,' but healing is not possible because, following Hegel's dialectical advance of history, 'the *Muselmaenner* are not left behind' when thought moves through their silent testimony to resistance.[422]

Hegel would have acknowledged the absolute distinction between thought and life because his thought recognizes a 'speculative Good

Friday'; it recognizes that Easter includes within itself as thought the Crucifixion. What is more, Hegel acknowledges Judaism's recognition of the absolute distinction: in his understanding of Jews as a collective Job, Hegel acknowledges that the movement by which one moves from the universal to the particular is through the negation of the negation, the initial recognition of God as Absolute Other, which culminates in the restoration of the finite by God. In Hegel's understanding, Judaism understands free action as remaining within the constraints of God's will; moreover, despite any historical circumstance, Jews continue to believe. Although at times claiming that Jews pray to a God who no longer exists, in Fackenheim's reading, Hegel – because Jews insist on the absolute distinction between eternity and history, yet continue in their belief – cannot quite dismiss Judaism entirely.

Just as Hegel's synthesis would be fragmented as a result of the Holocaust, so too Jews must find, in political terms, the balance between worship and self-defence, both of which terms exist within the context of a theological commitment that is not necessarily a commitment to God or to secularism. Because thought has the capacity to destroy both itself and empirical reality, Fackenheim concludes that the new theology must be not simply religio-secular, as was Hegel's, but rather religious and/or secular, always fragmented. While Hegel, by recognizing the partial truth of each world view, attempts to synthesize them into an absolute world view, Fackenheim recognizes that the human being lives in a fragmented world; that the synthesizing of world views is accomplished through the asking of questions; that each world view is a partial truth in terms of the historical moment at which it is experienced, espoused, and finitely lived, and at the same time a whole truth.[423] Fackenheim's work in Christian–Jewish relations suggests belief as the basis of one's world view; at the same time, his promotion of the commonality of the Jewish birthright suggests that existential reality is the basis. The discrepancy reflects his understanding of the re-fragmentation of Hegel's absolute world view. It is this fragmentation that is the beginning of dialogical openness to the world view of each philosophy and revelatory theology and that marks the end of Hegel's post-Christian theological and political supersessionism, or what Fackenheim calls his 'residual Constantinianism.'[424]

Fackenheim's attempted synthesis of reason and revelation will be the point of disagreement between him and Buber, on the one hand, and Strauss, on the other. Buber's thought, he argues, falls short of the present need because it cannot account for, or create, God's action in and through secular history.[425] Strauss, as we shall see in the following two chapters, is concerned about the destruction of both Judaism and philosophy, both revelation and reason, that results from the introduction of historicism into thought. Strauss will conceive of a Judaism that is reduced, on the one hand, to the brute fact of revelation, and, on the other, to Law, reaffirming a Judaism (Maimonidean) that from Fackenheim's point of view is deeply problematic. Fackenheim believes that Buber and Strauss each are both too sanguine or optimistic about evil in the world,[426] and also not optimistic enough about the ability of human beings to, so to speak, restore ourselves.[427] But, given that reason and revelation cannot be synthesized, and are not synthesized, can one be 'too optimistic' within the terms of philosophy? or 'too hopeful' within those of revelatory theology?

4 The Problem of Historicism

Introduction

We have seen in chapters 2 and 3 Strauss and Fackenheim's diagnosis of the crisis of modernity: the lack of an authoritative standard by which to judge morality. Both thinkers trace the crisis to the post-Enlightenment attempt to synthesize reason and revelation, a synthesis that applied the idea of progress and a new definition of 'nature,' introduced by Machiavelli and the promoters of the new science, to the revelatory sphere; or, more broadly, that introduced the anthropocentric stance of modern rational thought to the revelatory sphere.[1] The result was historicism: the idea that changes in human thinking literally change the object of thought, or the conviction that the foundations of human thought are rooted in particular historical circumstances. The crisis of modernity reaches its apex in the doctrine of historicism. What was begun by Machiavelli, who, by positing human freedom, posited the idea of history, was developed to its height by Heidegger, who posited that human freedom extends to human self-creation.

Jewish thinkers as well, from Spinoza to Rosenzweig, adopted the progressive, or, more ultimately, historicist, stance. This was even more devastating to Jews than the Christian or post-Christian adoption was to Christians or post-Christians.[2] In the case of Spinoza, it entailed, according to Strauss, a complete break with Judaism,[3] and according to Fackenheim, the inability to recognize that there might be cases in which even Jews as men would not be accepted into the modern liberal state. In the case of Rosenzweig, it entailed, according to Strauss, the impossibility of discovering an orthodoxy unqualified by modernity,[4] and according to Fackenheim, an inability to open his 'absolute empiricism' to Jewish experience.[5] Modern Jewish thought, and its adoption of historical consciousness, or of the doctrine of historicism, has, according to both thinkers, meant the defeat of both Judaism and Jews.

The most dangerous aspect of the doctrine of historicism, as we shall see below,[6] is that it blinds its adherents: once the doctrine is accepted, there is no means by which to counter it. Both Strauss and Fackenheim diagnose the acceptance of historicism as a crisis of authority: historicism both denies the brute fact of the existence of objects and also precludes the discovery of definite standards external to human reason. The acceptance of the doctrine of historicism has led to the loss of common sense. Both thinkers reject the doctrine and seek a means by which to extricate the modern mind from its teachings. Strauss seeks to discover a means by which to 'return' to the distinct claims of the two bases of Western thought: reason and revelation. He seeks to return to pre-modern thought, to the rediscovery of natural right and also therefore of conventional (or divine) law, and in this return to rediscover a definite, and non-dogmatic, standard of morality that restores the authority of reason and of revelation and the tension between them. But Strauss will be forced to recognize that this return, simply because it is a return, cannot replicate the older position. He therefore suggests an interim period wherein human thinking uses historical studies as a means of re-establishing the context necessary for a return to Plato's cave.[7]

Fackenheim also seeks a return to the affirmation of the distinct realms of reason and revelation, and to common sense. However, as we saw in chapter 3,[8] he, returning instead to Hegel, attempts his own synthesis of reason and revelation. As we shall see in this chapter and the next, this apparent contradiction is accounted for when one recognizes that, for him, the return to reason and revelation must be undertaken within a stance of 'covenantal affirmation.'[9] Fackenheim rejects Strauss's return to Plato's cave and instead promotes a reaffirmation of the possibility of revelation in history. He works to provide a means by which to conceive of the perpetuation of pre-modern revelatory experience into and through the present and therefore opts to incorporate the modern historicist sensibility into his thought. Fackenheim's historicism, however, as was previously mentioned, issues as much from modern philosophical thought as from the Jewish concern for history, and is therefore a quasi-historicism, open to even radical changes in the definition of nature, but only those that can be recognized theologically as (possibly) issuing form the Sinaitic God.[10] As we shall see in chapter

5, Fackenheim's historicism, like Strauss's, is necessary perhaps only for the time being.

Before exploring the issue of historicism in the work of Strauss and Fackenheim, we must lay a brief groundwork. Both thinkers trace the emergence of the doctrine of historicism to the belief that reason and revelation can be synthesized, or that God can be internalized, or, more broadly, to the mistaken understanding that there is no definitive tension between reason and revelation. The rejection of at least the most radical form of the doctrine by both thinkers begins with their affirmation that, while neither reason nor revelation can be validly made to speak in the terms of the other, each is one strain from which Western thought and experience is derived. To understand Western thought and experience – indeed, to recognize the authority of each reason and revelation – one must recognize that each must be fundamentally 'open' to the claims of the other.

The Necessity of 'Openness' in Philosophic and/or Religious Thought[11]

> Philosophy as such is nothing but genuine awareness of the problems, i.e., of the fundamental and comprehensive problems. It is impossible to think about these problems without becoming inclined toward a solution, toward one or the other of the very few typical solutions. Yet as long as there is no wisdom but only quest for wisdom, the evidence of all solutions is necessarily smaller than the evidence of the problems. Therefore the philosopher ceases to be a philosopher at the moment at which the 'subjective certainty' of a solution becomes stronger than his awareness of the problematic character of that solution. At that moment the sectarian is born.[12]

Fortin writes: 'By showing that modern science has not replaced God and that History has not replaced philosophy, or by showing as no one has done in four hundred years that the claims of Reason and Revelation are inherently untouched by modernity, Strauss may have performed as great a service for theology as he has for philosophy.'[13] He suggests that Strauss's work exposes both the rational irrefutability of revelation and also the self-destructive result of modern philosophy's dependence on history. What is at stake is the status of both revelation and reason: if revelation either succumbs to, or seals itself off from, the claims of reason, its content, which claims the greatest relevance for human life, is dismissed as having no relevance; if reason proceeds as if it has refuted the *inner* claims of revelation, and not merely its external claims,[14] it grounds itself in an irrational assertion. Strauss's work highlights that, despite the modern belief in the progress of reason over and against revelation, a return to a non-historicized philosophy will reveal that there has been no progress; there has, in fact, been a self-induced blindness to the fact that the battle between reason and revelation has not been resolved.

According to Strauss, the claims of philosophy and revelatory theology cannot be reconciled. One reason for this irreconcilability stems from the usurpation of philosophy by modern science. Modern science progresses on the assumption that its 'every result ... is provisional and subject to future revision, and this will never change.'[15] Implicit in science's self-definition is that the object of modern science ('everything that is – being'[16]) is beyond its grasp and scope. In this sense, implicit in the progress of the new science is the recognition that 'being is mysterious.'[17] The new science understands itself as not addressing the claims of revelation, or the claims to the mystery of being; there can be no means of incorporating those claims into modern science without distorting those claims and, indeed, science itself. At the same time, Strauss recognizes that it is at this point, in the realm of the mysterious, that reason and revelation 'do not meet exactly, but where they come within hailing distance.'[18]

The 'hailing distance' into which reason and revelation come defines the theoretic realm in which reason and revelation may coexist. Most important, because this realm exists – if only in theory – and because in practical terms reason and revelation stand in opposition, reason and revelation, in order to reveal, in any sense, being as such, must each remain 'open' to the claims of the other.[19] Reason and revelation are, in Strauss's estimation, on the practical level, mutually irrefutable; however, reason and revelation each suggest one way of understanding or recognizing their ultimate, theoretic, almost-common ground:

> If orthodoxy claims to know that the Bible is divinely revealed, that every word of the Bible is divinely inspired, that Moses was the writer of the Pentateuch, that the miracles recorded in the Bible have happened and similar things, Spinoza has refuted orthodoxy. But the case is entirely different if orthodoxy limits itself to asserting that it believes the aforementioned things, i.e., that they cannot claim to possess the binding power peculiar to the known.[20]

The claim of revelation is the claim that it does not exist in the realm of the knowable; it cannot therefore be refuted by reason. Yet, because revelation's position can be only a claim to belief, not an assertion of knowledge, equally revelation cannot dispute reason. Although philosophy and revelatory theology are and must remain practically separate as each irrefutable by the other, they are ultimately mutually dependent for meaning.[21]

Strauss works as a philosopher, but he is a philosopher in the tradition of Maimonides. That is to say, he works within the tradition of theistic rationalism. Because he finds common ground for both reason and revelation in the mystery of being, knowledge of which is impossible for reason, and expression of which is impossible for revelation,[22] he is able to demarcate the practical boundaries of each, even as he explores the 'hailing distance' between them. His thought eschews any prior commitment, to either philosophy or revelatory theology, because the priority of such a theoretic commitment is a means both to self-delusion and to the self-destruction of both reason and revelation. The question of which choice Strauss made as a practical matter – philosopher or theologian, Jerusalem or Athens – is the subject of much debate.[23] In his writings, he attempts as far as possible to represent his thought as philosopher *and* theologian, Jerusalem *and* Athens.[24] One might suggest that he chooses this means of expression in order to emphasize the importance he places on the separation of these two realms as a means of maintaining political stability and of safeguarding philosophy and revelation from the authority of the state, even as his affirmation of their mutual interdependence is kept as an esoteric matter.

Fackenheim, too, chooses neither philosophy nor theology. The importance of Strauss's work regarding the relationship between reason and revelation is exemplified in his early thought[25] and, indeed, in his life: when Fackenheim, in practical terms, works as a theologian, his work takes on relevance in the modern world because it acknowledges the distinct claims of both reason and revelation. When he works as a philosopher, his work is informed either by revelation in general or by the particular claims of Jewish revelation. Indeed, Fackenheim's earlier work recognizes that all thought, philosophical and theological, must be informed by the recognition both that its practical expression can be only partial and that its theoretical meaning must rest its openness – reason to revelation, revelation to reason.[26]

Fackenheim, when working as a philosopher, uses Strauss's discovery of the practical separation and theoretic interdependence of philosophy and revelatory theology in order to introduce philosophical rigour into theological thought.[27] '[T]he philosopher, *qua* philosopher, should suspend judgment as to the actuality of revelation.'[28] This is not to say that the philosopher should work as though revelation is, or is not, an actuality. Rather, Fackenheim proposes that the philosopher who is open to revelatory theology adopt the use of a 'sympathetic phenomenological reenactment, [which] remains bound to the limits of philosophical detachment, while at the same time seeking a sympathetic understanding of truths accepted only on the basis of a commitment.'[29] For him, 'detached thinking might understand some of the meaning of committed faith,' and, furthermore, might recognize that 'a leap from detachment to commitment' need not be 'wholly blind.'[30] The openness to revelation of Fackenheim's earlier philosophy grounds itself in the claims of revelation to commitment.

So, too, the openness of Fackenheim's earlier theology to philosophical reason stems from his assertion that 'religions begin with committing experiences, not with universal ideas ...'[31] In Fackenheim's theology, openness serves to perpetuate, insofar is it is possible, the rabbinic meaning of Jewish revelation.[32] 'Jewish theological thought ... has always remained open to present and future, and this openness includes vulnerability to radical surprise.'[33] Theological openness, to be genuine, must issue in surprise: the outcome of an open encounter must be unknown, the future unpredicted. The introduction of modern science and, more generally, of the historical sense, has made such surprise all but impossible;[34] but Fackenheim, adopting Strauss's identification of both the blinding effects of the introduction of these elements into thought and also the mutual interdependence of philosophy and revelatory theology, recognizes the possibility of perpetuating rabbinic teachings, even as the modern claims of reason inform his theology.[35]

Fackenheim, working within both the theological and philosophical world views, is convinced by Buber's work of the spuriousness of subjectivist reductionism.[36] But Buber's work is not enough: modernity requires that the claims of religion be brought to *prove* that philosophical arguments against the possibility of revelation are insufficient. Buber offers an alternative model of the relationship between the scientific, the I-It model, and the whole of reality, the I-Thou model. Fackenheim, through his philosophy, seeks to offer a 'positive assertion of the possibility of revelation.'[37] He seeks to move beyond Buber's thought to a doctrine suitable to modern Jews. While Buber suggests that the present be open to God's incursion, Fackenheim alters the biblical category of the hiding of God's Face in such a way as to make it possible to affirm the need for philosophy as the means by which to allow real change to occur in the present. In Morgan's formulation, revelatory theology needs philosophy as the means by which to provide a bridge from the subjective to the objective, from which in turn one can return to the subjective.[38]

Fackenheim's early adoption of Strauss's identification of the necessity of openness between philosophy and revelatory theology, however, should not be taken to mean that he blurs the distinct claims of each. Philosophy continues to work, detachedly, in the realm of the knowable, even as, through its commitment to experience, it remains open to the possibility of radical surprise. But it would be possible to systematize revelatory theology only if knowledge about revelation were believed to be complete. This cannot happen: 'a theology that does not rest on revelation is part of philosophy.'[39] The openness of Fackenheim's philosophical and his theological thought is dialogical and ends in fragmentation. 'I am thus left with no doctrine, but only with openness to Jewish-Christian dialogue. But what is a religious recognition which does not recognize the other in the terms of his own self-understanding? The heart of dialogue, it seems to me, is to refuse to give an abstract answer to this question, and instead risk self-exposure.'[40]

The Problem of Historicism: Strauss's Return to Natural Right

In his tribute to his teacher Leo Strauss, Allan Bloom spells out the problem as uncovered by Strauss:

> He was looking at the two great alternative standpoints beyond the cave – nature and history. Nature, and with it natural right, had been rejected as a standard in favor of history. Strauss dared to make that rejection, which was accepted as certain, a problem; and he did this by studying the perspective in which these standards come to light, political common sense. In short, Strauss returned to the cave. Its shadows had faded; but when one loses one's way, one must go back to the beginning, if one can.[41]

Strauss returns to the beginnings of philosophy in an attempt to provide a definite standard from which modern historicist thought might be assessed. According to his account of the emergence of philosophy, the doubt of authority spurred the project of distinguishing between those things which are natural and those which are made by human beings. The ancients discovered nature, and this discovery spurred the recognition that some things were not by nature, but were, rather, by convention. By beginning with doubt, Strauss seeks to critique the authority of historicist thought.[42] Furthermore, by rediscovering nature, so to speak, Strauss seeks to reaffirm the possibility of the existence of natural right. Machiavelli, we recall, had revolutionized 'nature' by looking to how human beings actually live for its definition, rather than to an ideal to which the human being may aspire – by looking, in other words, to the human being's beginning rather than his end.[43] Only by rediscovering nature as connected to the human being's perfection, or by looking, not to the 'extreme case,'[44] but, rather, like Aristotle, to what is true for most human beings in most cases, can natural right be rediscovered. By rediscovering the distinction between the natural and the human made, Strauss can (re)begin this process: because philosophy begins with the discovery of nature, the rediscovery of philosophy serves to bring to light the existence of natural right. Strauss's return to the beginnings of philosophy is motivated by his throwing into question, as Bloom suggests, history as a standard in favour of nature, and with it the quest for natural right. From the rediscovery of the existence of natural right, political common sense – the recognition of the claims of divine or conventional law – and a definite standard of morality may be derived.

Strauss's lecture 'Natural Right and the Historical Approach'[45] is a depiction of the genesis of historicism.[46] A review of its genesis will provide its own critique, as historicism is viewed in the light of philosophy proper. The denial of natural right did not happen immediately in early modern thought; rather, Enlightenment thought remained '... under the protection of the belief that knowledge, or at least divination, of the eternal is possible.'[47] This belief was gradually undermined until historicism emerged in its full-blown radical form in the twentieth century. At its beginnings, even as it retained the belief in the existence of the eternal, it laid the groundwork for the refutation of that belief: the modern argument defined natural right as both discernible by human reason and also universally acknowledged. When confronted with history, natural right, as understood by the moderns, was thought to be disproved: since there are an indefinite variety of notions of natural right, there are no immutable principles of justice.[48]

According to Strauss, this argument is spurious for three reasons. First, it misdefines natural right, which has known always that different ideas of justice in different times and places exist. This knowledge marks the beginning of political philosophy, whose aim, in contradistinction to the aim of philosophy proper, is to evaluate the best possible regime within the limitations of human knowledge.[49] Second, it presumes the idea of history in order to prove its argument in favour of history: the discovery of a variety of notions of natural right is the impetus for the quest for natural right, not proof of its non-existence. The modern argument against natural right, therefore, is a philosophical argument 'somehow connected to "history."'[50] Third, natural right may exist, but may be indiscernible by reason. So, for instance, Aristotle refutes the knowability of natural right, but not its existence,[51] whereas Hobbes recognizes that natural right is not known where reason is not cultivated.[52] Hobbes continues to understand the distinction between the authority of the state and the authority of philosophy.

The heart of Strauss's lecture attempts to allow philosophy in its original sense – as opposed to what was understood by the ancients as political philosophy; or alternatively, as opposed to the new, public philosophy introduced by Machiavelli[53] – to emerge, to speak according to its own self-understanding, and to cast serious doubts on the validity of the historicist project. Strauss begins his refutation of the modern argument against natural right by returning to the ancients, in whose texts he discovers that the critique of natural right began in the form of classical conventionalism. Philosophy begins with a fundamental distinction between nature and convention. Through convention, or opinion, as manifested in public dogma, one can ascend to nature, or knowledge, which is private, true, and eternal. The conventionalists base their argument against natural right not in nature, but rather in convention: since all attempts to grasp the whole are inadequate and are therefore arbitrary, validity rests always in the conventional. The argument against natural right as waged by classical conventionalism is not an argument against the existence of natural right or its fundamental distinction from convention, but only against its inadequacy in grasping the eternal. At the same time, simply by virtue of recognizing the inadequacy of natural right, conventionalism acknowledges its existence; and, simply by virtue of grounding its refutation in convention, conventionalism makes room for the equal claim to validity of natural right.

The return to classical conventionalism would mean a return to an acknowledgment of the existence of natural right, even as one recognizes the validity of public dogma.[54] The modern critique of natural right, however, according to Strauss, '... seems to begin with the contention that the variety of notions of right proves the nonexistence of natural right or the conventional character of all right.'[55] The critique of natural right posed by the early moderns begins with either the 'the rejection of the distinction between nature and convention ('man and his works ... [are] as equally natural as all other real things'[56]), or the trivialization of nature in favour of convention.[57] This trivialization may take the form of positing a dualism between nature and history: as natural beings, man manifests nature in the realm of freedom; what is more, this manifestation is more profound than nature itself because man is rational. In this way, 'human creativity is exalted far above nature.'[58] The basis of the modern critique, as distinct from the basis of classical conventionalism's critique, is a rejection of the idea of philosophy in its original sense: the fundamental distinction between natural right and convention through which one comes to know the eternal. In its place, the modern critique posits the idea that all human thought, including philosophical thought, is historical. All philosophical thought belongs to the historical world and remains within the world view of its particular civilization or culture.[59]

At this point in the lecture, Strauss reminds the reader that Plato had understood thought that is bound to a particular world view as the product of prisoners in the cave. The modern adoption of the historical sense not only is based on a misguided amalgam of philosophy and history that in effect replaces all of philosophy with a particular form of political philosophy – or that relies on nature in order to deny or trivialize nature – but also is a self-perpetuating delusion. It is, as Strauss suggests elsewhere, 'a deep pit beneath the cave.'[60]

The pit beneath Plato's cave, dug with tools invented by means of the adoption of the historical sense,[61] is characterized by a redefinition, and trivialization, of both philosophy and nature. The break with the classical notion of philosophy, begun by Machiavelli, was completed, paradoxically, by the historical school of the nineteenth century. The historical school, in reaction against the French Revolution, had attempted to oppose this break, to 'preserv[e] or continu[e] the traditional order';[62] but because the historical school presumed the redefinition of the natural implicit in the modern critique of natural right – nature as inclusive either of man's works or, more broadly, of the conventional – its efforts were self-defeating. Under its guidance, the historical sense, originally introduced as a critique of classical natural right, developed so as to lose its 'subterranean' affirmation of the possibility of knowledge of the eternal and its connection with philosophy as an idea perpetually beyond historical achievement.[63] The historical sense became historicism. The development of the historical sense into historicism was accomplished by the wholehearted acceptance of history, an acceptance that excluded the original formulation of the historical sense as existing uneasily with the idea of history or with a universal norm by which to guide history.

Strauss traces the development of historicism from the eighteenth-century historical sense, as contained in its critique of classical natural right, to its mature form in the historical school, to its radical form. As Strauss makes apparent, this development was spurred on, not by ever-increasing awareness of the authority of history, but rather by its opposite: the historical sense was pushed into historicism as a result of self-contradictions, which arose as a result, first, of its amalgamation with philosophy, and then, of its redefinition of philosophy as historically bound.

The development from the eighteenth-century critique of natural right to modern historicism was accomplished by the contradiction implicit in the nineteenth-century historical school. Because the early modern critique of natural right understood philosophy as seeking knowledge in connection with the conventional, nature – classically understood as providing the standard for universal norms – became, for the revolutionists, associated exclusively with the individual. But this created for the historical school a paradox: the revolutionists, while denying the existence of universal norms, had affirmed the natural right of every individual to 'pursue not just his happiness but his own version of happiness.'[64] Paradoxically, there was a new universal norm that each individual had the right to his particular happiness. Consistency demanded that this new natural right of the individual be adopted but at the same time rejected as universal and unnatural. The conservatives of the historical school adopted a middle strategy as a means of resolving the paradox: they recognized neither the uniformity of classic natural right, nor the 'anti-social individualism' of the revolutionists; rather, they established the existence of '"historical" rights,' such as the rights of Englishmen.[65] Implicit in such an establishment is the affirmation that 'the local and the temporal have a higher value than the universal.'[66] The conservatives not only failed to establish a connection with the traditional order but also radicalized the position of the revolutionists by deriving their preservation of that order from the latter's critique of it. Just as the assertion of the inability of nature to provide a universal norm was reinforced, so too the amalgamation of philosophy and history reinforced the affirmation that philosophy could not provide a universal norm.

The complete break with the classical tradition was accomplished inadvertently by those who sought to oppose that break. Most profoundly, the revolutionist effort against the transcendence of the eternal, whether of God or of the ideal political regime, and the success of that effort as accomplished by the conservatives, '... destroyed the only solid basis of all efforts to transcend the actual.'[67] Because the existence of universal norms was denied, there remained no authority by which to contextualize the surface of things.[68] The effort of the historical school served not to stem the acceptance of historicism, but rather to radicalize its this-worldly aspect.

The historical school, according to Strauss, attempted to remain objective, without recourse to universal norms, even as this objectivity was connected to the relativity of particular historical times and places. It failed to realize, however, that it retained the assumptions of the eighteenth-century critique of natural right, assumptions that undermined the traditional notion of philosophy as the quest for the eternal.[69] With the undermining of this notion, the historical school was able to '... assume that nations or ethnic groups are natural units, or it assumed the existence of general laws of evolution, or it combined both assumptions.'[70] Nature was understood by the historical school either as not fundamentally distinct from convention, or as less important than convention; philosophy was understood as fundamentally connected to history. Again, consistency required that these ethnic groups, ever-evolving in accordance with natural laws, could not be defined as both particular (or conventional) and universal, as both according to nature and not according to nature. The historical school abandoned the assumptions of the eighteenth-century critique of natural right, the assumptions that posited at least the possibility of the existence of the eternal, and '... the infancy of historicism came to its end.'[71]

Unwittingly, the historical school abandoned the claims of nature as superior or even equal to convention, and of philosophy as a means of informing thought. 'Historicism now appeared as a particular form of positivism, of the school which held that theology and metaphysics had been superseded once and for all by positive science or which identified genuine knowledge of reality with the knowledge supplied by the empirical sciences.'[72] This identification came about because the empirical method, for consistency, had itself to be understood as historically bound. Other sciences that used the empirical method, such as psychology and sociology, were deemed inferior to the study of history because, just as the subject matter of history is concerned exclusively with man and his pursuits, so too the empirical method rejects all theory and metaphysics. The historical school had established its authoritative claim to knowledge because the knowledge being sought was 'knowledge of what is truly human, of man as man ...'[73]

The historical school had claimed its ability to derive objective standards that did not rely on universal norms, but it was unable to deliver on that claim. There is no means by which to translate particular historical facts to a universal norm. On the other hand, to accept all historical facts as norms obfuscates the obvious fact that there is no standard by which to justify the superiority of progressing toward, rather than resisting, the future. The attempt to eliminate the human being's need for transcendence in order for him to gain understanding, and thus to make him master of his knowledge and his future, resulted, ironically, in he himself becoming, as it were, transcendent in his world. It led to his complete alienation from the world.[74] The 'historical process' has no meaning; it is simply a collection of chance data; it is 'a tale told by an idiot.'[75]

Despite its theoretical failings, historicism has taken grip on the modern mind because its delusion is self-perpetuating. Strauss writes: 'But the manifest failure of the practical claim of historicism, that it could supply life with a better, a more solid, guidance than the prehistoricist thought of the past had done, did not destroy the prestige of the alleged theoretical insight due to historicism.'[76] Although the ancients had held that the historical process could not issue in meaning – and this view was 'still powerful in the eighteenth century'[77] – the theoretical premise of historicism retained its authority, despite its inability to establish authority, because the historical process had shown that authority itself is based in variability. According to the theoretic premise of historicism, 'the foundations of human thought are laid by unpredictable experiences or decisions.'[78] What historicism teaches, ironically, is the variability of its own teaching. There are no universal standards; the human situation is one in which all thought is bound to historical circumstance; thought itself cannot transcend experience and cannot approach the true.

One cannot simply dispute this claim because the tools required for such a dispute lie outside historicism itself. The necessary procedure from here would be, according to Strauss, to conduct two critiques to evaluate the validity of the historicist claim. The first would be, in continuation of Kant and Hume, a critique of reason, which would determine to what extent the human mind is capable of metaphysical or philosophical thought.[79] If the human mind can validly conceive of, say, nature, or natural right, so too it can conceive of a standard that transcends one's immediate historical situation. This critique is necessary at this point in order to evaluate the theoretic claim of historicism from a philosophical perspective, so as to remove the possibility that human thought is based not on 'history' but rather on 'evident principles accessible to man as man.'[80] The second critique that is required at this point is to evaluate whether the positive sciences – the empirical method itself – are based on metaphysical foundations. If they are, this would undermine one argument from which historicism claimed its authority – the congruence of its subject matter and its methodology. There would be no philosophical validity for the claim to authority of either historicism or the empirical method.

The arguments in favour of historicism, that 'up to now, all thought has proved to be in need of radical revisions or to be incomplete or limited in the decisive respects';[81] that '... when a given limitation was overcome by a progress of thought, earlier important insights were invariably forgotten as a consequence of that progress,' with the consequence that 'on the whole, there was then no progress, but merely a change from one type of limitation to another type'[82]; and that '... any effort of thought which led to the overcoming of specific limitations led to blindness in other respects'[83]; appeal to the modern mind, according to Strauss, because they appear to fight dogmatism, 'the inclination "to identify the goal of our thinking with the point at which we have become tired of thinking."'[84] However, Strauss suggests that historicism may in fact be the 'guise in which dogmatism likes to appear in our age.'[85] The historicist 'experience of history' is not experience of the world, but rather is a sort of meta-experience. From the pit beneath the cave, one experiences not even shadows of human artifacts, but only chance images of thought whose only context is its disconnection with past thought and its equal value with all thought past and future. By the time radical historicism is introduced, even this minimal context is eliminated.[86]

Historicism presumes that each epoch, with its new insights, becomes blind to the insights of the past, and so we can neither grasp the whole nor assess any epoch as having greater or lesser value than another. But if, in fact, the experience on which historicism bases this presumption is defined already by an acceptance of historicism, one must raise serious doubts about it. Historicism bases itself on the various answers of different epochs to the fundamental human questions, rather than on the questions themselves; such a basis would be conceivable only in an era during which thinkers were unable to experience the surface of things, and experienced instead only interpretations of those things. Despite the attempt to define the experience of history as a comprehensive experience that includes thought, the experience of history by which historicism defines itself is really an experience of the history of thought.[87] Were one to experience history itself, Strauss suggests, one would be convinced that '... all human thought, and certainly all philosophic thought, is concerned with the same fundamental themes or the same fundamental problems, and therefore that there exists an unchanging framework which persists in all changes of human knowledge of both facts and principles.'[88] Most important, since the fundamental problems persist through history despite various solutions and approaches, human thought at each epoch is in fact capable of transcending its history.

Historicism concludes that because one cannot know natural right, it does not exist; but, were it to examine the fundamental questions, rather than its various answers, it would find that, in principle, human thought can acquire '... genuine, universally valid, final knowledge within a limited sphere or genuine knowledge of specific subjects.'[89] Furthermore, historicism, despite its denial of this capability, presumes it: by positing that all thought is historical, historicism posits also that there is at least one universally and perpetually valid principle.[90] Historicism claims both that it, as a human thought, is true only in a given historical epoch and also that it is transhistorically true. This contradiction is resolved by positing yet another contradiction: the history of thought, insofar as it proceeded aimlessly from one epoch to another, with the exception of historicist thought, is at its end. Strauss dramatically concludes that 'the historicist thesis is self-contradictory or absurd.'[91]

The radical historicist, however, because he recognizes a distinction between 'thought that recognizes the relativity of all comprehensive worldviews'[92] and thought that itself claims a comprehensive world view, denies the self-contradictions implicit in historicism. He denies that historicism makes claims to a transhistorical truth. He denies, furthermore, the possibility of transhistorical truths, and with this, the possibility of theoretic analyses of comprehensive views. The foundation of this position of the radical historicist, according to Strauss, was laid by Nietzsche,[93] who recognized the gap between life and its analysis:

analysis is defined by objective detachment, life, by commitment. For Nietzsche, life must be preserved. According to Strauss, two options were open to Nietzsche: he could either reaffirm the Platonic noble lie, 'insist on the strictly esoteric character of the theoretical analysis of life ... or else he could deny the possibility of theory proper and so conceive of thought as essentially subservient to, or dependent on, life or fate.'[94] Strauss, as has become clear, would choose the former option; Nietzsche's successors, however, chose the latter.[95]

The radical historicist eliminates the necessity of theoretic analyses of life by suggesting that the world view in which knowledge of each epoch is constructed is adopted, not through any rational guidance, but through commitment.[96] The ultimate grounding of reason cannot be legitimated through reason. One must make a commitment to a comprehensive world view because only commitment itself, the input of life itself, provides meaning. But once again, human thought is bound to impersonal fate: according to the radical historicist, one does not choose one's commitment; rather, one must commit to one's individual, or societal, fate. The freedom defined by eighteenth-century thought is reduced to the disposition with which we accept our fate.[97]

On the flip side of his assertion that the grounding of reason cannot be rationally validated, the radical historicist claims that only through the commitment to the world view that life has thrust on one can one come to know '... the true meaning of the "historicity" of all genuine thought ...'[98] Rational refutations of this position are dismissed as incapable of accessing the true meaning of thought: its relevance for life. The self-contradiction implicit in historicism – that it posits the transhistorical truth of the historicity of all knowledge, even as it denies the existence of all transhistorical truths – is resolved: the claim of the historicity of all knowledge is not transhistorical because it is bound essentially to the particular fate in which one's thought is thrust. This essential boundedness is not simply that one's thought is limited by the intellectual horizons of one's historical situation; rather, more fatally, the intellectual horizons of one's historical situation are the source of one's knowledge of the historical character of all thought.[99]

The historicist insight is not 'accessible to man as man.' Rather, it is dependent on man's commitment to his historical fate. Natural rights doctrines, on the other hand, are based on the claim that the fundamental principles of justice are accessible to man as man, that a basic truth persists through time. In rejecting this position, the radical historicist is able to assert both that there are no permanent truths and also that failure to recognize this fact previously was due to the limitations of previous historical situations. Fate had not yet decreed that it should be known that all human thought is limited, not by the essential unknowability of the whole, but by fate itself. While, as does all thought, historicist thought depends on fate (according to the radical historicist), only historicist thought has come to recognize this dependence. Thought need not transcend history in order to recognize its dependence on history: fate itself has bestowed the 'unforeseeable gift' of 'a privileged moment, an absolute moment in the historical process, a moment in which the essential character of all thought becomes apparent.'[100] There is no contradiction in historicist thought in its assertion that through all time there is no transhistorical truth. Rather, its assertion of an absolute moment in history – during which moment it was fated to be revealed that all thought is dependent on historical fate – suggests that the contradiction that exists, exists in reality itself, and not in thought about reality.

Strauss suggests that the historicist assertion of an absolute moment in history, though explicitly at odds with Hegel's assertion that history has ended (in yet another example of the self-contradictory character of historicism), implicitly follows Hegel.[101] For the historicist, the absolute moment in history defines the end of history because 'no possible future change of orientation can legitimately make doubtful the decisive insight into the inescapable dependence of thought on fate ...'[102] Hegel had based his assertion of the end of history on theoretical metaphysics: his moment in time defined, according to him, the moment at which philosophy had succeeded in attaining wisdom. While affirming that there is no further need to seek wisdom,[103] Hegel affirmed also the supreme value of philosophy.[104] The alleged historicist insight, however, that thought cannot transcend one's historical horizons, cannot survive the claim of theoretical philosophy's existence, and of the possibility of attaining wisdom in the philosophical sense.[105] Historicism defines its absolute moment as the moment at which thought comes to know its dependence on fate, its inability to achieve knowledge of fundamental principles, and its recognition that fundamental principles do not exist.

Strauss finds the historicist denial of the existence of philosophy (the existence of 'the attempt to replace opinions about the whole by knowledge of the whole'[106]) as characterized by dogmatism. One can recognize the insolubility of the fundamental riddles of thought and still recognize the foundations of the philosophical enterprise. For instance, the sceptical tradition that has coexisted with philosophy from its inception affirms this possibility. Unlike scepticism, which asserts that all claims are uncertain and therefore arbitrary,[107] and unlike philosophy in the above sense, for which there exist non-arbitrary metaphysical foundations, historicism asserts that all claims but its own are arbitrary. By asserting that all claims are arbitrary, historicism contradicts itself in claiming at the same time that its claim is non-arbitrary in each time and place. Philosophy, according to the historicist, is absurd because its foundations, on which it hopes to erect a monument to knowledge, rest on opinion. While the sceptical tradition is both non-historicist and non-dogmatic (in the sense that it does not deny the foundations of philosophy), historicism, in its attempt to go beyond scepticism, dogmatically denies the validity of both scepticism and philosophy.

The most influential process by which historicism has denied the validity of philosophy's dogmatism, according to Strauss, comprises five steps. First, according to this critique, philosophy 'presupposes that the whole is knowable.'[108] Therefore, second, the whole becomes identified as an object, an intelligible. Third, since the whole is identifiable as an object of thought, being itself is objectified; and fourth, everything that cannot be considered as an object is disregarded. Fifth and finally, because there exists a whole, or because the whole is knowable, '... the whole has a permanent structure ...'[109] through which, by means of thought, it is possible to predict the future of the whole. Philosophy presupposes that the whole is knowable because it dogmatically identifies '"to be" in the highest sense with "to be always,"' or '... understands "to be" in such a sense that "to be" in the highest sense must mean "to be always."'[110] The dogmatic character of philosophy, according to the historicist, blinded the philosopher to historicity. In fact, according to the historicist, philosophy's presupposition is invalid: the whole is not really a whole because it is always changing; the whole is unintelligible because it is not an object; '"to be" in the highest sense cannot mean – or, at any rate, it does not necessarily mean – "to be always."'[111]

We are, according to Strauss, indebted to radical historicism for bringing to light the necessity of re-examining the fundamental presuppositions of philosophy. We must return to the roots, to the premises on which the 'impressive edifices'[112] of traditions are built. During this necessary re-evaluation, two questions must remain open. First, we must suspend judgment as to whether the need for this work is superfluous or dictated by the historical situation in which we live. Second, because the validity of a doctrine of natural right rests on philosophical presuppositions, we must suspend judgment as to its existence. To

furnish ourselves again with the tools necessary for this re-evaluation
– a re-evaluation that will issue in 'a nonhistoricist understanding of
nonhistoricist philosophy'[113] – we must read classical philosophy, so
far as it is possible, in its own terms, in the way in which it understood
itself. Just as the foundations of philosophy must be reconsidered in
the light of radical historicism, so too the foundations of historicism,
equally dogmatic or arbitrary, must be reassessed in the light of classical philosophy.

One must, according to Strauss, return to the question, not to the answer: What can be known by human thought? And, by doing so, one
returns already to philosophy, to the awareness of both the fundamental
problems and also the various solutions available to human thought.[114]
'In grasping these problems as problems, the human mind liberates itself from its historical limitations.'[115] By submitting the historicist concept of the experience of history to critique, one would arrive at the
conclusion that it is but one interpretation of human experience, one
interpretation of experience that is accessible to man as man. Furthermore, the very act of undertaking the critique would return one both to
the fundamental problems and also to the act of philosophizing itself.
It would be 'a nonhistoricist understanding of historicism, an understanding of the genesis of historicism that does not take for granted the
soundness of historicism.'[116] History, far from being a discovery, may in
fact be an 'invention,' may in fact be but 'an artificial and makeshift solution to a problem that could arise only on the basis of very questionable
premises,'[117] a problem not at all fundamental, but itself issuing from
the inconsistency of the eighteenth-century doctrine of natural right.

The import of the modern crisis of historicism is that its impact is not
limited to philosophy as such. Because, beginning in the seventeenth
century, philosophy has become politicized[118] – because the separation
of philosophy from the authority of the state has been eliminated, or,
alternatively, philosophy has been brought into the public realm – the
crisis of historicism has become a political crisis. Since it is political philosophy that made the 'discovery' of history, this history concerns itself
with the conventional. It has denied the existence of natural right; and
this, in turn, has made principles of justice elusive, as well as minimized
our ability to discern the experience of everyday right and wrong. By
being unaware of the tension between philosophy and political authority, one[119] remains a victim of the delusion of historicism: one's thought
remains guided by the reigning, or conventional, interpretation of experience.[120]

The Problem of Historicism: Fackenheim the Philosopher's Return to History

While Strauss's critique of the historicist project is thoroughgoing, we note three places where he recognizes implicitly, as a present-day corrective, alternatives to a return to the classical understanding of philosophy and its concept of natural right. First, he recognizes the need for tools by which to raise ourselves out of the pit beneath Plato's cave. These tools are to be distinguished from the tools by which we imagine our progress: by eliminating from our thought our belief in the superiority of the present to the past, we eliminate also the cyclical nature of the self-justification of historicism. Second, the thrust of Strauss's lecture is his affirmation of the need for the possibility of human thought to transcend its particular time and place, so that it may recognize both the existence of natural right and also the context in which to understand the surface of things. While his lecture traces the process by which *philosophy* destroyed this transcendence, it does not address the issue for theological thought.[121] Third, in what will provide the basis for Fackenheim's mature thought on the encounter between historicism and revealed religion, Strauss recognizes in his lecture the difference between Hegel and the historicist's claims of an absolute moment in history.[122] While Fackenheim denies Strauss's affirmation that Hegel had pronounced philosophy finished,[123] he recognizes in Hegel's thought a moment at which both philosophy and history, both nature and convention, claim equal validity.[124] While Hegel adopted the historical sense, he did not, implicitly or explicitly, confuse philosophy with the modern form of political philosophy, nor did he trivialize philosophy proper.

Fackenheim's return to Hegel,[125] like Strauss's to the ancients, is a return to philosophy proper.[126] The question of whether his at least partial adoption of the historical sense is a philosophical or a theological decision will be explored below.[127] First, through a close reading of his responses to the doctrine of historicity in 'Metaphysics and Historicity' (1961), with a glance at 'The Historicity and Transcendence of Philosophic Truth' (1967),[128] it will be uncovered whether Fackenheim's philosophical work is adequate to the present need – whether it frees itself from the historicist self-delusion. The relationship between these two works is that 'Metaphysics and Historicity' focuses on the issue of selfhood, whereas 'The Historicity and Transcendence of Philosophic Truth' focuses on the later Heidegger's historicism. Both papers were written under the influence of Strauss, the former perhaps indirectly, but 'The Historicity and Transcendence of Philosophic Truth' was written specifically in response to Strauss's critique of 'Metaphysics and Historicity,' in which he suggested that Fackenheim needed both to reassess the later Heidegger's historicism and also to not so quickly dismiss the possibility of a more thorough return to the ancients.[129]

Second, I shall explore the particular problem faced by Fackenheim as a thinker who describes his stance as one of 'covenantal affirmation.'[130] Fackenheim attempted to incorporate philosophical rigour into his theology in, for instance, his essay 'Judaism and the Meaning of Life,'[131] an essay he considered to be his clearest example of this attempt in his early work. The particular problem for a Jewish existentialist thinker, as he phrased it in another essay, involves a dilemma:

> It cannot, on the one hand, seek to establish what is true and valid by independent philosophical or scientific criteria. For why should such thought be called Jewish? ... On the other hand, it is equally impossible for modern Jewish and Zionist thought to abandon Jewishly independent criteria and principles and, in an attempt to achieve Jewish validation, simply to immerse itself in the Jewish past. This is, indeed, possible for orthodox Jewish thought, for it finds in revelation an authoritative past ... But any non-orthodox thought which attempted to immerse itself in the Jewish past ... would simply arrive at declaring the whole past, indiscriminately, valid for the future. On what basis could it distinguish between the essential and the unessential, the profound and the trite, the living and the dead?[132]

Jewish existentialist thought must involve itself in Jewish history, but it must, at the same time, evaluate philosophically that history. The consequence of this dilemma for Fackenheim is an attempt, in his earlier thought, to do something 'akin to philosophy,'[133] and in his later thought (after 1967), to acknowledge that the Holocaust has threatened the continued validity of existentialist thought in particular: while the Holocaust occurred in history, it is unintelligible because its grounding is not in history, but in Hitler's transcendent world view. This chapter will focus only on Fackenheim's pre-1967 work, in an attempt to elucidate the practical consequences of his existentialism.[134] I will begin to explore the way in which Fackenheim's theological thought adopted or adapted, not historicism as generated from the modern critique of natural right through Heidegger, but rather history that can be judged objectively to be Jewish.[135] I shall explore to what extent his qualified historicism grows out of modern philosophical-historical developments and to what extent it grows out of what is organically Jewish.

Fackenheim's 'Metaphysics and Historicity' was written to explore as sympathetically as possible the doctrine of historicity according to its own criteria.[136] According to its own account, its 'chief purpose ... was to ask whether, in case *the very human condition is* itself *historical*, a transcendence of history is still possible.'[137] Immediately at the beginning of 'Metaphysics and Historicity,' one detects Strauss's influence on Fackenheim.[138] Just as Strauss had suggested that, in order to understand the experience of history as distinct from the experience of the history of thought, one's thought must be able to transcend that experience in order to provide for it context, so too Fackenheim writes, 'in order to act in history [man] must seek to rise above it.'[139] Man must accept 'timeless truths.' Yet like Strauss, Fackenheim recognizes that the ability of thought to rise above one's situation, despite the human being's best effort, may be only somewhat successful: 'opinion' often overtakes truth; the 'fashion' of one's contemporary situation often overtakes the authority of eternity.[140] And, like Strauss, he recognizes that the development of 'historical self-consciousness' has compounded the problem.

While Fackenheim's thought in this lecture is influenced by Strauss's critique of historicism, Fackenheim works, not from and within the tradition of Plato, but rather, the tradition of German Idealism.[141] Unlike Strauss's lecture, Fackenheim's is a description not of the genesis of historicism, but of the effects of historicism on man's 'spiritual' life.[142] We must begin with Fackenheim in his own terms, learn his intellectual vocabulary, before comparing his thought with Strauss's. The difference in vocabulary is immediately apparent in his use of the word 'scepticism.'[143] Strauss had suggested that historicism is not a development within scepticism but, rather, is at odds with the sceptical tradition, which, unlike historicism, denies the adequacy but not the existence of philosophy proper. Fackenheim seems to foreshadow his conclusion that acceptance of the doctrine of historicity need not imply the denial of the existence of a philosophy based on timeless truths: the historicization of scepticism does not necessarily deny the existence of classical philosophy.

Fackenheim is willing to undertake this historicization. From its beginning, we detect a difference between Strauss's lecture and Fackenheim's. While Strauss's critique self-consciously opposes its own historicization, Fackenheim's work begins in the present, in the very present, in the post-Holocaust moment, when it is commonly understood that historicism has led to disastrous results, but when we have not yet managed to escape its delusion. We are, according to Fackenheim, in an era defined by the step from historical self-consciousness to 'historical scepticism,' which he defines as 'the despairing view that history discloses a variety of conflicting *Weltanschauungen*, with no criterion for choice between them anywhere in sight.'[144]

Despite its issuing in despair, this step, according to Fackenheim, has often been taken, and for those who have taken it, there are three typical effects on their attitude toward spiritual life. First, one may end up in a position of 'sceptical paralysis,' which results in both the recognition that 'wherever there has been a great purpose there has been a great faith,' and also that one is incapable of making such a commitment.[145] Second, one may live a life of 'pragmatic make-believe,' in which one does not, but pretends to, believe.[146] Finally, the step from historical self-consciousness to historical scepticism may lead to the 'most ominous form of modern spiritual life: ideological fanaticism.'[147] Ideological fanaticism is a situation in which one asserts his belief with the absoluteness of faith, even as one knows that his ideology is ultimately not true, but is only the product of one moment in history. As a consequence, a historically conscious ideology must end in fanaticism: since it is not true in any objective sense, it must *make* itself true, it must 're-creat[e] history in its own image'[148] and destroy all ideologies opposed to it.

At this point, Fackenheim asks the philosophical question:[149] Must the step from historical consciousness to historical scepticism be taken? Is the step a necessary consequence of a metaphysical presupposition, a presupposition based on the affirmation that human thought can transcend its time and place? Or is it a product of human confusion and cowardice? Metaphysics has always affirmed 'that the predicament of history, however grave, is not wholly beyond human remedy; that at least when engaged in metaphysical discourse, man can rise above history to a grasp of timeless truth.'[150] By suggesting that there exists a basic disagreement between Aquinas, on the one hand, and Descartes, Kant, and Hegel, on the other, with regard to whether man can rise above the predicament of history,[151] Fackenheim argues that, despite metaphysical differences, all agreed that 'metaphysical truth is independent of any age.'[152] This view was first challenged in the mid-nineteenth century, and the possibility put forward – that metaphysics is essentially tied to history – opened up the possibility of a radical transformation of metaphysics.[153] Fackenheim sees this position not as a denial of metaphysics but rather as a historicization of metaphysics that, insofar as it is *commonly* held by various twentieth-century 'metaphysicians,'[154] perpetuates the metaphysical tradition.

The doctrine of historicity must be taken seriously, according to Fackenheim. Has it not always been the case that metaphysicians, even while commonly affirming the existence of metaphysics, have disagreed? Can one not then understand the common assent of various thinkers to the doctrine of historicity as an affirmation of metaphysics? Because metaphysical truth, in this sense, is not necessarily denied by the doctrine of historicity, this doctrine can be perpetuated, even as the idea of permanent human nature is replaced by the permanence of the inseparability of man's being and his history. Metaphysical truth, according to Fackenheim, would persist, even as it perpetually changed from one period to another.

Yet just because the doctrine of historicity *may* be true does not prove its truth and the necessity of its acceptance. One cannot turn to empirical history to prove it because empirical history cannot address man's 'very being,' which is, and remains, the subject matter of metaphysics.[155] On the other hand, simply because it cannot be proved does not prove that it is false. One cannot use the tools of traditional metaphysics to disprove what is outside its scope – indeed, what denies metaphysics any scope at all. Fackenheim suggests that 'before the metaphysician asks whether or not the doctrine of historicity is true he must be sure to have understood it in the terms it requires.'[156] His lecture will proceed in two parts. First, in order to make sure that he understands the doctrine of historicity in its own terms, he will 'seek to elicit the metaphysical assumptions without which the doctrine of historicity cannot arise.'[157] Second, he will seek to state 'the metaphysical categories without which it cannot be maintained.'[158] By gaining an understanding of the doctrine in itself, Fackenheim is able to address 'the question which concerns' him most: 'whether the doctrine of historicity necessitates the surrender of the age-old idea of timeless metaphysical truth.'[159] The deviation between the positions of Strauss and Fackenheim on historicism – Strauss accepting less (or none) of it, Fackenheim more – is reflected in their separate approaches to the issue. Strauss accounts for historicism historically; Fackenheim accounts for it metaphysically.

Fackenheim begins by defining the metaphysical presuppositions by which the doctrine of historicity was able to emerge. Like Strauss, he begins – and, as we shall see below in his 'Epilogue,' ends – with the surface of things, in his case, with terms that are 'close to common sense.'[160] The first presupposition that he identifies stems from Collingwood's distinction between 'natural event and historical action,' or what happens 'outside' human beings and what happens both 'inside' and outside of them.[161] The distinction presumes that the human being is capable of free action; that there are times when what human beings believe to be the reasons for their actions are in fact the reasons. This is, at least, a practical assumption, if not a theoretical one, because even the positivist will assent to it while he is in the process of attempting to explain the sequence of an action. At the same time, it is an assumption because it can be denied with some plausibility.[162] What is more, the assumption is necessary in order to lay the groundwork for the doctrine of historicity because historicity requires the definition of a separate realm of history, utterly distinct from and irreducible to nature.

At this point in the lecture, Fackenheim reminds the reader that in both secularist understandings of history and those of faith, there need be no contradiction between human free will and a third category that is neither natural event nor human action. The Bible, for instance, posits human free will and God's action in history. Human beings might be used as instruments, so to speak, of God's will, even as those used have their own intentions. Also, the Bible presupposes human free will in its affirmation of divine reward and punishment. Secularist understandings of history, on the other hand, may suggest that human free will can be reduced to fate. But this conclusion derives from a misunderstanding that makes of history a self-contradiction: when man has become so alienated from his purposes, as Strauss suggested, has become himself homeless by making his thought wholly this-worldly, man seems not to have free will because he becomes a victim of the unforeseen consequences of his own actions. The misunderstanding is a misunderstanding of the relationship between a metaphysical presupposition and history, between the *assumption*, on the one hand, of the distinction between natural event and human action, and, on the other, the *experience* of history as wholly human and wholly fated. Fackenheim, following Hegel, suggests that 'freedom in history is real enough to give rise to the most momentous consequences, although, because human freedom is finite, these consequences are always partly, and often wholly, other than those intended.'[163]

Even so, were one to accept the distinction between natural event and human action, one may still reject the doctrine of historicity. One may, in fact, argue that, because man is capable of action, he is capable of having a history; and it is the latter capability that indicates that man has a non-historical, or fixed, nature. Aristotle, Fackenheim reminds us, had suggested that history is even less philosophical than poetry because history deals only with particulars, not with universals.[164] The study of the accidents of history might be a field for a historian, but metaphysics, or ontology, would have no interest in it. Therefore, a second presupposition is needed in order for the doctrine of historicity to emerge: the doctrine must posit that there are no permanent human natures and that there is no permanent human nature. Human nature itself is a historical process. Since human being is inherently historical, history is a valid subject matter for ontology.

The doctrine of historicity requires both assumptions. First, that there is a distinction between history and nature, between what man does and what happens to or in man; second, that human acting is not distinct from human being – man's 'nature' is not fixed, but is rather 'itself the product of his acting ... *In acting, man makes or constitutes himself.'*[165] The doctrine of historicity asserts specifically that 'apart from history, man's very being, *qua* being and *qua* human, is deficient.'[166] What makes man human is itself historical, and what makes the historical is human action.[167]

Fackenheim concludes this section with the suggestion that the crucial assumption – the assumption without which the doctrine of historicity could not emerge – is that 'human being ... is a self-making or self-constituting process.'[168] With this assumption, which, he reminds us, is but a hypothesis without proof,[169] metaphysics itself, or at any rate, the ontological study of man, may become the study of history. And Fackenheim cites two ways in which the ontologist may turn into the historian, either as the speculative historian, as Hegel became, or as the 'historian pure and simple,' in the way of Croce and Collingwood.[170] Having accepted the hypothesis, one must accept a direct connection between being and action, or ontology and history. Without this acceptance, a scholar would either arrive at a 'mere abstract and empty possibility,' or he 'would mistake for a permanent nature what is in fact a specific historical product.'[171]

Fackenheim is now ready to understand the doctrine of historicity itself. To begin, he questions the extent to which the concept of a self-making process is intelligible, reminding the reader that its unintelligibility may exist only from the perspective of a rival metaphysics.[172] He captures the unintelligibility of a *causa sui*, or a self-making process, when he reminds us of Schopenhauer's suggestion of the absurdity of 'the story of Baron von Münchhausen, who claimed that, having fallen into a swamp, he pulled himself out by his hair.'[173] Yet he suggests that the concept of self-making is not new to metaphysics: there are two metaphysical traditions, one major, one minor, that have coexisted. The major tradition of metaphysics – that is, Scholasticism – understands God as Pure Being and as creator *ex nihilo* and is strictly ontological; the minor understands God as 'Pure Freedom who, in creating *ex nihilo*, Himself passes *ex nihilo in aliquid*,' and is meontological.[174]

Fackenheim cites Aquinas as representative of the major tradition and of the principle *operatio sequitur esse*, and Schelling and Hegel, among others, as representative of the principle *esse sequitur operationem*.[175] So, for instance, Aquinas works in the ontological tradition because, both in the *Summa Theologica* (I, 75) and especially in *Summa Contra Gentiles* (II, 21 and III, 42), he posits that 'the perfection of the operation follows the perfection of the substance.'[176] Being precedes process. The meontological tradition, on the other hand, posits that process, or pure freedom and the desire to become something, becomes something in its moving both backward and forward. So, for instance, Hegel: '"The supreme form of Nought as a separate principle would be Freedom."'[177] Fackenheim suggests that the ontological tradition, in its rejection of the meontological tradition, grounds itself on the principle of the four causes[178] – an efficient cause cannot cause itself, unless, absurdly, it could exist prior to itself. In the meontological tradition, on the other hand, the Nothing, or the Process, 'would have to be at once material and efficient cause, and be creative of the formal and final [cause].'[179] Given the presuppositions of the meontological tradition, the ontological tradition would have to abandon the principle of the four causes, and could therefore no longer sustain its argument as incontrovertible.

To address his major concern in this lecture – whether metaphysics must be abandoned with the adoption of the doctrine of historicity – Fackenheim at this point explores the possibility that the doctrine of historicity may emerge organically out of the metaphysical tradition; that the doctrine does not break from, but rather perpetuates, traditional metaphysics, if only in its minor representation. He therefore describes the meontological tradition and, by assessing its intelligibility, assesses also the intelligibility of the doctrine of historicity for ontological metaphysics.

In the meontological tradition of metaphysics, God is a process of pure making by which the possibility within nothingness becomes actualized as differentiation (*ex nihilo in aliquid*). Furthermore, because by this process the God of meontological metaphysics makes itself, it establishes its identity by means of nullifying the otherness into which it passes. In its self-making, from the point of view of ontological metaphysics, the God of meontology is both efficient and material cause, even as it defines its own final and formal cause. Finally, the process of pure making in the meontological tradition is absolute; therefore, it actualizes from nothingness *all* possibilities.[180] Fackenheim concedes that this description of meontology is unintelligible within the static terms of ontological metaphysics. At the same time, he suggests that to dismiss it based solely on the logic defined by those static terms would be to grant that logic autonomy – to have an experience of the history of thought, rather than an experience of history. Logic itself may be metaphysically grounded – may be an outgrowth of the system of thought from which it is derived – and meontology, while unintelligible in terms of ontological logic, may have an intelligible logic independent from or even at odds with it. One must understand meontology within the terms of its own logic: one must assess the validity of the ontological and meontological traditions not through a confrontation of their logics, but rather through a confrontation of their metaphysics.[181]

Meontology, according to Fackenheim, generates a logic of its own that qualifies it as a valid metaphysics.[182] Because it involves process, the terms of that logic vary. Indeed, the process that defines meontology involves a circular movement: it constitutes itself absolutely only by moving forward into otherness *and* moving backward as a means by which to integrate its new identity, so to speak, with its past manifestations.[183] Still, despite its circularity, it is a valid logic that springs organically from its metaphysical assertions. What is more, it is through this logic that one can begin to understand the doctrine of historicity in its own terms, terms that do not necessarily expel metaphysics from its coexistence.

When one reconsiders the meontological conception of God, according to Fackenheim, one recognizes that, although to be historical, a process must be understood as self-constituting, there may exist a self-constituting process that is not necessarily historical. He defines this situation as 'quasi-historical.'[184] It is, in some sense, historical both because there are distinguishable moments in the process by which *nihil* is transformed into *aliquid* and because the process constitutes an identity, which raises the status of the process from the merely temporal. At the same time, it is, in some sense, eternal because the self-constituting is a holistic process; an identity persists through the process, even as it is a process.[185] The only means by which this overt contradiction can be symbolized is as circular motion, but it is not strictly motion at all; or rather, it is both motion and eternity: the end of the process, while distinct from its beginning, is, in terms of the persistent identity, a return to the beginning.[186]

The doctrine of historicity must be distinguished from both temporality and the 'quasi-historicity of eternity.'[187] The first distinction is accomplished by the concept of self-making: because it is self – a persistent identity that is constituted – historicity cannot be mere temporality. Mere temporality is distinguished from history proper in three ways, corresponding to past, future, and present. In the case of the past, history proper is 'capable of present appropriation and reenactment'; while in the case of temporality, the past is 'present only as the present effect of past events.'[188] The doctrine of historicity teaches that man's actions are connected to his being *qua* being. Because man is self-constituting – because the process by which man is man requires appropriation and reappropriation of the past – man's being is historical.

Furthermore, historicity proper is distinguished from mere temporality in the way in which the future is present. From the latter perspective, the future is present only insofar as 'the present is pregnant with but limited possibilities.'[189] The historical future, on the other hand, is present as 'anticipation … a projecting-into-future.'[190] The historical future presumes the existence of free will, while the temporal future does not. Historicity presumes a historical future, and furthermore, by positing human being as self-making, posits the entry of the future into the present ontological constitution of human being.

Historicity distinguishes itself also from the temporal present, which is 'a vanishing point of passage.'[191] The historical present, on the other hand, integrates 'future possibilities' and past actualities into present action.'[192] The historical present is not simply the context in which one performs actions – which context provides no essential information regarding man's being – but rather is the moment in which man's present being is constituted. Because historicity equates man's being with his acting, man's present actions constitute what he is.

The second distinction – between historicity and quasi-historical eternity – requires the introduction of historicity's second most important concept, that of 'situation.'[193] Man's self-making must take place in a 'situation' in order for it to be possible to understand the process ontologically. The reason for this is as follows. Historicity is distinct from the quasi-historical and eternal, again, in terms of its understanding of past, future, and present. First, because the historical past exists as a present appropriation and reenactment of the past, it is by definition distinct from what it appropriates and reenacts. Second, the anticipated future of historicity is distinct from the actual future because the former involves planning, while the latter does not; the actual future may or may not conform to the planned future. Again, because the doctrine of historicity identifies man's being with his actions, the historical past and future are ontologically distinct from the actual past and future: the historical is not eternal and quasi-historical. Finally, the distinction between the historical and the quasi-historical and eternal with regard to the present is that any given moment of the historical present is, by definition, incomplete; it is 'fragmented by the loss of a past which it cannot recapture, and by the refractoriness of a future which refuses to be subdued into presentness.'[194] The actuality of the past and of the future sets limits to which the historical present must conform and provides a situation in which the historical present occurs. Situation distinguishes historicity from quasi-historical eternity.

While Fackenheim recognizes that the forms of situation 'are many and varied in kind,'[195] he suggests that the ones to which he has so far referred in the lecture are 'natural'; 'all historical acting occurs in a *natural situation*.'[196] This natural situation is defined by what actually happens, regardless of how the past is appropriated and reenacted, regardless, that is, of how the future is anticipated. It is situation that upholds Collingwood's distinction between the historical and the natural – indeed, it is what provides the means by which the historical can arise. In the quest for ontological understanding of man, the appropriate relationship between the historical and the natural is one in which the historical transcends temporality and also remains finite, one in which the historical freely aspires to humanity and is naturally limited to the human.[197]

Fackenheim suggests that an often overlooked but crucially important aspect of the doctrine of historicity is the distinction between situation and situated self-making.[198] Self-making must be finite because its lapse into the eternal would deny it the humanness of both its choosing what of the actual past to reappropriate and reenact, and also its anticipation of or planning for the future. Yet, as Fackenheim points out, in order to retain the finitude of self-making, there must be an ontological distinction between self-making and the situation in which this self-making occurs. If no such distinction exists, self-making would be capable of self-transcendence; self-making could free itself from the natural limitations imposed by situation. On the other hand, situated self-making cannot be *wholly* other than situation, or else it would be either simply a product within situation or ontologically impervious to situation.[199] This latter condition would be a denial of historicity itself, a denial of the identification of man's being and his acting.

There is a 'dialectical' relation between situation and situated self-making, a relation that retains both the otherness and the sameness of the two elements. It is crucial to remember the distinction between them in order to avoid a 'lapse into the kind of idealism which regards all limitation of the self as the self's own limitation.'[200] Without retaining the otherness, one cannot retain the limitations that are externally imposed on the self. On the other hand, there is a partial identity between the two elements, and not to recognize it is 'to lapse into the kind of naturalism for which the self is, in the end, the mere product of its environment.'[201] One may suggest a third option: a 'dualistic doctrine' that affirms that, while the self is subject to external limitations, it is ontologically unaffected by these limitations. A dualistic doctrine may suggest that the self is *actually* subject to limitations, a position that upholds the otherness of situated self-making and situation but that is *unaware* of these limitations and remains self-consciously non-other than its situation. To affirm such a doctrine, one could suggest that as the self becomes conscious of the natural limitations to which it is subject, it incorporates them into its ontological self-making.

Fackenheim rejects the last option. On the one hand, the self, by the definition of historicity, is a self-making, and it cannot, at any moment, be simply a passive element of its own constitution. On the other hand, self-awareness cannot wholly characterize the activity of the self because if it did, the self would, through awareness alone, transcend its limitations. The activity of the self must include more than self-awareness if self-awareness is to have subject matter. There would be, as Fackenheim points out, 'no difference between self-awareness and self-images created at random.'[202] Having exhausted the options for the means by which situation and situated self-making relate, and having warned the reader of the dangers of a particular kind of idealism or naturalism that results from relating them inappropriately, Fackenheim concludes that their relation is a dialectical one, one that upholds both the finitude and the transcending capabilities of the self.

As Fackenheim enters the centre of the lecture, he introduces a third concept necessary for the doctrine of historicity: to the concepts of self-making and natural situation, he adds the concept of historical situation. It is 'obvious' to affirm that not only natural events, but also other human actions, limit the possibility of human action.[203] But it is not so obvious that one's historical situation affects one's very being. Another way to put the question: Does the human being have a permanent nature? If he does not, then the historical situation in which he acts would affect his very being, and historical situation would be, not only a historical concept, but an ontological one as well.[204] If the human being does not have a permanent nature – if his being is self-constituted – Fackenheim suggests that two distinct concepts of historical situation as required by situated self-making are needed. First, because man's acting determines, and is determined by, man's very being, *all* of man's past acts of self-making must affect his present acts at least to some degree. Second, and more obviously, what other men have done in the past affects present man's being, as, for instance, 'Mozart has created possibilities of experience which but for his work would not exist.'[205] Mozart has defined a realm of possible experience – a historical situation – for those after him, and therefore his work 'circumscribes also what contemporary man can be and is.'[206]

Just as the relation between situation and situated self-making is a dialectical one, so too the relation between historical situation and historically situated self-making is dialectical. The natural situation can do nothing beyond limiting the situated; it cannot provide freedom to the situated except insofar as the latter can choose to accept the limitation. The historical situation, on the other hand, because it is itself defined by human acting, cannot simply limit human acting: it must, even while it limits human acting, also augment human acting.[207] This augmentation takes the form of the situated 'appropriating … aspects of the situating, to the integrating of these into its own process of self-constitution.'[208] Unlike natural situation, which provides limitations that involve no acting on the part of the situated, historical situation gives to the situated the freedom to appropriate aspects of itself, which aspects in turn become at once part of the self-constituting of the situated.[209]

The relation between historical situation and historically situated self-making is dialectical insofar as historical situation both limits and augments historically situated self-making. Again, the dangers of the loss of history are clear. The historically situated might appropriate all of its historical situation, in which case it would transcend history.[210] The historically situated might become unable to appropriate any of its historical situation, in which case it would 'fall below history.'[211] Fackenheim concludes that 'every historical situation, then, *qua* historical, is a conjunction of limitation and opportunity; as it were, of fate and freedom.'[212]

There is no aspect of historical situation that is accidental; even what is new of a given historical situation is essential to it. Fackenheim, having laid the groundwork – having, in an effort to compare the logics of traditional metaphysics and historicism, returned to the common sense by which one differentiates the experience of history and the experience of the history of thought – returns to a more precise formulation of his original question, which was, we recall, whether the idea of a timeless metaphysical truth must be abandoned in the face of the doctrine of historicity. Now Fackenheim formulates it this way: 'If human being is an historically situated self-making, must all its activities be historically situated – metaphysics included?'[213]

Fackenheim begins by recounting 'the case against the metaphysical claim to timeless truth.'[214] First, whether metaphysics creates its truths or rises to them, the knowledge to which metaphysics gives rise must be part of the self-making process. The knowledge is transhistorical and is, therefore, as part of the process, a transhistorical form of self-making. This argument, however, cannot be sustained: since the self-making process must presume that 'all aspects [of human being] are integrated into a single whole,'[215] there can be no distinction between the human capacities for transhistorical knowledge and for finite knowledge. Second, there can be no distinction between natural and historical situation, either because civilizations differ one from another in the attitudes of their citizens regarding their natural limitations, or because natural limitations are in some part affected by history. Fackenheim concludes that the only way to sustain a doctrine of self-making is by positing that human being is '*radically* historically situated; that there are no aspects of a man's being which are wholly unaffected by the historical situation in which he exists.'[216] Even the transhistorical truth of metaphysics must integrate itself with the historical; the distinction between the transhistorical and the historical 'appears absolute only to a standpoint which is itself historically situated.'[217]

The historicity of transhistorical truth is, according to Fackenheim, a revolution in metaphysics. What was once understood as the quest for timeless truth is now understood as the quest for what only seems to be, from a historically situated standpoint, timeless truth. 'All metaphysics ... is reduced to a sequence of historically relative *Weltanschauungen*.'[218] Because the metaphysician cannot recognize the relativity of his particular *Weltanschauung* yet continue to live by it, and because the historian recognizes the relativity of all *Weltanschauungen*, history supersedes metaphysics. 'The historian's history of *Weltanschauungen*,' while remaining as incomplete as the story of the whole can be at any given moment, is 'forever complete' in this sense: 'it leaves no room, beyond the history of metaphysics, for an independent inquiry into metaphysical truth.'[219] This is the position, as Fackenheim defines it, of historicism. 'Historicism, in the classical sense, is the position which asserts that all philosophical questions are superseded by historical questions. It is the assertion that the fundamental distinction between philosophical and historical questions cannot in the last analysis be maintained.'[220]

Historicism cannot, according to Fackenheim, be sustained because historicism must posit an exception to its historicization of knowledge: 'the act by which self-making recognizes itself as self-making, and as historically situated.'[221] As he, and indeed Strauss, point out, without this exception, historicism collapses in self-contradiction.[222] Were it to posit that history supersedes philosophy, the basis on which historicism establishes itself is contradicted by historicism itself; were it to renounce all philosophical assumptions, historicism would be reduced to history. Fackenheim concludes that the ontology that historicism requires, a foundation in the metaphysical affirmation that the recognition of the fact of historicism is timelessly true, renders historicism false.[223]

Historicism, as a development from the doctrine of historicity, posits a radically historically situated self-making. Its failure is traced to the radicality of this situating: it attempts to rid itself of its need for timeless metaphysical truth by historicizing that truth, but the historicization of that truth itself dramatizes a timeless truth. Fackenheim's distinction between historicity and historicism seems to suggest that, while he agrees with Strauss that historicism is a fatalistic dogmatism or self-delusion, he is seeking to develop historicity in an alternative direction,[224] one that, stemming from Hegel, recognizes the distinction between the transcendence of situation and what is beyond history, and the fundamental distinction between the questions of history and those of philosophy. Fackenheim's historicity, like Strauss's return to Plato, will recognize that one must begin with the phenomena, with common sense. Fackenheim requires this in order to compare different kinds of metaphysics, rather than the different logics that emerge from them, and to recognize the logical difference in kind between statements about truth. Yet he will go beyond Hegel, who, by conceiving the distinction between nature and history to be exhaustive, was able to transcend both; Fackenheim will recognize the possibility that these categories are not exhaustive, that there may exist a third category, in which persists timeless truth and in relation to which the self is both passive and active.

The doctrine of historicity, to be sustainable, must allow for the co-existence of what is recognized from the historical standpoint as 'trans-historical possibilities of self-making.'[225] In a statement reminiscent of Strauss's suggestion that 'transcendence is not a preserve of revealed religion,'[226] Fackenheim suggests that the possibility of transcendence even within the doctrine of historicity is not a preserve of philosophy.[227] Since transcendence remains a possibility after the 'discovery of history,' one must recognize, along with Kierkegaard, that 'Christianity, if a possibility at all, must be substantially the same possibility in the nineteenth century as it was in the first.'[228]

Having refuted historicism to his satisfaction, Fackenheim attempts to respond to the challenge it poses. To do so, one must speak in the terms of historicity – one must return to the roots from which histori-cism emerged – to respond adequately to the full challenge posed by it.[229] Ironically, according to Fackenheim, Hegel provided a response to historicism, even before it emerged. 'Hegel perceived with the utmost clarity a truth wholly beyond the comprehension of historicism.'[230] Hegel derived this perception from his recognition of the paradox at the basis of human existence: if human being is a self-making, it has both finite and infinite aspects; it is both human and also is capable of philosophical self-recognition. While the aspects of man's being must integrate themselves in order to create a self-identity, they are unable to do so. Were the infinite aspect to reduce itself to finitude, 'the result would be a relapse into historicism.'[231] Were the finite to 'reduce itself to the infinite aspect, man would cease to be human.'[232]

While Fackenheim recognizes in Hegel's thought a powerful re-sponse to the challenge of historicism, he recognizes also that the latter thinker failed to sustain the 'struggle' between the infinite and finite aspects of human being as historically situated self-making, a strug-gle implicit in the latter's response to historicism.[233] Because he feared that philosophy would otherwise become impossible, Hegel affirmed the primacy of man's infinite aspect and sublated man's finite, into his infinite, aspect.[234] Ironically, according to Fackenheim, it was not philo-sophical considerations that destroyed Hegel's 'transhistorical synthesis of the historical and the transhistorical,' but rather 'the recalcitrance of subsequent history.'[235] Hegel's failure in this regard has enormous ramifications: his failure to retain the tension between the infinite and finite aspects of man's being resulted in the emergence of historicism even after Hegel had offered an adequate refutation of it. Because historicism did in fact emerge from the doctrine of historicity, historicism has had its effect: human being, according to Fackenheim, has inalterably changed as a result of its historically situated self-making during the historical situation of the Holocaust, during which time 'the intellect … lost its basic quality: its transcendence.'[236] Hegelianism cannot be salvaged, cannot be brought up to date, because of the very process that it, by its failure, set into motion.[237]

Fackenheim spends the remainder of the lecture discussing 'whether the doctrine of man-as-unresolved-struggle must in fact lead back to historicism.'[238] He begins by affirming that the struggle of man's infinite and finite aspects both seeking and fleeing each other is not only unresolvable, but also, insofar as human being is a self-making, constitutes what man is: the aspects must seek each other in order to establish an integrated self-identity, yet must flee each other in order to avoid either a self-contradictory historicism or transcendence above history. Philosophic understanding is still possible because, while human being manifests itself as struggle in various forms, one (or some) of the forms of human being is distinct from its other forms: 'human being *recognizes* itself as a struggle which is in principle unresolvable.'[239] And this recognition must itself be part of human being's struggle, so that it does not resolve the struggle.

The doctrine that teaches this qualitative difference among forms of human being cannot assume the traditional standpoint of metaphysics, which views the object of knowledge as a detached subject. Rather, because the struggle that is human being must be preserved, this standpoint is invalid. On the one hand, the object must be understood as an 'object-for-understanding,' not as an object, which, incapable of self-understanding, is separable from the struggle; on the other, the subject cannot be detached if it is to remain part of the struggle. Knowledge gleaned from a detached standpoint cannot issue in human self-understanding because, if human being is self-making, knowledge of reality must come in the form of human self-definition. The only means by which to gain this sort of knowledge is, according to Fackenheim, through 'existential attempts at radical self-transcendence, in which human being, seeking to rise above the unresolvable struggle which is its essence, recognizes its radical limitations by foundering in the attempt.'[240]

While the attempts must be 'made by each person for himself ... the knowledge attained through them is radically universal.'[241] The knowledge gained is not simply knowledge of one's own situation; rather, it is knowledge that, like all human being, one is both situated and also able to recognize that one is situated. The knowledge attained, while not detached, is universal; and he who has attained it has attained 'philosophical self-understanding.'[242] It is recognition not of natural or historical situation, but rather of *'human situation.'*[243] Human situation is known only when an individual recognizes it as his own even though, at the same time, human situation is recognized as universally human. Unlike natural and historical situation, it does not provide additional limitations to human being, but neither does it eradicate those limitations: human situation is, rather, the root of natural and historical situation, into which it is individuated. Human situation 'is achieved when the natural and the historical situation are understood ... as specific manifestations of a universal condition.'[244] Human situation is the ontological basis of historically and naturally situated human self-making.

One comes to recognize human situation when natural and historical situation are radicalized. This radicalization provides the philosophic basis for the doctrine of historicity insofar as it issues in knowledge that is both universal and timelessly valid. Natural situation may disclose itself as one's recognition of one's necessary development from childhood to older age; historical situation may disclose itself as knowledge of the particular 'limitations and opportunities' of one's age.[245] Human situation, on the one hand, discloses itself as recognition that *all* human being is subject to 'temporality and mortality'; on the other, that *'all* history is a conjunction of compulsion and freedom, and that to be subject to the one and to be challenged to realize the other is universally part of the human condition.'[246]

The implications of this existential concept of human situation, for Fackenheim's present purpose, are twofold. First, there is a 'need for a radical revision of the whole doctrine of self-making.'[247] While natural situation exists in dialectical relation with human being, it cannot provide aspects that are 'distinctively human.'[248] And, again, while historical situation provides to self-making something other, it does not provide something 'other-than-human but merely other than the particular self-making which it situates.'[249] Without the concept of human situation, natural and historical situation alone could provide all the terms necessary for self-making; this would render philosophical self-transcendence both impossible and irrelevant. There would be neither means nor desire to rise above the other-than-human.[250] The acceptance of the concept of human situation, however, provides the basis for means and desire: to natural and historical situation it adds something that is both qualitatively other and more than human. And because of this addition, which adds to human self-making both situation and content for its activity, human self-making cannot be wholly autonomous.[251]

The radical revision to the doctrine of self-making that is required is that the *'human being must be understood as something more than a mere product, and yet as something less than a self-making. Instead of a self-constituting, it must rather be the accepting or choosing of something already constituted, and yet also not constituted, because the accepting or choosing is part of its essence.'*[252] The dialectic thus posited between human situating and the humanly situated issues in the existentialist distinction between the self and the authentic self. The self, through self-choice, becomes authentic self. Again, while the self both must remain separate from its activity of self-choice and also must incorporate into itself its self-choosing, the act of self-choice must create a choosing self. The acceptance of self through self-choice, which is the choosing of something qualitatively other than human, or 'myself in my eternal validity,'[253] defines authentic self. This choosing, according to Kierkegaard, is a choosing of the self as 'absolute,' it is the choosing itself, which choosing is limited by natural and historical situation: 'it is freedom.'[254]

Fackenheim, in his introduction of the existentialist concept of human situation, is not bringing Hegel up to date. Rather, he is adding to Hegel's concept of the Absolute a distinctively human grounding.[255] Human infinitude, in, for instance, Kierkegaard's sense, is not comparable to Hegel's sense.[256] Hegel's human infinitude, we recall, is a synthesis of human finitude and infinitude and is not limited by human situation; the finite and infinite aspects of human being for Hegel no longer flee each other. For Kierkegaard, man can neither succeed at self-transcendence nor deny the limitations imposed on human self-making by something wholly other than human. For Kierkegaard, the 'authentic' acceptance of one's finitude, which can be attained only through the acceptance of the inability of one's infinitude of becoming Hegel's Absolute, is absolute in the sense that one freely chooses one's finitude.[257]

Recognition of the dialectical relation between self and authentic self effects a 'replacement of the doctrine of self-making with a doctrine of self-choosing.'[258] And this replacement, according to Fackenheim, affects metaphysics as a whole. If human being is regarded as self-making, the activity of human speculation must be considered also a part of the process of self-making. One must, in that case, consider that metaphysical truths are affected by human self-making, 'that man has at least a share in creating the realm to the knowledge of which his metaphysics rises.'[259] But once the concept of human situation is introduced; once human being is understood as humanly situated self-choosing; once it is recognized that humanly situated self-making cannot be wholly autonomous and must, therefore, give way to humanly situated self-choosing; the possibility that the realm of metaphysics is humanly created is excluded. 'For what situates man humanly is not produced by man but on the contrary the condition of all human producing.'[260] It is the ground from which man's natural and historical situations arise.

Strauss understands the quest for this grounding as the quest for the mystery of being.[261] Fackenheim refers to it as 'the Other par excellence.'[262] For Fackenheim, the only thing that can be known of this Other is its otherness. This is because to know it, man could no longer be situated by it; yet to know nothing of it, man could not rise to philosophy. Fackenheim writes:

> We have seen that existential metaphysics originates in the recognition of man's human situation, as a dialectical mystery. We now see that this metaphysics culminates in pointing, as to a vastly greater mystery, to the ultimate Other which situates man humanly. And this pointing-to is itself dialectical. It expresses an ignorance which knows the grounds of this ignorance, or a knowledge which knows that it is ignorant, and why. The Other that is pointed to thus remains undefined, and is yet given names. But the names express Mystery. They do not disclose It.[263]

An obvious difference between Strauss's and Fackenheim's concepts of this ground, this mystery, is that the latter suggests that the 'pointing-to-the-Other, the last achievement of unaided philosophical thought, need not be regarded in existential thought as necessarily the last achievement of man: if the Other is God who reveals Himself.'[264] Strauss, while not denying the possibility of God as the mystery of being, would not ascribe to His revelation the possibility of historical content. Put another way, Strauss's thought remains undogmatic because his thought remains a *quest* for and not a doctrine of the mystery of being.[265] For Fackenheim, if the Other is God, human being becomes involved with Him through love; the Other no longer remains an object of philosophy, or rather, objectified by philosophy. One must think about the difference between philosophy's love of the true object and religion's love in relation to and with Another. This difference seems to stem from the difference between Plato's categorization of dialectic as logical, and Hegel's as metaphysical: once dialectic affects being itself, the mystery of being can no longer be wholly unknown; it must be brought into relation with being.

Fackenheim concludes that 'the doctrine of historicity requires the assumption that human being is a self-constituting process.'[266] Finally, in the last few pages of the lecture, he addresses the fundamental question for our purposes: Is there a reason that this assumption should be granted? While Fackenheim suggests that time constraints preclude him from addressing this question adequately (the paper under discussion was delivered as a lecture), he stresses the importance of addressing it more fully in the future. To begin, it was, ironically, Kant who, while not accepting it himself, influenced the development of the doctrine of self-making. Kant rejects the doctrine because 'he regards the metaphysical knowledge of man as a task which transcends human power.'[267] The doctrine was accepted as a means, most simply put, of fighting empiricism, of refuting ideologies that reduce the self to a material object.[268] In this battle, the doctrine has been successful.

Yet according to Fackenheim, the doctrine of human self-making has not necessarily succeeded against the doctrine of a permanent human nature.[269] Kant's immediate successors did not necessarily reject that there exists a specifically permanent human nature, but they did reject that a self could exist prior to the self's own activity. Fichte, for instance, held that it is 'metaphysically and morally intolerable'[270] to regard the self as anything other than wholly self-produced. The extremism of Fichte's position was rejected almost immediately: 'already Schelling and Hegel insist that the self requires a background other than itself for its self-constitution.'[271] Even so, in both their thought the doctrine of historicity remains bound to idealism, insofar as both posit that 'in the highest form of the self's self-constitution no aspect of otherness remains.'[272] Kierkegaard, according to Fackenheim, was the first to deny idealism altogether as a necessary coexistent with the doctrine of historicity. For Kierkegaard, the self is indeed a process of self-activity, and it is 'a responsibility rather than a given fact.'[273] But, at the same time, the otherness of the self-making process is not supplied by a natural background, as it is for Schelling and Hegel; rather, the otherness is supplied by 'existential limitations' – by the fact that the self is a gift that, through appropriation or self-choosing, becomes itself.[274]

By suggesting at this point that one consider the return to the doctrine of a permanent human nature – considering the almost immediate retreat from the extremism of Fichte's position – Fackenheim comes as close as he will in the lecture to Strauss's position.[275] One could, for instance, following Aristotle, recognize the process of self-constitution as a process of the actualization of potentialities implicit in permanent human nature. Fackenheim suggests that Kierkegaard, Jaspers, and Buber would object to this return based on its necessary objectification of the self.[276] Because the self self-constitutes within the human situation, the self can be understood only through encounter. Yet perhaps the classical doctrine can answer this objection; its 'counter-attack' would be 'based on the indispensability of speculative thought.'[277] As Strauss had suggested, one can understand neither the surface of one's own situation, nor the self in that situation, without an ability to ascend from the particularities of one's time and place. Furthermore, existential philosophy itself relies on speculative thought: Can this reliance be justified? And how accurate is its conception of the self, when it defies its own position against the self's objectification?[278] Fackenheim does not retreat from either the classical or the existential position; he suggests that the appropriate step from here is to put the two positions into 'metaphysical dialogue.'[279] The concept of a metaphysical dialogue is oxymoronic, or at least fragmentary, in the sense that the subject of its existential conversation is timeless; but at the same time, existentialism and classical metaphysics share the idea that 'a reality other than man has a share in the constitution of human being *qua* being and *qua* human: a reality which cannot be either nature which is less than human, or historical action which is only human.'[280]

Fackenheim dramatizes the imagined dialogue in his Epilogue to the lecture. Coleridge, in the British Museum, reads a copy of a book by Schelling, written while the latter was under the influence of Fichte's extreme concept of human self-constitution, according to which there is no otherness present in human self-constitution. 'Schelling writes: *"Ich bin, weil ich bin. Das ergreift jeden plotzlich."* "I am because I am. This truth seizes hold, all of a sudden, of everyone."'[281] In reaction, Coleridge writes in the margin of the book: '"*Jeden?*" Everyone? I doubt it. Many may say: I am because God made me.'[282] This anecdote incorporates two of Strauss's theses. First, it parallels the paradox that guided the historical school, that a truth that is universal must be true also of individuals only. Second, because Fackenheim describes Coleridge's comment as both 'naive' and also 'profound,'[283] he attributes to Coleridge's thought its foundation in what Strauss had called common sense. One rises to metaphysical truth only by *remaining with* the surface of things, with the phenomena. The dialogue between the doctrine of historicity and the doctrine of permanent human nature takes place beyond, so to speak, the capability of their respective metaphysics, and below, so to speak, their respective logics.

The Problem of Historicism: Fackenheim the Theologian's Return to History

In 'Metaphysics and Historicity,' Fackenheim argues for the coexistence of the doctrine of historicity – which he sees as the inevitable, human situation in which philosophy presents itself – and timeless truth. The question that he poses toward the end of the lecture – whether a return to the metaphysics of Aristotle might be more desirable than a return to Hegel – opens up the question of why Fackenheim chooses the latter.[284] He seems to imply an answer when he suggests the particular temptation of the doctrine of historicity for the theologian:[285] the theologian wants, in order to preserve an enduring relationship with God – a relationship that is personal and unique yet is enacted with the universal and the enduring – to affirm that Being alters with each time period. For Fackenheim, who arrives at the conclusion that human being has changed as a result of the emergence of historicism in conjunction with situating historical events,[286] the Jewish God must remain the Sinaitic God, yet the relationship – Jewish theology itself – must be redefined. At the same time, his Jewish theology perpetuates rabbinic theology in its conception of hope:[287] Fackenheim establishes a new relationship to the old God by means of a doctrine of historicity that dialectically affirms the possibility[288] of both the revelation of the Sinaitic God and also a reappropriation and reenactment of the event of revelation as it is presented in rabbinic tradition.

But does Fackenheim's theological acceptance of the doctrine of historicity grow out of his critique of a metaphysics that objectifies the self and the other? Does it grow out of his sense of the rupture in thought effectuated by, alternatively, Hegel's or the Holocaust's, indelible alteration of human nature? Does it grow out of a conception of Jewish history that is fundamentally distinct from historicity but that informs historicity with Jewish self-understanding? Or is it all of the above?

Is the fragmentation of his response a manifestation of the need for 'something more than human' as Fackenheim humanly situates himself?

The problem implicit in such questions is clear enough to Fackenheim. Just as Strauss had concluded, so too he recognizes that theology cannot resolve the self-contradictions of philosophy, nor can philosophy those of theology. Fackenheim's 'Other *par excellence,*' or Strauss's mystery of being, cannot be disclosed either philosophically or theologically. Fackenheim writes that 'the theologian impairs the philosopher's freedom if he speaks on his behalf, as well as his own freedom when he makes faith and theology dependent on specific philosophies.'[289] Fackenheim might, as a *philosopher,* agree with Strauss's possible assessment of his theological work as analogous to the self-destructive work of the historical school, which, by adopting the eighteenth-century critique of natural right, elevated history above nature even as it sought to preserve the natural right tradition.[290] The destruction of the universal norms derived from nature, or implicit in classical conventionalism, may be understood to apply also to the application of the historical sense to revealed religion.[291] However, if, as a *theologian,* Fackenheim can find within the rabbinic tradition[292] a different conception of history, one from which a doctrine of historicity may be organically developed, and into which a timeless God may enter – if what he seeks to preserve is historically based already – the analogy between his work and the work of the historical school will not be applicable.

The problem between philosophy and theology goes two ways.[293] In good philosophical conscience, one might dismiss the rabbinic tradition as, in Strauss's sense, delusion-inducing, as removing human being from the phenomenon of revelation on which the tradition is based. On the other hand, one might recognize in the rabbinic tradition, or adapt from it, a specifically Jewish historical sense, based neither on objectification nor on the experience of thought, but rather on action involving an absolute Other and one's human self. These positions, of course, are not mutually exclusive, nor are they, for Fackenheim, clearly distinct. The possibility of a historicity, in Fackenheim's sense, developed organically out of rabbinic thought and not out of 'secularist interpretations of history,'[294] might issue in a historicism that poses no threat to the timeless truths experienced through rabbinic self-understanding.

Fackenheim chooses, in his thought since 1957,[295] to stand within what he refers to as 'covenantal affirmation.'[296] By standing within covenantal affirmation, he does not imply that he chooses theology over philosophy but only that his work as either a philosopher or as a theologian takes place within this commitment.[297] His justification for this choice is twofold:

> First, philosophy, no longer subject to theological exigencies, is free to go its own way, and encounters between philosophy and Judaism – if and when they occur – are more likely to be genuine ones; they are no longer suspect of being theologically staged. Second, theology, freed of its polemical posture, is freer to inspect its own domain, and philosophical thinking, *or something akin to it*, can take place within that domain.[298]

Fackenheim follows Strauss in his recognition of the need to return to the roots of both philosophy and revelatory theology, which bases reveal the fundamental distinctions between them. Even so, while he recognizes the mutual irrefutability, and mutual dependence, of philosophy and revelatory theology,[299] he concludes that revelation is 'not wholly' inaccessible to philosophical reason: revelation, within the limits of philosophy, is yet open to truths accepted only on the basis of commitment.[300] Fackenheim readily admits the ambiguity of this position: Can one who is a believer really be indifferent when philosophizing? Can one who is not, really be open to commitment?[301] Following, in a way, Strauss's articulation of the rediscovery of the authority of the surface of things, he posits the existence of an 'essence' of Judaism,[302] despite existentialist protests,[303] as the means by which to provide limitations to what can and cannot be assimilated to Judaism; but parting ways from Strauss, he seeks with this essence also to disclose an 'inner logic' of Judaism.[304] Fackenheim, in other words, resituates Strauss's project in the realms of metaphysics and theology.

   The positing of the essence of Judaism, at this stage in his development, is crucial for Fackenheim. First, it provides resistance against the reduction of revealed religion to historical religion, or the dissolution of history as it is conceived in rabbinic self-understanding into history as understood, for instance, by the historical school.[305] By positing that Judaism has an essence, Fackenheim, following Strauss, insists on the preservation of the distinction between revelation and philosophy, even though he does not limit, as Strauss does, revelation to the Bible.[306] At the same time, he provides a basis, within the stance of covenantal affirmation, from which something 'akin to' philosophy might emerge. Second, Fackenheim's positing of an essence of Judaism provides boundaries to the extent to which Judaism may allow historical events to inform its self-construction.[307] Judaism can endure, according to Fackenheim, only by being open to secular historical experience;[308] the positing of limitations to what can be assimilated into it safeguards Judaism's preservation even as Judaism remains open to secular historical experience. Openness to both historical events and philosophical thought becomes the basis for a historically based Judaism, even while the positing of an essence of Judaism provides the safeguard against its reduction to historicism.[309]

Of primary importance is the dialectic that emerges from the positing of an essence of Judaism in and of history: to be radically open to secular history is to recognize the limitations to thought within it. For instance, Heidegger's existentialism, though it purports to be based in empirical history, is, according to Fackenheim, unable to confront the possibility that a committed stance toward the Bible or religious traditions might inform knowledge. Heidegger dismisses any insight gained by Christian and especially Jewish sources.[310] It is Hegel who more appropriately, in Fackenheim's reading, approximates existentialism: by guessing 'that the World Spirit might emigrate from Germany and Europe to America Hegel's outlook is open. Heidegger merely updates ideological aberrations [for instance, that Europe, Germany, Nazism, are the centre of the world's fate] that have plagued the German mind ever since the Napoleonic wars, and certainly since the death of Hegel.'[311] By discovering a historically based Judaism within an era that defines itself as historicist, Fackenheim discovers also a tension between Judaism's openness and non-openness to its being informed by historical events: the 'inner logic' of Judaism must be informed by revelation as the means to its recognition of its need for 'something more than human,' and revelation must be informed by reason as the safeguard of the 'Other *par excellence.*'[312]

Fackenheim points us to his theological essay 'Judaism and the Meaning of Life'[313] as the clearest example of "philosophizing, or something akin to it."'[314] This essay emerges before his more mature thought, in 1966, but is instructive for our purposes because it both establishes the stance of covenantal affirmation that Fackenheim will assume for the remainder of his work and also provides a clear, early example of the direction of his thought with regard to the relation between philosophy and revelatory theology and the role of history in Jewish thought. While what Fackenheim conceives to be the understanding of history most consonant with Judaism's central tenets is ruptured with his later radical awakening to the Holocaust,[315] a look at his understanding of a philosophically conceived Jewish history will suggest the qualifications he means to apply to the doctrine of historicity.

Fackenheim begins the essay by stating that one of the ways in which religions differ is in their understandings of the boundaries, or even the possibility, of the divine–human encounter. This beginning is, of course, to provide a context, but also one notes that Fackenheim begins the essay from a position of neutrality. He then proceeds to define the primordial experience of Judaism as a 'mystery' in which the infinite, transcendent God 'bends down low so as to accept and confirm man in his finite humanity; and man, though met by Divine Infinity, yet may and must respond to this meeting in and through his finitude.'[316] The foundation of Judaism is defined by a dual or dialectical action: by encountering man, God distances him from Himself; by encountering God, man recognizes, yet also attempts to transcend, his finitude. Again, Fackenheim returns to neutrality: 'some scholars,' through 'modern prejudice,' deny that the God of early Judaism was infinite.[317] The process of Fackenheim's defining 'something akin to philosophizing' begins here, in his suggesting that these scholars confuse logic with religious reality. What matters as a *philosophic* position arising out of a standpoint of commitment is that even at its beginnings, the Jewish God was, objectively speaking, 'experienced and conceived as the all-demanding God.'[318] Again, as in 'Metaphysics and Historicity,' Fackenheim, following Strauss, critiques the failure of these scholars to begin below the logic, so to speak, with the surface of things. Yet, in contradistinction to Strauss, he points out the ontological significance of metaphysics.[319]

Fackenheim allows that, at its beginning, Judaism posited, not monotheism, but monolatry, or the acknowledgment of the existence of other gods, even while only one God is worshipped. But he suggests that the development into monotheism was 'only a question of time.'[320] This point is illustrative because Fackenheim claims also that progress from this primordial experience is illusory. Neither God's fundamental infinity, nor man's fundamental finiteness, has altered.[321] There is no progress beyond the meeting because nothing finite can be more ultimate than the meeting of the finite with the infinite.[322] Again, this meeting is an experience, a presence, of God, not a comprehension of a Cohenian God-idea. Progress has been made in the realm of logic, but not in the realm of metaphysics: the move from monolatry to monotheism was warranted once the experience of the 'all-demanding God' was reflected upon. But it is a return to the experience itself, away from the history of the experience of thought as manifested in idolatry, that issued in this progress.

Judaism's essence or core is the paradox implicit in the divine–human encounter. Because the relation between God and man, or infinity and finiteness, is dialectical, Fackenheim suggests that the core of Judaism is one 'marked by a fundamental tension.'[323] Modern attempts to impute to Judaism the notions of man's potential or partial divinity are antithetical to Jewish faith because they are 'unassimilable' to the 'miracle of miracles' at Judaism's core.[324] Rather than resolve the tension, as, for instance, ancient Epicureanism and modern Deism did by denying the possibility of the meeting, or understanding the meeting as a 'mystical conflux' in which man loses himself in infinity, Judaism resisted resolution of its fundamental tension.[325] Furthermore, this fundamental tension permeates all aspects of Judaism and, in consequence, establishes 'whatever meaning life acquires.'[326]

Philosophy, on the other hand, seeks to resolve tensions. Philosophical concepts such as progress, or philosophy in general, cannot recognize the meaning of Jewish history because the meaning for human life derived from the dialectical encounter is not wholly finite and cannot be understood in wholly finite terms. However, despite the ultimate inexpressibility of the divine–human encounter, the encounter assumes in Judaism 'structure and content,'[327] and it is this structure and content that will provide for Fackenheim a means of philosophizing (or something akin to it) about Jewish history. Again, the structure and content of Judaism is a dialectic between God and man, a covenantal relation in which God commands, and man obeys, while yet he is free to rebel; in which God is at times far, and at times near, a relationship that allows God's commands to be freely chosen.[328]

At this point in the essay,[329] Fackenheim begins discussion of the topic that is most pressing to our concerns: the Jewish understanding of history. Universalism and particularism are united in this understanding of history: history is not an abstraction; rather, it is comprised of particular, unique events, and, at the same time, comprises a coherent or universal whole.[330] When God enters history, in Jewish understanding, He, while remaining transcendent, singles out individuals and issues commands for the particular here-and-now in which a prophet lives. Each new incursion of God is connected to the past incursion at Sinai and leaves open its ultimate future meaning: the meaning of Jewish history as a whole is directionality.[331] 'A crucial dimension of meaning in Judaism is therefore historical.'[332] Furthermore, the Jewish concept of historical is not the same as that of modern philosophy: history in Jewish terms is both experiential and beyond experience. While modern philosophy (empiricism, positivism or 'left-wing Hegelianism,' the internalization of God[333]) has attempted to resolve fundamental contradictions by presuming that all is explicable, Fackenheim suggests that this presumption cannot *disprove* the meaning of Jewish history: it merely *precludes* the possibility of its having meaning. Judaism, in order to continue to issue in meaning for Jewish life, must retain the fundamental paradox of its core.[334]

As mentioned above, Fackenheim does not mean to suggest that because there is no progress from the experience of the all-demanding God, there is no progress in the logic by which human beings come to know this experience. The understanding of history changes from, for instance, the Book of Judges;[335] but while Fackenheim, following Buber, takes seriously the Bible as an independent account of revelation, his choice to stand within covenantal affirmation[336] means that, moving beyond Buber, he accepts as authoritative those changes as conceived and modified by the rabbinic tradition.[337] According to Fackenheim, the rabbis reflected explicitly on 'the inextricable connection between Divine-human mutuality and Divine unilateralness.'[338] Although the rabbis of the Talmud recognize the contradiction between human freedom and Divine omnipotence, they do not resort to philosophy; they accept the fundamentally paradoxical nature of the experience of revelation in history.[339] History is 'wholly in Divine hands'; but at the same time, 'man has a share in making it'; the meaning of history applies both to the 'domain of pure spirit' and also to 'worldly fortune, good or ill.'[340]

One notes the similarities between Fackenheim's understandings of the need for transcendence at the heart of the doctrine of historicity and of the paradoxical mystery that is the core of history in Jewish self-understanding. It is impossible, in Fackenheim's thought, to separate the meaning of and in the historical present – a present that includes the doctrine of historicity as informative of that present – from the meaning of and in the Jewish historical present because the meaning of Jewish history must, paradoxically, include its connections to both the Jewish past and future, and also to objective criteria by which to find meaning. It is therefore impossible to determine whether his philosophical concern with the doctrine of historicity is informed by his theological concern for Jewish continuity, or whether his understanding of the meaning of Jewish history is informed by his philosophic concern for the doctrine of historicity.[341] Insofar as he applies the standards derived from Strauss, Fackenheim philosophizes, but his philosophizing is only 'something akin to philosophizing' insofar as he remains concerned by the particularity of Jewish self-understanding.[342]

Conclusion

Fackenheim discovers through Strauss's work the necessity of the return to the roots of philosophy in order to avoid the self-destruction of philosophy, revelatory religion and, indeed, standards of justice. Strauss traces this self-destruction to the acceptance of historicism, which, as he defines it, 'is nothing other than the petrified and self-complacent form of the self-criticism of the modern mind.'[343] The adoption of the historical sense and, most important, of the belief in the superiority of the present, according to Strauss, has led to an idealism that defies the authority of the surface of things – and, indeed, common sense – by attempting to elicit knowledge from the mind without input from external phenomena; or, alternatively, by defining knowledge as what is gleaned from the experience of the history of thought. This knowledge surreptitiously undermines the mutual irrefutability of the claims of reason and revelation because the experience of thought is its exclusive source.[344] In its most radical form, historicism undermines all authority, and Strauss seems at times to simply identify it with nihilism.[345] At other times, he seems to identify the adoption of the historical sense with the source from which 'pseudo-philosophies' emerge.[346]

By adopting a philosophic stance in his quest to discover the claims of revelation, Strauss discovers also a ground neutral to Judaism and Christianity. Paradoxically, the rediscovery of the separate claims of revelation, by providing limits to what man can know rationally, serves also to reveal the claims of a philosophy of timeless truths.[347] Philosophy in the classical sense may be articulated, and the passions inspired by revelatory religion may be abated. Strauss finds this neutral ground in natural theology, which he takes to be questions about God and divine things whose answers are limited by the human ability for reason. Furthermore, only by formulating natural theology as neutral to the revelatory religions can Maimonides, for instance, remain an authority for Judaism.[348] According to one thinker, 'Strauss's theism ... explains his anti-historicism in general.'[349] His rediscovery of the classical notion of natural right implies his application of reason to the question 'What is God?' to ascertain an objective measure of duties, rather than a sidestepping of the question by adopting an anthropocentric, historically bound measure of rights, as, for instance, we see the beginnings of in Machiavelli and Hobbes.

Furthermore, there is an inherent connection between Strauss's antihistoricism and his hermeneutics: there is, according to him, 'no reason to question a thinker of the past unless his problems are our problems and unless we are ready to admit the possibility that, for example, Plato was right.'[350] Strauss's hermeneutics consist of two principles. First, a reader should follow, not guide, a writer. Readers must return to the surface of a text, to the way arguments are presented, and to the phenomena on which the permanent questions of philosophy are based. When a reader criticizes a thinker of the past by going outside the framework the writer himself has established, he is superimposing 'his own notions of the past onto the past even before he discovers what the ancients thought of a particular issue,'[351] and he is presuming implicitly the superiority of the modern point of view.[352]

Second, a reader should remain aware that a writer may omit his most important point, either for reasons of censorship or persecution, or simply because he 'accepts the distinction between esoteric and exoteric thought.'[353] The historicist method of reading a text – exemplified in Collingwood's idea that the knowledge or thought of a given time is valid for that time and, therefore, when we study a text of the past, our study is foreign to the interests of that period[354] – has it exactly backward. For Strauss, a philosophical text does not express or reveal a given society, but rather protects philosophy against a given society or is written despite the existence of a given society.

Strauss rejects historicism as neither rationally nor theologically authorized, nor as able to provide a hermeneutic through which to either establish authority or become cognizant of alternative authorities. Through his discovery of the natural as the means to the permanent human problems, Strauss suggests the possibility of an alternative viewpoint from which to view the historical sense.[355] He notes that the attainment of this viewpoint may exist only according to philosophy's own self-interpretation. His choice of nature, then, is not so cleanly cut: he recognizes that, as a modern, he may find it impossible to escape the historical sense. His return to classical natural right may be an act of will, guided by knowledge. What is more, his return requires the stopgap measure of accepting, to a limited extent, a historical sense, as a means of returning to the original cave.

Fackenheim, for his part, adopts Strauss's recognition of the injustice that can result when history is made to claim universal validity instead of being restricted to a particular object of study of which only certain examples have been chosen – and furthermore, the injustice that can result by claiming universal validity through a process that understands the past through the criteria of the present. For him, as well as for Strauss, knowledge must remain bound to its roots, to its surface, must remain ultimately self-limited by philosophy's inability to incorporate the claims of revelation, and by revelation's, of philosophy.[356] His qualification of his historicism, manifested in his earlier work by his recognition of the need for transcendence within experience, and in *To Mend the World* as his 'proof' that resistance is an ontological category, may be seen as a consequence of this self-limitation.[357]

While Fackenheim recognizes the possibility of Strauss's choice of returning to the doctrine of natural right as the means of limiting the scope of historicism, he chooses to return to the root of history as a means to same end. He retains Strauss's affirmation that knowledge must issue from the root of things, even as he defines the fundamental root of history as revelation. His return to the root of history has as its impetus the possibility of providing the human being with a relationship with the Absolute. One might understand Fackenheim's work as involving a dilemma different from Strauss's less than absolute choice between nature and history.[358] For Fackenheim, the choice is rather between history as understood within and without what he defines as the 'midrashic framework.'[359] He does not so readily accept Strauss's position that Jewish philosophy is an oxymoron; rather, he attempts to join together these two things, even as he recognizes the irreconcilable opposition between reason and revelation.

In order to understand Fackenheim's thought with regard to history and historicism, one must recognize that he chooses to work within the stance of covenantal affirmation. His goal is to adapt the living rabbinic tradition to the claims of both a non-historicized philosophy and also the possibility of revelation as a present actuality. Nature as an organizing principle cannot be a choice for him because it presupposes a world view that begins and ends outside what he recognizes as the rabbinic framework. One might suggest that Strauss's practical choice of nature is a choice that organizes knowledge through reason that remains open to the possibility of revelation; for Fackenheim, knowledge is organized through revelation, made reasonable – or reason, informed with general or Jewish revelation – but having its ultimate source in God.[360]

For Fackenheim, two considerations mandate the return to Hegel. First, from the perspective of the philosophical, Hegel, through his reconciliation of the philosophical concern for eternity and the religious concern for history, begins the process through which philosophy is informed by the historical sense. Second, from the perspective of the historical, Hegel's reconciliation issues in the fact that experience itself is informed by thought. Hegel's thought begins a process of dialogical openness between philosophy and history, which, if maintained, both need not decay into historicism and also can be, in a sense, self-corrective.[361] 'All genuine dialogical thought begins not in a vacuum but "where one is." Its post-Hegelian setting makes this "where one is" more than an arbitrary personal given but also, and at the same time, a given in the Western religious-secular situation.'[362] For Fackenheim, as long as thought remains connected to its roots, though those roots be based in history, radical historicism can be avoided.[363]

Strauss himself seems to allow the possibility of Hegelianism as an immediate measure by which to challenge the relativism that results from the adoption of historicism:[364]

> The situation [of their not existing eternal verities based on empiricism] would be entirely different if one could assume the possibility of a peak of experience, of an absolute moment in history, in which the fundamental condition of man is realized for the first time and in principle fully. But this would also mean that in the most important respect history, or progress, would have come to its end.[365]

While Strauss rejects the 'decayed Hegelianism'[366] of an optimism preserved after the abandonment of its authority, and rejects also the existentialism that serves to overcome the resultant relativism, he does not explore – for reasons that may at this point be apparent – the possibility of Hegel's conception of history (as opposed to his philosophy) as legitimate. This is Fackenheim's starting point. And while Fackenheim, for his own reasons, rejects Hegel's Absolute Idealism, he does not reject his work as a historian: Hegel's conception of the infinite within history resonates to him as the Jewish conception of history, modernized insofar as the empirical data that give rise to this history inform secular history as well, but also retained insofar as, in the decisive respect, there is no progress from moment to moment, that each moment reflects the possibility of a moment of encounter with the Sinaitic God and so, the end or fulfilment, so to speak, of history.[367]

5 Reason and Revelation: Jewish Thought after Strauss and Fackenheim

Introduction

We saw in the last chapter that Fackenheim works as both a philosopher and a Jewish theologian and the problems that arise when he attempts to join together Jewish theology and philosophy. This chapter will explore more deeply the problematic involved: Strauss argues that philosophy and revelation are mutually irrefutable and that their separation is one means of retaining the vitality of the West. This chapter will begin with a discussion of the problem and the means by which Strauss and Fackenheim following him resolve it. Both thinkers, first of all, re-examine the roots of Western civilization, reason and revelation.[1] Second, both thinkers acknowledge the necessity of mutual openness between reason and revelation.[2] Third, both recognize the problematics involved with the adoption of modern idealism.[3] But Strauss's rejection and Fackenheim's quasi-adoption of the rabbinic tradition insofar as it is dramatized in the 'midrashic framework'[4] will issue in dramatic differences in the way in which each thinker achieves his ends. Because in Strauss's view, a practical choice must be made between philosophy and revelatory theology, the section 'Strauss: Jerusalem and Athens' will explore which choice, if either, Strauss made. The chapter will then discuss Fackenheim's critique of Strauss's recovery of Plato. Implicit in this discussion is the problem of evil, which for believers in an omnipotent and good God is a fundamental problem. It is not as fundamental for those who consider evil (vice, defect) as the natural opposite of good.

Both Strauss and Fackenheim recognize the need to avoid dogmatism in any form. Strauss attempts to recover philosophy as a way of life that is, on the theoretic level, above hope and fear, a life in quest of the good life. He writes:

> If there is no standard higher than the ideal of our society, we are utterly unable to take a critical stance from that ideal. But the mere fact that we can raise the question of the worth of the ideal of our society shows that there is something in man that is not altogether in slavery to his society, and therefore that we are able, and hence obliged, to look for a standard with reference to which we can judge of the ideals of our own as well as of any other society.[5]

For Strauss, the theoretic solution takes the form of moving away from religious constructions of hope and despair and rediscovering the priority of the intelligible realm.[6] Because knowledge of the intelligibles cannot reveal the practicalities of how to be a good citizen of a particular *polis*, there needs as well to be a recognition that one follow the laws of one's society. Those citizens who know the intelligibles must be discreet and must stay away from government.[7] Strauss's solution, following Maimonides, is to carve out a space for philosophical thought even while affirming ascription to Law.[8]

Strauss adopts and addresses the classical problem of the relationship between the good citizen and the good state[9] – or between the practical and the theoretical. According to him, two things move human beings: love of the good and love of one's own. There is only one case in which these loves coincide, and that is in the case of the best (ideal) regime. Since all other regimes are less than perfect, there exists a tension between love of the good and love of one's own. In theoretic terms, then, there is no separation between them: one must go through love of one's own to arrive at love of the good. In practical terms, however, this goal cannot be achieved. In *Natural Right and History*, Strauss suggests that love of the good is higher and corresponds to our intellectual part; but love of one's own is primary. It corresponds to what Plato calls our spirited part (*thumos*),[10] and in order to love virtue, one must love it spiritedly. One might understand the relationship between love of the good and love of one's own as each both necessary and more important from the perspective of the other.[11] In Thomas L. Pangle's formulation:

> The dialectic of the *Laws* needs to be complemented or completed by the dialectic of the *Republic*. But it has this key advantage over that of the *Republic*: certain essential first principles which are taken for granted in the

Republic are not taken for granted but are instead demonstrated dialectically in the *Laws*: 'in the *Republic*, reason or intellect guides the foundation
of the city from the beginning.'[12] The *Laws*, it would seem, is understood
by Strauss to exemplify the art of conversational examination by which
one can ascend from the quarrel between reason and revelation to its resolution.[13]

Knowledge of the intelligibles, according to Strauss, has no direct practical influence on the state, nor can it alone issue in knowledge of the
mystery of being.

Fackenheim, on the other hand, believes that there can be no ideal to
which to aspire because idealism is implicitly antithetical to Judaism;
it is implicitly idolatrous.[14] Hegel's attraction for Fackenheim is his attempt to synthesize the timeless truths garnered through philosophy
with the hope implicit in the religious concern for history. Strauss attempts to forestall the adoption of modern idealism by recovering, for
instance, Platonic thought in its self-understanding, which is thought
that manifests a dialectical relation between its ideals and its self-mock-
ery of those ideals, or between its theoretical ideal state – which it self-
consciously knows cannot be implemented in reality – and its practical
resolution of theory and practice. Fackenheim's philosophy, or 'something akin to it,'[15] is precluded from reverting to idealism through its
incorporation of Hegel's concern for history, or through the application
to Hegelianism of Hegel's historically self-corrective philosophy.[16]

By building on the universality not of philosophic thought, but of
the possibility of actual religious experience for Jews and for Christians, Fackenheim furthers a 'new thinking' that is built on hope. His
philosophy is an overcoming of the despair of Auschwitz even as – at
least in his later thought – it, so to speak, brings the despair into the
present and is, at the same time, a mending of the religious differences
that inspire and promote historical calamity. Fackenheim works within
the stance of covenantal affirmation even as he adopts from Strauss
the critique of modern liberal idealism, a critique that issues both in
the recovery of the surface of things and in the fundamental openness
that mutually informs the more ascended forms of reason and revelation. For Strauss, Fackenheim's stance within covenantal affirmation
cannot lend itself to the surface of things as understood by philosophy
because it is known only from hearsay or alternatively, because it presumes already the foundation of Judaism: that God is a person or that
God created the world out of nothing.[17] For Fackenheim, Judaism, be-

cause it intertwines, for instance, belief and action, defines committed experience as the surface of things.[18] The choice of the philosophical way of life, in Strauss's view, requires an openness to the possibility of revelation, but the converse is not true: revelation can be open to philosophy only as its handmaiden. Fackenheim disagrees: because God is a person, experience of God is genuine; the transmittal of the tradition through reenactment translates hearsay into what one sees with one's own eyes.[19] Only through the rabbinic tradition, albeit opened up to the secular experience that defines contemporary life, can Judaism persist and can Jews continue to hope that they may have an *actual* experience of God, and further, that this actual experience will be with the same God who appeared at Sinai.

Whereas Fackenheim makes a commitment to ground Judaism in the simultaneity of revelation and revelatory theology – though, again, that revelation and that theology may be irretrievable and/or contentless in the present – Strauss rejects such grounding as a misconception of the nature of authority: it is only through doubt of authority that philosophy – knowledge based on common sense or the surface of things – can arise. Fackenheim cannot formulate his religio-secular Judaism in this way because for him, Judaism cannot be understood within the context of religion-in-general: Judaism's theological tradition, for one instance, does not separate the particularism of the election of the Jews from the universal of humankind. Working as a philosopher, Strauss humanly understands – or redefines – revelation within the terms of natural theology; his thought about revelation moves in the realm of philosophy, and he is able to affirm the existence of religion-in-general. With this affirmation, he is able to promote the claims of revelation because he is able to establish for those claims a common sense basis; they are able to serve as a source of authority.[20] In this sense, Strauss's natural theology is not identical with atheism: paradoxically, his affirmation of natural theology as the ground of religion promotes the authority of the claims of revelation.[21]

For Strauss, although truth itself remains elusive, the activity of loving truth renders existent the good life. The practical choice of philosophy over revelatory theology has less to do with one's determination of whether to manifest one's thinking as experience than with the decision to carve out a realm whose determination remains distinct from the revelatory theological and whose content remains permanently valid. For Fackenheim, truth rests ultimately in the *relationship* with God, the source of all existence – even if God does not exist. The quest for truth consists in being not good, but rather holy, because God is holy. His is not a search for the permanent but rather imitation and observance of the holy within temporal limits. Although, according to Fackenheim, the Holocaust has ruptured the flow and permutations of revelatory theology within history – indeed has raised the possibility of God's non-existence – to minimize or even dismiss the relevance of the historical or experiential dimension is to preclude the existence of the holy and the possibility of the Jews and the Jewish God to inform the realm of existence. Strauss rejects the historical prejudice and rejects also the grounding of thought on experience, Jewish or otherwise (although Jewish experience may have important implications for human existence). Fackenheim's dialectic of thought and experience renders pertinent to philosophy both human evil against Jews and also Jewish responses against human evil; Strauss's rejection of the historical sense safeguards philosophy from the escalation of passions that results from the experience of evil.

Strauss: Jerusalem and Athens

> We see at once that each of the two claims to be true wisdom, thus denying to the other its claim to be wisdom in the strict and highest sense. According to the Bible, the beginning of wisdom is fear of the Lord; according to the Greek philosophers, the beginning of wisdom is wonder. We are thus compelled from the very beginning to make a choice, to take a stand.[22]

As we have seen above,[23] the claims of reason are dependent on those of revelation. Strauss recognizes that philosophy must grant (in the absence of refutation) the possibility of revelation: philosophy cannot demonstrate or prove revelation false. For Fackenheim, the claims of reason and revelation are mutually interdependent: just as philosophy cannot disprove revelation, the Bible recognizes that it must represent God in (alien) human terms.[24] Because, according to Strauss, as a practical matter one must choose whether to be a philosopher or a theologian, the question arises whether he chose ultimately Jerusalem or Athens.[25] Although he clearly was not a theologian and did not work on rabbinic texts,[26] Strauss's reading of the Bible was conducted with a respect equal to the respect that he afforded the great thinkers of philosophy.[27] So, for instance, Strauss inspired in at least one student what one might call a theological approach to the Bible: '[Leon R. Kass] consistently treats the biblical text as richer than any rational interpretation we can offer – and yet he himself mines those riches so well that he invites his skeptical readers to ignore or forget his humble, even pious, stance. He charms the skeptic into respecting and then embracing Genesis as a source of wisdom.'[28] The importance of this inspiration cannot be overstated: Strauss is combating Spinoza's dismissal of the biblical text as a source of authority.[29] He writes of Spinoza that 'the result of his criticism can be summarized as follows: the Bible consists to a considerable extent of self-congratulatory assertions, of remnants of ancient prejudices or superstitions, and of the outpourings of an uncontrolled imagination; in addition it is poorly compiled and poorly preserved.'[30] Spinoza suggests that 'our ignorance of the power of nature disqualifies us from ever having recourse to supernatural causation.'[31] But Spinoza's position, according to Strauss, ignores the fact that 'the positive mind, applying precise observation and stringent analysis, is incapable of perceiving miracles.'[32] The introduction of Spinoza's biblical hermeneutics, which preclude without validation the possibility of miracles, marks the beginning of the modern dissociation from the common sense on which revelatory authority – and indeed reason – are based.[33]

Despite Strauss's obvious respect for the biblical text and his recognition that 'in the case of revelation, there are no impartial observers ... All witnesses are adherents, and all transmitters were believers,'[34] he does not read the Bible through the eyes of the rabbis, that is, through the experiential component of the transmitters.[35] For Strauss, the authority of revelation can be recognized only from the human perspective: the Bible does not include the mystery of being itself. One may recognize its authority as the *record* of the mystery of being. The Bible's authority is necessarily translated into what is accessible to common sense.[36] When Strauss translates revelation into the *idea* of revelation – or strips from revelation its 'historical' component – he is not diminishing but rather augmenting the claims of revelation and the claims of the mystery of being itself.

What are accessible in the Bible to common sense are those things in it that are based in natural law. In the Bible's own terms, there is no recognition of natural law: 'there is no Hebrew-biblical term for nature, the Hebrew word being derived very indirectly from a Greek word which is an equivalent of "nature" in Greek, *charakter*, *teva* in Hebrew.'[37] But from the perspective of common sense, one can find in the Bible things based in natural law. Strauss reads the medieval thinkers in order to discover a distinction between natural law as conventional and therefore irrational and natural law as rational precepts and therefore necessary.[38] What one can know of the claims of revelation must be disentangled from its conventional (political) context. Just as philosophy comes into being through doubt of authority, so too the claims of revelation are illuminated when one recognizes the distinction between the authority of the mystery of being and revelatory theology. According to one scholar, '[Strauss's] theory of natural law is essentially an interpretation of theism as attainable through reason.'[39]

While Strauss upholds the claims of revelation in his hermeneutics, one may or may not choose to uphold the authority of religion in practice. Of al-Farabi,[40] Strauss writes that he 'virtually denied all cognitive value to religion, and yet considered conformity with the laws and the beliefs of the religious community in which one is brought up as a necessary qualification for the future philosopher.'[41] Strauss creates, one might say, an artificial realm in which the idea of revelation coexists with philosophy; and from this realm – because theory must be open to practice – a Jew may choose to live as a Jew and think as a philosopher.[42] Strauss's commitment to Judaism is not trivial; it is the necessary outcome of recognizing that if philosophy is to be the search for wisdom, it must recognize that its wisdom is self-limited, that it begins, of necessity, with a denial of revelation on its own terms. Strauss, according to one of his students, 'made many of his students, both Jews and Gentiles, take their religious heritage seriously.'[43] This is the dimension of his thought that Fackenheim picks up: when Strauss writes that 'Emil Fackenheim is among American Jews the one best equipped by virtue of his devoutness and his knowledge to pave the way for future Jewish thought,'[44] he accords to Fackenheim the recognition that revelatory theology must acknowledge the claims of both Jerusalem to devoutness and Athens to knowledge.

Strauss's examination of the antagonism and common ground between the Bible and philosophy must – because it is a philosophic question – move in the realm of philosophy. To begin, he argues for the philosophic position that 'only through knowledge of the good can [man] find the good that he needs.'[45] The question by which philosophy opens itself to the claim of revelation is whether a person can know the good through his own natural reason or whether he requires divine revelation. Strauss argues that 'philosophy or science in the original sense of the term' is characteristic of the pursuit of natural reason, whereas the Bible is characteristic of the need for divine revelation.[46] Because the Bible claims 'a life of obedient love' as the only thing the human being needs, whereas philosophy claims 'a life of free insight' as the only thing he needs, there can be no harmonization and no syn-thesis of these two means of pursuing knowledge of the good.[47] The at-tempt to make such a synthesis has always sacrificed one to the other.[48] As Strauss formulates it, 'philosophy, which means to be queen, must be made the handmaid of revelation or vice versa.'[49]

Were we to step back from the syntheses and harmonizations be-tween philosophy and the Bible that have been attempted to resolve what Strauss calls 'the secular struggle between philosophy and the-ology,'[50] we would see clearly that neither has succeeded in refuting the other. Strauss's use of the word 'secular' suggests that he is refer-ring only to the this-worldly harmonizations; his implication is that philosophy and theology may exist within 'hailing distance' of each other beyond what can be put into this-worldly, or human, terms.[51] Phi-losophy refutes revelatory theology only when philosophy is presup-posed; revelatory theology refutes philosophy only when revelation is presupposed.

Strauss suggests that revelation seems ultimately to refute philoso-phy. First, since revelation cannot convince 'unassisted reason' of its authority, the human being seeks through 'free investigation ... [to] articulat[e] the riddle of being.'[52] Yet because he recognizes the limita-tion of human knowledge, the human being recognizes that he is need-ful of seeking divine guidance, 'and the possibility of revelation cannot be refuted.'[53] 'Philosophy has to grant that revelation is possible.'[54] The problem with this position is that it denies philosophy's basic premise: that its pursuit provides the possibility of the one thing needful to the human being. Philosophy cannot provide the one right life because it would rest on the principle that philosophy itself is not necessary, that is, that revelation is a possibility; 'philosophy ... would itself rest on an unevident, arbitrary, or blind decision.'[55] Philosophy would seem to have proved revelation's thesis that revelation's pursuit provides the only 'possibility of consistency, of a consistent and thoroughly sincere life.'[56] Since philosophy claims the sphere of refutation, and since phi-losophy cannot refute revelation, philosophy, so to speak, disproves itself. Strauss sums up succinctly: 'The mere fact that philosophy and revelation cannot refute each other would constitute the refutation of philosophy by revelation.'[57]

The conclusion above outlined, however, is based only on how things seem – motivated, perhaps, by the desire for consistency or a completed system of knowledge. In his lecture 'Progress or Return?' Strauss sug-gests that 'the whole history of the West presents itself *at first glance* as an attempt to harmonize, or to synthesize, the Bible and Greek philoso-phy.'[58] The misunderstanding garnered by this first glance arises from the fact that, although the two roots of Western civilization cannot be harmonized or synthesized, each philosophy and the Bible can use the 'one thing needful' posited by the other.[59] So, for instance, 'Greek phi-losophy can *use* obedient love in a subservient function, and the Bible can *use* philosophy as a handmaid.'[60] Because philosophy and the Bible are able to engage each other in order to disagree, Strauss discovers that there must be an area of agreement that is more than formal between them. He locates this agreement in what he identifies as 'the problem of divine law'; their disagreement is the means by which each resolves that problem.[61]

Strauss suggests that the Bible and Greek philosophy agree in their rejection of what would become elements of modernity such as anthro-pocentrism, the primacy of rights over duty (which replaces virtue with freedom and posits ultimately that human-ness must be acquired), and the nineteenth-century dependence on history, a dependence freely created as the limitation on freedom by the human being's past use of freedom.[62] He reduces this agreement to 'only an implicit one' and suggests that 'we should rather look at the agreement as it appeared directly in the texts.'[63] Strauss argues for the recovery of the surface of the texts in order to recognize the respective authorities from which their ideas arise. To adopt only their implicit argreement would be to adopt a historical sense with which to approach the texts. The Bible and Greek philosophy agree, according to Strauss, 'regarding the im-portance of morality, regarding the content of morality, and regarding its ultimate insufficiency. They differ as regards that "x" which sup-plements or completes morality, or, which is another way of putting it, they disagree as regards the basis of morality.'[64]

Strauss suggests, in agreement with some theologians, that 'the sec-ond table of the Decalogue, as the Christians call it,' may be identified with natural law as understood in Greek philosophy.[65] Both Aristotle and Moses knew 'that murder, theft, adultery, etc., are unqualifiedly bad.'[66] Also, both Greek philosophy and the Bible promote the patriar-chal family as the means to frame moral behaviour. Women are deemed inferior in both texts. Neither Greek philosophy nor the Jewish Bible permits the worship of any human being. Justice, understood 'primari-ly [as] obedience to the law' – both human law and moral and religious law – is promoted by both texts as a virtue.[67] Because obedience to the law means, for both the Bible and Greek philosophy, obedience also to a moral and religious law, obedience to the prescripts of either text means the adherent must be guided in all aspects of his life by this law. Strauss concludes that in both the Bible and the Greek texts, law and justice are understood as divine law and divine justice; both systems of life are theocracies. Both praise humility, and both affirm the reality of divine retribution. Furthermore, 'the Bible and Greek philosophy agree not merely regarding the place which they assign to justice, the connection between justice and law, the character of law, and divine retribution. They also agree regarding the problem of justice, the difficulty created by the misery of the just and the prospering of the wicked.'[68]

Strauss suggests at this point in the lecture that the reader note that he has 'tacitly replaced morality by justice, understanding by "justice" obedience to the divine law.'[69] This replacement will mark the fundamental discrepancy between biblical and Greek thought. But also this hint serves as a means of dramatizing the 'hailing distance' between Greek philosophy and the Bible: the place where they agree – their recognition of justice and its primary importance – is precisely the place where they disagree, as each tries to resolve the problem of the inadequacy to human life of this concept of justice.[70]

Rather than proceeding directly in the lecture to spelling out the root of the antagonism between the Bible and Greek philosophy, Strauss first 'enumerat[es] some of its consequences.'[71] This procedure issues from Strauss's beginning with things as they appear to us, that is, with the texts insofar as each is an authority from which ideas may ascend. He begins with Aristotle's *Ethics*, 'as the most perfect, or certainly the most accessible, presentation of philosophic ethics.'[72] Aristotle crowns his ethics with two virtues, justice and magnanimity. Each justice and magnanimity comprises all the other virtues, but justice does so 'insofar as the actions from them relate to other men,' magnanimity, 'insofar as they enhance the man himself.'[73] The reader now discovers that the 'close kinship' between Greek and biblical conceptions of justice refers to the first virtue that comprises all the other virtues: how one treats others. Magnanimity is alien to the Bible: 'biblical humility excludes magnanimity in the Greek sense.'[74] Biblical humility mandates that right human action be circumscribed by obedience to God. So, for instance, when Saul disobeys God by sparing Agag, God rejected him; and when Jonathan does not vie with David for kingship of Israel, though Jonathan be a 'perfect gentleman,' God elected David, who was not.[75]

Furthermore, the Bible rejects the Greek concept of magnanimity by emphasizing one's duty to the poor as a duty to be fulfilled precisely *because* it is commanded by God. While the Greek philosophers, according to Strauss, also did not worship wealth, Socrates, for instance, recognized that 'as far as the general run of men is concerned, virtue presupposes a reasonable economic underpinning.'[76] In contrast, the Bible goes so far as to identify the terms 'poor' and 'pious' or 'just,'[77] eliminating altogether the possibility of magnanimity figuring into its conception of justice. And this rejection is deep: 'Magnanimity presupposes a man's conviction of his own worth. It presupposes that man is capable of being virtuous, thanks to his own efforts.'[78] Greek philosophy, according to the biblical perspective, is 'heartless'; it considers it beneath the virtuous human being to be conscious of his own shortcomings.[79] While Strauss recognizes that 'the Greek philosophers differed as to whether man can become fully virtuous,' he who would deny this possibility 'merely replaces the self-satisfaction or self-admiration of the virtuous man, by the self-satisfaction or self-admiration of him who steadily progresses in virtue.'[80] Furthermore, it is because the Greek philosophers reject the sense of shame in the good man that Plato, for instance, disallows tragedy in his best city[81] and that Aristotle allows tragedy for the purpose only of catharsis of the multitude's fear and pity. Without fear and pity, Strauss suggests, feelings of guilt may not arise.

Religion, on the other hand, from the human point of view, arises from feelings of fear and pity. One fears God, who unites humankind in brotherhood and thus enables and sanctifies pity.[82] For Aristotle, one must be liberated from these feelings in order to turn oneself 'wholeheartedly to noble action.'[83] Again, from the religious perspective, 'Greek philosophy has frequently been blamed for the absence from it of that ruthless examination of one's intentions which is the consequence of the biblical demand for purity of the heart.'[84] In contradistinction to this demand, Greek philosophy affirms the necessity of knowing oneself, to 'know what it means to be a human being, know what is the place of man in the universe, examine your opinions and prejudices, rather than "Search your heart."'[85]

Despite the antagonism between them, and putting aside the Bible's rejection of magnanimity, the Bible and Greek philosophy agree that the attainment of either a pure heart, or of knowing oneself, cannot be achieved by moral demands alone. It is in their solutions to the insufficiency of morality that the Bible and Greek philosophy differ. For the Greek philosophers, contemplation or understanding completes morality; for the Bible, 'humility, a sense of guilt, repentance, and faith in divine mercy' complete morality.[86] The difference in these resolutions affects how the moral demands are understood. So, for instance, the Bible completes morality with humility, and so on, which serve to promote the existence of the community of the faithful; the Bible 'necessarily strengthen[s] the majesty of moral demands.'[87] On the other hand, since the Greek philosophers complete morality with contemplation – which is an individual or asocial activity – the force of moral demands tends to be weakened. The source of this weakening is that 'this demand is not backed up by divine promises.'[88] The Greek philosopher does not live in hope, and his wisdom does not begin in fear. Rather, he lives 'above hope,' and his wisdom begins in a sense of wonder.[89] Strauss remarks on the 'serenity' with which the Greek philosopher is able to live. For contrast he notes that in the Bible, David, who breaks the terms, so to speak, of God's promise to the human being, is 'seriously and ruthlessly rebuke[d]' for one murder and one act of adultery; in Greek thought, on the other hand – for instance, in Xenophon's *Hiero, or, On Tyranny* – a Greek poet-philosopher attempts to convince a tyrant who has committed many murders that 'he would derive greater pleasure if he would have been more reasonable.'[90] In Greek thought, since there is no divine promise to back up moral demands, one must rely on one's own reasonable efforts to achieve morality. A second example of the difference made when moral demands are backed up by divine promises is the biblical story of the Akeda (Genesis 22), in which obedience – because a command is issued from God – is more highly valued than intelligibility. In Greek thought, without the backing of divine promise, Socrates is moved rather to examine the unintelligible saying of the Delphic oracle.[91]

The greater the God who issues the divine promise, the greater the force of moral demand on human action. The Bible, to strengthen the force of the divine promise, teaches that God is omnipotent. It presumes that God is the highest being: He is omnipotent insofar as all that exists, exists by virtue of God's will. For the Bible, 'the first cause is ... a person,'[92] and because God is a person, God is concerned with human beings absolutely. Furthermore, the Bible bases its teaching that religious experience is genuine, and that one therefore lives in hope and/or fear of the fulfilment and/or withdrawal of the divine promise, on its recognition of God as, so to speak, an omnipotent person.

Greek philosophy rejects the concept of God as either a person or as concerned for human beings absolutely as problematic; and this is true 'for every Greek philosopher.'[93] Greek thought teaches that although the gods can do anything, they do so by knowing the natures of things independent of themselves, and therefore 'they are capable of using all things properly.'[94] Greek thought establishes that there exists always 'an impersonal necessity higher than any personal being.'[95] Connected to its teaching of the impersonal necessity that exists above the gods, Greek thought teaches also 'the eternity of cosmos or chaos';[96] it therefore recognizes the soul as prior and self-generating.[97] Greek thought would at least suspend judgment as to whether to interpret religious experience as genuine.[98]

Strauss argues that the Bible's promotion and Greek thought's rejection of the role of experience in ascertaining truth marks a radical difference between them – not only with regard to each one's affirmation of its conception of the good life, but also with regard to the way in which a reader should approach each text. In the Bible, the only means by which God is known is through His actions and His revelations. 'The book, the Bible, is the account of what God has done and what He has promised.'[99] This means that human experience of God is the means by which God is known: 'This experience, and not reasoning based on sense perception, is the root of biblical wisdom.'[100] Furthermore, the Bible is a recording of religious experience. What Strauss labels the 'literary character' of the Bible is a dramatization of the priority of experience of the divine: the Bible is a compilation, and as such continues a tradition wherein few modifications have been made.[101] The human being does not of himself make a beginning; the beginning is ultimately God. The right way of life according to the Bible's teaching – in both its content and its form – is a life in imitation of God. The root of Greek wisdom, on the other hand, is demonstration, or sense perception and *noesis;* one can search for wisdom in Greek thought even in bypassing the gods. In addition, by suspending judgment as to whether experience is genuine, Greek thought expresses itself in books written by individual authors, books that each have a beginning in an individual. Its concept of the right way of life lies outside of experience and cannot therefore imply imitation.

At the root of the difference between the Bible and Greek thought regarding the interpretation of religious experience as genuine experience is the means by which each solves the problem of the insufficiency of divine justice. Strauss recognizes 'the equation of the good with the ancestral [a]s the primeval question,'[102] the answer to which defines the way in which each the Bible and Greek thought resolves the problem. The notion of custom or way as the regular manner in which, for instance, fire behaves is found in both the Bible and pre-philosophic Greek thought. And both biblical and pre-philosophic Greek thought equate one's own way with the good because one's own way is old. The ancestors, then, were superior. This superiority defines the ancestors 'as gods, or sons of gods, or pupils of gods.'[103] The right way is recognized by both the Bible and pre-philosophic Greek thought as the divine law. The Bible and Greek thought, however, deviate in how they develop from this common understanding, and this deviation is deeply problematic because each presumes that its right way is the only right way.

Greek thought, once it recognized the variations among cultures, according to Strauss, 'transcend[ed] this whole dimension, to find one's bearings independently of the ancestral.'[104] It realized that there is a distinction between the ancestral and the good although they at times coincide. How, then, does one 'find one's bearings in the cosmos'[105]? Strauss argues that philosophic Greek thought emerged as a result of the distinction between what one sees with one's own eyes and hearsay. It became clear, however, that what one demonstrates about the cosmos is of no avail unless there were a connection between the cosmos itself and the thinking of beings; in order for man to identify and separate those things that are manmade from those things that are 'natural,' the universe must have been made by thinking beings.[106] The process of demonstrating what one sees with one's own eyes and the ascent from it becomes the dimension from which the cosmos is understood. Divine law, understood by the Bible as the code of a personal God, is translated by Greek thought into what would be called the 'natural order,' or the quest for rational beginnings accomplished through a rational, or philosophic, methodology.[107] 'So the divine law, in the real and strict sense of the term, is only the starting point, the absolutely essential starting point, for Greek philosophy, but it is abandoned in the process.'[108]

The Bible, on the other hand, does not abandon its affirmation of the equation of the right way and divine law. It maintains that its view is the one true divine law. Other codes are manmade. It differs from myth,[109] because the Bible, like pre-philosophic Greek thought, recognizes 'the problem of the variety of the divine laws.'[110] As a consequence, the biblical author or authors incorporated the conditions that would be absolutely necessary to claim its code as the one true divine law. These conditions are 'it must be a personal God; the first cause must be God; He must be omnipotent, not controlled and not controllable.'[111] Because to know God would mean to control Him, later biblical thought incorporated the idea that God's essence is not knowable. The biblical understanding of essence, however, differs from the Greek understanding: for the Bible, essence is complete freedom, or unpredictability;[112] for Greek philosophy, essence is what something is eternally.[113] The connection between God – who is utterly inaccessible – and human beings is trustworthy from the human point of view because God has freely bound Himself to human beings through a covenant with them. Human beings have no necessary and no intelligible relationship to God; furthermore, the force of the divine promise is strengthened insofar as human beings did not enter into their relationship with God freely – they are commanded to enter into it.

The fact that Greek thought and the Bible share the problem of divine law emerges from each one's recognition of the variety of divine laws. They deviate in how they resolve that problem: Greek thought attempts to find an essential point of view from which to transcend the equation of the ancestral and the good – an equation by which various divine codes come into absolute conflict – and so to abandon the notion of divine law in the strict sense of the term. The Bible, on the other hand, retains its affirmation that its code is the one divine code and posits a personal and omnipotent God with whom its authors have made a covenant. The equation between the ancestral and the good is retained.

Strauss provides two examples to demonstrate their respective recognitions of the problem – although he recognizes, of course, that the Greek philosophers and the biblical authors did not know each other. It is striking that both texts or sets of texts recognize that there exists the 'alternative' of the divine.[114] On the one hand, from the Greek point of view, Strauss points out that the biblical injunction against rebellion from God is found in certain passages in Aristotle, wherein 'he speaks of certain very crude notions in Greece which pointed fundamentally to what we know in the Bible in a more developed form.'[115] On the other hand, the Bible expounds clearly and consistently, in two accounts of Creation, the message that 'man is not meant to be a theoretical, a knowing, a contemplating being; man is meant to live in childlike obedience.'[116] The Bible modifies this position subsequently, and Strauss traces this modification to its incorporation of certain trends in Greek thought. So, for instance, the city is denigrated in the Bible, first by its becoming the dwelling place of Cain and his descendants, and then by the fact that the Torah was given in the desert. Later on, the city and kingship in general – although rebellions from God – are accepted by God insofar as they 'become dedicated to the service of God and thus become holy.'[117] The Bible adapts the Greek affirmation of reason – ascertainable by what one sees with one's own eyes – as the basis of divine law by affirming that God gave human beings knowledge in order to understand His commands, or alternatively, that human knowledge is good if it is dedicated to God. In this way, philosophy emerges out of biblical thought: the adherent to the Bible, by separating knowledge from service, at the same time frees his understanding from his service to God. But the antagonism between the Bible and Greek thought remains: in the Bible, knowledge is subservient to fulfilment of God's commands and exists for that purpose.

While both Greek philosophy and the Bible begin with the equation of the ancestral and the good – and the consequent problem of divine law – each recognizes the solution of the other. Greek philosophy begins with divine law only to abandon it, but its abandonment is not complete: Aristotle, as has been mentioned, makes reference to certain notions in Greece that prize obedience over knowledge; the Bible retains divine law but makes room for philosophy insofar as its adherent might understand his service to God. Yet the antagonism remains between Greek philosophy and the Bible regarding the means of living the good life. For Strauss, this antagonism should not be abandoned: it defines 'the vitality of Western civilization.'[118] Because this conflict surrounds what is the right way of life, it occurs in the very fabric of our living; to give up that antagonism is to defeat Western civilization itself. While in the practical realm each person must decide whether to uphold the good life as the Bible or as Greek thought understands it, the conflict itself must be preserved in the theoretic realm in order for Western civilization to remain vital. One must remain 'open' to the claims of the other.[119] This means, according to Strauss, that one must live the conflict between these two codes.

The maintenance of this tension is aided by the self-understandings of both the Bible and Greek philosophy: 'the Bible refuses to be integrated into a philosophical framework, just as philosophy refuses to be integrated into a biblical framework.'[120] So, for instance, as we have seen, the Bible is written by various unknown authors. For its part, Greek philosophy – though written as individual books by individual authors – retains a fundamental openness regarding its own insights. Strauss traces this openness to, for instance, Greek thought's relationship to revelation. The Greek philosopher cannot accept revelation because it does not present itself as evident; yet because as a practical question, revelation is 'of utmost urgency' to human life (from the biblical point of view), his suspension of judgment with regard to it is *de facto* a rejection of it.[121] Despite the seeming self-contradiction with which the Greek philosopher seems to be faced – the rejection of revelation without refutation – 'the philosophers of the past were absolutely certain that an all-wise God would not punish with eternal damnation, or with anything else, such human beings as are seeking the truth or clarity.'[122] The philosopher of the past might validate his suspension of judgment regarding revelation by maintaining his way of life – his quest 'animated by a peculiar passion, the philosophic desire or *eros*' – as the good life.[123] The question, then, for both the student of the Bible and the student of Greek philosophy is the question of how one should live. Because within Greek philosophy's self-understanding, 'all solutions are questionable'[124] – even the solution as to what is the right way of life – this philosophy never understood itself as a completed system: if one possesses a completed system, one has wisdom and therefore there is no further need of the quest for wisdom.[125] Unlike modern philosophy,[126] which is compatible with the biblical way of life insofar as it is made into a tool or a system,[127] classical philosophy remains incompatible with the Bible because, like the Bible, Greek philosophy establishes itself as a way of life. By living the good life as he understands it, the Greek philosopher, while not denying the possibility of revelation, dramatizes the right way of life as the philosophic life in practical terms: the fact of his ignorance of the most important things is the evidence for philosophy being the right way of life.

Philosophy, in the original sense of the term, because it remains – through its own terms – open to serious alternatives for which serious arguments can be made regarding the right way of life, can never lead to the acceptance of another way of life as the good life. The antagonism between the Bible and philosophy in the original sense is profound: each claims to be the right way of life, claims, that is, to inform man of the way he should exist in every aspect of his life. Strauss suggests that the tension between the biblical and the philosophic right ways of life dramatizes the 'fundamental dualism' in man, a 'dualism of deed and speech, of action and thought,'[128] where 'deed' and 'action' are reflected in the Bible and 'speech' and 'thought' in the philosophical quest. As Strauss writes, 'philosophy and the Bible are the alternatives or the antagonists in the drama of the human soul.'[129]

Strauss argues for the possibility of a return from modern philosophy – which, understanding itself as a tool or completed system, has become compatible with the Bible – to philosophy understood as a never-ending quest. With the latter understanding of philosophy, it becomes possible to reaffirm, against modern science, the priority of the philosophic way of life. Strauss argues not simply that the claims of revelation be open to those of philosophy and vice versa, but also that philosophy, so understood, has a positive claim on the right way of life.[130] All thinking must be rooted in the common (theoretic) ground of the Bible and Greek philosophy, a ground from which the (practical) choice of neither revelation nor reason is entirely valid or alternatively, from which each revelation and reason has a positive claim on human thought.[131]

Again, Strauss finds common ground between Greek thought and the Bible:

> In the crucial respect there is agreement between classical philosophy and the Bible, between Athens and Jerusalem. According to the Bible man is created in the image of God; he is given the rule over all terrestrial creatures: he is not given the rule over the whole; he has been put into a garden to work it and to guard it; he has been assigned a place; righteousness is obedience to the divinely established order, just as in classical thought justice is compliance with the natural order; to the recognition of elusive chance corresponds the recognition of inscrutable providence.[132]

By recognizing the common ground from which the ideas of righteousness and justice spring, Strauss seeks to discover, like Plato, a standard of action that is independent of a completed metaphysics. Even so, unlike Plato, this standard, because Jerusalem serves also to inform it, can be no longer eternal: Strauss seeks to discover *nous*, which possession allows a glimpse of 'the noetic idea of the good,'[133] in order to rediscover the idea of a human condition that is permanent. The human condition can be understood no longer as eternal because philosophy, while recovering its classical definition as the right way of life, must, if the West is to remain vital, remain open to the claims to the right way of life of the Bible. The common ground between Jerusalem and Athens is the conformity to a pre-given order; they differ about this as the divinely established order differs from the natural order.

Strauss seeks to preserve both the Bible and Greek philosophy as he understands it. Like Greek thought, he moves in the realm of philosophy; he seeks a point of view that transcends the problem of divine law, even as he remains open to the possibility that this pursuit may not be the ultimate right way of life.[134] But Strauss, in his adoption of Athens, does not abandon Jerusalem: 'But while being compelled, or compelling myself, to wander far away from our sacred heritage, or to be silent about it, I shall not for a moment forget what Jerusalem stands for.'[135] And his procedure of wandering far from the Jewish heritage, Strauss implies, has its precedent in Maimonides. As one colleague writes: 'The secret position of the philosopher within Judaism (as the example of Maimonides demonstrates) is that of speaking of reason in the world of faith, of defending reason in the name of those who respect and understand faith but do not share it. In essence, this is the secret role that Leo Strauss, a disciple of Maimonides, had assigned himself.'[136] According to this scholar, Strauss had a 'primitive need to understand clearly the tradition of the fathers and the sense of their secular sacrifice. Few men have loved the faith of the fathers with so much austere love as Leo Strauss, who understood it but did not share it.'[137] Understanding the 'faith of the fathers' (patriotism) is essential for political philosophy.

Strauss does not presume that the recovery of Greek thought is necessarily possible or impossible,[138] but in his rejection of the historical sense – or his articulation of classical natural right – he argues that one must make at least the attempt at recovery in the theoretic realm. His recognition that one must attempt something whose highest attainment may not be possible leads to the paradoxical result that the recovery itself is influenced by contemporary concerns.[139] Strauss, while taking seriously Platonic thought, does not adopt what would seem to be its basic premise: the finding of a metaphysics.[140] This is due to his recognition of the separation of theory and practice: political theory is theory about practice. As a philosopher, then, Strauss had to concentrate on the evidence for any position he preferred, that is, he had to think hard about how his personal situation might prejudice his judgment. As a modern man, and a Jew, he addresses modern people and Jews and writes in such a way as to gain their sympathetic understanding of his understanding of their problems, which were his problems. It has been suggested that Strauss's reading of Plato is 'idiosyncratic, perverse or simply bizarre,'[141] that he has incorporated into his thinking on Plato his 'historical understanding, the revitalization of earlier ways of thinking.'[142] This conclusion is not lost on Strauss himself: 'a secession from this world might again become necessary for Jews and even for Christians.'[143] The context of his statement suggests that escape from shallow secularist conformism could become a reasonable alternative as well as a religious one. Strauss recognizes the necessity of historical consciousness and, through this recognition, responds to the charge of escapism.

Yet for Strauss, exile is and has been always ultimately political. It has its roots in both Greek and Jewish thought. One's recognition of one's ultimate exile from reality begins in one's actual experience that, for instance, there can never – or hardly ever – be an identity between the good citizen and the good man. For Strauss's Plato, the surface of things – the *eidē* – indicates the intelligibles; there is a correlation between this world and the real: one's glimpsing of the good is necessarily *through* one's immanent experience of the less than good. In the same way, the Bible teaches that exile is ultimately political. For instance, in Leviticus 26, God says that He will 'walk contrary' to those who have 'walked contrary'[144] to Him – those who have not kept His statutes. Exile from God results from disobedience within the political realm: one's understanding of this world and one's actions within it bear directly on whether or not there exists a connection with God. Because Greek and biblical thought share this ultimate point that is at once exile and intimacy, Strauss suggests that beginning one's relationship to reality in exile is neither despair nor hope, but rather, simply is.

Fackenheim's Rejection of the Return to Greek Thought

In Fackenheim's formulation:

> [T]he foundations of our civilization are Athens and Jerusalem, and philosophy is the critical self-consciousness of a civilization. If one assents to these two propositions, one must also charge modern philosophy with the task of doing to Jerusalem no less a justice than to Athens ... [Modern philosophy] ... cannot escape the task of seeing Jerusalem through her own (as well as through other) eyes. And the persistent failure to do so would be tantamount to having somehow failed our civilization as a whole.[145]

For Fackenheim, as for Strauss, one goal of philosophy is not to uncover certainties or truths *per se*, but rather to improve civilization, to live the right way of life. Furthermore, in his allusion to 'our civilization as a whole,' Fackenheim seems to adopt Strauss's notion of the tension between Athens and Jerusalem as the secret to the vitality of the West. But Fackenheim seems here to distort Strauss: by defining philosophy exclusively in terms of 'civilizations,' he defines it through the lens of historicism. For Strauss, the philosopher is primarily an *individual* devoted to the quest for knowledge of the whole; he is so devoted not only for practical reasons but also, as he writes, to 'find his satisfaction, his bliss, in free investigation, in articulating the riddle of being.'[146] Nevertheless, in Fackenheim's formulation, because the modern world has discovered self-consciousness, Jerusalem needs Athens. Also, Athens needs Jerusalem because it needs to know the limit of the proscription against idolatry.[147] Self-consciousness must be bounded by knowledge of what is ever beyond its scope, both the transcendent God of revealed religion and the contingent realities of freedom and existence. It is these latter realities that can result in the actuality of evil. Jerusalem must interact with Athens; Athens must interact with Jerusalem. Most important, the results of Jerusalem's incorporation of Athens, and Athens's of Jerusalem, must interact because, even while revelation and reason are mutually irrefutable and mutually interdependent, our existence within modernity demands an openness to the possibility of beginning within the stance of Jerusalem or of Athens. '"The reform party wished to assimilate the Torah to Hellenism; the Maccabees wished to incorporate Hellenic culture in the Torah." Here is the core of the self-exposed, self-mediating response of Jerusalem to the challenge of Athens and all her works.'[148]

While Fackenheim's affirmation of the interdependence of Athens and Jerusalem may develop from – and apparently is not at odds with – Strauss's thought, Fackenheim rejects what he understands as Strauss's return to Athens, for two primary reasons.[149] First, while Greek thought may lead to the good, it can never lead to the holy as holy. Strauss argues that Greek thought accepts the holy as *politically* necessary for those who cannot fathom moral seriousness through philosophy alone; Greek thought includes philosophic politics: 'In what then does philosophic politics consist? In satisfying the city that the philosophers are not atheists, that they do not desecrate everything sacred to the city, that they reverence what the city reverences, that they are not subversives, in short, that they are not irresponsible adventurers but good citizens and even the best of citizens.'[150] But for Fackenheim – recognizing primarily the metaphysical and not the political aspects of Greek thought – the Greek concern for the eternal precludes the Jewish concern for history. Strauss might counter that he disregards the surface of things – the political exigencies of the moment: Fackenheim's 'history' may be informed by the idea of history. Second, the claim that 'men as men' are free to be philosophers in any civil society so long as they keep their distance from the government has been shown to be false: Jews were not free to be philosophers during the tyranny of the Nazis, regardless of whether they considered themselves to be exclusively 'men as men.' This is perhaps the more important issue because here we see the informative value of Fackenheim's historicism; surely people have been philosophers through very bad times, yet philosophy has persisted. But Fackenheim identifies what he considers to be the urgency of the moment: the combined effects of 'Hitler's shadow' (modern historical self-consciousness) and atomic power (weapons of mass destruction) threaten Jewish survival.[151]

For Fackenheim, then, Strauss's return to Greek philosophy as a way of life defeats Judaism and Jews in two ways. First, while it does not deny Judaism as a way of life – insofar as one may continue to observe the commandments – it denies Judaism as a way of thought. In other words, it questions the theoretic basis of the public expression of Judaism.[152] Since for Fackenheim Judaism cannot separate action and thought, Strauss's affirmation of Greek thought is a *de facto* denial of Judaism's imitation of the holy.[153] In this disagreement we see the practical dimension of what Strauss discovers as the tension between philosophy and theology. Second, its refusal to recognize evil as a transcendent existent[154] precludes post-Holocaust Jews from beginning their thinking from within the stance of covenantal affirmation, be it ever so adapted in the present circumstances. Fackenheim fears not only the annihilation of Jews but also the loss of Jewish eschatological hope and a standard by which to judge and direct right action.[155] But Maimonides, Strauss discovers, while writing with restraint, nevertheless at times stood outside the revelatory tradition because he saw it, given his political context, as politically exigent.

But Fackenheim rejects esoteric reading: for him, the suggestion that there is a hierarchy from existence to essence, and a hierarchy within existence – from, for instance, the exoteric to the esoteric – minimizes the things, events, and people of this world. It is, for him, a form of evasion of what he considers to be the most urgent practical question, and it is an evasion that will persist no matter the magnitude of evil in this world. Ironically, it is Fackenheim's attention to the Holocaust that frees him from this evasion: the assessment of this world as below reality itself, or the good, begins one's relationship to reality in a form of exile from the good. His suggestion that one must attend to evil in order to connect with the good, or with God, is an attempt at beginning one's relationship to reality as a coexistent, that is, without exile. This stance, without adopting idealism, counters despair. It is a stance that begins in hope.[156] But it must be added here that this position may not be precluded by Strauss's argument that the philosopher might both live the right way of life and also attend to his own bliss; Fackenheim's position may be simply a reflection of a different practical choice.

Fackenheim rejects the return to the eternal of Greek thought (or to the permanent) as both a denunciation of the holy and an unwarranted escapism from the real. Whereas Strauss argues for the timeless truths of philosophy and the rediscovery of natural theology – a position that is incompatible with atheism – Fackenheim maintains a commitment to revelatory theology. The distinction between these two positions does not mean necessarily that Fackenheim abandons the quest for timeless truths any more than it means that Strauss abandons the claims of revelation. But Strauss bases his rediscovery of natural theology – of the surface of things on which natural theology is based – on the primacy of what one sees with one's own eyes over hearsay.[157] Fackenheim, working within the stance of covenantal affirmation, rejects the ultimacy of this distinction: through reenactment, hearsay is seen with one's own eyes. More specifically – through, for instance, the reenactment of the Exodus – Jews participating in the seder see with their own eyes what had previously been only the hearsay of the Bible, the rabbis and the ancestors. In this sense, not only is the historical realm the arena in which phenomena representing the timeless truths appear to human beings, but also, conversely, the timeless truths become timely and bestow ultimate meaning on the present.[158] Furthermore, Fackenheim rejects Strauss's teaching regarding how to read the medieval thinkers. There are two related reasons for this, which, as will be spelled out, issue from his more fundamental position that philosophy 'is the critical self-consciousness of a civilization.' First, thought itself is no longer what once it was: the rupture in thought effectuated by the Holocaust has made an unqualified return to pre-Holocaust thought impossible. Second, Hegel's introduction of historical thought into philosophical thought has altered not only the dimension of thought but also the dimension of existence.

First, Fackenheim rejects Maimonides as a model for modern Jewish thought (though Strauss, it would seem, argues not for 'models of thought,' but rather against the modern historical prejudice that precludes the ability to take seriously Maimonides's texts in their own terms). While he recognizes what may be called the Jewish core of Maimonides's thought – his powerful affirmation of the transcendence of God[159] – Maimonides cannot serve as a model for modern thought because thought, after the Holocaust, must be specific; it must recognize the individual. The Holocaust is unintelligible because the Nazis, while creating and adopting a *Weltanschauung*, sabotaged their cosmic goal by continuing, for instance, to run the trains to the death camps when they did not have the resources.[160] The Holocaust must be confronted with total self-exposure – from within the human existence of the integrated human being. Strauss might argue that the Holocaust may be intelligible in the sense that it can be omitted from philosophical pursuit – just as all evil can and must be. Fackenheim suggests that such an omission, insofar as it circumscribes the Holocaust and removes it from the reality of human existence, transforms the event into an idea – or, perhaps, into an anti-idea. The Holocaust cannot be confronted with 'any sort of mediation: it can be confronted only by uncompromising opposition.'[161] Furthermore, 'such a radical opposition is offered by every Jewish survivor by his mere decision to remain a Jew; and this decision is normative because, by virtue of it, the survivor has become the paradigm of the whole Jewish people.'[162]

Second, since Hegel, human thought includes the specific accidents of history. Somewhat paradoxically, Hegel both proposed the inclusion into thought of 'empirical history,'[163] and also thereby altered empirical history by informing it with models of thought. Hegel brought the representations of God, or the models of philosophy, into history and thereby, according to Fackenheim, altered our conception of what historical experience is. Because contemporary historical experience is profoundly not Maimonides's historical experience – is not recognized by us in the way Maimonides understood historical experience – Maimonides cannot provide for us a methodology for thought but can only guide us through an encounter with him as his specific moment in history. The Holocaust, according to Fackenheim, as *our* particular historical experience, has therefore *conclusively* demonstrated that there is no permanent human nature: by creating an anti-world, the Holocaust has established the reality of the anti-world. While 'the medieval Jewish thinker must confront Greek (i.e., pagan) philosophy only insofar as it conflicts with his Judaism,'[164] in the modern period – because Hegelianism claims comprehensiveness – the Jew must confront philosophy with total Jewish self-exposure. In the modern period, according to this historicist or quasi-historicist understanding, the Jew must confront all models of philosophy not simply in the realm of thought, but in the realm of life as well.

Fackenheim's rejection of the return to Greek thought is, positively put, a rejection of the inability of Greek thought to provide human life with models of holiness:[165]

The God of Greek philosophy is timeless, unchanging, and indifferent toward all but Himself. Man can relate himself to Him only by means of thought. This thought, if true, is timelessly true; and it is a truth indifferent toward the thinker's individuality. Indeed, in Aristotle the thinker, *qua* thinker, ceases to be an individual and becomes pure thought.

The Biblical God, too, may be timeless. But He is known only through His revelation; and that is *not* timeless. It is addressed not to man as such, but to *this* man, or *this* people, here and now. Moreover, the content of this revelation does not consist of timelessly true propositions; whether it is God's commandment, His promise, or God Himself, it is not abstractable from the moment to which it belongs, nor from those to whom it is addressed. Clearly, then, Biblical man's thinking about God cannot be detached from his person.[166]

Goodness can be achieved alone, but since it ultimately concerns only eternity, it cannot point to models of individual human behaviour. Knowledge attained in the sight of God, however, can 'prove' God's existence, and what is more, in its 'proof,' it performs *tikkun*: it fights evil. Jewish theology's proof of God culminates in its pointing to the fighting of evil[167] and the bringing of holiness into the world. The god of Greek thought, on the other hand, can exist only in thought and can never be proved. For Fackenheim, the god of Greek thought is insufficient: it denies the existence of both holiness and unholiness because it does not bring God into the world. Most urgently, it cannot fight evil, which for Fackenheim, is now the primary, or even exclusive, function of philosophy.

Results from Beginning with Fackenheim's Position

The positive obligation to live as Jews, as Fackenheim conceives it, is complicated by a number of factors. First, according to him, the greatest threat to the survival of Jewish faith in the modern period is what he labels secular messianism.[168] Secular messianism – the positing of messianic redemption in this world through human effort – is premature messianism and poses a great threat to Jewish survival because it is a rival faith. To place the Jewish messiah within the modern idea of historical progress is a form of idealism that claims that Jewish messianism has been superseded; to claim that Jewish messianism has been superseded is to affirm implicitly that 'the genuine Jewish destiny [is] ... self-dissolution in mankind.'[169] One can of course hope, but one's hope must be rooted in empirical reality because only with this root is it possible to be open to the goal of hope: God and/or redemption. One must be fully aware not of the extent of evil in the world, but rather of the fact that evil is a self-contained – one might say transcendent – principle and that it must be subdued or neutralized, if necessary, with force.[170] For Fackenheim, the distinction between hope and idealism, and the acceptance of hope and rejection of idealism (as idolatrous), are crucial.

Indeed, whereas Fackenheim argues against modern idealism as a source of what Strauss labels 'delusion,' one might suggest that his parting of ways with Strauss is his position that without hope there cannot be philosophy. 'The high,' in other words, cannot exist without hope. For support, he cites the Bar Kochba rebellion, which, although terrible, was not a catastrophe: because Akiba had hope, Jewish theology could be sustained. The Holocaust, in contrast, effectuated a break between the high and the low, between the transcendent – or the aspiration for the transcendent – and the reality of human experience. Hope was systematically destroyed; so too philosophy was destroyed. In this position, however, we note both Fackenheim's historicism and his completion of morality – as Strauss might formulate it – with the biblical alternative.

Second, the positive obligation to live as Jews is complicated by present historical circumstances. Since Hegel, according to Fackenheim, history itself critiques thought, and therefore 'it is on secular terms, and on secular terms alone, that in modern times those international bonds will be created without which the human race will not long survive.'[171] Fackenheim attempts to resolve Strauss's characterization of the Jewish problem: 'progress beyond' Judaism is identical with 'denial of' Judaism.[172] To this end, he suggests that Judaism – both despite and because of secularism and the Holocaust – must, qualifiedly, progress beyond its original conception. 'One's thought [must now] be vulnerable to history.'[173] Fackenheim understands the Holocaust as rupturing philosophy, Judaism, and Christianity. Philosophy is ruptured because it did not have the resources to resist the Holocaust's *idealization* of genocide: from its beginning in Plato, philosophy connects the intelligible with the good.[174] Christianity and Judaism are ruptured because Christianity did not live up to its teaching of love, and the experience of Jews may, with good reason, lead Jews to despair of Judaism and God. All three, philosophy, Judaism, and Christianity, must confront with total self-exposure both the event of the Holocaust and secularism in order to persist.

Yet these ruptures can, according to Fackenheim, be mended:[175] '*only because of particular historical acts [committed] during ... the Holocaust*'[176] – acts that rose above the destruction – can philosophy, Judaism, and Christianity survive. The mending of these ruptures entails, to a certain extent, redefinitions of Judaism,[177] Christianity, and philosophy: the foundation of future thought must be 'action-concepts,'[178] concepts that at once permeate and establish the truth of human existence.[179] Fackenheim finds these action-concepts in Jewish theology as *teshuvah*[180] and *tikkun*; and while in his earlier thought, the State of Israel provides the means for Jewish redemption, in his later work, action-concepts – the *tikkun* that took place in the death camps – become the foundation for his thought. It is with a vulnerability to history, an awareness both of the ultimate destructiveness of the modern philosophical project of internalizing the transcendent God and also of the interconnectedness of Jewish thought and experience[181] that Fackenheim's thought critiques German philosophy. The encounters that Fackenheim proposes presume that reason – despite modern rationality's self-definition – is not 'autonomous and all-encompassing':[182] because philosophy could not address the Holocaust, the only response is action. Yet action cannot determine truth: the witnesses in the camps did not abandon God. Fackenheim's explorations will leave him to espouse a religious existentialism that is open to experience, yet finds limitations in how that experience is understood.

Fackenheim's argument for the need for existentialism in modern thought is this: by positing the concept of man as the starting point for future thought, the Jew must 'first abstract himself out of the ongoing covenant between God and the Jewish people.'[183] For him, it is a deception to deny faith only to arrive at it. Jewish theology is possible only after a commitment is made to Jewish existence; therefore, election is and must always remain the starting point for Jewish theology.[184] In other words, 'the Jewish thinker is deluded when he begins with essence rather than existence. He is not a man-in-general, an impartial spectator who may choose between religious options in an existential vacuum. He exists already as a Jew, and is singled out as a Jew, and he cannot make an authentic religious commitment unless he relates it to his singled-out Jewish condition.'[185] At the same time, because this election occurs in history, at Sinai, so too must the starting point of Jewish theology be within the empirical realm, wherein each moment is new and must be able to respond to 'epoch-making events.'

For Fackenheim, the contemporary Jew finds himself confronted with two such epoch-making events: the Holocaust and the State of Israel.

Like Strauss, Fackenheim suggests that philosophical theory has practical consequences. Unlike Strauss, who argues for a recovery of a philosophy in quest of the permanent human problems, Fackenheim argues – beginning perhaps in *God's Presence* (1970) or *Encounters* (1973) and reaching its culmination in *To Mend the World* (1982) – that philosophy must dialogue with Judaism if philosophy, now a realm where thought and life must be integrated, is to survive. So, for instance, one might argue that the singled-out condition of the Jew is both a religious and an experiential position; but that argument does not cover the range of what the Jewish experience might be, that is, it is neither an empirical position nor a philosophical one. Fackenheim reads Kant, Hegel, and Heidegger not necessarily on their own terms: by being made to dialogue with the Jewish tradition, they are shown to be partial and limited. What is more, he critiques Heidegger and Sartre for their unwillingness or inability to open their existentialism to a confrontation with the Jewish existentialism of Rosenzweig and Buber. The case of Heidegger, with his never-renounced Nazism, is more obvious.[186] But even Sartre, who thoughtfully attempted to diagnose the disease of 'anti-Semitism,' failed to inform the definition of the 'Jew' of *Anti-Semite and Jew* with Buber's religious self-definition, instead allowing his 'Jew' to be defined through the eyes of the 'anti-Semite.'[187] Rosenzweig and Buber's attempt to establish this confrontation, or 'dialogical mutuality,' was all one-sided.[188] Fackenheim argues that existentialism must confront Jewish existentialism, which he conceives, at the time of *Encounters*, as beyond the scope of the book.[189] And in 1994, long after having completed *To Mend the World*, Fackenheim writes, 'I wonder whether the truly *radical* response required in either discipline is not still largely missing.'[190]

Both Strauss and Fackenheim agree that the interchange between philosophy and revelatory theology is dialogical and that so too the reassessment of the philosophical and religious traditions must be dialogical. For Fackenheim, it is not enough to establish a secular realm of thought with Christians because such a realm – since Jewish existentialism must begin with the Jew as human being within covenantal affirmation – becomes specifically post-Christian. Jews must inform post-Christian thought with relationship, with covenant, in order to create a philosophy that includes Jewish empirical experience. Jewish

philosophy is defined by the historical context of the Jewish philosopher – as the experience revealed by the Jew who exposes himself in
moments in history both to the Jewish tradition and to philosophy. In
this way, one brings both the Jewish God and the Jews back into history. Strauss argues against the historicism implicit in this formulation,
and perhaps we see here what may be a limitation of Fackenheim's
philosophy: how can it include *all* serious empirical and non-empirical
experience, that is, all that is able to be experienced?

Fackenheim's return to the roots of history means a return to the
foundation of belief in revelation as the source from which human action is dictated.[191] In practical terms, this return means that Jews, if they
are to survive, must return *both* to Judaism's source in faith and *also* to
the surface of things as presented in their contemporary history. Returning to these roots, Fackenheim is presented with a choice: either
revelation is real and faith is validated, or the Holocaust is real and
faith is discredited. He chooses a third option: returning to what he
understands to be the 'essence of Judaism,'[192] especially as dramatized
in the 'midrashic framework,'[193] he finds faith *and* doubt. The return to
the roots of history is for Fackenheim a return to history as it revealed
itself *in*, and reveals itself *through*, nature.[194]

Strauss asks a philosophic question; but as we have seen, he suggests
that reason and revelation must each have a fundamental openness to
the other.[195] His practical choice of philosophy – or, more precisely, his
rediscovery of Greek philosophy as (in its self-understanding) a quest
that provides the right way of life – is informed by his contemporary
concerns.[196] Strauss argues for natural right as a theoretic guide for
practical action: natural right aims at tempering passions and promoting the necessity of moral action.

Philosophy, Strauss advises, is the method by which to 'view the low
in the light of the high';[197] by recovering cosmocentric or theocentric
thought, we can see past not only the autonomy that results from anthropocentric thought, but also the idea of history as an entity that arose
as a consequence of the understanding of human nature and human
experience as subjects of inquiry; without the idea of history, there can
be no (to use Fackenheim's term) ruptures. Strauss attempts to resolve
the modern Jewish problem created by Spinoza – who made a 'break'
from Judaism rather than a progression from it[198] – by reassessing both
anthropocentrism and the relationship between knowledge and historical change.[199] Fackenheim, in his self-understanding, follows Strauss
in this: 'After the unique rupture that has occurred, the high is acces-

sible only through an *act of recovery*, and this must bridge what is no mere gap but rather an abyss: the necessary recovery must be a *Tikkun*. Indeed, Strauss's own philosophical efforts, so it would seem, must be understood in such terms.'[200] In what seems to be a misrepresentation of Strauss, who recognized only the temporary need for historical studies, Fackenheim argues that the recovery must, like the break, occur in and through the idea of history.

For Strauss, the action necessary in and through the idea of history is only a stopgap measure: it provides only the tools by which to return to the original cave. This is a recovery of history in its Greek sense of inquiry or study. Fackenheim, in contrast, argues in the first place, that Judaism and the Jewish God cannot exist ahistorically[201]; and in the second place, that faith can be known only from within the stance of faith. The failure of the modern world, according to Fackenheim, is not so much its anthropocentrism or historical sense, but rather the failure of the relationship between Jews and Christians (as culminated in the Holocaust). Jews, according to Fackenheim, must continue the work on this side of the covenant, so to speak, in order to find God again, and they require Christians to do the same work: 'How would it be if a Jewish-Christian reading-together [of the Old Testament] came about – one that has never happened before? Doubtless this would have to struggle with difficulties as yet unknown. But how would it be if here, too, a human beginning, made by us here below, were to find a divine response, from above?'[202]

The Present Writer's Position

> [W]hen one is attacked as a Jew one must defend oneself as a Jew, not as a German, not as a world citizen.[203]

In his self-assessment, Fackenheim recognizes that, with the exception of his work in Hegel, he was not the scholar that Strauss was.[204] Scholarship, however, may not be the most urgent present need. Strauss would agree that the thing most needful right now is a return to philosophy as a quest, even if this return, as has been suggested, issues in a reading of Plato that is more reflective of contemporary need than of Plato's self-understanding. (More likely, Strauss's understanding of Plato is the ever relevant practical or methodological aspect of philosophy – history as inquiry.) Toward the end of his life, Fackenheim spoke to the present writer about a subject that was urgently on his mind:

'philosophy and grandchildren.'[205] I understood his implication to be that, despite any desire or scholarship to the contrary, the removal of one's thought from both its political ramifications and its historical entry into the world is impossible.

Fackenheim recognized his great debt to Strauss for rediscovering that philosophy is a questing after the permanent human questions. The great question posed by philosophy to revelatory theology, as Novak sums up Strauss's formulation, is whether the revelatory tradition is reliable.[206] And the asking of that question, for Fackenheim, is the existential moment in which post-Holocaust Jews find themselves. Philosophy cannot validate the revelatory tradition, but it can 'elucidate [theology's] *conditio sine qua non*, its minimal condition, without judging its *conditio per quam*, its ultimate ground.'[207] This minimal condition is defined by the hailing distance within which reason and revelation may come – beyond human comprehension, within the mystery of being. But again, for Strauss, even asking this question is problematic: as Jenny Strauss Clay writes, 'If I understand him correctly, Strauss would consider a conference and then a volume devoted to Jerusalem and Athens paradoxical, if not impossible. For if such an enterprise were to go beyond a presentation and exposition of respective claims and foundations to a genuine confrontation of those claims and those foundations, by which I mean a reasoned dialogue represented by this book, then wouldn't Athens have already won?'[208]

According to Fackenheim, Strauss's thought provides a haven – or better, a home within their exile – for Jews who stand, either esoterically or both esoterically and exoterically, outside the stance of covenantal affirmation. Fackenheim's stance within covenantal affirmation draws not only on Jewish conceptual categories, but also on Jewish experience. So, for instance, he points to Soviet Jews who, without any knowledge of Jewish categories, heroically remained Jewish.[209] He argues for the secular component of Jewish experience as a means of informing new Jewish categories; Jews have a right, and after Hitler, an obligation, to survive as Jews. In this light, Strauss's suggestion that Jewish chosenness is a reminder to the world that it is not yet redeemed[210] makes one's blood freeze. But if Strauss's goal is primarily the rediscovery of the permanent truths of philosophy and not the preservation of Judaism – or, more precisely, if his means of preserving Judaism is by recovering philosophy – then his depiction of the Jewish condition as only the most exposed of the human condition achieves a certain neutrality.

Strauss's work points to the most focused critique of Fackenheim's thought: his adoption of the qualified historicism of Rosenzweig and Buber destroys the boundaries between divine and non-divine revelation and blurs the line between revelation and reason.[211] In Jewish and Islamic medieval thought, with its theocentric world view, such a blurring was relatively inconsequential; but today the anthropocentric elements of such a blurring – according, at any rate, to Strauss – perpetuate the crisis of modernity.[212] Fackenheim's exploration of the ontological status of history as a means to reaffirm both the possibility of revelation and the ontological status of radical evil issues in a philosophy that is problematic insofar as it necessarily incorporates aspects of historicist thinking and provides no means by which to judge the reliability of the revelatory tradition.

In practical terms, one might ask what the status of Torah can be in the light of anthropocentrism. As freedom in the modern world is itself sanctified – which sanctification, according to Strauss, is the primary ingredient of modernity's hermetic idealism – does the seder commemorate the Exodus and God's consequent overseeing of human life, or does it in fact celebrate the sanctification of freedom, even of human rebellion?[213] Does Fackenheim's at least partially anthropocentric reading of Torah inform Judaism with the means by which to ensure its own self-destruction? Furthermore, can one base the content of revelation simply on Jewish survival and not on dictated specific action?[214] Without an absolute, timeless yet humanly accessible standard of action, what happens if Jews are once again expelled, so to speak, from empirical history: how do they persist as Jews? Seeskin recognizes these issues when he suggests that 'to the degree that we rely on historically situated individuals to give vitality to ideas, we risk trivializing those ideas.'[215]

Fackenheim's understanding of the Holocaust (and the founding of the State of Israel) as epoch-making events presupposes that Jews are God's chosen people; but by suggesting that Hitler's singling out of Jews necessitates a redefinition of religious election, he delegitimizes the authority of election as part of a wise God's plan.[216] Moreover, he delegitimizes experience itself, as, for example, Armenian or Rwandan empirical experience – not to mention Mizrahic or Sephardic empirical experience – may be excluded from his new 'Jewish philosophy.' Philosophy, Strauss would remind us, articulates the principles of all serious empirical (and non-empirical, that is, non-sensuous) experience: empirical experience is experience that is *able* to be experienced. Fackenheim's formulation of the Holocaust as a rupture in thought precludes the philosophy to which Strauss was pointing, as ancient Jewish philosophy or medieval Jewish philosophy – ancient or medieval philosophy in general – is not validated as part of the 'empirical' experience to which Fackenheim points. His stance, somewhere between reason and revelation, is more the stance of one who wants to defend revelation with philosophy, and the danger, of course, is the distortion of both. Moreover, and perhaps more urgently, his stance risks the creeping in of dogmatism regarding the boundaries of what he defines as experience. Perhaps we see something like dogmatism in his working definition of 'the Holocaust' as a specifically and uniquely 'Jewish' event.

But Fackenheim's concern for historical experience is, like Hegel's, a concern for the possibility of religious faith – whereas Hegel 'mak[es] peace with religion,'[217] Fackenheim makes peace with philosophy. Contingency must persist, if revelation is to remain a possibility. His suggestion that the progression of Spirit in Hegel is grounded in contingency is a means of suggesting that, while Spirit has in some sense a history, at the same time, insofar as it shares in existence, it remains as always. While the contingent must to a certain extent engage in what Robert Penn Warren calls the 'impure,'[218] or a certain level of self-destruction, in order not to intoxicate and disembody – we must confront in both thought and experience the evil of the Holocaust – the contingent is never superseded by the eternal. After all the philosophy, all the discursive 'old thinking,' the contingent remains. Most profoundly, Fackenheim's return to Hegel is not a return, but rather an intimation that the contingent stands somehow in identity with the eternal, if only by the self-negation of its 'pure' elements. Just so, what I have referred to as Fackenheim's quasi-historicism may point to something altogether beyond historicism; it may be a recognition that in order to recognize the contingent in its strictest sense – to be open to all possibilities of experience, including the experience of the true God – we must *first* recognize the self-destructive capacity of the contingent and *then* incorporate this recognition into our understanding of the eternal. Secular and religious experience are identical when *at once* we have interpreted and appropriated Torah *after* we have listened to Torah.[219]

Fackenheim, then, argues that his blurring of the boundaries of philosophy and of revelation is not really a blurring. The identity of the concerns for eternity and for history is accounted for once the historical has been superseded.[220] Because there is an identity between revelation and going beyond the revelation, one may, as a *philosophic* position, begin in revelation, in the experience of having glimpsed already the eternal. Fackenheim would argue that this having gone beyond is neither strictly historical nor a blurring of eternity and history. Rather it is in one respect true to the human, discursive nature; in the other, to the more divine, better angel of our nature. Fackenheim responds to the challenge of translating our idealism with regard to modern philosophy into faith with regard to our profound moral commitments. While it has been suggested that his results issue from his hermeneutic,[221] one might argue rather that his results issue from his beginning his thought within the stance – a profoundly open stance – of covenantal affirmation.

For Fackenheim, the immediate need is the reaffirmation or readoption of faith in Judaism, whatever that Judaism comes to look like. His work is to reaffirm divine authority within a profoundly secular context. This is by definition a paradoxical goal, and more traditional understandings of both philosophy and revelatory theology will be threatened by Fackenheim's synthesis. Questing after knowledge is, as Fackenheim writes as a theologian in his earlier work, 'walking on the narrow ridge of risk.'[222] Because ultimately, in his formulation, philosophy and revelatory theology can be synthesized only in the contingent realm, this synthesis can take place – and be sustained – only in a given particular moment. By reaffirming the presence of God in history – that all knowledge, religious and secular, is at any moment fragmentary – Fackenheim creates the possibility that one may credibly adopt the standpoint of faith without necessarily having faith. This issues in a profoundly unfinished understanding of Judaism or, in Morgan's conception, a Judaism of 'engaged waiting.'[223] But Fackenheim means no evasion:

> The answers must be answered clearly, straightforwardly, and without evasion. But answers will inevitably seem evasive when no evasion is intended; complex and ambiguous when what is aimed at is clarity and simplicity; above all, they will seem far harsher and more dogmatic than their author actually is. Judaism is a spiritual life – dynamic, open, and whole. Answers to a questionnaire cannot capture that life but only open a door.[224]

This book, by looking at what Yaffe has called Fackenheim's 'self-distancing' from Strauss,[225] raises the question of whether the Jewish concept of election can be informed by secular thought and/or experience without distortion of both rabbinic Judaism and philosophy. But it also enables us to see that Fackenheim takes seriously the unqualified claims of revelation and of philosophy and the possibility that we might rediscover those claims. I imagine that he would respond to the critique that he blurs the boundaries of reason and revelation by suggesting that fundamental to his thought is openness to continual empirical experience: just as Hegel would not today be an Hegelian, perhaps Fackenheim would not at some time be a Fackenheimian. Fackenheim's self-distancing from Strauss is, perhaps, a bridge by which one might discover Strauss's thought.

Strauss himself acknowledged that Fackenheim's is the 'model better suited for future Jewish thought.'[226] Not every Jew is a philosopher; not every Jew can read Maimonides with an eye toward philosophical thought; and not every Jew experiences the 'bliss' that may accompany the articulation of 'the riddle of being.' Fackenheim's work revalidates rabbinic Judaism by making space (in the form of a modified midrash[227]) for it to face head-on the incomprehensible experience of the Holocaust. His working within covenantal affirmation carries with it the practical fight against Hitler's attack on Judaism, and this fight was, for many Jews, a necessary fight, as, in the secular, post-Holocaust world, Hitler loomed larger than God.

Fackenheim told me many times that his favourite prophet was Jeremiah, who loved a good fight and spoke out for God and His works. The same can be said of him.

Notes

1. Background and Introduction

1 Emil L. Fackenheim, personal interview, August 2003. The conversations between Strauss and Fackenheim, incidentally, were conducted in English.

2 Leo Strauss, *Persecution and the Art of Writing* [PW] (Chicago: University of Chicago Press, 1980), 155.

3 Strauss's work on Hobbes was not limited to the latter's attacks on traditional orthodoxy. Positively put, Strauss was interested in Hobbes's philosophy as a means of clarifying the grounding for modern philosophy. See below, pp. 52–6.

4 For more on Fackenheim's relationship to Germany, see Emil L. Fackenheim, 'Reminiscences: From Germany to Canada (Growing Up in Germany),' reprinted, with changes, from 'An Interview with Emil Fackenheim' by William Novack in *New Traditions* 3 (Summer 1986), in *The Jewish Thought of Emil Fackenheim: A Reader*, ed. Michael L. Morgan (Detroit: Wayne State University Press, 1987).

5 Emil L. Fackenheim, 'Leo Strauss and Modern Judaism,' in *Jewish Philosophers and Jewish Philosophy* [JPJP], ed. Michael L. Morgan (Bloomington: Indiana University Press, 1996), 98.

6 Fackenheim cites Strauss as concluding that 'Rosenzweig's *Star of Redemption* is the philosophical equal of Martin Heidegger's *Being and Time*.' Emil L. Fackenheim, *Encounters between Judaism and Modern Philosophy: A Preface to Future Jewish Thought* [EJM] (New York: Schocken Books, 1973), 257n1. Also, that while Maimonides' *Guide* is 'primarily not a philosophical book but a Jewish book, Rosenzweig's *Star of Redemption* is primarily not a Jewish book but a "system of philosophy."' Ibid., 132, cited from Leo Strauss, Preface to the English Translation, *Spinoza's Critique of Religion* [SCR] (New

York: Schocken Books, 1982). Although Strauss only rarely referred directly to the Holocaust – a lapse that Fackenheim takes issue with – his statement that the Nazis 'had no other clear principle than murderous hatred of the Jews, for "Aryan" had no clear meaning other than "non-Jewish"' was profoundly meaningful to Fackenheim. Ibid., 166; see also *SCR*.

At least one scholar, Martin D. Yaffe, sees Fackenheim's work as a 'self-distancing' from Strauss's thought. See Martin D. Yaffe, 'Historicism and Revelation in Emil Fackenheim's Self-Distancing from Leo Strauss,' in *Emil L. Fackenheim: Philosopher, Theologian, Jew*, ed. Sharon Portnoff, James A. Diamond, and Martin D. Yaffe (Boston: E.J. Brill, 2008).

7 Michael L. Morgan, Introduction to Part I, in *JPJP*, 4.
8 Emil L. Fackenheim, *To Mend the World: Foundations of Post-Holocaust Jewish Thought* [*MW*] (Bloomington: Indiana University Press, 1994), 38–45.
9 See, for instance, Emil L. Fackenheim, *The Jewish Bible after the Holocaust: A Re-reading* (Bloomington: Indiana University Press, 1990), 7, 8, 9, 12, 14; *The Jewish Return into History: Reflections in the Age of Auschwitz and a New Jerusalem* [*JRH*] (New York: Schocken Books, 1978), 257; and *What Is Judaism? An Interpretation for the Present Age* (New York: Summit Books, 1987), 26, 27, 78, 79–80, 92.
10 *JPJP*, 97–105.
11 *PW*, 95–8.
12 Leo Strauss, 'On Natural Law,' in *Studies in Platonic Political Philosophy*, intro. Thomas L. Pangle (Chicago: University of Chicago Press, 1983), 138.
13 Leo Strauss, *Natural Right and History* [*NRH*] (Chicago: University of Chicago Press, 1965), 81.
14 Ibid. I repeat Strauss's use of the Christian name for the Bible in an attempt to read him literally enough.
15 As will become clearer in the course of this book, Fackenheim's understanding of the 'rabbinic' or 'midrashic' tradition is not altogether traditional. In the first place, to the extent that he had some facility with biblical and midrashic Hebrew (in the 1940s and 1950s), he may not have relied overly much on it. Morgan concludes that 'his grasp of Hebrew and use of it was basic, even after he made aliyah.' Michael L. Morgan, e-mail to the author, 14 September 2004. Second, Fackenheim uses a concept of an essence of Judaism – its election and its proscription against idolatry – to argue that a tradition that is in some way perpetuated from the rabbis can be adopted even while momentarily stripped of its particular content. For a discussion of Fackenheim's concept of the essence of Judaism, see below, pp. 196–7. For problems associated with his alteration of traditional categories, see Robert Eisen, 'Midrash in Emil Fackenheim's Holocaust

Theology,' *Harvard Theological Review* 96, no. 3 (July 2003): 369–92; and
Zachary Braiterman, *Theodicy and Antitheodicy: Tradition and Change in Post-
Holocaust Jewish Theology*, PhD diss., Stanford University, 1995. On page 56,
Braiterman argues that 'imprecise readings of classical Jewish texts have
confounded post-Holocaust religious thought.' Seeskin and Shapiro also
argue that Fackenheim's midrash is pushed too far. See Kenneth Seeskin,
'Emil Fackenheim,' in *Interpreters of Judaism in the Late Twentieth Century*
(Washington: B'nai Brith, 1993), 55; and Susan E. Shapiro, 'The Recovery
of the Sacred: Hermeneutics after the Holocaust, PhD diss., University of
Chicago, 1983, 212, 262–6.
16 Leo Strauss, 'The Three Waves of Modernity,' in *An Introduction to Political
Philosophy: Ten Essays by Leo Strauss*, ed. Hilail Gildin (Detroit: Wayne State
University, 1989), 83.
17 See below, pp. 155–9 and 209–24.
18 See below, p. 221.
19 Fackenheim himself uses the designation the 'quasi-historicity of eternity.'
See his *The God Within: Kant, Schelling, and Historicity*, ed. John Burbidge
[*GW*] (Toronto: University of Toronto Press, 1996), 131.
20 In Fackenheim's earlier work, his historicism is qualified by transcendence; but whether he adopts historicism altogether in *To Mend the World*
remains an open question. For a discussion of his historicism qualified by
transcendence, see below, pp. 172–94.
21 Emil L. Fackenheim, *Quest for Past and Future: Essays in Jewish Theology*
[*QPF*] (Boston: Beacon Press, 1968), 8.
22 See Shapiro, 'The Recovery of the Sacred,' 321.
23 *JPJP*, 104.
24 Kenneth C. Blanchard, Jr, 'Philosophy in the Age of Auschwitz: Emil Fackenheim and Leo Strauss,' in *Remembering for the Future: Working Papers and
Addenda*, vol. II, 'The Impact of the Holocaust on the Contemporary World'
(New York: Pergamon Press, 1989).
25 See below, pp. 172–94.
26 The rabbinic conception of the permanence of the *yezer harah* (the human
evil inclination) would seem to support this position, though Fackenheim would suggest that the rabbis never faced the possibility of the *total*
slaughter of Jews.
27 See below, pp. 248n75 and 223.
28 Strauss's return is a return to the appearance, *eidos*, from which an idea
arises. See Leo Strauss, 'What Is Political Philosophy?' in *What Is Political
Philosophy? and Other Studies* (Westport: Greenwood Press, 1959), 74–7, esp.
75. Strauss's return is a return to philosophy through its basis in common

human experience. Fackenheim returns to the Sinaitic revelation *and* to the possibility of present revelation as the basis of common Jewish experience.

29 See Leo Strauss, 'Progress or Return? The Contemporary Crisis in Western Civilization,' in *Jewish Philosophy and the Crisis of Modernity: Essays and Lectures in Modern Jewish Thought [JPCM]*, ed. Kenneth Hart Green (Albany: SUNY Press, 1997), esp. 87–91.

30 *JPCM*, 154.

31 Strauss's relationship to Judaism is the topic of much scholarly debate. Does he, for instance, concern himself with Judaism *per se*, or does his interest in Jews and Judaism simply reflect their being the most exposed instance of the human theologico-political problem – that is, the problem of retaining particular providence even while adopting the modern liberal state? For the former position, see Hillel Fradkin, 'Philosophy and Law: Leo Strauss as a Student of Medieval Jewish Thought,' in *Leo Strauss: Political Philosopher and Jewish Thinker*, ed. Kenneth L. Deutsch and Walter Nicgorski (Lanham: Rowman and Littlefield, 1994); for the latter, see Steven B. Smith, 'Leo Strauss: Between Athens and Jerusalem,' in the same volume.

32 See Emil L. Fackenheim, 'Holocaust and Weltanschauung: Reflections on Athens, Jerusalem, and the Western Academy,' in *JPJP*.

33 See, for instance, Michael L. Morgan, 'The Curse of Historicity: The Role of History in Leo Strauss's Jewish Thought,' and 'Leo Strauss and the Possibility of Jewish Philosophy,' both in *Dilemmas in Modern Jewish Thought: The Dialectics of Revelation and History* (Bloomington: Indiana University Press, 1992).

34 Kenneth Hart Green, 'Editor's Introduction: Leo Strauss as a Modern Jewish Thinker,' in *JPCM*, 2.

35 Allan Arkush, 'Leo Strauss and Jewish Modernity,' in *Leo Strauss and Judaism: Jerusalem and Athens Critically Revisited,* ed. David Novak (Lanham: Rowman and Littlefield, 1996), 111–30.

36 Ibid., 124.

37 Implicit in my use of the term 'revelatory theology' is a distinction – an essential one, as will become clearer in the course of this book – in the thought of both Strauss and Fackenheim, between the brute fact of revelation and its human interpretations. This distinction became necessary when Strauss raised the question of whether the revelatory tradition was reliable, and Fackenheim set out to affirm its reliability insofar as he is successful in constructing a Jewish philosophy.

38 *NRH*, 82.

39 Note that Strauss writes: 'What is "first for us" is not the philosophic un-

derstanding of the city but that understanding which is inherent in the city as such, in the pre-philosophic city, according to which the city sees itself as subject and subservient to the divine in the ordinary understanding of the divine or looks up to it. Only by beginning at this point will we be open to the full impact of the all important question which is coeval with philosophy ... the question *quid sit deus.*' Leo Strauss, *The City and Man* (Chicago: University of Chicago Press, 1978), 241.

40 See Laurence Berns, 'The Relation between Philosophy and Religion: Reflections on Leo Strauss's Suggestion Concerning the Source and Sources of Modern Philosophy,' *Interpretation: A Journal of Political Philosophy* 19, no. 1 (Fall 1991): 43–4.

41 *NRH*, 124.

42 Ibid., 125.

43 Strauss would argue that exceptions to this goal, such as the Wisdom Literature, do not reflect the Bible's primary intention. His reading of the Bible to a more or less consistent purpose cannot be traced to lack of Jewish knowledge.

44 *NRH*, 81. Fackenheim cites the following from *Pirke Avot* (3: 11, 12): 'He whose fear of sin precedes his wisdom, his wisdom shall endure; he whose wisdom precedes his fear of sin, his wisdom shall not endure. He whose deeds exceed his wisdom, his wisdom shall endure; he whose wisdom exceeds his deeds, his wisdom shall not endure.' Emil L. Fackenheim, *What Is Judaism? An Interpretation for the Present Age* [*WJ*] (New York: Summit Books, 1987), 158.

45 See, for instance, Deuteronomy 4:6.

46 One notes, at this point, that Strauss's reading of the Bible or of Plato suggests, if not each's knowledge of the other, then each's recognition of the whole from which its position is derived (and from which the other's is precluded or excluded). Strauss traces the tension between reason and revelation to its roots in the two primary sources of Western thought: Greek philosophy and the Bible.

47 See Leon Kass, *The Beginning of Wisdom: Reading Strauss* (New York: The Free Press, 2003), 31–6.

48 See below, pp. 155–9 and 221–4.

49 See Genesis 9:27: 'God enlarge Japheth [Greeks] and let him dwell in the tents of Shem [Jews].' See also Kass, *The Beginning of Wisdom*, 215.

50 *JPCM*, 131.

51 Thomas Hobbes, *The Elements of Law Natural and Politic, Part I: Human Nature, Part II: De Corpore Politico with Three Lives*, ed. J.C.A. Gaskin (New York: Oxford University Press, 1999), 99.

52 According to Jaffa, as cited by Novak, 'the very term "natural law" is itself an oxymoron in ancient pagan philosophy, for *natura* or *physis* is the opposite of *lex* or *nomos*.' In David Novak, 'Philosophy and the Possibility of Revelation: A Theological Response to the Challenge of Leo Strauss,' in *Leo Strauss and Judaism: Jerusalem and Athens Critically Revisited*, ed. David Novak (Lanham: Rowman and Littlefield, 1996), 184. See Novak 190n48. See also *NRH*, 165–251, esp. 186–92; Strauss, *Studies in Platonic Political Philosophy*, 137–46; and *PW*, 95–8.

53 See Thomas Aquinas, *Treatise on Law*, intro. Stanley Parry (Chicago: Henry Regnery, undated), 110–13 (q. 97, art. 3).

54 Strauss, *Studies in Platonic Political Philosophy*, 144. Here Hobbes follows and modifies Machiavelli.

55 Ibid.

56 Francis Bacon, *The Masculine Birth of Time: Or the Interpretation of Nature*, trans. Laurence Berns, from chapter 1, 'The Legitimate Mode of Handing On [the Torch of Science]' (unpublished).

57 Francis Bacon, *The New Organon and Related Writings*, ed. Fulton H. Anderson (Indianapolis: Bobbs-Merrill Educational Publishing, 1980), 39.

58 Strauss discovered that there remained in the thought of the Enlightenment thinkers a 'subterraneous' affirmation of the possibility of knowledge of the eternal. See *NRH*, 13.

59 See Fackenheim, 'Kant's Philosophy of Religion,' in *GW*.

60 So, for instance, the modern reader reads Machiavelli having already accepted his premises; Cohen, even as he recognizes the separate claims of reason and revelation, cannot recognize their mutual irrefutability. See below, pp. 46–52 and 72–4.

61 See below, pp. 107–11.

62 Spinoza recognized this outcome in his attempt to separate philosophy from revelatory theology. He writes of those who attempt to prove theology mathematically that '… they invoke the aid of reason for her own defeat, and attempt infallibly to prove her fallible. While they are trying to prove mathematically the authority and truth of theology, and to take away the authority of natural reason, they are in reality only bringing theology under reason's dominion …' Benedict de Spinoza, *A Theologico-Political Treatise and A Political Treatise*, trans. R.H.M. Elwes (New York: Dover Publications, 1951), 197–8.

63 *JPCM*, 90.

64 See, for instance, Spinoza's argument: 'From this fact therefrom, that is, that the power whereby natural things exist and operate is the very power of God itself, we easily understand what natural right is. For as God has

a right to everything, and God's right is nothing else, but his very power, as far as the latter is considered to be absolutely free; it follows from this, that every natural thing has by nature as much right, as it has power to exist and operate; since the natural power of every natural thing, whereby it exists and operates, is nothing else but the power of God, which is absolutely free.' Spinoza, *A Theologico-Political Treatise and A Political Treatise*, trans. R.H.M. Elwes (New York: Dover Publications, 1951), 291–2. 'Natural right' in this sense would seem to have been invented by the moderns as a means of reacting against the ancients by reaffirming the sanctity of the individual without bringing in the biblical God.

65 See, Leo Strauss, Introduction, in *Philosophy and Law: Essays toward the Understanding of Maimonides and His Predecessors,* trans. Eve Adler (Albany: SUNY Press, 1995). See also Strauss, *What Is Political Philosophy?* 47.

66 *NRH*, 170. By idealistic, Strauss is referring to the modern notion – spelled out by Spinoza, who articulated contemplation as man's end – that the ideal is the work of human beings and is not 'an end imposed on man by nature.' *SCR*, reprinted in *JPCM*, 156.

67 *NRH*, 170.

68 Fackenheim remarked that, unlike Hegel, Heidegger failed to even consider Spinoza's thought, as is evidenced by the absence of reference to Spinoza's thought in Heidegger's works. Fackenheim, personal interview, August 2003. This failure on Heidegger's part reveals not only the latter's quest for 'freedom' but also his anti-Jewish animus, insofar as the Jewish God alone is precluded as a possible world view. See below, pp. 115–19. Interestingly, Strauss spoke of Heidegger's ignoring Shakespeare and the English in general.

69 As cited in Berns, 'The Relation,' 55.

70 Fackenheim, 'The Revealed Morality of Judaism and Modern Thought: A Confrontation with Kant,' in *QPF*, 206. Strauss's return to Maimonides will be, in a sense, a readoption of these 'additional' assumptions. Strauss will emphasize that the 'hailing distance' into which reason and revelation come is beyond theoretic conception, even as in practical terms reason and revelation each inform our living with the goal of justice. See below, pp. 209–24, esp. 212–13. Strauss traces the modern loss of faith in reason and revelation to the loss of a realm of philosophy distinct from the realm of political philosophy, from the realm in which right action is described.

71 Hobbes, *The Elements of Law*, 144.

72 See Spinoza, *A Political Treatise,* esp. chapters 4 and 5. One notes, however, that to understand Spinoza as anti-Maimonidean or even as being against

the ceremonial laws is but one way to read this thinker, who exists somewhere between medieval and modern thought. See also *JPCM*, 163–5.

73 This is why Strauss argues that, if we are to return to the original cave of philosophy, Spinoza must be refuted in every respect; and furthermore, that such a return might be a return to that lost core, to an unqualified orthodoxy.

74 See, for instance, Fackenheim, 'Hermann Cohen – After Fifty Years,' in *JPJP*, 41–56; *QPF*, 204–28; and Emil L. Fackenheim, *The Religious Dimension in Hegel's Thought* [*RD*] (Chicago: University of Chicago Press, 1967), 10–11.

75 Strauss may or may not concur with this evaluation: he reads Plato as recognizing the contingent insofar as he claims to be presenting the right way of life; but at the same time, he recognizes that his reading of Plato – following Plato! – incorporates contemporary concerns. See, Plato, *The Republic* 473a: action gets hold of truth less than speaking does. For Fackenheim's disagreement with this position, see below, pp. 224–9.

76 Aquinas, however, writes that nothing is in the intellect that is not first in the senses.

77 *RD*, 11.

78 Ibid., 10.

79 See, for instance, Fackenheim's discussion of Nazism as 'modern idolatry' in *EJM*, 201–29.

80 See, for instance, *JPJP*, 41–56; and Graeme Nicholson, 'The Passing of Hegel's Germany,' in *Fackenheim: German Philosophy and Jewish Thought*, ed. Louis Greenspan and Graeme Nicholson (Toronto: University of Toronto Press, 1992). One might suggest also that this radical self-confidence is at the heart of Strauss's critique of Cohen's reading of Spinoza; that is to say, Cohen was not able, according to Strauss, to read Spinoza 'literally,' because he could not recognize that Spinoza himself was not an idealist. See *JPCM*, 156–71.

81 But just as the acknowledgment of mystery at the basis of revelatory theology remains nonetheless a presence in, for instance, the receptacle in the *Timeaus*, so too, as Fackenheim points out, does radical doubt remain an element in the Bible, for instance, in *Ecclesiastes*. See Fackenheim, 'A Retrospective of My Thought,' in *JPJP*, 226.

82 The identification of the permanent problem of Jew hatred in the West – and, more specifically, of 'the radical difference between the requirements of social life and the requirements of intellectual life' (*JPCM* 95) – is the theme of Strauss's essay 'Progress or Return?' See *JPCM*, 87–136.

83 *JPCM*, 90. While one could argue that Spinoza's thought is more of a tran-

sition than a break, Strauss – for reasons that will become more apparent – chooses to emphasize its radical characteristics.

84 Spinoza writes, for instance: 'It is thus abundantly evident that religion among the Hebrews only acquired the form of law through the right of the sovereign rule; when that rule was destroyed, it could no longer be received as the law of a particular kingdom, but only as the universal precept of reason.' Spinoza, *Treatise*, 248. Strauss points out, however, that the new religion that Spinoza attempts to create for the modern liberal state is decisively *not* a religion of reason (*JPCM*, 91).

85 Spinoza, *Treatise*, 248.

86 See ibid., chapter 16.

87 Hobbes, *The Elements of Law*, chapter 25. As Strauss and others have pointed out, Spinoza's position with regard to his near equation of Judaism with democracy may be belied by his statement that 'if the foundations of their religion [Judaism] have not emasculated their minds they may even, if occasion offers, so changeable are human affairs, raise up their empire afresh, and … God may a second time elect them.' Spinoza, *Treatise*, 56. In addition, as Cohen pointed out, Spinoza's advocacy of democracy is suspect when one considers the latter's explicit statement that he is writing only for philosophers. See *JPCM*, 158.

88 Spinoza understands piety as adherence to the true religion and, conversely, impiety as external adherence to what is no longer sacred. The biblical text has shown its ineffectiveness in the right directing of human lives and is no longer sacred. See Spinoza, *Treatise*, chapter 12.

89 Ibid., 207.

90 One sees the desire for Jews to be included in the modern liberal state in, for instance, Spinoza's discussion of the meaning of biblical narratives, wherein he argues that 'the narratives in the Old and New Testaments surpass profane history, and differ among themselves in merit simply by reason of the salutary doctrines which they inculcate.' Ibid., 79. Jewish and Christian *experience* differs, but one can 'surpass' this experience through the philosophical understanding of the universal divine law.

91 Fackenheim, for reasons that will become clearer in the course of this book, reads Spinoza through a historicist lens. His argument that 'Spinoza emerges not as the founder of biblical criticism but rather as the founder of "Old Testament" criticism only' (*MW*, 44) is not supported by Strauss, who argues that he does 'not find that [Spinoza] was more opposed to Judaism than to Christianity.' *JPCM*, 90. For Strauss, reading Spinoza as an esoteric writer, Spinoza's attempt rather is to dismiss all revelation in order to found a state based on the Noachide laws. See ibid., 88–9.

92 *JPCM*, 89.

93 Ibid., 130.

94 Furthermore, Spinoza does not claim to refute revelation: 'It is not my purpose here to refute the assertions of those who assert that the natural light of reason can teach nothing of any value concerning the true way of salvation.' Spinoza, *Treatise*, 80. It is unclear whether Spinoza was, as Novalis argued, 'God-intoxicated,' or whether he was Machiavellian insofar as he recognized that the best way for Jews to be granted religious tolerance was to deprecate Judaism – that he was in fact an atheist appealing nonetheless to religious prejudices. Strauss argues that Spinoza begs this fundamental question, but Spinoza may have thought that he had shown in the *Treatise* that the Bible aimed primarily at positing moral and political principles.

95 One sees this zeroing in on the problem in Cohen's stunning critique, amidst what Strauss describes as the near unanimous celebration, of Spinoza. See *JPCM*, 154–61.

96 See *JPJP*, 47–9. Strauss formulates Cohen's failure as his succumbing to idealism: the latter is unable to move from the interpretation of the experience of history to the experience of history itself.

97 Strauss suggests this very startling irony in the Preface: Spinoza attempts to solve the Jewish problem of their exclusion from the state by promoting a modern liberal democracy wherein Jews and Christians will be united in thought. But Spinoza's two resolutions – the assimilationist model and the Zionist model – not only fail to solve the problem of Jewish exclusion from the state, fuelled by the perpetuation and protection of private Jew hatred, but also introduce a new problem: Jews now have no unequivocal recourse to their heritage.

98 *JPCM*, 104.

99 See *PW*, 154–8.

100 Spinoza, *Treatise*, 197.

101 *JPCM*, 92.

102 See below, pp. 159–71.

103 Perhaps, however, Jews and Judaism stand as only the most exposed form of this 'theologico-political' problem.

104 For a fuller discussion of the differences between Strauss and Fackenheim on the rejection or acceptance of historicism, see chapter 4.

105 Strauss calls into question that concern by exposing modern philosophy to a radical 'deconstruction,' suggesting that the more fundamental problem is the relation of Jewish thought to philosophy, not just modern philosophy.

106 Spinoza writes, for instance: 'It is quite certain that the expressions, "the hill of God," and "His tents and the dwellers therein," [Psalms 15 and 24] refer to blessedness and security of soul, not to the actual mount of Jerusalem and the tabernacle of Moses ...' Spinoza, *Treatise*, 71. While not necessarily denying that Spinoza uses esoteric writing, Fackenheim is more concerned with the actualities that issued from Spinoza's exoteric speech.

107 *MW*, 44–6.

108 The *Muselmaenner* were the 'living dead' who made up the mass of inmates at the Nazi death camps. They ultimately died of exhaustion, 'covered with filth and lice.' *WJ*, 265. See also, among other places, *MW*, 25, 99–100; and *JRH*, 246–7.

109 *JPCM*, 172.

110 Catherine H. Zuckert, *Postmodern Platos: Nietzsche, Heidegger, Gadamer, Strauss, Derrida* (Chicago: University of Chicago Press, 1996), 109.

111 Fackenheim notes, however, that 'in an unpublished lecture given just prior to his death, Strauss not only argued for the irrefutability and moral nobility of traditional Orthodoxy ... but also admitted his inability to regard it as more than a noble illusion.' *MW*, 89n. The reference is probably to 'Why We Remain Jews,' published for the first time in Kenneth L. Deutsch and Walter Nicgorski, eds., *Leo Strauss: Political Philosopher and Jewish Thinker* (Lanham: Rowman and Littlefield, 1994), 60 (reprinted in *JPCM*).

112 Strauss is, of course, a political philosopher, but he discovers that 'what is "first for us" is not the philosophic understanding of the city but that understanding which is inherent in the city as such, in the pre-philosophic city, according to which the city sees itself as subject and subservient to the divine in the ordinary understanding of the divine or looks up to it. Only by beginning at this point will we be open to the full impact of the all-important question which is coeval with philosophy although the philosophers do not frequently pronounce it – the question *quid sit dues.*' Strauss, *The City and Man*, as cited in ibid., 3.

113 Zuckert, *Postmodern Platos*, 111.

114 See, for instance, Leo Strauss, *On Tyranny: Including the Strauss–Kojeve Correspondence*, rev. and exp., ed. Victor Gourevitch and Michael S. Roth (New York: The Free Press, 1991).

115 See below, p. 225.

116 Fackenheim, 'These Twenty Years,' in *QPF*, 8. 'Covenental affirmation' becomes a technical term in Fackenheim's thought. It is at once an affirmation of the ongoing covenant made between God and the Jewish people and an acknowledgment that that covenant may be emptied of all content

specificity. Fackenheim affirms the necessity of commitment to 'Judaism' even as he leaves open both whether that Judaism is a perpetuation of the Sinaitic covenant and also what that Judaism may look like. See below, pp. 194–201.

117 See below, pp. 129–30.

118 While Buber finds it sufficient to affirm the epistemological validity of revelation, or the I-Thou relationship, Fackenheim feels it necessary to affirm the presence of God in and through secular history, or to account for the possibility of God's action within secular experience. See below, pp. 145–6.

119 See, for instance, Fackenheim, 'Elijah and the Empiricists' in *EJM*.

120 This statement must be qualified. Both Steven B. Smith and Deutsch and Nicgorski note that Strauss wrote on Jewish topics throughout his life, 'namely commentaries on Maimonides, Halevi, Spinoza, Hermann Cohen, Franz Rosenzweig, the Bible, and Zionism.' Deutsch and Nicgorski, *Leo Strauss*, 4. See also Smith, 'Leo Strauss,' 81–2. Strauss's work in political philosophy, however, may be understood – insofar as it serves to promote both pre-modern philosophy and revelation – also as work in Jewish thought. See below, pp. 209–24. Strauss himself writes: 'I believe I can say, without any exaggeration, that since a very, very early time the main theme of my reflections has been what is called the "Jewish question."' Strauss, 'Why We Remain Jews,' reprinted in *JPCM*, 312.

121 See below, pp. 39–41; 81; and 112–13.

122 See below, pp. 91–106.

123 Strauss, *On Tyranny*, 205, as cited in Werner J. Dannhauser, 'Athens and Jerusalem or Jerusalem and Athens?' in *Leo Strauss and Judaism*, ed. David Novak (Lanham: Rowman and Littlefield, 1996), 161.

124 A brief comparison of Strauss and Fackenheim's contextualizations of Spinoza and Cohen is illustrative. Strauss contextualizes Spinoza's *Treatise*, not within the rabbinic framework, but in increasingly tolerant Amsterdam; he concludes that Spinoza's text is based in history and that one must therefore read the text historically. This historical contextualization reveals to Strauss the fallacy of Cohen's argument that Spinoza was a traitor to the Jews: while Spinoza may have hated Judaism, he did not hate the Jews. Spinoza's intention, conveyed esoterically, was to ameliorate the Jewish political situation. Although Strauss recognizes that Spinoza plays '"a most dangerous game," even an "amazingly unscrupulous" one' (*SCR*, 19 and 21, cited in Steven B. Smith, *Spinoza, Liberalism, and the Question of Jewish Identity* [New Haven: Yale University Press, 1997], 18), he discovers that Spinoza continues to recognize both the necessity of reli-

gion for political stability, and also that the philosopher, who eschews all religions, takes refuge from political authority. Furthermore, Strauss argues that 'it is of the essence of the wise man that he is able to live under every form of government.' *PW*, 180. But I have omitted from the citation its first word: 'if.' Because Strauss begins this sentence with the conditional, and furthermore is addressing in this sentence the specific need for esoteric writing, it is unclear that Fackenheim's understanding in this matter, as laid out below, is warranted.

Fackenheim, on the other hand, concludes, along with Cohen, that Spinoza was a traitor to the Jews, but his intellectual path is not, like Cohen's, guided by an exoteric reading based in idealism. Rather, to Fackenheim, Spinoza's *Treatise* is a failure because it does not recognize that there might exist political authorities that would preclude Jews as human beings from living as philosophers. See *MW*, 99 and 38–58. Fackenheim's reading of Spinoza is informed by Strauss's recognition that texts base themselves in a given authority; but his reading also parts ways from Strauss in its recognition of the historical, religio-secular consciousness of Jews. See, for instance, Fackenheim, 'Judaism and the Meaning of Life,' in *QPF*, 245: because he did not 'stop short' of 'embracing mysticism[,] ... Spinoza ... pass[es] beyond the bounds of Judaism.' Fackenheim's reading of Spinoza's *Treatise* is both a critique of Cohen's idealistic reading, and also – while recognizing that the text is historically based – a recontextualization of the text within a proposed historical perpetuation of the rabbinic tradition. For Strauss's reading of Spinoza, see below, pp. 65–72; for Strauss's reading of Cohen, below, pp. 72–5; for Fackenheim's reading of Spinoza, below, pp. 129–33.

125 Both thinkers were German Holocaust refugees, but Strauss left Germany before Hitler rose to supreme power (in 1932). Fackenheim spent three months in Sachsenhausen after *Kristallnacht* (November 1938–January 1939).

126 See below, pp. 91–106 and 148–58.

127 See below, pp. 155–9 and 209–24.

128 Strauss, *Studies in Platonic Political Philosophy*. The import of the central placement of this essay is spelled out by Zuckert: 'According to the rules of reading Strauss formulated almost two decades after he published his first study of Spinoza, the central chapter, item, or discussion is often the most important.' Zuckert, *Postmodern Platos*, 300n8.

129 See below, pp. 228–9. The question of whether it is possible for a way of thinking to end, as Fackenheim attempts to effectuate, is beyond the scope of this book. Within its scope is the question of whether or to what

extent Fackenheim's religious existentialism – insofar as it remains concerned with the permanent human questions – is utterly new.

130 For a discussion of whether Fackenheim accepts an unqualified historicism in *MW*, see Michael L. Morgan, 'Philosophy, History, and the Jewish Thinker: Jewish Thought and Philosophy in Emil Fackenheim's *To Mend the World*,' in *Dilemmas in Modern Jewish Thought*, ed. Louis Greenspan and Graeme Nicholson (Toronto: University of Toronto Press, 1992).

131 Fackenheim himself suggested this formulation to me. Fackenheim, personal interview, August 2003.

132 *EJM*, 69.

133 W.B. Yeats, 'The Second Coming,' in *The Collected Poems of W.B. Yeats* (New York: Macmillan, 1959), 184.

134 *JPJP*, 226.

135 See *MW*, 91–100, esp. 94ff.

136 See, for instance, David Novak, ed., *Leo Strauss and Judaism: Jerusalem and Athens Critically Revisited* (Lanham: Rowman and Littlefield, 1996); Deutsch and Nicgorski, *Leo Strauss*; Susan Orr, *Jerusalem and Athens: Reason and Revelation in the Work of Leo Strauss* (Lanham: Rowman and Littlefield, 1995); Kenneth Hart Green, *Jew and Philosopher: The Return to Maimonides in the Jewish Thought of Leo Strauss* (Albany: SUNY Press, 1993); *JPCM*; and Morgan, *Dilemmas*, 40–54, 55–67.

137 I am grateful to Laurence Berns, a student of Strauss, for this characterization.

138 Baum, for instance, argues that Fackenheim is far more effective in directing Christian than Jewish theology. He writes: 'Fackenheim is a brilliant theologian for Christians but an uncertain guide for Jewish believers.' See Gregory Baum, 'Fackenheim and Christianity,' in *Fackenheim: German Philosophy and Jewish Thought*, ed. Louis Greenspan and Graeme Nicholson (Toronto: University of Toronto Press, 1992), 180. On the other hand, Krell argues that there was a shift in Fackenheim's relationship to Christianity from one of 'appreciation' to one of 'antagonism' after the Six Day War. See Marc A. Krell, 'Post-Holocaust vs. Postmodern: Emil Fackenheim's Evolving Dialogue with Christianity,' *Journal of Jewish Thought and Philosophy* 12, no. 1 (2003): 69–96.

139 Consider, for example, just one of Fackenheim's tributes to Strauss: 'Ever since my student days, it was Leo Strauss – first, the author of books, later also the personal mentor, this even when I no longer saw him, but often kept thinking of him – whose example has convinced me, more than that of any other Jewish thinker alive in my own lifetime, of the possibility, and therefore the necessity, of a Jewish philosophy for our age.' *MW*, x.

140 See below, pp. 115–17.

141 See *NRH*, 169.

142 'Nature to be commanded must be obeyed.' Bacon, *The New Organon*, 39.

143 See, for instance, *NRH*, 35–80, esp. 60–1n22.

144 Deutsch and Nicgorski, *Leo Strauss*, 12.

145 Fackenheim, 'On the Eclipse of God,' in *QPF*, 232.

146 Ibid., 235–6.

147 Ibid., 239.

148 Fackenheim considered his work in Christian–Jewish relations to be his most pressing work toward the end of his life. Fackenheim, personal interview, August 2003.

149 Fackenheim, 'These Twenty Years,' 8.

150 See Michael L. Morgan, *Interim Judaism: Jewish Thought in a Century of Crisis* (Bloomington: Indiana University Press, 2001), 22–7.

151 Indeed, Strauss's commitment to openness with regard to the practical choice between philosophy and revelatory theology is evident in the fact that Fackenheim, his younger protegé, chose not to abandon revelatory theology.

152 *MW*, 4–5.

153 Strauss, correspondence to Glikes, reprinted on back cover, *MW*.

154 I mention in this regard Harvey C. Mansfield's statement on the back cover of Leo Strauss, *Thoughts on Machiavelli* (Chicago: University of Chicago Press, 1978): 'When studying Machiavelli, every time that I have been thrown upon an uninhabited island I thought might be unexplored, I have come across a small sign saying, "please deposit coin." After I comply, a large sign flashed in neon lights that would have been visible from afar, with this message: "Leo Strauss was here."'

155 See, for instance, Strauss on Cohen: 'Cohen read Spinoza on the one hand not literally enough and on the other hand much too literally; he understood him too literally because he did not read him literally enough.' *JPCM*, 167.

156 Strauss, *Thoughts on Machiavelli*, 13.

157 Note that Thomas Aquinas recognized that human law is necessary for the wicked as a means to restraint. Aquinas, *Summa Theologica* q95 art1. Yet he also recognized that the eternal law is imprinted on all of nature (ibid., q93 art5) including wicked human beings. In this way, Aquinas in effect equated reason with revelation. This may solve the problem of the peculiarly modern distortion of revelation; even so, for Fackenheim, a new relationship between reason and revelation must be developed be-

cause, while Aquinas may solve the problem of evil, he does not solve the problem of *radical* evil.

For Strauss, on the other hand, Aquinas may solve the problem of evil in his own medieval philosophical terms: 'laws may be unjust through being opposed to the Divine good: such are the laws of tyrants inducing to idolatry.' Ibid., q96 art4. But he does not solve the problem of philosophy's enthrallment to theology.

158 Regarding the 'old' versus the 'new' thinking, Fackenheim writes: 'The difference is rather that the "old" thinking, having carried the mind above time and existence, carries it to dwell in eternity, whereas the "new," having carried the mind to things eternal, perceives these latter to be empty abstractions, and is plunged by this perception back into existential limitations, now *known* to be untranscendable.' *MW*, 63.

159 Fackenheim makes little mention of Moslems.

2. Strauss's Formulation of the Relationship between Reason and Revelation in Modern Thought

1 Leo Tolstoy, *Anna Karenina*, trans. Rochelle S. Townsend, vol. 1 (New York: E.P. Dutton, 1943), 239–40.

2 David Janssens, *Between Athens and Jerusalem: Philosophy, Prophecy, and Politics in Leo Strauss' Early Thought* (Albany: SUNY Press, 2008), 175.

3 Ibid., 174–5.

4 See Leo Strauss, *Jewish Philosophy and the Crisis of Modernity: Essays and Lectures in Modern Jewish Thought*, ed. Kenneth Hart Green [*JPCM*] (Albany: SUNY Press, 1997), 137.

5 So, for instance, Strauss points to Maimonides as the exemplary model for the relationship between reason and revelation. Maimonides deviates both from the inference made, for instance, by Aristotle for the eternity of the world and also from the reliability of the tradition of Creation. See, for instance, Maimonides, *Guide for the Perplexed*, trans. Shlomo Pines (Chicago: University of Chicago Press, 1963), I:13–25, esp. chapters 14 and 25. See also Hillel Fradkin, 'Philosophy and Law: Leo Strauss as a Student of Medieval Jewish Thought,' in *Leo Strauss: Political Philosopher and Jewish Thinker*, ed. Kenneth L. Deutsch and Walter Nicgorski (Lanham: Rowman and Littlefield, 1994).

6 Strauss, *Thoughts on Machiavelli* (Chicago: University of Chicago Press, 1978), 13.

7 Arnaldo Momigliano, 'Hermeneutics and Classical Political Thought in Leo Strauss,' in *Essays on Ancient and Modern Judaism*, ed. Silvia Berti,

trans. Maura Masella-Gayley (Chicago: University of Chicago Press, 1994), 188. This hermeneutics includes a tendency to presume modernity superior by refusing to allow pre-modern texts to speak in their own non-historicist terms. See below, pp. 38–40 and 48–9.

8 Strauss, for instance, finds in the ancient texts a paradox: their politics was utopian in that it began with the discovery of the permanent nobility of human nature, yet at the same time, these thinkers knew that the actualization of this ideal could not be accomplished. 'According to Strauss, all classical thought represents a noble attempt to come close to th[e] impossibility [of utopia].' Momigliano, 'Hermeneutics,' 183. So, for instance, Plato pokes fun at himself. But because this paradox is never stated outright, Strauss concludes that these thinkers wrote esoterically. See ibid., 183–4.

Umphrey formulates the paradox in the following way: 'There is much evidence that Strauss sought to revive political philosophy in the original, full sense of the term. But there is also evidence of a strong inclination, on his part, toward a positive natural right teaching.' Stewart Umphrey, 'Natural Right and Philosophy,' in *Leo Strauss: Political Philosopher and Jewish Thinker,* ed. Kenneth L. Deutsch and Walter Nicgorski (Lanham: Rowman and Littlefield, 1994), 288.

9 See below, pp. 209–24.

10 Strauss is more interested in the commonalities between Plato and Aristotle – and indeed, all the ancients – than in their differences. He claims, for instance, that despite their 'profound differences,' both 'agree in regard to the most fundamental point: both admit that the distinction between nature and convention is fundamental.' Leo Strauss, *Natural Right and History* [NRH] (Chicago: University of Chicago Press, 1953), 11. His emphasis on the commonalities among the ancients serves to underline the quarrel between the ancients and the moderns as primary. See below, pp. 47–8 and 73–5.

11 *NRH*, 123.

12 See, for instance, Plato's simile of the divided line: one ascends from knowledge arrived at through use of the 'originals of the visible order' to that arrived at through use 'solely by and through the forms themselves' only when one recognizes his assumptions as assumptions. Plato, *The Republic,* trans. Desmond Lee, rev. 2nd ed. (New York: Penguin Books, 1987), 252 (510b). Only with the recognition that wisdom begins and must remain in the surface of things can one arrive at conclusions that comprise true knowledge of the permanent things. Strauss discovers, for instance, that for both Plato and Aristotle, 'there is a universally valid hierarchy of ends, but there are no universally valid rules of action.' *NRH*, 162.

13 Ibid., 82.
14 Likewise, Strauss's critique of the idea of liberalism – or, more generally, of progress – circumscribes all ideas adopted from within the idea of liberalism. See below, pp. 166–71.
15 *NRH*, 84–5.
16 Leo Strauss, *The City and Man* (Chicago: University of Chicago Press, 1978), 22.
17 *NRH*, 123.
18 See below, pp. 155–9 and 209–24.
19 As we shall see, Fackenheim attempts, while affirming the primacy of the surface of things, to firmly establish this doubt within the revelatory tradition. See below, pp. 194–201.
20 *NRH*, 120.
21 See ibid., 146.
22 Strauss points out that the natural right doctrine that was developed in the seventeenth century must be distinguished from this classic natural right doctrine. See below, pp. 159–71.
23 Strauss argues that Socrates' innovative focus is rather a return to 'common sense.' *NRH*, 123. In reference to Maimonides, who 'remember[s] the darkness' in which knowledge of things may suddenly be glimpsed, Gilson defines common sense as an 'intellectual modesty, which differs alike from presumption and skepticism.' Étienne Gilson, 'Homage to Maimonides,' in *Essays on Maimonides: An Octocentennial Volume*, ed. Salo Wittmayer Baron (New York: Columbia University Press, 1941), 27.
24 See, for instance, Aristotle: 'One must begin from what is known, but this has two meanings, the things known to us and the things that are known simply [i.e., as first principles]. Perhaps then we, at any rate, ought to begin from the things that are known to us.' Aristotle, *Nicomachean Ethics*, trans. Joe Sachs (Newburyport: Focus Publishing, 2002), 4 (1095b). For Fackenheim, however, the separation of what one sees with one's own eyes and what one knows from hearsay may not be ultimate. These elements may coexist, albeit in tension, under the rubric of revelation: through reenactment, what one knows with one's own eyes *is* what one knows from hearsay. On the question of what is at stake in Strauss's beginning with the separation of the natural from the conventional, see below, pp. 159–71.
25 *NRH*, 123.
26 One sees suggested in Strauss's study of classic natural right both his desire for a return, after the tyrannies of the first half of the twentieth century, to common sense, to the common understanding of things human; and

also his discovery of the openness necessary between philosophy (thought based in nature) and revelatory theology (thought based in the divine), since what alone is accessible to human beings is the surface of things. Note the revolutionary/reactionary character of Strauss's reading of Plato: the stereotypical understanding of Plato as perhaps too quickly vast is replaced with that of a thinker continually grounded in the immediately accessible.

27 Sometimes, according to Strauss, in order to understand a philosopher's position with regard to the permanent human problems, a text will require that it be read according to its surface, as in Machiavelli; and sometimes it will require that it be read 'against' its surface, so to speak, as in Hobbes. See below, pp. 46–56.

28 Laurence Berns, 'The Relation between Philosophy and Religion: Reflections on Leo Strauss' Suggestion Concerning the Source and Sources of Modern Philosophy,' *Interpretation: A Journal of Political Philosophy* 19, no. 1 (Fall 1991): 43–5.

29 Ibid., 45. In Greek thought there is no divine promise backing up the human striving for morality. The imperative in Greek thought is 'know thyself,' which places the burden of morality exclusively on the human being. Although Plato in the *Laws* tries to devise a standard of fear based on the acceptance of the more excellent, because that more excellent remains human, there is no guarantor for that limit. Greek thought lives in wonder, but without fear and without hope. See, for instance, *JPCM*, 128.

30 See below, pp. 209–24. Strauss suggests that biblical revelation has no word for doubt and that therefore the tension between natural and revelatory religion continually persists. Fackenheim, on the other hand, will find doubt in the rabbinic tradition. Adopting Strauss's insight, he will retain the tension between natural religion (or secular experience) and Judaism.

31 Strauss understands conventionalism as 'the contention that the variety of notions of right proves the nonexistence of natural right or the conventional character of all right.' *NRH*, 10. Classical conventionalism, while in disagreement with Plato's discovery of classic natural right, agrees with the validity of the distinction between nature and convention. For a fuller discussion of the distinctions between classical and modern conventionalism, see ibid., 9–34; and below, pp. 159–71.

32 *NRH*, 9.

33 Aristotle, *Nicomachean Ethics*, 1134b24-7, as cited in ibid., 10.

34 For more on Strauss's critique of modern historicism and its delusional aspects, see below, pp. 159–71.

35 This is not to suggest that all modern thinkers make this critique. Strauss

points to Hobbes as an example of a thinker who argues that where reason is not cultivated, natural right will not be known universally. See Hobbes, *De Cive* 2:1, as cited in *NRH*, 9.

36 So, for instance, Aristotle argues that nature, or natural right, is not immediately accessible to the individual; rather, nature is transformed into society, from which and in which the individual finds definition.

37 The ascent from the realm of convention, which is defined by public dogma, to the realm of nature, understood as the quest for the eternal, situates philosophy as a private activity. *NRH*, 12. This is why Strauss understands the basis of the distinction between Jerusalem and Athens as the distinction between public law and private philosophy. Fackenheim will dispute this distinction on the basis of Judaism's interconnection between the public and the private, or the law and *kavanah*. This latter position will suggest further to him that the historicism that results from the seeming dismissal of the distinction between convention and nature is a matter distinct from the idea of history within Jewish thought. See, for instance, Emil L. Fackenheim, 'Judaism and the Idea of Progress,' in *Quest for Past and Future: Essays in Jewish Theology* [*QPF*] (Boston: Beacon Press, 1968). For more on the distinctions between Strauss and Fackenheim with regard to historicism, see chapter 4 of this book.

38 *NRH*, 11.

39 Strauss writes, for instance, that '"philosophy" designates primarily, not a set of dogmas … but a method, or an attitude.' Leo Strauss, *Persecution and the Art of Writing* [*PW*] (Chicago: University of Chicago Press, 1980), 105n29.

40 In this, Strauss follows Heidegger. See below, pp. 56–60.

41 See *JPCM*, 87–136. For Strauss's conception of the coexistence of Greek philosophy and biblical thought, see below, pp. 209–24.

42 Niccolo Machiavelli, *The Prince*, trans. Harvey Mansfield (Chicago: University of Chicago Press, 1998), 4. See also ibid., 59, 72, 98.

43 Drury, for instance, suggests that Strauss 'probably used Machiavelli as his mouthpiece.' S.B. Drury, 'The Esoteric Philosophy of Leo Strauss,' *Political Theory* 13, no. 3 (August 1985): 318, 323. Her misunderstanding of Strauss's work on Machiavelli stems from her not reading Strauss (or Machiavelli) literally enough: for Strauss, the crucial point about Machiavelli is the latter's *denial* of the classical tradition, even if that denial is in keeping with the traditional antagonism between the city and philosophy. The most important sentence in his book on Machiavelli is his assessment of Machiavelli's remaining with the surface of things: 'The problem inherent in the surface of things, and only in the surface of things, is the heart of things.'

Strauss, *Thoughts on Machiavelli*, 13. Strauss, of course, favoured a return to the classical tradition.

44 *NRH*, 61n22.

45 In the re-establishment of this conversation, Strauss argues also that, like the permanent human problems, history itself cannot be known within a historical basis. See below, pp. 159–71.

46 See below, pp. 209–24.

47 See *NRH*, 180.

48 For a classically informed (albeit anachronistic) refutation of Machiavelli's view of Fortune, see Dante (Alighieri), *The Divine Comedy*, trans. Laurence Binyon, notes C.H. Grandgent, in *The Portable Dante*, ed. Paolo Milano (New York: Viking Press, 1947), 38–9 (*Inferno* 7:61–96).

49 Strauss, *Thoughts on Machiavelli*, 176.

50 Ibid., 177.

51 Both Machiavelli and Socrates, for instance, corrupted the young in order to free philosophy from sophists, or relativists. But unlike Socrates, 'Machiavelli's philosophizing … remains on the whole within the limits set by the city qua closed to philosophy.' Ibid., 296. See also below.

52 Ibid.

53 Strauss discovers that Machiavelli's willingness 'to give advice with equal competence and alacrity to tyrants as well as to free peoples' was only 'apparent': it disregards the most basic fact that Machiavelli remained always aware of the changing expediency of the political realm. Ibid., 4.

54 Leo Strauss, 'Relativism,' in *Relativism and the Study of Man*, ed. Helmut Schoeck and James W. Wiggins (New York: Van Nostrand, 1961), 148.

55 Strauss, *Thoughts on Machiavelli*, 9. So, for instance, he attributes crucial importance to a 'mistake' made by Machiavelli in *Discourses* I, 26, *because* it is made in chapter 26. See Dante Germino, 'Blasphemy and Leo Strauss's Machiavelli,' in *Leo Strauss: Political Philosopher and Jewish Thinker*, ed. Kenneth L. Deutsch and Walter Nicgorski (Lanham: Rowman and Littlefield, 1994), 298–9.

56 See below, pp. 159–71.

57 *PW*, 155.

58 Strauss, *Thoughts on Machiavelli*, 296.

59 Strauss and Cropsey, as cited by Germino, 'Blasphemy and Leo Strauss's Machiavelli,' 299. It is in this sense that Machiavelli is not simply a thinker promoting or encouraging or introducing evil, but rather a teacher of evil. The reader is, so to speak, a convert to Machiavellianism without consciously recognizing as much.

60 Strauss, *Thoughts on Machiavelli*, 12.

61 Machiavelli, 49.

62 Ibid., 24.

63 See ibid., 68–70 (Chapter 18).

64 Chiron is the wisest of the centaurs and became the teacher of Aesculapius and others. After his death, he was placed among the stars in the constellation of Sagittarius (as the Archer).

65 Machiavelli, *The Prince*, 61.

66 Ibid., 69.

67 Ibid., 4, 59, 72, 98.

68 Ibid., 69.

69 See Xenophon, 'Hiero or Tyrannicus' and 'On Tyranny,' both in Leo Strauss, *On Tyranny: Including the Strauss–Kojeve Correspondence*, rev. and exp., ed. Victor Gourevitch and Michael S. Roth (New York: The Free Press, 1991). Strauss mentions also the Platonic characters Callicles and Thrasymachus and the Athenian ambassadors of Thucydides as examples of similar teachings that remained covert. Strauss, *Thoughts on Machiavelli*, 10. See also above, pp. 41–6.

70 Strauss, *Thoughts on Machiavelli*, 11.

71 Ibid., 10.

72 Classical philosophy, Strauss discovers, does not deny that philosophers might view revelatory religion as deriving its authority from the human being, but nor does such philosophy *reveal* this insight.

73 Against this position, Germino argues 'that Machiavelli was not guilty of "impious irreverence" but instead explicitly condemned blasphemy.' Kenneth L. Deutsch and Walter Nicgorski, eds., Introduction to *Leo Strauss: Political Philosopher and Jewish Thinker* (Lanham: Rowman and Littlefield, 1994), 36. See also Germino, 'Blasphemy and Leo Strauss's Machiavelli.'

74 Strauss, *Thoughts on Machiavelli*, 10. In terms that will become more pressing in the later chapters of this book, one might see in Machiavelli's ambiguous stance with regard to religion, and with regard to the state, also his ambivalent stance with regard to history: while 'Machiavelli and Hobbes dethrone classical philosophy and revert to pragmatic history as the best teacher man can have in planning and conducting his life, they still cling to a two-dimensional history to build their own political philosophy.' Jacob Klein, 'History and the Liberal Arts,' *St. John's Review* 47, no. 2 (2003): 17. As Klein maintains, this 'two-dimensional' history enables Machiavelli to retain the Leibnizian distinction between the true and the certain, a distinction that still allows the possibility of a non-historical perspective or standard of justice.

75 Machiavelli, *The Prince*, 69.

76 Ibid., 21–5.

77 See above.

78 See Strauss, 'Restatement on Xenophon's *Hiero*,' in *What Is Political Philosophy? and Other Studies* (Westport: Greenwood Press, 1959), 102.

79 Machiavelli, *The Prince*, 102.

80 '[You] can put [yourself] at the head of this redemption. This is not difficult if you summon up the actions and lives of those named above [i.e., Moses, Cyrus, Romulus, and Theseus]. And although these men are rare and marvelous, nonetheless they were men ... their undertaking was not more just than this one, nor easier, nor was God more friendly to them than to you.' Ibid., 102–3.

81 Ibid., 22.

82 Strauss, *Thoughts on Machiavelli*. 12. One might consider Buber or Fackenheim's formulation of 'subjectivist reductionism,' the reduction of religion to either an empirical fact or a subjective feeling on the part of the believer. Either position allows the dismissal of religion as either irrelevant or untrue. See below, pp. 129–33 and 140–8.

83 Strauss emphasizes the importance of recognizing the distinction between Aristotle and Machiavelli: 'Machiavelli denies natural right, because he takes his bearings by the extreme situations in which the demands of justice are reduced to the requirements of necessity, and not [as in Aristotle] by the normal situations in which the demands of justice in the strict sense are the highest law.' *NRH*, 162.

84 Strauss sees the following development: modern atheism leads to recognition that human beings can conquer nature through the new science, which in turn points to the distinction between natural and human sciences – a distinction that ultimately led to historicism.

85 One might argue that Heidegger's use of the transhistorical to solve this problem serves ultimately to seemingly destroy the eternal verities absolutely. Strauss writes that 'for Heidegger there is no security, no happy ending, no divine shepherd; hope is replaced by thinking; the longing for eternity, belief in anything eternal is understood as stemming from "the spirit of revenge," from the desire to escape from all passing away into something that never passes away.' Leo Strauss, *Spinoza's Critique of Religion* (New York: Schocken Books, 1982), 11. See below, pp. 56–60.

86 Strauss, *Thoughts on Machiavelli*, 296.

87 Machiavelli, *The Prince*, 99.

88 As noted above, Machiavelli is the initiator of this process but not its final

word. History would replace completely the natural order as the standard by which to judge human action only in the later modern perid.

89 Strauss, *Thoughts on Machiavelli*, 174. I base my argument that Strauss recognizes this as the ultimate lesson for Machiavelli's readers on the fact that this statement occurs near the centre of his book. As Zuckert, as well as others, have pointed out, the rules for reading Strauss include that the central part of each of his books is the most important. Zuckert, *Postmodern Platos*, 300. One should here consider his odd formulation: Machiavelli does not write that what cannot be said ought not be said, but the reverse. How does one know what ought not to be said if one cannot be so taught? If my line of thinking is correct (i.e., that Strauss discovers that Machiavelli's greatest evil is his dissemination of philosophy in the public realm), might this formulation argue for Machiavelli's revolutionizing of the art of esoteric writing?

90 It is not simply the historical sense that Strauss contests, but rather also its development into historicism: 'Historical understanding, the revitalization of earlier ways of thinking, was originally meant as a corrective for the shortcomings of the modern mind. This impulse was however vitiated from the outset by the belief which accompanied it, that modern thought … was superior to the thought of the past … Historical understanding loses its liberating force by becoming historicism, which is nothing other than the petrified and self-complacent form of the self-criticism of the modern mind.' *PW*, 158. For a fuller discussion of Strauss's critique of historicism, see below, pp. 159–71.

91 Momigliano, 'Hermeneutics,' 186. Hobbes's debt to Thucydides includes the latter's demonstration of 'the omnipresence of war in the real city.' Ibid., 184. But Hobbes fails to recognize that Thucydides's work served to 'reaffirm the utopian character of the city built by philosophers.' Ibid., 184. He fails to account for the paradox at the heart of Thucydides's project, a paradox that is the impetus for the esoteric level of the latter's work.

92 Ironically, Strauss characterizes the ideal of the Enlightenment as 'atheism with a good conscience,' a vehement denial of God paired with an 'intellectual probity' that is the 'descendant of the tradition grounded in the Bible.' Leo Strauss, *Philosophy and Law: Essays toward the Understanding of Maimonides and His Predecessors*, trans. Eve Adler (Albany: SUNY Press, 1995), 37. In the sense that the Bible provides a way of thinking used by modern philosophy, Strauss discovers that, even while modern philosophy attempted to free itself from the need for biblical thought, it continued to move in accordance with biblical thought. Ibid., 37.

93 Strauss argues that the modern anthropocentric world view goes hand
in hand with the modern beliefs in progress and the idea of history. The
transition from the medieval theocentric, to the modern anthropocentric,
model, not only – in a philosophically arbitrary way – shifted the primacy of authority from God to the human being, but also, on the model
of natural science, introduced the idea of progress. Precisely because the
anthropocentric world view is subsequent to the physiocentric and theocentric world views, it is presumed to be superior. See *JPCM*, 102–4.

94 See below, pp. 56–60.

95 Again, following Leibnitz, we distinguish between the certain and the
true.

96 Laurence Berns, 'Putting Things Back Together Again in Kant,' *Interpretation: A Journal of Political Philosophy* 28, no. 3 (Spring 2001): 209.

97 Fackenheim, on the other hand, accepts the idea that historical consciousness has to a limited extent informed thought. Thus, simply *because* moderns read Hobbes without recognizing his higher aspirations, this is how
he *should* be read by moderns. Hobbes's exoteric critique of religion (if I
may fairly apply Fackenheim's thoughts on Spinoza to him) not only undermines the belief in religious rites, but also precludes Jewish inclusion
– or inclusion of Jews as Jews – from participation in the modern liberal
state. See below, pp. 129–33 and 172–94.

98 *NRH*, 168.

99 Martin D. Yaffe, 'Autonomy, Community, Authority: Hermann Cohen,
Carl Schmitt, Leo Strauss,' in *Autonomy and Judaism: The Individual and the
Community in Jewish Philosophical Thought*, ed. Daniel H. Frank (Albany:
SUNY Press, 1992), 154. For a discussion of the similarities and differenc-
es between Strauss and Schmitt, see Susan Shell, 'Taking Evil Seriously:
Schmitt's "Concept of the Political" and Strauss' "True Politics,"' in *Leo
Strauss: Political Philosopher and Jewish Thinker*, ed. Kenneth L. Deutsch and
Walter Nicgorski (Lanham: Rowman and Littlefield, 1994).

100 Abraham Lincoln, 'First Inaugural Address, March 4, 1861,' in *A Documentary Portrait through His Speeches and Writings*, ed. Don E. Fehrenbacher (Stanford: Stanford University Press, 1964), 160.

101 Momigliano, 'Hermeneutics,' 186.

102 Hobbes recognized that he wrote at a momentous time, when he could
set the agenda for future political thought.

103 Klein, 'History and the Liberal Arts,' 17. See above, pp. 46–52. Strauss
referred to this ambiguity in Hobbes as his having 'Aristotelian eggshells'
– that bits of the shell cling to the chick at its birth. Laurence Berns, tele-
phone conversation, 4 November 2004.

104 Strauss, *Thoughts on Machiavelli*, 176.
105 Thomas Hobbes, *The Elements of Law Natural and Politic, Part I: Human Nature, Part II: De Corpore Politico with Three Lives*, ed. J.C.A. Gaskin (New York: Oxford University Press, 1999), 144.
106 Ibid., 148.
107 *SCR*, 104, italics in original.
108 Strauss, 'How to Study Spinoza's *Theologico-Political Treatise*,' in *JPCM*, 216. See also below, pp. 65–72. Strauss refers to Hobbes's suggestion that he would not have had the courage to speak as openly as Spinoza. See Strauss, 'On the Basis of Hobbes's Political Philosophy,' in *What Is Political Philosophy?* 171.
109 One might argue that Strauss's use of Judaism, and his near silence about Christianity, amount to implicit indictments of Christianity's nearly total dismissal of the political realm. His critique of Christianity is far harsher than that of Judaism because Christianity – as already an interpretation of Judaism – has more limited relation with the surface of things. Belief in Christianity may be, like belief in the pre-philosophical world, belief in the authority of one's own. See also Susan Orr, *Jerusalem and Athens: Reason and Revelation in the Work of Leo Strauss* (Lanham: Rowman and Littlefield, 1995), 128–30.

A comparison here with Fackenheim is instructive. Fackenheim might argue that while Christianity is perhaps one form of extending Judaism, to make the extension is to destroy the core of Judaism. This core for him rests principally in two areas. First, Judaism teaches hope and not idealism: what ought to be is external to what is, and not within it awaiting actualization. Idealism is inherently idolatrous and therefore inherently anti-Jewish. Second, Judaism – especially Fackenheim's conception of midrash – exists with no attempt to resolve its contradictions. The unity of Judaism is a unity not of Christian or post-Christian universalism, but rather of particulars – even in contradiction – within unity. Furthermore, if the return to nature as Hobbes might have it is a return to pre-Christianity, Jews must *first* give up Judaism and *then* adopt natural right, while no such requirement is made of Christians. This sets up Jews as trailblazers for the secular state and – Fackenheim might argue – is yet another extension of the Christian misconception of Jewish election. On this last point, see Emil L. Fackenheim, *Jewish Philosophers and Jewish Philosophy*, ed. Michael L. Morgan [*JPJP*] (Bloomington: Indiana University Press, 1996), 41–56. See also below, pp. 224–9.

Strauss, on the other hand, while providing, in a sense, the bases for Fackenheim's aforementioned critiques, works not within the stance of

covenantal affirmation, but rather in the broader context of revelation
in general, or revelation as it is 'accessible to man as man.' Fackenheim
would deny, on the surface of it, the existence of such a context. See below, pp. 194–201.

110 Hobbes, *The Elements of Law,* 141, 156.

111 Ibid., 156.

112 Strauss, *Thoughts on Machiavelli,* 13.

113 Heidegger, of course, does not conceive of this as a break.

114 One basic difference between Heidegger and Aristotle is that Heidegger
does not separate, theoretically or practically, intelligibility from action.
Understanding, in Heidegger's sense and in contradistinction to Aristotle,
is necessarily historically based. Heidegger's integration of thought and
action becomes the basis of Strauss's criticism of Fackenheim's *Metaphysics and Historicity,* which attempts to refute Heidegger using only theoretical criteria. See below, pp. 111–20 and 172–94.

115 See Charles B. Guignon, 'Martin Heidegger,' in *The Cambridge Dictionary of Philosophy*, 2nd ed. (New York: Cambridge University Press, 1999),
370–3.

116 Ibid., 370.

117 See, for instance, Martin Heidegger, *Introduction to Metaphysics*, trans. Gregory Fried and Richard Polt (New Haven: Yale University Press, 2000).

118 Dante (Alighieri), *The Divine Comedy,* trans. Laurence Binyon, notes C.H.
Grandgent, in *The Portable Dante,* ed. Paolo Milano (New York: Viking
Press, 1947), 24 (*Inferno* 4:131).

119 For a more thorough discussion of Strauss's critique of historicism, see
below, pp. 159–71.

120 Ralph Lerner, 'Leo Strauss (1899–1973),' in *American Jewish Year Book* 76
(1976) (New York: American Jewish Committee), 92.

121 Ibid., 91.

122 *NRH*, 5. There is, however, one limit to the toleration as adopted by
Heidegger: there is no tolerance of a value system based on absolutes.
Fackenheim derives his critique of Heidegger from this, pointing out that
his toleration includes all but monotheists. See below, pp. 111–20.

123 Ibid., 6.

124 Leo Strauss, 'An Unspoken Prologue to a Public Lecture at St. John's College (in Honor of Jacob Klein, 1899–1978),' *Interpretation: A Journal of Political Philosophy* 7, no. 3 (September 1978): 1–3.

125 Strauss, 'Relativism,' 151.

126 For more on the choice between nature and history as an organizing principle of knowledge, see chapter 4.

127 Strauss, 'Relativism,' 154.

128 Ibid., 154.

129 Note that this does not characterize Fackenheim's religious existentialism insofar as he upholds the value of metaphysics.

130 Strauss, 'Relativism,' 155.

131 Ibid.

132 Ibid.

133 Heidegger's return to the roots of philosophy provides for existentialism its 'hard core.' Ibid., 151.

134 Werner J. Dannhauser, 'Athens and Jerusalem or Jerusalem and Athens?' in *Leo Strauss and Judaism*, ed. David Novak (Lanham: Rowman and Littlefield, 1996), 161.

135 From a perspective within the rabbinic framework, Judaism holds as its foundation that, while God's Otherness exists in some way in the human being as God's 'image,' God's essence is ultimately and utterly Other than human. The challenge of Jewish philosophy is the maintenance of the conception of both God's transcendence and His immanence, the necessary silence about God and the contingent presences of God. God is not a *conception*, but rather an experience of relationship between self and other.

136 Strauss, 'Relativism,' 156.

137 According to Dannhauser, Strauss 'equates the religion of the Bible with revelation (and once even with "the brute fact of revelation"), with belief in the mysterious and omnipotent God, with the life of obedient love (versus the life of free inquiry), and with *faith* [italics in original].' Dannhauser, 'Athens and Jerusalem,' 158. Although his critique of Rosenzweig and Buber's neo-Orthodoxy is that it allows for only a qualified revelation (see below, pp. 75–9), Strauss's discovery of an unqualified revelation may be said to omit a basic aspect of Jewish revelation: its recreation and reenactment in and throughout moments of a Jew's life. Strauss, however, insofar as he argues that neither philosophy nor the Bible claims it can know the realm of Pure Actuality or the Transcendent God, and, furthermore, that a Jew must 'love one's own' even as he 'loves the good,' follows Maimonides and remains within the tradition of Jewish theistic rationalism. Hilail Gildin rejects Dannhauser's thesis that Strauss must be considered, ultimately, to be an atheist. See Hilail Gildin, 'Deja Jew All Over Again: Dannhauser on Leo Strauss and Atheism,' *Interpretation: A Journal of Political Philosophy* 25, no. 1 (Fall 1997): 125–33.

138 See, for instance, as Albert Keith Whitaker suggests, the centre of 'Progress or Return?' where Strauss argues that a common ground exists.

This is in distinction to the essay's end, where he argues that they exist in tension. Albert Keith Whitaker, 'The Bible and Philosophy: A Review of *The Beginning of Wisdom: Reading Genesis* by Leon R. Kass and *Political Philosophy and the God of Abraham*, by Thomas L. Pangle,' Claremont Institute, 25 November 2003, 8, at http://www.claremont.org/writings/crb/winter2003/whitaker.html. Likewise, Strauss's error in the centre of 'On the Interpretation of *Genesis*' suggests that there exists a common ground between the Bible and philosophy, whereas the essay's beginning and end suggest that there is no common ground.

139 Strauss may use the Christian term for the Bible for the same reason he does so in 'Jerusalem and Athens': he 'is merely imitating Cohen, who uses such Christian terms as the Old Testament for the Hebrew Bible, for example.' Orr, *Jerusalem and Athens*, 126. I imitate Strauss with the intention of reading him literally enough.

140 See, for instance, Genesis 8: 'The Lord said to Himself: "Never again will I doom the earth because of man, since the devisings of man's mind are evil from his youth; nor will I ever again destroy every living being, as I have done. So long as the earth endures / Seedtime and harvest / Cold and heat / Summer and winter / Day and night / Shall not cease."' (This, and all biblical translations, are from the JPS edition, Philadelphia: Jewish Publication Society of America, 1955.) The natural order, according to this text, is a decision by God to disallow chaos.

141 *NRH*, 81. Elsewhere Strauss refers to Matthew Arnold's famous pronouncement. See 'Review of J.L. Talmon, *The Nature of Jewish History – Its Universal Significance*,' in *JPCM*, 411. As Arnold puts it: 'The uppermost idea with Hellenism is to see things as they really are; the uppermost idea with Hebraism is conduct and obedience ... The Greek quarrel with the body and its desires is, that they hinder right thinking; the Hebrew quarrel with them is, that they hinder right acting. "He that keepeth the law, happy is he."' Matthew Arnold, 'Hebraism and Hellenism,' in *Culture and Anarchy*, chapter 4 (1869), as reprinted in *Matthew Arnold: Prose and Poetry*, ed. Archibald L. Bouton (New York: Charles Scribner's Sons, 1927), 315.

142 One is reminded of Lincoln, who argued that we must act consistent with 'firmness in the right' and also only insofar 'as God gives us to see the right.' Abraham Lincoln, 'With Malice Toward None: Second Inaugural Address, March 4, 1865,' in *A Documentary Portrait through His Speeches and Writings*, ed. Don E. Fehrenbacher (Stanford: Stanford University Press, 1964), 279.

143 Fackenheim rejects Strauss's return to Greek philosophy for these very reasons. Because Jews cannot opt out of the covenant in order to readopt

the covenant, he rejects also Strauss's return to revelation. See below, pp. 224–9.

144 'On the Interpretation of *Genesis*,' in *JPCM*, 374–5.

145 Jonathan Cohen, 'Strauss, Soloveitchik, and the Genesis Narrative: Conceptions of the Ideal Jew as Derived from Philosophical and Theological Readings of the Bible,' *Journal of Jewish Thought and Philosophy* 5, no. 1 (1995): 103.

146 See, for instance, Gildin, 'Deja Jew All Over Again.'

147 See Maimonides, *Guide for the Perplexed*, 65–7 (I:31).

148 *JPCM*, 361.

149 In a point the importance of which will become apparent below, Strauss's attention to the foundations of the Bible and philosophy is an argument for retaining the Bible's status as the non-historicized basis of Judaism. He rejects the attempt within modern philosophical thought to incorporate into itself the function of revelatory theology, which, by positing the self-creation of truth, leads to the historicization of the Bible. See below, pp. 75–9.

150 *JPCM*, 368.

151 Ibid.

152 Ibid., 367.

153 Ibid., 368. We recall that Strauss defines knowledge based on reasoning and sense perception – or, more fully, the noetic techne, that is, intelligence gained in the mind separate from sensuous data – as a specifically philosophical procedure. See ibid., 118–19.

154 Immanuel Kant, 'Conjectural Beginnings,' trans. Emil L. Fackenheim, in *On History*, ed. Lewis White Beck, trans. Lewis White Beck, Robert E. Anchor and Emil L. Fackenheim (Englewood Cliffs: Macmillan Publishing, 1963), 55.

155 For a summary of the sequence by which things are created according to Strauss, see *JPCM*, 366; or Leon R. Kass, *The Beginning of Wisdom: Reading Genesis* (New York: The Free Press, 2003), 34.

156 *JPCM*, 362.

157 Ibid., 367; and see Green's footnote in ibid., 376n16.

158 Elsewhere, Strauss defines the likeness between the Bible and Greek philosophy as only a 'hailing distance.' *JPCM*, 329. See also below, pp. 155–9.

159 *JPCM*, 367.

160 Strauss argues this distinction on the fact that heaven is the only created thing in Genesis 1 that is neither called good by God nor blessed by Him. Ibid., 369.

161 See ibid., 371.

162 Harry V. Jaffa as cited in Hadley Arkes, 'Athens and Jerusalem: The Legacy of Leo Strauss,' in *Leo Strauss and Judaism: Jerusalem and Athens Critically Revisited*, ed. David Novak (Lanham: Rowman and Littlefield, 1996), 4.

163 See ibid., 3–6.

164 Ibid., 4.

165 See Hillel Fradkin, 'Leo Strauss,' in *Interpreters of Judaism in the Late Twentieth Century*, ed. Steven T. Katz (Washington: B'nai B'rith, 1993).

166 Ibid., 346.

167 Strauss concludes that Spinoza's argument is both indebted to, and antagonistic toward, Maimonides's arguments against *kalam* and reads Spinoza against the backdrop of the *Guide for the Perplexed*. This complicated reading is, however, outside the more narrow purposes of this book. See Martin D. Yaffe, 'Leo Strauss's "Maimonideanism" in His Interpretation of Spinoza's *Theologico-Political Treatise*,' Annual Conference, Association for Jewish Studies, Boston, 23 December 2003.

168 For a fuller discussion of Cohen's critique of Spinoza, see below, pp. 65–72.

169 David N. Myers, *Resisting History: Historicism and Its Discontents in German-Jewish Thought* (Princeton: Princeton University Press, 2003), 125. See also *SCR*, 258–9.

170 Because Spinoza was acutely attuned to the surface of the text, yet seemingly dismissed revelation, Strauss concludes that the true rival of revelation is Spinoza: only if Spinoza were wrong in every respect can revelation be returned to. Spinoza does not refute revelation because such a refutation is impossible; therefore, any attempt would introduce an element of irrationality into one's position. Strauss rejects the possibility of a return to Rosenzweig's neo-Orthodoxy, because neo-Orthodoxy betrays rational inconsistency. Instead he argues that the only return possible is a return to an unqualified orthodoxy. See below, pp. 75–9.

171 *PW*, 193.

172 Ibid.

173 But while Spinoza recognized the *Treatise* as a philosophical confrontation with revealed religion within the context of his time and place, post-Spinoza scholars conducted the argument on a much more shallow level by treating the *Treatise* as only a product of Spinoza's time and place. See Yaffe, 'Leo Strauss's "Maimonideanism,"' 1–2.

174 Cohen bases his argument that Spinoza was a traitor to Judaism on his identification of a basic contradiction in the latter thinker: he claims to

be promoting democracy even while declaring that he is writing only for a minority. Cohen then wonders whether Spinoza was in fact seeking to establish a modern liberal state. Spinoza contradicts his teaching that one must read in the light of natural reason by directing his book to an audience of philosophers, those for whom the 'most fundamental teaching' is not necessarily the 'clearest' or the most often stated. *PW*, 162. Strauss, on the other hand, maintains that Spinoza was appealing to the historical circumstances in which he wrote and he therefore discovers that Spinoza was in fact attempting to ameliorate the Jewish condition. Strauss argues that Cohen was unable to see this because the latter thinker, working in the Kantian tradition, could recognize the state only as an ideal. See below, pp. 65–72.

175 Spinoza claims that he does not cite the New Testament frequently because of his insufficient knowledge of Greek – a claim that Strauss rejects. See Benedict de Spinoza, *A Theologico-Political Treatise and A Political Treatise*, trans. R.H.M. Elwes (New York: Dover Publications, 1951), 156. Strauss argues that Spinoza's 'relative reticence about specifically Christian subjects could be expected to protect him against persecution by the vulgar, while it was not likely to disqualify him in the eyes of the "more prudent" readers.' *PW*, 191.

176 The argument is, roughly, that since Jesus the Christ is no longer here to embody the true religion, subsequent external signs of religion are mere interpretation. Adherence to religion's external signs is impiety.

177 According to Cohen and Strauss, Spinoza himself provides the information that he must be read as an esoteric writer: he states explicitly that he writes not for the vulgar, but for philosophers, even as within his writing he calls for the establishment of a liberal democracy. *SCR*, 19.

178 Ibid., 20.

179 *PW*, 162.

180 Ibid., 168–9.

181 Critiquing the results of Spinoza's strategy of establishing civic equality between Jews and Christians, Fackenheim argues that, in effect, orthodox Christians are being asked to become liberal Christians, whereas Jews have no incentive to remain Jews. Emil L. Fackenheim, *To Mend the World: Foundations of Post-Holocaust Jewish Thought* [MW] (Bloomington: Indiana University Press, 1994), 49.

182 Again, Spinoza does not claim that he has refuted revelation. Spinoza, *Treatise*, 80.

183 See *PW*, 165–7.

184 Ibid., 166.

185 Ibid., 167n31.

186 The idea that each human being 'can be a Christ,' as I framed it here, is what Fackenheim labels Spinoza's construction of the 'man-in-general.' See below, pp. 129–33.

187 Furthermore, Strauss argues that Spinoza's discovery of Jewish prophets, law, and belief in providence (*Treatise*, chapters 3–5) illustrates the latter's argument for the need to separate philosophy from theology: the *Treatise*'s 'Jewish illustrations here are in service to the *Treatise*'s deliberate reworking of arguments drawn from the Islamic *kalam* showing the dependence of divine providence on revealed law and of revealed law on prophecy' Yaffe, 'Leo Strauss's "Maimonideanism,"' 4.

188 *JPCM*, 92.

189 Ibid., 143.

190 Ibid., 144.

191 See below, pp. 209–24.

192 *JPCM*, 90.

193 Ibid.

194 Spinoza, by replacing Aristotle's 'becoming' with 'progress,' in effect replaces revelatory religion with natural religion. Because Aristotle's universal is the end of natural religion, and not of revelatory religion, Spinoza brings into the world of becoming the necessary universal and defines the necessary universal, the end of nature, as the divine.

195 *PW*, 180. In this argument, Strauss and Spinoza agree: Strauss argues that if in Spinoza's text there exists a contradiction, one should accept as Spinoza's view the position most alien to the 'vulgar' point of view.

196 Again, Spinoza's stance in this matter is contradicted by his claim 'that the author of Genesis 1 had unstated ulterior motives for espousing the doctrine of creation' Yaffe, 'Leo Strauss's "Maimonideanism,"' 6.

197 David Novak, Introduction, in *Leo Strauss and Judaism: Jerusalem and Athens Critically Revisited*, ed. David Novak (Lanham: Rowman and Littlefield, 1996), xi.

198 *MW*, 99.

199 Leo Strauss and Jacob Klein, 'A Giving of Accounts,' as cited in Orr, *Jerusalem and Athens*, 124.

200 Unlike, for instance, his successors Bergson, Whitehead, Husserl, and Heidegger. See ibid.

201 For an explicit response by Strauss to Cohen, see Strauss, Introduction, in *Philosophy and Law*.

202 Orr, *Jerusalem and Athens*, 125.

203 One might rephrase this by saying that the state occupies a realm of a

new religion, one that is secular and philosophical in the modern sense. See above, pp. 52–6 and 65–72.

204 Strauss writes that 'not even Cohen and Rosenzweig acknowledged the original, "non-internalized" meaning of the basic tenets of the tradition.' Strauss, *Philosophy and Law*, 136n3. Cohen and Rosenzweig, following Enlightenment thought – or rather, returning to it – adopt the results of the attack launched by Hobbes and Spinoza against the '"externally" understood tenets of the tradition.' Ibid., 28. They do not, however, distinguish the success of the attack from an attack against, in the broadest sense of the term, the Bible's teaching of obedience.

205 Orr, *Jerusalem and Athens*, 149. See also Strauss, 'Jerusalem and Athens,' in *JPCM*, 200–2.

206 Orr, *Jerusalem and Athens*, 127. Strauss argues that Cohen's historicist outlook determined his understanding that Hegel had superseded Enlightenment thought. Furthermore, he argues that Cohen, and the nineteenth-century successors of Lessing, succeeded in reintroducing Enlightenment thought – without, however, addressing the fundamental conflict between Enlightenment and orthodox thought. This reintroduction was a radicalizing of Enlightenment thought. See Strauss, *Philosophy and Law*, 27–34, esp. 27–8. Yet even here, Strauss's admiration for Cohen is evident: he refers to Cohen's critique of Spinoza's *Treatise* as 'by far the most important critique of the Enlightenment that has emerged from the return movement.' Ibid., 137n6.

It is interesting that Cohen conceived of his own stance as anti-historicist. It is the consequent blending of historicism and anti-historicism in Cohen that issues in the strange outcome of a historicism that seeks to understand, not the past in its own context, but rather the future. For more on the development of Jewish anti-historicism, from Cohen and Rosenzweig to Strauss and Breuer, see Myers.

207 Strauss discovers that Cohen's imposition of an *interpretation* of the thing on the surface of the thing precludes him (i.e., Cohen) from reading texts literally enough. This is especially evident in the latter's critique of Spinoza, in which he could not see beyond Spinoza's exoteric disparagement of Judaism, a disparagement that, according to him, goes beyond even the Christian polemic against Judaism, a disparagement that leads him to suggest that 'by denying that the God of Israel is the God of all mankind Spinoza has blasphemed the God of Israel.' *SCR*, 18.

Cohen's mistake with regard to Spinoza is not that he contextualized the thinker, but rather that he misidentified the context in which Spinoza wrote the *Treatise*. He contextualized Spinoza in the Amsterdam Jewish community, a position that led him to understand Spinoza as reacting to his excommunication; Strauss discovers that the appropriate context in which to understand Spinoza is the broader struggle of philosophers in Protestant Holland 'to gain freedom from ecclesiastical authority.' Myers, *Resisting History*, 124. Because Cohen had misunderstood the context in which Spinoza wrote the *Treatise*, he misunderstood Spinoza. Cohen's critique did not pay sufficient attention to the political circumstances in which Spinoza wrote: he understood Spinoza too literally because he did not understand Spinoza literally enough.

208 See *JPJP*, 41–56.

209 Strauss's critique of Cohen in this regard, because it is based also in an idea of history, is ironical: he writes that Cohen had only to deal with Dreyfus and the pogroms of Czarist Russia; he did not live to see Nazi Germany. Strauss, 'Jerusalem and Athens,' as cited in Orr, *Jerusalem and Athens*, 201. Strauss explains the irony as follows: 'only the history of philosophy makes possible the ascent from the second "unnatural" cave, into which we have fallen less because of the tradition [of orthodoxy] itself than because of the tradition of polemics against the tradition, into that first, "natural" cave which Plato's image depicts, to emerge from which into the light is the original meaning of philosophizing.' Strauss, *Philosophy and Law*, 136n2. Strauss rejects the idea of history as an invalid means of obfuscating knowledge, yet at the same time he recognizes that at this particular moment, 'the "historicizing" of philosophy [is] justified and necessary.' Ibid. See also *PW*, 154–8.

210 Orr, *Jerusalem and Athens*, 132.

211 For contrast, note that according to Strauss's reading of Plato, implicit in the latter's works is the recognition that the ideal society for which he strives is utopian. The achievement of Plato's Republic is, at best, highly improbable, not simply because philosophers are too few – a position informed by the idea of history or progress – but rather because utopianism is beyond the grasp of human knowledge. See above, pp. 41–6.

212 Orr, *Jerusalem and Athens*, 133.

213 Yaffe, 'Autonomy, Community, Authority,' 144.

214 See, for instance, Kant, 'Conjectural Beginnings.'

215 Strauss argues that the appropriate stance regarding philosophical and revelatory thought is best exemplified by Maimonides, whose 'rationalism is the true natural model, the standard to be carefully protected from any distortion, and thus the stumbling-block on which modern rationalism falls.' Strauss, *Philosophy and Law*, 21. For a thorough discussion of Strauss's return to Maimonides, and the development of his thought in

regard to Maimonides's conclusions regarding the relationship between reason and revelation in the prophet/philosopher-king, see Kenneth Hart Green, *Jew and Philosopher: The Return to Maimonides in the Jewish Thought of Leo Strauss* (Albany: SUNY Press, 1993).

216 Strauss, *Philosophy and Law*, 27.

217 Eve Adler, Translator's Introduction, in Strauss, *Philosophy and Law*, 5.

218 Fradkin, 'Leo Strauss.'

219 Ibid., 349.

220 According to Rosenzweig, since divine revelation is a present possibility and not simply received opinion, its reality or its content can be genuinely known, and not simply dismissed by philosophy as mere belief.

221 So, for instance, Strauss dedicated his book on Spinoza to Rosenzweig. As Tanguay suggests, Strauss in his earlier work 'maintained some affinities of style and thought with the major theological renaissance that took place in Germany in the 1920s.' Daniel Tanguay, *Leo Strauss: An Intellectual Biography*, trans. Christopher Nadon (New Haven: Yale University Press, 2007), 196. This renaissance, which included Rosenzweig, reflected a strong reaction against the synthesis of revealed theology and modern idealism. In Strauss's mature thought, the critique of modern political philosophy began in the 'critique of the modern critique of religion.' Ibid. See above, pp. 75–9.

222 Leo Strauss, *Spinoza's Critique of Religion* [SCR] (New York: Schocken Books, 1982), 15.

223 Myers argues that Strauss is uncertain whether a return to pre-modern thought is possible. 'As would become clear over time, he was too much a modern to cast his lot fully with traditional orthodoxy. Conversely, he was too much a skeptic to embrace the facile truisms of modernity.' Myers, *Resisting History*, 120–1. See also Tanguay, *Leo Strauss*, 196.

224 For Strauss's understanding of this all-important term, see *JPCM*, 87–100.

225 Allan Arkush, 'Leo Strauss and Jewish Modernity,' In *Leo Strauss and Judaism: Jerusalem and Athens Critically Revisited*, ed. David Novak (Lanham: Rowman and Littlefield, 1996), 120.

226 Michael L. Morgan, *Dilemmas in Modern Jewish Thought: The Dialectics of Revelation and History* (Bloomington: Indiana University Press, 1992), 45. Morgan's essay is a critique of Strauss's argument that the return to Judaism must be a return to Jewish orthodoxy. See also *JPCM*, 152.

227 Another way to put this is that Rosenzweig attempts to replace, as primary in thought, nature with history. Fackenheim will follow him in this replacement, finding in rabbinic thought a basis for the reversal. See below, pp. 133–40 and 172–201.

228 Fackenheim, too, addresses this point. See below, pp. 133–40.

229 Arkush, 'Leo Strauss and Jewish Modernity,' 120.

230 Morgan, *Dilemmas*, 47. On this point, Fackenheim does not disagree with Strauss but questions if Rosenzweig would have retained his optimism had he lived to see the events that were about to unfold in his homeland.

231 In this position, Strauss follows Maimonides, who wrote, for instance, that 'only a person who has "filled his belly with bread and meat" is qualified to stroll in the *Pardes* (i.e., to delve into metaphysics). "Bread and meat" are the knowledge of what is permitted and what is forbidden and the details of the other mitzvos.' Rambam, *Mishneh Torah*, *Yad Hachzakah*, 'The Laws of the Fundamentals of the Torah (4:13),' trans. and annotated Rabbi Abraham Yaakov Finkel (Scranton: Yeshivath Beth Moshe, 2001), 33.

232 The 'affective fallacy' is 'a confusion between the poem and its *results* (what it *is* and what it *does*) ... It begins by trying to derive the standard of criticism from the psychological effects of the poem and ends in impressionism and relativism. The result ... is that the poem itself, as an object of specifically critical judgment, tends to disappear.' W.K. Wimsatt, Jr, and M.C. Beardsley, 'The Affective Fallacy,' *Sewanee Review* 57 (Winter 1949): 31–55, as cited in William Elton, *A Guide to the New Criticism* (Chicago: Modern Poetry Association, 1950), 10–11 (italics in original).

Note that in Fackenheim's conception of Jewish self-understanding, the surface of the text coexists *already* with its esoteric meanings: the rabbinic tradition, or Oral Torah, was revealed simultaneously with the Written Torah. More important, Oral Torah continues to be written in each generation, if not literally, then through the re-creations of the revelatory experience throughout the Jewish calendar. Strauss's critique of Rosenzweig's blindness to the surface of the text of the Torah may be a result of his adoption of theistic rationalism.

233 Arkush, 'Leo Strauss and Jewish Modernity,' 120.

234 Momigliano, 'Hermeneutics,' 186.

235 For a 'modest corrective' to Strauss's reading of Rosenzweig as an accommodationist, see Morgan, *Dilemmas*, 45–54.

236 See below, pp. 155–9.

237 See below, pp. 209–24.

238 *JPCM*, 116. Strauss's statement is echoed in the various critiques of Fackenheim's thought. These critiques are based ultimately in his not making a choice between philosophy and theology. See below, chapter 5, 'The Present Writer's Position.'

239 See *PW*, 154–8; and above, pp. 65–72.

240 See below, pp. 209–24.

3. Fackenheim's Formulation of the Relationship between Philosophy and Revelatory Theology

1 See below, pp. 224–9.
2 See Emil L. Fackenheim, *Jewish Philosophers and Jewish Philosophy*, ed. Michael L. Morgan [*JPJP*] (Bloomington: Indiana University Press, 1996), 104; Michael L. Morgan, Introduction to Part I, in ibid., 4; and below, pp. 224–9.
3 See, Emil L. Fackenheim, 'Metaphysics and Historicity,' in *The God Within: Kant, Schelling, and Historicity*, ed. John Burbidge [*GW*] (Toronto: University of Toronto Press, 1996), 128–30, and esp. 220–1n21; and below, pp. 172–94.
4 See below, pp. 159–71 and 209–24.
5 Note that throughout this chapter I will attempt to present Fackenheim's thought as far as possible as he himself understood it. Part of his understanding seems at times to be a misapprehension of Strauss's articulation of his rediscovery of the question of justice, of which natural right is a part. See chapter 5.
6 Emil L. Fackenheim, *What Is Judaism? An Interpretation for the Present Age* [*WJ*] (New York: Summit Books, 1987), 99.
7 Emil L. Fackenheim, *Encounters between Judaism and Modern Philosophy: A Preface to Future Jewish Thought* [*EJM*] (New York: Schocken Books, 1973), 37–40.
8 Ibid., 38–9.
9 Ibid., 39.
10 Ibid., 45–7.
11 *JPJP*, 46
12 *EJM*, 39.
13 *JPJP*, 47.
14 Ibid.
15 Ibid., 47–8.
16 Ibid., 48, italics in original.
17 Emil L. Fackenheim, *The God Within: Kant, Schelling, and Historicity*, ed. John Burbidge [*GW*] (Toronto: University of Toronto Press, 1996), 9.
18 Ibid., 16.
19 Ibid., 3.
20 See Laurence Berns, 'Putting Things Back Together Again in Kant,' *Interpretation: A Journal of Political Philosophy* 28, no. 3 (Spring 2001): 204. One might consider this apparent replacement of the God of revelation with a projection of the mind as Kant's ultimate failure in rising to Bacon's chal-

lenge to eliminate from human thought the 'idols of the mind.' See Francis
Bacon, *The New Organon and Related Writings*, ed. Fulton H. Anderson (Indianapolis: Bobbs-Merrill Educational Publishing, 1980), esp. aphorisms 44
and 65.

21 Immanuel Kant, 'Religion Within the Limits of Reason Alone,' in *The Philosophy of Kant: Immanuel Kant's Moral and Political Writings*, ed. Carl J. Friedrich (New York: Modern Library, 1949), 366–7.

22 See, for instance, Immanuel Kant, *Critique of Practical Reason*, trans. Werner
S. Pluhar (Cambridge, MA: Hackett Publishing, 2002); and *Grounding for a
Metaphysics of Morals, with On a Supposed Right to Lie Because of Philanthropic
Concerns*, 3rd ed., trans. James W. Ellington (Cambridge: Hackett Publish-
ing, 1993), 9–14.

23 See 'Kant and Radical Evil,' in *GW*. Strauss discovers that philosophy must
continue to understand 'the low in the light of the high,' in effect exclud-
ing a place in philosophical thought for transcendent evil. This will prove
to be one of the major disagreements between Strauss and Fackenheim,
who argues for an *actual* transcendent evil within the subject matter of
philosophical thought. See also Laurie McRobert, 'Kant and Radical Evil,'
in *Fackenheim: German Philosophy and Jewish Thought*, ed. Louis Greenspan
and Graeme Nicholson (Toronto: University of Toronto Press, 1992).

24 Emil L. Fackenheim, *To Mend the World: Foundations of Post-Holocaust Jewish
Thought*, First Midland Edition, [*MW*] (Bloomington: Indiana University
Press, 1994), 267–77.

25 Alexander Donat, *Holocaust Kingdom: A Memoir* (New York: Holocaust Library, 1978).

26 *EJM*, 253n157.

27 Kant, *Grounding for the Metaphysics of Morals*, 39.

28 According to Kant, an individual should let himself be martyred rather
than allow himself to be used as a means toward an end. *EJM*, 61. This
concept arises from Kant's insistence that an individual carries within him
the divine element, the moral law, and that he is thus sacred. Fackenheim
reminds us how chilling Kant's idea might be without an ultimate rational
(or transcendent) grounding: the Holocaust took away the capacity of Jews
for martyrdom as a means to deny the divine element in them. At the same
time, the divine element was destroyed as an actuality in the world by the
perpetrators.

29 One might ask why Fackenheim's prioritizing of the authority of empirical historical events does not extend to events that occurred during but
beyond the 'Holocaust kingdom.' The distortion implicit in this understanding of 'the Holocaust' – as though it were a monolithic entity – may

be part of Fackenheim's critique of post-Kantian thinkers: the relationship between universal ideas and particular events must remain a *question*, not, that is, in synthesis but in dialectical relationship.

30 *EJM*, 52.

31 McRobert, 'Kant and Radical Evil,' 34–5.

32 Ibid., 26. To put this in terms more useful to Strauss, Fackenheim's earlier formulation of the relationship between the moral and the religious fails to allow revelation to speak on its own terms: revelation is understood in terms of reason.

33 Ibid., 26, italics in original.

34 See below, pp. 133–48. Buber is related to Hegel insofar as both men depart from Kant's understanding of antinomy. *EJM*, 254n168. Both Buber and Hegel understand the relationship between the human and the divine as 'one double activity.' Ibid., 160. And in the thought of both, God remains Absolutely Other. In Hegel, when the synthesis between the human and the divine is absolutely complete, the divine and the human become one double activity. In Buber, the activity of God remains separate from the activity of human beings. While Judaism must testify against any such identity between human beings and God, Hegel is unable to be open to Judaism's testimony: the openness would elevate Judaism to a true religion and deny the eternity of God's Otherness in Christianity. Ibid., 161.

35 See Hermann Cohen, *Religion of Reason out of the Sources of Judaism*, trans. Simon Kaplan (New York: Frederick Ungar, 1972), 361–5.

36 *MW*, 9. Fackenheim defines Constantinianism as 'the theopolitical praxis of two beliefs: that the Christian revealed truth is the complete revealed truth; and that the truth itself is not divided into "religious" and "secular" but rather is one and indivisible.' Ibid., 127. While Fackenheim focuses primarily on Christian and post-Christian Constantinianism, he suggests the possibility that Constantinianism might apply as well to Islam. Ibid., 127.

37 See, for instance, *EJM*, 166: 'The same absolute anti-Spirit that has shattered Hegel's identity of the divine nature and the human had no other clear principle than murderous hatred of the Jews, for "Aryan" had no clear meaning other than "non-Jewish."' (In the latter part of the statement, Fackenheim quotes from Strauss's *Preface*.)

38 Fackenheim writes: 'The "being-toward-the future" of the religious Jew is secular in that Auschwitz has destroyed all "religious" illusions; and the secular Jew is "recovering" a religious heritage in his search for a present identity.' Ibid., 226. He adds that in order for Jews to continue to witness to 'Eternity in the midst of time' (ibid., 227), they have use of both the

'"secular" Bar Kochba' (to affirm being in history as the ability for self-protection) and the '"religious" Rabbi Akiba' (for guidance in distinguishing between false gods and the true God by finding in Him hope). Ibid., 226–7.

Along these lines, Fackenheim reveals what is perhaps his most chilling insight about post-Holocaust Jewry: one must choose between the religious obligation to raise Jewish children and the moral obligation not to expose one's heirs to the danger of genocide. See Emil L. Fackenheim, *God's Presence in History: Jewish Affirmations and Philosophical Reflections* [*GPH*], 1st Jason Aronson ed. (Northvale: Jason Aronson, 1997), 6.

39 Fackenheim, personal interview, August 2003.

40 Emil L. Fackenheim, 'Man and His World in the Perspective of Judaism: Reflections on Expo '67,' in *The Jewish Return into History: Reflections in the Age of Auschwitz and a New Jerusalem* [*JRH*] (New York: Schocken Books, 1978), 6–7.

41 *EJM*, 87.

42 Ibid., 87, italics in original. The intertwining of the universal and the particular is manifested in many of Fackenheim's writings. As one instance, in *GW*, both the introduction and the last two chapters consider the particular existential Jewish reality, the impact of the Holocaust. Between them are ten essays on Kant, Schelling, Hegel, and Heidegger. Also, Fackenheim uses this technique within various essays.

43 Ibid., 87.

44 As will become clear, Fackenheim, in rejecting Hegel's secular optimism, rejects also Hegel's attempt at synthesis in favour of understanding the interconnection of philosophy and religion as a dialectical interplay. We shall see in chapter 5 whether such a distinction can be sustained.

45 So, for instance, Hegel understands that the secular emancipation from religion was made possible by a religious emancipation in religion, that is, in Protestant Christianity. Fackenheim, 'On the Life, Death, and Transfiguration of Martyrdom: The Jewish Testimony to the Divine Image in Our Time,' in *JRH*, 238. Revealing, perhaps, of his understanding of Hegel's deeper motive, Fackenheim's working title for what became *Religious Dimension* was *Making Peace with Religion*. Fackenheim, personal interview, August 2003.

46 Elsewhere Fackenheim suggests that Hegel supersedes the dialectic between Judaism and Spinoza, who resolves the disparate aspects of the human into the One by synthesizing the acknowledgment of Absolute Otherness and the divine perspective within the human being. *MW*, 117–19.

47 *JRH*, 238.

48 Louis Greenspan and Graeme Nicholson, Introduction, in *Fackenheim: German Philosophy and Jewish Thought*, ed. Louis Greenspan and Graeme Nicholson (Toronto: University of Toronto Press, 1992), 5.

49 There is a change in Fackenheim's distinctions between left- and right-wing Hegelianism from the time of *Religious Dimension* to the time of *To Mend the World*. 'In *To Mend the World* ... the old Hegelian left wing [in *Religious Dimension*] has itself broken open into a left and a right wing – Marx and Kierkegaard, respectively.' W.A. Shearson, 'The Fragmented Middle: Hegel and Kierkegaard,' in *Fackenheim: German Philosophy and Jewish Thought*, ed. Louis Greenspan and Graeme Nicholson (Toronto: University of Toronto Press, 1992), 74–5.

50 Emil L. Fackenheim, *The Religious Dimension in Hegel's Thought* [RD] (Bloomington: Indiana University Press, 1967), 82.

51 *JRH*, 239.

52 In Hegel's philosophy, according to Fackenheim, self-making is a quasi-historical process: while the act transcends history, a historical process, a directionality, still occurs. At the same time, the process is not fully historical, because Idea, in Hegelian terms, need always return to Being. In addition, Hegel's concept of action as only quasi-historical leads to the split between left-wing Hegelians, who abandon eternity, and right-wing Hegelians, who abandon historical directionality.

53 *JRH*, 239.

54 'Redemption,' then, means the right governance of the world in accordance with the Protestant religion.

55 'Hegel on the Actuality of the Rational and the Rationality of the Actual,' in *GW*, 164–71.

56 The division of the actual and the merely existent is problematic because, through the overlooking of the latter from what is actual in history, the merely existent is overlooked also as a datum for thought. Fackenheim understands this as the outcome of secular optimism, which simply disposes of evil. For his part, Hegel, aware of empirical history, considers evil a relapse into barbarism. See ibid., 171.

57 As cited in ibid., 164.

58 As alluded to already, note that this is not a reversion to Neo-Platonism or Aristotelianism: although Hegel identifies God and the divine human perspective, the latter evolves as God more fully reveals himself through history.

59 *GW*, 166.

60 Ibid., 167.

61 As we shall see, Hegel's affirmation of the pre-philosophical religious

dimension of historical experience, while rationalizing it to make suitable the context for the synthesis between religion and philosophy, also limits his vision of historical experience.

62 See 'Demythologizing and Remythologizing in Jewish Experience: Reflections Inspired by Hegel's Philosophy,' in *JRH*, 114–20. Fackenheim, for instance, cites from Hegel's *Werke*: 'I am to make myself fit for the indwelling of Spirit. This is my labor, the labor of man; but the same is also the labor of God, regarded from His side. He moves toward man and is in man through the act of raising him.' Ibid., 114.

63 Quite possibly, Kant is aware of this inadequacy: it may be that he provides this explanation only for those who are incapable of appreciating the intrinsic dignity of the moral law.

64 *JRH*, 115.

65 The following discussion understands the word 'infinite' – both the human being's infinite perspective and God's infinite aspect – from a religious point of view, as distinct (as far as possible) from a philosophical one. That is to say, Fackenheim reads Hegel through the lens of his religious dimension: while philosophically – insofar as philosophy asks what the human being can know – neither God nor human beings are infinite, religion suggests that the human being can 'know' God as an Absolute Other (in His infinity) in moments of revelation. For Hegel, as has just been said, historical experience is essentially religious.

66 In Kierkegaard's 'immediacy after reflection,' thought points beyond itself to the divine, whereas in Hegel, the remythologizing of religion is necessary in order to reinstate the double aspect of religious experience – in other words, both the finite and infinite aspects of one's encounter with the divine. See *JRH*, 118–20. Hegel recognizes, as we shall see, that if religious life is no longer vital, the connection between history and thought would make the remythologizing of religion impossible: philosophy cannot create religion or religious symbols from within its own context. Ibid., 123.

67 Ibid., 115. In contrast, we recall Strauss's assertion that the main argument is not between Kant and Hegel, but rather between the ancients and the moderns.

68 *RD*, 17.

69 Ibid., 26.

70 Ibid., 37–44, 93–4.

71 Ibid., 37–44. See also Shearson, 'The Fragmented Middle,' 81.

72 *RD*, 19.

73 *JRH*, 116.

74 Ibid.

75 As cited in ibid., italics in original.
76 Note that Hegel alters Christianity in his attempt to unify it with secularity. See Shearson, 'The Fragmented Middle,' 82–3n5.
77 *JRH*, 116.
78 Graeme Nicholson, 'The Passing of Hegel's Germany,' in *Fackenheim: German Philosophy and Jewish Thought*, ed. Louis Greenspan and Graeme Nicholson (Toronto: University of Toronto Press, 1992), 50.
79 *RD*, 131–2.
80 See below, pp. 107–11.
81 *GW*, 232n53.
82 *EJM*, 124.
83 Ibid., 96.
84 'The Jew was to be permitted to remain a Jew "at home" – in the privacy of a purely religious conscience – on condition that he become "a man abroad," that he purge all remnants of Jewish national-cultural life from his public-secular existence.' Emil L. Fackenheim, *Quest for Past and Future: Essays in Jewish Theology* (Boston: Beacon Press, 1968), 332n12.
85 But one can hardly blame Hegel for his assessment of Judaism as unfree: the idea was first proposed by Spinoza.
86 *EJM*, 126.
87 Ibid.
88 Fackenheim notes that Hegel's failure to disavow his Constantinianism is a 'philosopher's failure'; because, although he as an historian recognizes the continued existence of Jews and Judaism, his philosophy can make no room for an alternative comprehensive world view. Ibid., 89.
89 So, for instance, Hegel attempts to overcome the multiplicity of *Weltanschauungen* by recognizing in each a partial truth. 'Epilogue: Holocaust and *Weltanschauung*: Philosophical Reflections on Why They Did It,' in *GW*, 184. So, too, Fackenheim does not deny the existence of eternal truths: there are ultimate truths graspable within human experience; but these truths, because they are necessarily historically bound, are necessarily and at every moment fragmentary.
90 *GW*, 170. By this distinction, Hegel's system rises or falls for Fackenheim because, if Fackenheim cannot remove it from Hegel's thought, then neither can he insist that all of human existence – including the merely existent, in which irrational realm evil exists – merits philosophical attention and theological care.
91 *EJM*, 86.
92 *QPF*, 207. See below, pp. 129–33.
93 *RD*, 12.

94 See below, pp. 107–11.

95 *EJM*, 160–1. See, also, Shearson, 'The Fragmented Middle,' 67.

96 *QPF*, 87.

97 See above.

98 Greenspan and Nicholson, *Fackenheim*, 6.

99 *EJM*, 166.

100 Shearson, 'The Fragmented Middle,' 80–2.

101 See *QPF*, 83–94; and below, pp. 194–201.

102 *EJM*, 166–7.

103 See, for instance, *MW*, 200. Fackenheim suggests that the Holocaust is wholly unintelligible because it is based on a *Weltanschauung* that is cosmic without being in any sense cognizant of worldly practicalities. Fackenheim, 'Holocaust and *Weltanschauung*,' in *GW*, 182.

104 In Strauss's formulation, Hegel's position reveals a misunderstanding of the nature of authority: Hegel begins with an idea of history in order to determine the political, rather than with the political in order to determine what is experience.

105 *JRH*, 113.

106 Fackenheim writes: 'Midrash is the profoundest and most indigenously Jewish and hence most authoritative theology ever to emerge within Judaism. What makes it both profound and indigenously Jewish is that it takes the form not of propositions and systems put forward (or perhaps even "demonstrated") as true, but rather of stories and parables: These never pretend to have all the answers; moreover, the beliefs expressed in them are not binding … [but] there are limits to the liberty of the Midrashic story teller … There are Midrashim relating that God weeps, is in exile, accuses Himself, or in other ways suggest that God has not, or could not have, prevented catastrophe. The divine powerlessness suggested here, however, is always only temporary, and the faith in God's redemptive power, to be sure, is tested but not destroyed.' *WJ*, 72. For Fackenheim, midrash provides the authority most relevant for Jewish thought and existence in our time because it precludes the idealism that can evolve from philosophical systems while at the same time affirming the hope necessary for the perpetuation of Judaism. See below, pp. 194–201 and 224–9.

107 *JRH*, 124. As we saw above, the fact that midrash continues to be written confirms for Fackenheim that Judaism survives, even in the context of secularism, for as long as Jews survive. What he calls the 'midrashic framework' (*GPH*, 20–1), which he hopes to preserve, comprises three points. First, midrash stresses God's action in human history, rather than

(for instance) God's extreme transcendence as described in Ezekiel 1. Midrash in Fackenheim's sense reflects on root experiences, or experiences that meet the above-stated criteria. Second, midrash becomes aware of the contradiction between divine transcendence and divine involvement, between divine power and human freedom, and between divine involvement with history and evil in history. Third, midrash stays within the context of the root experience and is unwilling to resolve these 'dialectical contradictions.' Thus midrash actually expresses the contradictions of human existence, which makes midrash fragmentary yet at the same time ultimate for human thought. Because midrash is in this sense ultimate, its fragmentation is in another sense an integrity, which suggests that these contradictions are destined for ultimate resolution. Fackenheim focuses on midrash because, since midrash can confront epoch-making events, the redefinition of its framework is one means by which to sustain the classic texts after the Holocaust.

To my knowledge, Fackenheim does not address the issue of whether these three qualities are exclusive to midrash. The lapse may be a result of a less exhaustive knowledge of other classic Jewish texts, or it may indicate that the question of the extent to which midrash is unique among Jewish texts is secondary to Fackenheim's primary purpose, which is to find a source of authority for post-Holocaust Jewish thought.

108 *JRH*, 113.
109 'The 614th Commandment,' in *JRH*, 22: '*the authentic Jew of today is forbidden to hand Hitler yet another, posthumous victory.*' Italics in original.
110 *RD*, 13–14.
111 See *JRH*, 244–51.
112 'Schelling in 1800–1: Art as Revelation,' 'Schelling's Philosophy of Literary Art,' 'Schelling's Philosophy of Religion,' and 'Schelling's Conception of Positive Philosophy,' all in *GW*.
113 See above, pp. 91–106; and below, pp. 111–20 and 194–201.
114 See below, pp. 111–20 and 172–94.
115 Strauss, for his part, recognizes Schelling's 'very profound understanding of what one would call the "substance" of Judaism.' Leo Strauss, *Jewish Philosophy and the Crisis of Modernity: Essays and Lectures in Modern Jewish Thought*, ed. Kenneth Hart Green [*JPCM*] (Albany: SUNY Press, 1997), 336. Green suggests that Strauss refers to Schelling's final philosophical stage (his 'positive' philosophy), in which he 'maintained the irreducible divine revelation to Israel. It has been responsible for conveying the Hebrew Bible, for bringing to light the profundity of the inexpressible divine name, and for bearing divine chosenness as the ground for God's special relation to man.' Ibid., 354n38.

116 While Kant argues that there is no access to God outside of experience, post-Kantians conclude – based on Schelling's early identification of experience and reality – that God is not outside experience. *GW*, 93–4.

117 Again, since Fackenheim's thought links idea and experience, Schelling's development is of interest insofar as it lays the groundwork for each stage of his thinking. Although Schelling's last phase – what may be called early or proto-existentialism – influences Fackenheim most directly, the very fact that his thinking proceeds in stages, each built one on the other, suggests to Fackenheim the essentially historical nature of thought. See *GW*, 50–2, 92–108, 110.

118 Schelling's philosophy of religion was rejected by both Kierkegaard and Hegelians, both his contemporaries and moderns. *GW*, 92.

119 John Burbidge, Preface, in *GW*, xii.

120 *GW*, 113. The question is of particular importance for Fackenheim because by posing it, Schelling returns thought to its first principles, which are coincident with the first principles of revelatory theology. This first question – 'Why something rather than nothing?' – sets up the moment of interaction or interdependence of philosophy and revelatory theology and, what is more, grounds each in historical facticity. For Strauss's influence on Fackenheim's emphasis on the return to the surface of things, see chapter 4.

121 *GW*, 113.

122 Ibid., 114.

123 Ibid., 112.

124 For the problem of establishing a one-to-one correspondence between essence and existence, or the endurance of God's identity though His Name may change in future revelations, see below, pp. 155–9.

125 *GW*, 50, 111. Schelling's understanding of Absolute Idealism as a negative philosophy is not simply a repudiation of it, but rather the adoption of it as a prerequisite for a new metaphysics. According to Fackenheim, Schelling's positive philosophy is not an anti- but rather a post-idealistic metaphysics. Ibid., 111.

126 Ibid., 112. Fackenheim suggests that Schelling has been ignored until recently because, while Hegelians could not accept the introduction of the undialectical aspects of existence into thought, Kierkegaard could not allow aspects of essence to be introduced. Ibid., 112.

127 Ibid., 114.

128 Ibid., 57n21, as cited in John Burbidge, 'Reason and Existence in Schelling and Fackenheim,' in *Fackenheim: German Philosophy and Jewish Thought*, ed. Louis Greenspan and Graeme Nicholson (Toronto: University of Toronto Press, 1992), 92. Burbidge points out that the word 'leap' is used not by

Schelling but rather by Fackenheim, following Lessing. Schelling uses the word 'ecstasy,' which lies within the capacity of reason. According to Burbidge, in Lessing the leap is impossible, and therefore Fackenheim's translation of ecstasy to leap 'is significant.' Ibid. Strauss, we recall, criticizes Lessing's followers for radicalizing Enlightenment thought, or for failing to break through the historicist delusion because they begin with an idea of history rather than with history itself. Fackenheim, it seems, is here proposing a means of breaking through that delusion.

129 *GW*, 51.

130 Burbidge, 'Reason and Existence,' 93.

131 *GW*, 115.

132 Burbidge, 'Reason and Existence,' 96. For a discussion of the meontological tradition in philosophy, see below, pp. 111–20 and 172–94.

133 Fackenheim, as we shall see, denies that existence has a rational grounding and that it is possible to anticipate the results of free action. Yet Schelling's principle – that self-creating takes place in the context of choosing – will recur in Fackenheim's thought in his critique of Heidegger, in which he counters Heidegger's historicity by claiming that one self-creates only within the parameters of the possible. See below, pp. 111–20.

134 *GW*, 118. The act of will becomes determinative for both Strauss's (under the influence of Nietzsche) and Fackenheim's returns to authority. See below, pp. 224–9.

135 *GW*, 51.

136 Fackenheim labels Schelling's attribution of will to the absolute existent 'metaphysical empiricism.' It is unclear that Schelling actually reinvokes an Absolute Other; more likely, he provides for human autonomy an extra-human means of conceiving and defining the reality of human existence. See *GW*, 116.

137 Burbidge, 'Reason and Existence,' 93.

138 Ibid.

139 *GW*, 121.

140 Ibid., 117.

141 Burbidge, 'Reason and Existence,' 93.

142 Fackenheim here reveals his adoption of existentialism insofar as experience is primary to idea. One cannot claim the Holocaust as a general human condition because thought must begin with the particulars of an individual existent and build to the concept of a universal human condition. See below, Fackenheim's critique of Heidegger, pp. 111–20; and below, pp. 224–9.

143 Burbidge, 'Reason and Existence,' 95. See also *QPF*, 83–95.

144 Fackenheim's affirmation of reason's inability, when isolated from existence, to provide comprehensive meaning, is an important source of comparison with Strauss. For Strauss, the ideals of philosophy can, perhaps,
continue to be discovered because reason is the means by which one
aspires to – even reaches toward – truth. There are some human beings
who, in Aristotelian terms, more closely approximate the great-souled
man. See Aristotle, *Nicomachean Ethics*, trans. Joe Sachs (Newburyport:
Focus Publishing, 2002), 4:2 (1122a–1123a). For Fackenheim, too, some of
us may have a capacity for reason that is more highly developed, but this
capacity in no way brings them closer to ideals – or even, alas, to reality.
For this reason, Fackenheim counters the ideal of the great-souled man
with informed and personal humility.

145 Fackenheim pointed out to me that he was often criticized for attacking
the philosopher (Heidegger) rather than the philosophy. His response: a
person must be accountable for his ideas, must live in accordance with his
ideas. Fackenheim, personal interviews, August 2003.

146 Fackenheim points out that the later Heidegger Judaizes philosophy by
redefining truth as the 'unconcealedness' of the Presence of Being 'accessible to an original "thinking," which is a "hearing" rather than a
"seeing,"' and which includes 'the whole being of the thinker.' *EJM*, 219.
Heidegger's later thought threatens not only Christian or post-Christian
thought, but also Jewish (or what may become post-Jewish) thought.
Jews may find the later Heidegger – the thinker who transcends the for-
getfulness of Being by recognizing it – more compelling than the early
Heidegger, the philosopher who has forgotten Being. Ibid., 218.

147 'The Historicity and Transcendence of Philosophic Truth,' in *GW*, 154.

148 To put this another way, one might say that after Hegel, one cannot be a
philosopher exclusively but must be open to theological thought, just as
Fackenheim, as a theologian, must be open to philosophical thought. See
below, pp. 155–9.

149 Fackenheim, 'Metaphysics and Historicity,' in *GW*. For a more thorough
treatment of the lecture, see below, pp. 172–94.

150 For a more comprehensive discussion of the doctrine, see chapter 4.

151 *GW*, 151.

152 Ibid.

153 Ibid.

154 Note that Fackenheim ends the lecture by suggesting that one may
choose, as did Strauss, 'the classical doctrine of a permanent human nature.' *GW*, 145. See below, pp. 172–94.

155 *GW*, 123.

156 This position undergoes a qualification after 1967 when, following the Six Day War, Fackenheim, by his own account, recognizes the Holocaust as a unique example of empirical history demonstrating the non-permanence of human nature.

157 *GW*, 138.

158 Ibid. See also ibid., 225n37.

159 *EJM*, 213.

160 Ibid.

161 *MW*, xiii.

162 *GW*, 160.

163 Ibid., 149–50. See also above, pp. 91–111. One notes here Rosenzweig's argument that one needs 'eternity in time' in order to confront history. For the concept of 'eternity in time,' see below, pp. 133–40.

164 *GW*, 158.

165 Ibid., 154. As we shall see, because the way in which Heidegger frames the relationship between thought and life presumes its answer, he only seems to be refuting historicism; indeed, he is prey to what Fackenheim terms 'radical historicism.' See below, chapter 4.

166 Nicholson, 'The Passing of Hegel's Germany,' 48.

167 *EJM*, 219–200, italics in original.

168 Ibid., 221.

169 Ibid., 213.

170 Ibid., italics in original. Fackenheim's earlier position was to look first toward *the* human condition in order to consider the Jewish condition – a position he later renounced. See, for instance, *QPF*, 101, italics in original: '*The analysis of the human condition constitutes the necessary prolegomenon for all modern Jewish and, indeed, all modern theology.*' As cited in *EJM*, 260n28.

171 *EJM*, 215.

172 Ibid.

173 Ibid., italics in original.

174 See below, pp. 140–8.

175 *EJM*, 221. Fackenheim suggests that Strauss, in his Preface, was unaware of this distinction in insecurities. Ibid., 262n51. One might wonder whether Strauss did not rather choose to focus on the political naivety that results from the inability of the citizens of the modern liberal state to distinguish between false gods and the true God, rather than on tracing the source of that naivety to a 'spurious Christianity.'

176 Ibid., 221–2.

177 Ibid., 221. Nor, according to Rashi, does he name all things without acknowledgment that it is God who has created them. Ibid., 262n53.

178 Ibid., 221.
179 Ibid.
180 Ibid., 223.
181 Ibid., 226.
182 As cited in ibid.
183 Ibid. See also ibid., 216. Even though Heidegger became a Nazi, and even though he gave 'Nazism his philosophical endorsement,' one must, according to Fackenheim, address his philosophy. Fackenheim suggests that an adequate position about Heidegger's attachment to Nazism is somewhere 'between the extremes [of the claim] that something in Heidegger's philosophy "compelled" a surrender to Nazism and that it was "unable to prevent" that surrender.' Ibid., 216.
      Hegel justifies human overreaching yet retains an Absolute Other in the act of grasping. There is in Hegel a certain openness. Fackenheim suggests that this openness is apparent in his 'guess that World Spirit might emigrate from Germany and Europe to America.' Ibid., 263n58. In contrast, because Heidegger eliminates the involvement of a Judeo-Christian divine nature, also he eliminates any openness to data that are either irrational, in the sense of being extra-rational, or simply external to his rational system. Heidegger therefore suggests that 'America and Russia are, "metaphysically considered," the same "frenzy of a boundless technology and a soil-less organization of human mediocrity."' Ibid. (Fackenheim notes that this citation and the following ones are from lectures Heidegger gave in 1935 but then reprinted, 'errors removed' by the author, in 1953.) The 'Germans are "the metaphysical people" *par excellence*,' Heidegger writes, and, most shockingly, 'there is an "inner truth and greatness" in the Nazi movement.' Ibid.
184 Ibid., 226.
185 Ibid., 216.
186 Ibid., 217.
187 Ibid.
188 Ibid.
189 Ibid.
190 Ibid.
191 By ignoring the Holocaust, Heidegger lapses into inauthenticity. See Kenneth Seeskin, 'Fackenheim's Dilemma,' in *Jewish Philosophy in a Secular Age* (New York: SUNY Press, 1990), 52–3. See also Seeskin's references to *MW* in ibid., 190–200; and *EJM*, 213–23.
192 *MW*, 166–7.
193 *GW*, 144.

194 Fackenheim suggests, rather eloquently, that '*to hear and obey the Commanding Voice of Auschwitz is an "ontological" possibility, here and now, because the hearing and obeying was already an "ontic" reality, then and there.*' *MW*, 25, italics in original.

195 See, for instance, Eugene B. Borowitz, 'Emil Fackenheim as Lurianic Philosopher,' in *Sh'ma: A Journal of Jewish Responsibility* 13, no. 254 (13 May 1983): 109–11. In *MW*, for instance, only two such explorations are made, at 9–13 and 181–8. See also Emil L. Fackenheim, 'The Uniqueness of the Holocaust,' in *The Jewish Thought of Emil Fackenheim: A Reader*, ed. Michael L. Morgan (Detroit: Wayne State University Press, 1987), 135–9.

196 'Transcendence in Contemporary Culture: Philosophical Reflections and a Jewish Testimony,' in *JRH*, 110.

197 Michael L. Morgan, 'Philosophy, History and the Jewish Thinker: Philosophy and Jewish Thought in *To Mend the World*,' in *Fackenheim: German Philosophy and Jewish Thought*, ed. Louis Greenspan and Graeme Nicholson (Toronto: University of Toronto Press, 1992), 150.

198 Strauss argues that in historicism, all philosophical questions are superseded by historical questions; there is no fundamental distinction between philosophical and historical questions. See, below, pp. 159–71.

199 See Borowitz, 'Emil Fackenheim as Lurianic Philosopher,' 109.

200 *EJM*, 228; and *MW*, 166–7, as cited in Michael Oppenheim, *What Does Revelation Mean for the Modern Jew: Rosenzweig, Buber, Fackenheim* (Lewiston: Edwin Mellon Press, 1985), 109–10.

201 Ibid., 110.

202 Fackenheim recognizes the great difficulty presented with his position: without a transhistorical standard, how is the human being to recognize God as absolute standard if and when He enters history? See below, pp. 155–9 and 172–201.

203 *EJM*, 223.

204 'The People Israel Lives: How My Mind Has Changed,' in *JRH*, 43. Fackenheim seems not to include within his conception of 'neo-orthodoxy' the observance of the commandments.

205 For Rosenzweig, God's Voice from the past continues into the present, but God no longer is speaking in history. Oppenheim, *What Does Revelation Mean*, 122. Buber confines 'the scope of the dialogue between God and man ... to those moments of encounter that the individual discovers in the midst of his living in the world.' Ibid., 123. See below, pp. 133–48. For more on *the* human condition, see above, pp. 111–20.

By recognizing the possibility of an encounter with the divine immanence throughout all aspects of human experience, Fackenheim shows an affinity with Protestant neo-orthodoxy in his understanding of Jewish neo-orthodoxy. This is at odds with Catholic neo-orthodoxy. 'For the [Catholic] neo-orthodox, God is ever the Word that stands over against us, never the ground that supports us, or the light that enables us to see, or the matrix out of which we are alive, or the vector along which we move forward.' Gregory Baum, 'Fackenheim and Christianity,' in *Fackenheim: German Philosophy and Jewish Thought*, ed. Louis Greenspan and Graeme Nicholson (Toronto: University of Toronto Press, 1992), 179.

206 Oppenheim, *What Does Revelation Mean*, 94.

207 Ibid., 123.

208 Ibid., 91. Oppenheim suggests that there were three stages in Fackenheim's theological thought, the second beginning in 1957 but really coming to fruition in 1967. Ibid., 91–2.

209 Ibid., 122.

210 Ibid., 123.

211 Nicholson, 'The Passing of Hegel's Germany,' 52.

212 The importance for Fackenheim of rediscovering an Absolute Other is to enable us to bear witness against idolatry in all its forms. See above, pp. 111–20.

213 *GPH*, 5. Such is the argument of one strand of Enlightenment thought.

214 Strauss characterizes this as the rehabilitation of the revelatory tradition.

215 *GPH*, 5. One might, for instance, see as an example Hegel's argument that God is equivalent to religious experience and history is the unfolding of God.

216 The antithesis between the modern world and religion is more prominent in Judaism than in Christianity. As Fackenheim points out: 'As portrayed in the New Testament, Jesus differs from the "scribes and Pharisees," not in interpreting the Torah, nor even in offering new interpretations, but rather in doing so on his own, personal authority. No corresponding claim was ever made on behalf of such as Hillel or Shammai, learned and pious though they were … [T]he rabbinic view was – *had* to be – that "both are the words of the living God."' *WJ*, 70.

217 Ibid., 78.

218 See above, pp. 91–106.

219 *QPF*, 36.

220 Ibid., 68.

221 Ibid.

222 Ibid., 36.

223 Ibid., italics in original. Elsewhere, Fackenheim refers to this prejudice as 'subjectivist reductionism.' See below, pp. 129–33.

224 *QPF*, 320n5.

225 Ibid., 45.

226 We note that Fackenheim has not yet in his theological development reached the point of recognizing the difficulties inherent in abstracting the human being into a representative of *the* human condition.

227 See below, chapter 4.

228 *QPF*, 115.

229 Borowitz, 'Emil Fackenheim as Lurianic Philosopher,' 109. This, in other terms, is the continuation of Hegel's mediation between Spinoza and the rabbis. See below, pp. 129–33.

230 In his only full book on the Bible, he suggests that Esther, with its parallels to the Holocaust, genocide, and the absence of God, is the most pertinent book for the contemporary Jew. See Emil L. Fackenheim, *The Jewish Bible After the Holocaust: A Re-Reading* (Bloomington: Indiana University Press, 1990), 60–2. In *MW*, he suggests the dramatic distinction between the needs of Esther's generation and those of our own: for Hitler, the murder of Jews was ultimately more important than the survival of the Reich; not so for Ahasverus, who saved Persia. See also, *WJ*, 84.

231 The anthropocentrism associated with revelation is squarely rejected by Strauss, who views this perspective as closing off the possibility of a return to an orthodoxy unqualified by the modern historical prejudice. See above, pp. 75–9; and below, pp. 159–71. Fackenheim does not view this perspective as simple anthropocentrism because for him, while the *interpretation* of Judaism may in a given context be anthropocentric, the event itself of revelation – or at least, the aspiration of the hope of such an event – is absolutely Other.

232 *QPF*, 110.

233 Ibid., 101.

234 In a later stage of his thought, Fackenheim recognizes that '*only* if the community could experience a fragment of His Presence in connection with the Holocaust, was His Presence in Halakha a possibility.' Oppenheim, *What Does Revelation Mean*, 128, italics in original.

235 *QPF*, 307.

236 Ibid., 309.

237 Ibid., 13.

238 Ibid.

239 Ibid., 115.

240 Ibid., 80.

241 Ibid., 115.

242 Ibid., 118.

243 Elsewhere, Fackenheim defines the structure of Jewish experience as a 'root experience': 'God's presence is immediately given in the event "for the abiding astonishment of the witnesses" ... [It] is both public and historical [and it] is accessible to later generations.' Oppenheim, *What Does Revelation Mean*, 100. For problems associated with Fackenheim's positing of 'root experiences,' see Susan E. Shapiro, 'The Recovery of the Sacred: Hermeneutics after the Holocaust,' PhD diss., University of Chicago, 1983.

244 As we have seen (above, pp. 111–20), Fackenheim understands the fact that God as Absolute Other was present in history as teaching subsequent generations to bear witness against idolatry in both its ancient and modern forms.

245 *QPF*, 117.

246 Ibid., 81.

247 Ibid., 315; see also *WJ*, 28, 98.

248 Fackenheim does not cite the source of this midrash. His knowledge of the classic Jewish texts was not exhaustive. While this may be one reason for his not providing citations of midrashim, Fackenheim's non-specific references to the 'rabbis' or to 'midrash' may have another explanation: Since his attempt to make a connection with the writings of the traditional texts entails his returning through the rupture of the Holocaust, his use of those texts tends toward generalities. The 'essence' of the rabbinic framework (see below, pp. 194–201) – the election of Israel to witness against idolatry – is reaffirmed in the 'election' of Jews by the Nazis. But it is reaffirmed also in the founding of the State of Israel. As Fackenheim puts it, salvation came, but it came too late. His return to the 'rabbis' is a return to the most basic aspect of 'covenantal affirmation' (*QPF*, 8), to the affirmation that something – and something wholly uncommunicable – happened at Sinai. See below, pp. 172–94.

Fackenheim insists on a return to Oral Torah, rather than only to Written Torah, because he insists on the reaffirmation of the mysterious as the primary source of authority (see chapter 4). So, for instance, in his discussion of the world to come, he suggests that the 'rabbis' held the doctrine to be true, even though there is no biblical justification for it, because 'so all important is the world to come that it simply *must* be contained in every single chapter of the Torah; and if we cannot find it there, it is because its mystery, this side of eternity, is impenetrable.' *WJ*, 270, italics in original.

249 Oppenheim, *What Does Revelation Mean*, 92.

250 See below, pp. 133–40.

296 Notes to pages 127–30

251 *MW*, 91, italics in original.

252 Martin Buber, 'Religion and Reality,' in *Eclipse of God: Studies in the Relation between Religion and Philosophy* (Atlantic Highlands: Humanities Press International, 1988), 23. See also Isaiah 45:15.

253 Oppenheim, *What Does Revelation Mean*, 122.

254 Robert M. Seltzer, 'Judaism According to Emil Fackenheim,' in *Commentary* 86, no. 3 (September 1988): 34.

255 *GPH*, 76, as cited in Oppenheim, *What Does Revelation Mean*, 97.

256 *MW*, 18.

257 See *GPH*, 8–14. Oppenheim points out that sometimes Fackenheim refers to the Holocaust as an epoch-making event because it challenges the continuity of the Jewish belief in the God of the past. Ibid., 16. Other times, he seems to refer to the Holocaust as itself a root experience because it is now a 'foundation of the Jew's belief in God's power and direction.' Oppenheim, *What Does Revelation Mean*, 100.

258 Ibid., 100–1. See also *GPH*, 83, as cited by Oppenheim, *What Does Revelation Mean*, 102.

259 For Fackenheim, God was both present and absent during the Holocaust. This position is, of course, problematic. How can God have been absent during the Holocaust yet His Covenant have been present? Fackenheim wants to find both secular and religious meaning in the event.

260 *QPF*, 117.

261 See ibid., 148–65.

262 Oppenheim, *What Does Revelation Mean*, 92.

263 See, among other places, *GPH*, 84–92; *JRH*, 22, 110; and *JPJP*, 193–4. Fackenheim later abandons this formulation as a commandment but does not abandon its mandate.

264 *JRH*, 251, italics in original.

265 *QPF*, 237.

266 *GPH*, 41–2.

267 Ibid., 42.

268 Note that 'Spinoza does not claim to have refuted revelation.' *MW*, 48. What is more, Spinoza 'endorses but [does] not definitively demonstrate' naturalism. Michael L. Morgan, 'Introduction: Part II The Early Stage: From 1945 to 1967,' in Fackenheim, *The Jewish Thought of Emil Fackenheim*, 34.

269 Fackenheim, 'These Twenty Years,' in *QPF*, 12.

270 *JRH*, 5.

271 Fackenheim argues that Rosenzweig's ability to create a Jewish system was at great cost: Jewish existence was made ahistorical. *MW*, 95.

272 Fackenheim, Introduction, in *JRH*, xi–xii.

273 Baum argues that with the insight that historical experience can prove philosophical positions, Fackenheim merely translates the problem of subjectivist reductionism into the problem of anti-Semitism. Baum, 'Fackenheim and Christianity,' 194.

274 *MW*, 49.

275 *EJM*, 122.

276 Ibid., 125.

277 For instance, Hegel's making immanent the transcendent God, Schelling's facticity, and Cohen's translation of God into the God-Idea are examples of the extension of God into the world and the attempt to recover His Otherness as empirical fact or as idea. See, above, pp. 91–111; and below, pp. 133–40.

278 Christianity, for Spinoza, according to Fackenheim, is the Christianity of Jesus and Paul. See *MW*, 38.

279 When Spinoza distinguished between Christianity and Judaism, he found the latter to be 'legalistic' (*EJM*, 89) – a finding that leads Hegel to understand Judaism as 'religious "positivity"' or '"unfreedom"': the Jew obeys purely on the basis of an external authority, without a will of his own. Ibid., 139. See above, pp. 91–106. Strauss, it seems, follows Spinoza, at least exoterically, in the conception of Judaism as revealed Law.

280 Fackenheim notes that Germany is 'a country in which Christianity, since Luther, has been prone to cut off the "inner" world reserved for Christian conscience from the "outer" world, handed over to Machiavellian princes and autocrats.' *QPF*, 281–2. And 'the profane-sacred, temporal-eternal dichotomy has always been alien to Judaism and Jewish existence.' Ibid., 283. This resonates with Strauss's characterization of the Jewish problem as the problem of the liberal state's inability to monitor the private realm. See *SCR*, 6.

Elsewhere, Fackenheim remarks on the assertion of Hans Jonas, 'effac[ing] his own Jewishness' (*EJM*, 220), of the 'traditional dichotomy between "*homo sub lege*" and "*homo sub gratia*"' – an assertion that, by distinguishing law from Grace, rejects the possibility of 'Grace *in* the Torah.' Ibid., 261n46, italics in original. Is Jonas's statement a dramatization of the essentially Christian, or post-Christian, nature of the public realm?

281 Ibid., 125.

282 Ibid.

283 *QPF*, 4.

284 *EJM*, 126.

285 Ibid. Kant recommends euthanasia for Judaism, while Hegel demon-

strates that Judaism is anachronistic. Ibid., 89. But it should be noted that Fackenheim suggests that Kant understands Judaism as legalistic because he learned it from Spinoza and Mendelssohn. According to Fackenheim, 'Kant undoubtedly would have had a profound regard for Judaism had he possessed an adequate knowledge of it.' *QPF*, 323n3.

286 See, below, pp. 133–40.
287 *MW*, 95.
288 Ibid., 98–9.
289 Ibid., 118.
290 Ibid., 113.
291 Ibid., 118.
292 Ibid., 109.
293 Ibid., 120.
294 Ibid., 108.
295 To stay with the world after the Holocaust, however, threatens the attempt to synthesize Spinozistic and rabbinic thought. Fackenheim wrote *MW* to find out if, after the Holocaust, Rosenzweig could return to the rabbinic conception of revelation, and if Spinoza could *not* return. After all, Spinoza's unity in thought is questionable when one considers the inability to think while in a Nazi work camp. Fackenheim, personal interview, August 2003.
296 While Hegel mediates between Spinoza and the rabbis, Fackenheim mediates between Spinoza and Rosenzweig, whom he considers to be the rabbis's neo-orthodox representative. Spinoza, in his 'old thinking,' and Rosenzweig, in his 'new thinking' each strives to create a system; and for Fackenheim, Spinoza represents one end of the spectrum, the secular, and Rosenzweig the other, the return to revelation. Fackenheim puts these two thinkers into dialogue to arrive at a position that incorporates both positions. See *MW*, esp. 31–101.
297 *EJM*, 202.
298 Oppenheim, *What Does Revelation Mean*, 123.
299 *WJ*, 80.
300 Ibid., 81.
301 By my use of the word 'affirm' here, I mean to suggest that Rosenzweig is, like Fackenheim to a certain extent, a historicist thinker.
302 Oppenheim, *What Does Revelation Mean*, 127.
303 Ibid., 124.
304 Ibid., 117.
305 Ibid.
306 The greatest attack of the 'new thinking' on the 'old thinking,' Facken-

heim argues, is its confidence that it can overcome the fear of death through thought; since the only way we can think of being is as *within* time, any moment of being is rooted in being-toward-death. *MW*, 162–3. Fackenheim rejects this Heideggerian stance, instead seeking, not a return to the 'old thinking,' as Strauss did, but rather a qualification of the 'new thinking.' See below, pp. 224–9.

307 'Franz Rosenzweig and the New Thinking,' in *The Jewish Thought of Emil Fackenheim,* 64n2.

308 Ibid., 59.

309 Ibid., 64.

310 Ibid., 61.

311 Ibid., 62.

312 Ibid., 61.

313 See below, pp. 140–8.

314 Fackenheim, 'Franz Rosenzweig and the New Thinking,' 62.

315 *EJM*, 131.

316 Fackenheim, 'Franz Rosenzweig and the New Thinking,' 59.

317 Regarding Rosenzweig, Fackenheim writes that 'the bridge between radical subjectivity and objective validity is the concept of revelation.' Fackenheim, 'Review of N. Glatzer, *Franz Rosenzweig: His Life and Thought'* (1953), as cited by Morgan in *The Jewish Thought of Emil Fackenheim,* 35.

318 Ibid., 62.

319 Fackenheim laments the 'wide-spread misconceptions' about existential-ism that imagine the existentialist as he who would 'escape the rigours of logic and system.' Ibid., 63.

320 Ibid.

321 Ibid.

322 *EJM*, 132.

323 As cited in ibid., 257n1.

324 Ibid., 132.

325 Ibid., 131.

326 Ibid., 132.

327 Ibid.

328 Ibid.

329 Ibid., 131.

330 Hegel had imagined that the First World War could not happen. Ibid.

331 Nicholson, 'The Passing of Hegel's Germany,' 45–6.

332 Ibid., 57–8. Nicholson adds that by the 1830s and 1840s Jews were per-ceived to be 'the most mercenary' of peoples. Ibid., 58.

333 Oppenheim, *What Does Revelation Mean,* 122.

334 *EJM*, 133.

335 Rosenzweig can thus argue that, although Spinoza is partly successful in disproving biblical revelation, he does not in any way disprove the possibility of revelation-in-general because the secular state has formed itself on foundations different from those of biblical revelation.

336 Fackenheim notes that, whereas Kant 'takes no serious look at … Judaism' (*EJM*, 89), Hegel, because his system must include, at least philosophically, the reality of post-biblical Jewish history (ibid., 125), must include an image of Judaism in his philosophy. Ibid., 242n9. Yet Hegel's 'image' of Judaism is necessarily, following Spinoza, as legalistic (ibid., 89), because, if it were not, Hegel would not be able to sustain his assertion of the identity of the human and the divine in the moment of absolute completion and his assertion of Christianity as the absolute religion. Furthermore Fackenheim rejects Rosenzweig's '"double covenant" theory, according to which all except Jews (who are "with the Father") need the Son in order to find Him' (*QPF*, 22) because it denies truths to non-Christian religions.

337 Oppenheim, *What Does Revelation Mean*, 123. See Fackenheim, 'Israel and the Diaspora: Political Contingencies and Moral Necessities; Or, The Shofar of Rabbi Yitzhak Finkler of Piotrkov,' in *JRH*.

338 Rosenzweig suggests that the beginning of authentic religion is fear of death. Oppenheim, *What Does Revelation Mean*, 91.

339 Ibid., 122.

340 *EJM*, 133.

341 Ibid., italics in original.

342 Ibid. Note that the fact that Fackenheim conceives of aspects of Rosenzweig's thought as anachronistic in no way delegitimizes it: because empirical fact informs thought, thought may arrive at different aspects of truth in different empirical historical moments.

343 I use the term advisedly since – as Oppenheim points out – Fackenheim rejected the existentialism of, for instance, Kierkegaard, because it ignores the historical and communal context of human existence. Oppenheim, *What Does Revelation Mean*, 118. See below, pp. 229–34.

344 Fackenheim defines Rosenzweig's absolute empiricism as 'a leaping-to-fact to which *a priori* construction itself leads, by reaching its limits.' Fackenheim, *The Jewish Thought*, 63.

345 Indeed this idea, to which Strauss often refers, originates with Kant, who wrote in *First Critique* (B370) that 'posterity often understands an author better than he understood himself' – a position that marks the end of the art of esoteric writing and serves also to foster the optimistic belief in progress that underlies historicism.

346 *MW*, 63.
347 *EJM*, 133.
348 Ibid., 248n101.
349 Fackenheim, following Strauss, argues against Rosenzweig's reading of the later Cohen. Rosenzweig contends that 'Cohen's work breaks through the circle of idealism.' *JPJP*, 53. For Fackenheim, Cohen's 'loving God, His acts of forgiveness, His correlation with man which preserves human individuality, are all necessary Ideas.' Ibid., 55. The circle of idealism must be broken, according to Fackenheim, for philosophy to gain a grounding in the reality of historical existence. Ibid., 53. See below, chapters 4 and 5.
350 *MW*, 85–8. Fackenheim adds that 'Rosenzweig's thought, though situated in history, rises above it ... Heidegger's thought ... *remains* in history, unable to rise above it.' Ibid., 320, italics in original.
351 Martin Buber, 'The Man of Today and the Jewish Bible,' as cited in *WJ*, 91.
352 *WJ*, 88.
353 Ibid.
354 Ibid., 89.
355 Ibid., 88.
356 Ibid., 89.
357 Ibid., 90.
358 Ibid.
359 Ibid.
360 Ibid.
361 Ibid., 91.
362 *JPJP*, 61.
363 Ibid., 59.
364 See, for instance, *QPF*, 235–6; and *GPH*, 35–66.
365 *QPF*, 291.
366 *JPJP*, 62.
367 For instance, in *GPH*, 44, Fackenheim writes: 'Buber places immediacy above reflection, for this latter, cut off from the divine Presence, is left with the mere feeling which is its by-product; thus is preordained the impotence of reflection to dissipate the divine Presence.'
368 *JPJP*, 69.
369 *QPF*, 242.
370 Buber's image of an eclipse of God 'evokes the familiar biblical "hiding of His face."' Neil Gillman, *Sacred Fragments: Recovering Theology for the Modern Jew* (Philadelphia: Jewish Publication Society, 1990), 206. In the Bible, the image most often is a sign of God's punishment, but 'sometimes – Psalm 13 is an excellent example – it represents a mysterious ebb in the divine–human relationship that the human being simply can not fathom

but experiences as palpably real and terrifying.' Ibid. It is this latter use that Buber invokes.

371 QPF, 315.
372 MW, 196.
373 Ibid., 197.
374 Ibid., 196.
375 QPF, 273–4. For more on Fackenheim's understanding of idolatry, see EJM, 173–98.
376 As cited in EJM, 220–1. To contrast Buber's understanding of the prophets' insecurity with Heidegger's, see above, pp. 111–20.
377 Ibid., 221.
378 Ibid.
379 See, above, pp. 111–20.
380 QPF, 272.
381 Ibid., 302.
382 JPJP, 64, italics in original.
383 Ibid., 63.
384 Ibid., 62–3.
385 See the comparison between excerpts from Bertrand Russell's My Philosophical Development and excerpts from Buber's Eclipse of God. QPF, 238–40. Fackenheim writes that Russell's position is a representative of the subjectivist reductionist view. See ibid., 239.
386 Ibid., 240.
387 JPJP, 64, italics in original.
388 Fackenheim writes, for instance: 'His [Buber's] treatment of Hasidism shows him to be a thinker capable of practicing the empathetic openness which he preaches.' QPF, 326n13.
389 MW, 4.
390 Oppenheim, What Does Revelation Mean, 123.
391 MW, 196.
392 This critique echoes Fackenheim's critique of Strauss: Buber's image of an eclipse is at once too optimistic and not optimistic enough. On the one hand, it does not take evil seriously enough because it does not acknowledge the possibility that there no longer exists a guarantee of God's Presence behind God's absence; or, in the terms of his dialogue with Strauss, it does not question whether the revelatory tradition is reliable. On the other, it does not take God's Presence seriously enough because it does not acknowledge that the God of the Bible, if He exists, is the God of secular history as well. See below, pp. 224–9.
393 Oppenheim, What Does Revelation Mean, 123.

394 Fackenheim points out that 'precisely to the degree to which his [Buber's] thought has been influential has it also been emasculated, wittingly or unwittingly, of its Jewish content.' *EJM*, 257n1. He seems to be suggesting that his thought is acceptable to Heidegger and Sartre only insofar as it argues for – as the latter thinkers do – the human condition as the foundation of authentic thought.

395 *JPJP*, 60.

396 Like Strauss, Buber might deny the necessity of taking Fackenheim's next step of moulding a Jewish philosophy. There is, on the one hand, an inherent (and ultimate) connection between reason and revelation, and Buber acknowledges this connection by recognizing I-Thou knowledge as a valid form of knowledge (or, as Fackenheim puts it, when he succeeds in establishing a doctrine). But on the other hand, reason and revelation cannot be synthesized within the realm of human comprehension or existence. Buber's choice to retain the separate realm of revelation, like Strauss's of reason, preserves, perhaps, a more sustainable Judaism. A full exploration of this issue with regard to Buber is beyond the scope of this book; for a fuller discussion of it with regard to Strauss, see below, pp. 159–71 and 209–24.

397 *JPJP*, 64.

398 Ibid., 70–1.

399 This alternative seems to have its source in Schelling's 'positive philosophy' and can, perhaps, be traced to the meontological tradition of metaphysics. See above, pp. 107–11 and 172–94.

400 One might say, along with Strauss, that philosophy, if it is to endure, must remain aware of the persistence of the ultimate mystery at its inception and its end.

401 Fackenheim concedes that Jewish philosophy will always be fragmented: in the theological context, one 'proves' the existence of God through one's right living. The only intelligible 'proof' of God's existence is a 'pointing to,' which by definition remains fragmentary. Yet this fragmentation represents the limit of both philosophy and revelatory theology – philosophy because, although God is one and in some sense intelligible, He is transcendent; and revelatory theology because, although God is transcendent and is not intelligible, also He is One. For a discussion of the problem of Jewish philosophy, as Fackenheim conceives it, see, for instance, *QPF*, 204–28; and 'What Is Jewish Philosophy? Reflections on Athens, Jerusalem, and the Western Academy,' in *JPJP*, 165–84. For the necessity of fragmentation, see below, pp. 155–9; for knowledge or wisdom as defining the right way of life, see below, pp. 209–24.

402 Oppenheim points out that perhaps Fackenheim 'transforms his endeavor to hear into a hearing.' Oppenheim, *What Does Revelation Mean*, 112. This is a misunderstanding of the nature of authority: Fackenheim does not attempt to answer whether there is a hearing, only to describe and affirm the stance necessary to listen.

403 *MW*, 196.

404 *QPF*, 302.

405 Fackenheim points out that Buber, when faced with the apparent contradiction of God being at once in a moment and also eternal and infinite, can only respond that 'the relation between divine address and human response is an antimony which thought cannot resolve.' *JPJP*, 69.

406 Fackenheim's critique of Buber, with regard to Buber's overemphasis on the present even while he does not alter the religious centre of the biblical category of the hiding of God's Face, is, ironically, similar to his critique of those who would overemphasize the past or the eternal: the present must be recognized as both distinct from and connected to an utterly transcendent truth.

407 *JPJP*, 69.

408 See, for instance, *EJM*, 257n1; and *MW*, 190–5.

409 *MW*, 195.

410 *RD*, xi.

411 *MW*, 20.

412 *EJM*, 202.

413 *GPH*, 76, as cited in Oppenheim, *What Does Revelation Mean*, 97.

414 See Borowitz, 'Emil Fackenheim as Lurianic Philosopher,' 109–11.

415 *Teshuvah* translates as both 'return' and 'repentance.' Fackenheim defines *teshuvah* as a 'basic Jewish idea … a turning and returning in which the old is renewed.' *WJ*, 58. He claims that '*teshuvah* is the ultimate source of Jewish life and renewal.' Ibid., 211; see also Lamentations 5:22. The present age, in its attempt to revalidate both God's existence and His absence at Auschwitz, requires a 'radical *t'shuvah* [*sic*] – a *turning* and listening to the God who can speak even though He is silent.' *QPF*, 315, italics in original. As will become clearer in chapter 5, this concept is essential for Fackenheim's contention that a 'return' to Hegel, and to 'rabbinic' thought, is possible because in human experience, the absolute and the contingent exist – at least in part – in identity. See Fackenheim, '*Teshuva* [*sic*] Today,' in *The Jewish Thought of Emil Fackenheim*.

Strauss suggests that a Jewish 'return' in the above sense is impossible because Spinoza has accomplished a complete break with Jewish thought. One may 'return' to an unqualified Jewish orthodoxy, but one cannot incorporate historical categories to accomplish this return. See Strauss, 'Progress or Return?' *JPCM*, 87–136. See also below, chapters 4 and 5.

416 *Tikkun olam* translates as 'mending of the world' and defines the appropriate form of post-Holocaust resistance to radical evil. *Tikkun* of the ruptures created by the Holocaust, while impossible, is necessary. It is like *teshuvah* in the sense that the return to the moment of these ruptures both mends and does not mend them; for instance, the *Muselmaenner*, or living dead in Auschwitz, are both left behind and not left behind. See *MW*, 336n13. The evil of Auschwitz cannot 'retroactively justify … the evil that it was to mend.' Fackenheim, 'Resistance and *Tikkun Olam*,' in *The Jewish Thought of Emil Fackenheim*, 188.

417 Fackenheim, 'On the Self-Exposure of Faith,' 293, italics in original.

418 *QPF*, 18.

419 *MW*, xiii.

420 Fackenheim, personal interview, August 2003.

421 See *EJM*, 7–29.

422 *MW*, 336n13.

423 This discussion is more fully developed in chapters 4 and 5, where it is formulated as the necessity for reason and revelation to be open toward each other. See, below, pp. 140–8.

424 Ibid., 127–30.

425 See above, pp. 133–40.

426 Fackenheim was troubled both by Buber's too early return to Germany (1953) and by Strauss's inattention to the Holocaust. He accounted for the former by recalling Buber's advanced age and for the latter by suggesting that Strauss 'did not live long enough.' Fackenheim, personal interview, August 2003.

427 See below, pp. 224–9.

4. The Problem of Historicism

1 Following Strauss, one might say, more specifically, that when the art of esoteric writing was lost, so too was lost the Enlightenment distinction (in such writers as Hobbes and Spinoza) between the critiques of the outer and the inner truths of religion. Revelation was subsequently incorporated erroneously into the public (secular) realm.

2 Although I do not develop this thought here, one might turn to the residual Christianity in the post-Christian goal of universalism, or to the traces of the Incarnation in univeralism's goal of human self-perfecting. Clearly, post-Christianity is not Christianity; yet for Jews to become

post-Christians, they must break with Judaism, whereas Christians need (minimally) only a privatization of Christianity, or (maximally) a development from Christianity. See, Leo Strauss, 'Progress or Return?' in *Jewish Philosophy and the Crisis of Modernity: Essays and Lectures in Modern Jewish Thought*, ed. Kenneth Hart Green [*JPCM*] (Albany: SUNY Press, 1997), 87–136; and above, pp. 129–33.

3 See above, pp. 65–72.

4 See above, pp. 75–9.

5 See above, pp. 133–40.

6 See below, pp. 159–71.

7 Strauss argues for the development of a 'genuine history of philosophy,' whose elements would be understanding the thinkers as they understood themselves, rather than a history of the historical circumstances that produced their thought.

8 See above, pp. 148–52.

9 Emil L. Fackenheim, *Quest for Past and Future: Essays in Jewish Theology* [*QPF*] (Boston: Beacon Press, 1968), 8.

10 See below, pp. 172–94.

11 For a more complete discussion of the relation between philosophy and revelation in Strauss's thought, see below, pp. 209–24.

12 Leo Strauss, *On Tyranny: Including the Strauss–Kojeve Correspondence*, rev. and exp., ed. Victor Gourevitch and Michael S. Roth (New York: The Free Press, 1991), 196. Also cited – in different translation – in Kenneth L. Deutsch and Walter Nicgorski, eds., Introduction to *Leo Strauss: Political Philosopher and Jewish Thinker* (Lanham: Rowman and Littlefield, 1994), 7 (citing Stanley Rosen, 'Leo Strauss and the Quarrel between the Ancients and the Moderns' in *Leo Strauss's Thought: Towards a Critical Engagement*, ed. Alan Udoff [Boulder: Lyenne Rienner Publishers, 1991]).

13 Ernest L. Fortin, 'Rational Theologians and Irrational Philosophers: A Straussian Perspective,' in *Classical Christianity and the Political Order: Reflections on the Theologico-Political Problem*, ed. J. Brian Benestad (Lanham: Rowman and Littlefield, 1996), 295.

14 The external claims are the rites of religion; the inner claims are its truth content. The refutation of the external claims, as in the work of Strauss's Spinoza – the Spinoza who writes esoterically for the amelioration of the Jewish political condition – is rationally consistent. The refutation of the inner claims of religion – the rational judgment of whether religion is true – is based on the irrational assertion that reason has the authority to make this judgment, even though it cannot rationally prove its authority.

15 *JPCM*, 328.

16 Ibid., 329.

17 Ibid.

18 Ibid. As we shall see, the hailing distance between them is that philosophy is the *search* for the right way of life, while religion claims to *possess* the right way of life. See below, pp. 209–24.

19 Both Strauss and Fackenheim use the word 'open' to describe the necessary theoretic relationship between reason and revelation. See, for instance, *JPCM*, 117ff; *QPF*, 10, 16, 22; and Emil L. Fackenheim, the title of Part One of *The Jewish Return into History: Reflections in the Age of Auschwitz and a New Jerusalem* [*JRH*] (New York: Schocken Books, 1978). Buber also uses the word to describe 'the opened abyss' in which the prophets proclaim 'the unwished for God,' an abyss created through the shattering of all human security. See Martin Buber, *The Eclipse of God*, as cited in Emil L. Fackenheim, *Encounters between Judaism and Modern Philosophy: A Preface to Future Jewish Thought* [*EJM*] (New York: Schocken Books, 1973), 261n48.

20 *JPCM*, 170.

21 Both Strauss and Fackenheim recognize the need for mutual openness between reason and revelation also as a political necessity. For Strauss, a thinker who is living, for instance, under an ecclesiastical authority must be able to express his thought in accordance with the external claims of that authority, even as his more covert meaning may defy it. Fackenheim's adoption of Strauss's openness stems not simply from the desire to preserve the claims of both revelation and reason, but also from his insistence that the human being must neither flee from the world nor can bear to be totally immersed in the world.

22 See, for instance, Ezekiel 1–3.

23 See below, pp. 209–24.

24 So, for instance, Strauss includes intentional errors in his work; structures his work so as to place the subject worthy of most study in the centre, or even contradicts his beginnings and endings with his centres; and seems to speak from the perspective of either reason or revelation in the first part of a sentence, before extending the sentence to speak from the other's perspective.

25 In his later work, when he no longer wants to be 'compartmentalized,' Fackenheim attempts to join these two strains: philosophy and Jewish revelation.

26 While the insistence on this openness became more profound in Fackenheim's work as he became more and more aware of the 'ruptures' in thought and life created by the Holocaust – as, for instance, in his *To Mend the World: Foundations of Post-Holocaust Jewish Thought*, First Midland Edi-

tion [*MW*] (Bloomington: Indiana University Press, 1994) – my argument is that this openness stems from Strauss's critique of the idealism inherent in the modern liberal state, and is evident in Fackenheim's thought as far back as *QPF*. See, for instance, Zachary Braiterman, *Theodicy and Antitheodicy: Tradition and Change in Post-Holocaust Jewish Theology* (PhD diss., Stanford University, 1995), 207–11.

27 For the 'clearest example of "philosophizing, or something akin to it" within Judaism' (*QPF*, 317n11), see Braiterman, *Theodicy and Antitheodicy*, 244–62.

28 *QPF*, 207.

29 Ibid., 208. Elsewhere, in relation to Buber, Fackenheim understands this 'sympathetic phenomenological re-renactment' as a third kind of knowledge from which Jewish philosophy might be developed. This knowledge would transcend I-It knowledge and point to I-Thou knowledge. See *JPJP*, 70–1; and above, pp. 140–8.

30 *QPF*, 208. Fackenheim's philosophical commitment to revelatory theology will differ from Strauss's, however, insofar as his commitment is not to revelation in general, but to Jewish revelation in particular.

31 Ibid., 117.

32 For the necessity, in order to avoid 'modern idolatry,' of this kind of limitation of the openness of theology, see above, pp. 111–20. For a fuller discussion of the distinctions between standing inside and outside the rabbinic framework, see below, pp. 194–201.

33 Ibid., 16.

34 See Emil L. Fackenheim, *Encounters between Judaism and Modern Philosophy: A Preface to Future Jewish Thought* [*EJM*] (New York: Schocken Books, 1973), 7–29.

35 For Fackenheim, theological thought must begin in commitment, and, simply by virtue of living in the modern world, one is committed to modern philosophy. For this reason, modern philosophy – even with its blindness-inducing historical sense – must inform revelatory theology. On this point – whether, or to what extent, the historical sense should inform thought – Strauss and Fackenheim disagree. See the remainder of chapter 4.

36 See above, pp. 140–8.

37 Emil L. Fackenheim, *Jewish Philosophers and Jewish Philosophy*, ed. Michael L. Morgan [*JPJP*] (Bloomington: Indiana University Press, 1996), 64. Fackenheim's development of Buber derives from Schelling's distinction 'between a "positive" philosophy which is based on a commitment, and a "negative" philosophy which is a dialectical argument for this commitment.' Ibid., 254n47.

38 Michael L. Morgan, *Dilemmas in Modern Jewish Thought: The Dialectics of Revelation and History* (Bloomington: Indiana University Press, 1992), 114.

39 *MW*, 4.

40 *QPF*, 22.

41 Allan Bloom, 'Leo Strauss: September 20, 1899–October 18, 1973,' in *Giants and Dwarfs: Essays 1960–1990* (New York: Simon and Schuster, 1990), 241–2. Thomas Paine writes: 'In the following pages I offer nothing more than simple facts, plain arguments, and common sense; and have no other preliminaries to settle with the reader, than that he will divest himself of prejudice and prepossession, and suffer his reason and feelings to determine for themselves; that he will put *on*, or rather, that he will not put *off*, the true character of a man, and generously enlarge his views beyond the present day.' Thomas Paine, *Common Sense*, intro. Isaac Kramnick (New York: Penguin Books, 1986), 61, italics in original. For Strauss, political common sense is the recognition that public dogma is necessary for political stability.

42 Fackenheim, too, as we shall see, begins with doubt; but because he begins also with a commitment to Jewish survival, he locates this doubt within the rabbinic framework.

43 See above, pp. 46–52.

44 Leo Strauss, *Natural Right and History* [NRH] (Chicago: University of Chicago Press, 1965), 179.

45 Ibid., 9–34.

46 One can only suggest that the immense intellectual density of the lecture, and the consequent diligence with which the reader must attend to it, is one means by which Strauss fights historicism, which he understands as a complacency of the tired mind.

47 *NRH*, 12.

48 See above, pp. 41–6.

49 Failure to make this distinction will result in a denial, not only of the existence of philosophy in its original sense, but also of the possibility of thought that contradicts or transcends the political authority under which one lives. See below, pp. 167–9ff., on the role of 'fate' in radical historicism.

50 *NRH*, 10.

51 Aristotle, *Nicomachean Ethics*, trans. Joe Sachs (Newburyport: Focus Publishing, 2002), 5:7, as cited by *NRH*, 10.

52 Thomas Hobbes, *De Cive or The Citizen*, ed. Sterling P. Lamprecht (New York: Appleton-Century-Crofts, 1949), 31–2 (2:1), as cited by *NRH*, 9.

53 See above, pp. 46–52. Again, Strauss suggests that Hobbes's solution, building on Machiavelli's objection to ancient utopianism, 'was to main-

tain the idea of natural law but to divorce it from the idea of man's perfection.' *NRH*, 180.

54 Furthermore, public dogma, or the antithesis between public dogma and political philosophy in the classical sense, provides for Strauss common sense, the 'surface' from which to ascend to, or the authority in which to contextualize, his esoteric readings.

55 *NRH*, 10.

56 Ibid., 11.

57 Conventionalism in this sense marks the beginning of a particular form of political philosophy, a political philosophy that has untethered itself from its acknowledgment of the existence of philosophy proper.

58 *NRH*, 11.

59 Ibid., 12.

60 Leo Strauss, *Persecution and the Art of Writing* [PW] (Chicago: University of Chicago Press, 1980), 155.

61 Strauss acknowledges the need for historical studies insofar as, since, in our pit beneath the cave, we have lost the entrance to Plato's cave, human beings must devise tools with which to raise themselves to the natural cave. The 'new and most artificial tools unknown and unnecessary to those who dwelt in the natural cave' (ibid., 155) – the invention of history – might have worked as a corrective to the limitations of modern thought, or might have worked as a means of resolving the self-contradictory character of historicism, had they not been accompanied by the belief 'that modern thought (as distinguished from modern life and modern feeling) was superior to the thought of the past' (ibid., 158). This belief, by affirming the supposed progress of modern thought, merely reinforced its own presupposition.

62 *NRH*, 13.

63 The historical sense, as manifested, for instance, in the eighteenth-century idea of progress, while 'profoundly modif[ying]' the affirmation of the existence of the eternal as a standard of judgment, continued to preserve it. Ibid., 15. Strauss points the reader to Kant's 9th Thesis in the latter's 'Idea for a Universal History,' in which Kant suggests the tension, at this stage of the development of historicism, between philosophy and history. Ibid., 15n6. Kant writes: 'That I would want to displace the work of practicing empirical historians with this Idea of world history, which is to some extent based upon an a priori principle, would be a misinterpretation of my intention. It is only a suggestion of what a philosophical mind (which would have to be well versed in history) could essay from another point of view.' Immanuel Kant, 'Idea for a Universal History from a Cosmopolitan

Point of View,' trans. Lewis White Beck, in *On History*, ed. Lewis White
Beck (Englewood Cliffs: Macmillan Publishing, 1963), 25.

64 *NRH*, 14.

65 Ibid.

66 Ibid., 15.

67 Ibid. Strauss writes: 'Transcendence is not a preserve of revealed religion.
In a very important sense it was implied in the original meaning of political philosophy as the quest for the natural or best political order.' Ibid.,
15. Strauss's critique of the destruction of the universal norms either derived from nature or implicit in classical conventionalism applies also to
the application of the historical sense to revealed religion. See below, pp.
194–201.

68 Furthermore, without recognition of the surface of things, one cannot ascend beyond that surface; moreover, one is unable to be informed about
that surface. By denying the existence of transcendence, one can neither
understand the immediately accessible nor judge the accuracy of thought
within the immediately accessible.

69 For Strauss's notion of philosophy as a quest, see below, pp. 209–24.

70 *NRH*, 16.

71 Ibid.

72 Ibid.

73 Ibid., 17.

74 This alienation is at the heart of the theologico-political predicament as
Strauss sees it: not only Jews but all human beings are in exile within the
world. See Leo Strauss, *Spinoza's Critique of Religion* [*SCR*] (New York:
Schocken Books, 1982).

75 *NRH*, 18. This allusion to *Macbeth* is especially dramatic when one considers the play's theme: Macbeth first chooses death, and the play dramatizes
the events by which he constructs his wished-for fate. Just so, the historicist chooses nihilism and then claims proof for his choice. Furthermore,
if we recall Strauss's analysis, in which he recognizes philosophy as the
replacement of impersonal fate, or myth, with nature and intelligible necessity, one might say that the adherence to historicism is a regression from
philosophy. Generally speaking, this regression is the pit beneath the cave;
more specifically, the pit is the consequence of the belief in progress – the
absolute superiority of modern thought.

76 Ibid., 18.

77 Ibid.

78 Ibid., 19.

79 See Plato's *Theaetetus* 152a.

80 *NRH*, 19.
81 Ibid., 20.
82 Ibid., 21.
83 Ibid.
84 Lessing's letter to Mendelssohn of 9 January 1771, as cited in ibid., 22n8.
85 Ibid., 22.
86 Ibid.
87 Strauss suggests that Heidegger's return to the roots of philosophy provided for existentialism its 'hard core.' Leo Strauss, 'Relativism,' in *Relativism and the Study of Man*, ed. Helmut Schoeck and James W. Wiggins (New York: Van Nostrand, 1961), 151.

   As will become more apparent below, the question with regard to Fackenheim's work is whether it is based on an experience of history or an experience of the history of thought – in his case, the thought of the rabbis. Because Fackenheim works within the rabbinic tradition – a tradition based in part on the history of thought – he attempts to connect these two concepts. In the realm of philosophy, Fackenheim focuses on Hegel as the moment at which the connection between experience and thought is defined. In the realm of theology, he begins with the laity's experience, from which his thought ascends. In both cases, Fackenheim, in an attempt to eliminate the possibility of falling into what Strauss has shown to be a self-perpetuating intellectual delusion, retains the tension between the experience of history and the experience of the history of thought. See below.
88 *NRH*, 23–4.
89 Ibid., 24.
90 Fackenheim's 'Metaphysics and Historicity' centres on this contradiction implicit in historicism. Emil L. Fackenheim, 'Metaphysics and Historicity,' Thomas Aquinas Lecture, under the auspices of the Aristotelian Society of Marquette University (Milwaukee: Marquette University Press, 1961). See below, pp. 172–94.
91 *NRH*, 25.
92 Ibid., 26.
93 According to Strauss, Nietzsche recognized that the Hegelianism of his day had decayed through its acceptance of 'history,' even while rejecting the philosophical basis of 'history.' It is interesting to note here 'Nietzsche's sway over [Strauss] during his most formative years' (as indicated in correspondence between Strauss and Karl Löwith, as cited by Frederick G. Lawrence, 'Leo Strauss and the Fourth Wave of Modernity,' in *Leo Strauss and Judaism: Jerusalem and Athens Critically Revisited*, ed. David Novak [Lanham: Rowman and Littlefield, 1996], 132), and the impact this

may have had on Strauss's conclusion that the historical sense must necessarily end in decay.

94 *NRH*, 26.

95 Deutsch and Nicgorski suggest that 'Strauss had chosen, by an act of
his will, not to have faith in any doctrine, opinion, or any of the conflicting traditions of divine revelation, but to pursue a quest for wisdom by
means of his own unaided reason.' Deutsch and Nicgorski, *Leo Strauss*,
11. Note Strauss's adoption of the Nietzschean concept of will. See below,
chapter 5. Fackenheim, on the other hand, will deem it necessary – because Jews cannot, so to speak, opt back into the covenantal relationship
once having opted out – for Jews to begin with a commitment to their
survival as Jews.

96 *NRH*, 27.

97 Again, having regressed to the realm of myth from the possibility of ascending from Plato's cave to philosophy, we are mired in the pit beneath
the cave.

98 *NRH*, 27.

99 Ibid., 28.

100 Ibid.

101 Ibid., 29.

102 Ibid.

103 As we recall, Fackenheim explicitly rejects the reading that Hegel affirms
there is no further need to seek wisdom, citing the latter's suggestion
that World Spirit may have been transferred to the New World. See *EJM*,
263n58; and above, pp. 91–106.

104 Strauss understands this paradox at the heart of Hegel as stemming from
the latter's transformation of philosophy from a quest or way of life to a
completed system. Hegel's is 'one very special form of philosophy: it is
not the primary and necessary form of philosophy.' *JPCM*, 121.

105 Strauss's recognition of the radical distinction between Hegel's thought
and historicism suggests that Fackenheim's adoption of Hegel's thought
as a starting point for his refutation of historicism is not invalid. See below, pp. 194–201.

106 *NRH*, 30.

107 Ibid., 20.

108 Ibid., 30.

109 Ibid.

110 Ibid., 30–1.

111 Ibid., 31.

112 Ibid.

113 Ibid., 33.
114 As to whether this can be understood, as well, as a return to revelation, see below, pp. 209–24.
115 *NRH*, 32.
116 Ibid., 33.
117 Ibid.
118 Ibid., 34. One might consider, for instance, Machiavelli's establishment of philosophy as a public enterprise. See above, pp. 46–52.
119 Strauss refers here to 'an intellectual' who fails to make this distinction. In connection with the 'intellectual,' he uses the word 'fatal' – an allusion to the overwhelming role of fate in the thought of the 'intellectual.' Strauss's suggestion seems to be that fate must always dictate the abdication of independent thought.
120 Despite the claim of historicism that the 'experience of history' refutes the evidence in favour of the existence of natural right, this 'experience' ignores the simple, everyday, human experiences of right and wrong. Because it defines these experiences as both historical and philosophical, as both action and the interpretation of that action, historicism blinds itself to the possibility of experiences that are accessible to man as man, and with it to the possibility of the existence of natural right to which those experiences point.
121 Strauss writes, for instance, that 'transcendence is not a preserve of revealed religion.' *NRH*, 15. Yet in this lecture, he fails to account for the effect that historicism might have on revealed religion. For Strauss's thought on the effect of historicism on religion, see his essay 'Progress and Return,' in *JPCM*, 87–136, and his Preface to *SCR*.
122 Furthermore, the distinction between the thought of Hegel and that of the historicists becomes one basis for Strauss's insistence on the return to the experience from which an idea emerges. Strauss cites Hegel: 'The manner of study in ancient times is distinct from that of modern times, in that the former consisted in the veritable training and perfecting of the natural consciousness. Trying its power at each past of its life severally, and philosophizing about everything it came across, the natural consciousness transformed itself into a universality of abstract understanding which was active in every matter and in every respect. In modern times, however, the individual finds the abstract form ready made.' Leo Strauss, 'Political Philosophy and History,' in *What Is Political Philosophy? and Other Studies* (Westport: Greenwood Press, 1959), 75.
  Strauss comments: 'Classical philosophy originally acquired the fundamental concepts of political philosophy by starting from political

phenomena as they present themselves to "the natural consciousness," which is a pre-philosophic consciousness. These concepts can therefore be understood, and their validity can be checked, by direct reference to phenomena as they are accessible to "the natural consciousness."' Ibid., 75.

The preservation by Hegel of the natural consciousness, as Fackenheim understands him, will become important to Fackenheim's anti-historicist thought and will provide the justification for its beginning in the thought of Hegel. Nevertheless, Fackenheim rejects ultimately the exhaustiveness of the distinction between the natural and the historical consciousness.

123 As will become clear below, this is because Fackenheim understands Hegel's philosophical thought as intrinsically bound to his historical thought.

124 In Strauss's reading, convention becomes higher because it is more 'free,' that is, self-imposed.

125 Indeed, the shadow of Hegel hangs over 'Metaphysics and Historicity,' as evidenced by Fackenheim's numerous (sixteen in all) long footnotes referring to Hegel's work, and his dedication of a section of this lecture to Hegel's thought.

126 Indeed, Fackenheim's 'return' to Hegel is paradoxical: he attributes to Hegel's thought the very alteration of human nature; yet at the same time, this alteration itself is what precludes a return to Hegel proper. See below.

According to Fackenheim, Hegel concedes that perhaps philosophy must retreat from history: philosophy, though it try, cannot defeat history. This statement, made to this writer toward the end of Professor Fackenheim's life, was exceedingly poignant: Fackenheim's faith, not his blindness, allowed the reaffirmation of the existence of philosophy proper within the modern historical context. Fackenheim, personal interview, August 2003.

127 At this point, however, we note that regardless of whether Fackenheim is motivated by philosophical or theological considerations, or by both, he recognizes that authority is in the surface of things, not in proclamations conducted, as it were, *ex cathedra*. So, for instance, he writes: 'While philosophy assuredly cannot remove this need for choice it cannot escape from its own responsibilities by becoming itself an authority. At least part of the task of philosophy – existential philosophy included – must consist of argument, however inconclusive, such as the systematic elaboration of presuppositions and implications.' Emil L. Fackenheim, *The God Within: Kant, Schelling, and Historicity*, ed. John Burbidge [*GW*] (Toronto: University of Toronto Press, 1996), 228n45.

128 Both essays appear in *GW*.
129 See *GW*, 150–1.
130 *QPF*, 8. The change in Fackenheim's stance to one of covenantal affirmation took place in 1957.
131 Ibid., 244–62.
132 Emil L. Fackenheim, 'Martin Buber on Israel and Palestine,' in *The Jewish Thought of Emil Fackenheim: A Reader*, ed. Michael L. Morgan (Detroit: Wayne State University Press, 1987), 66.
133 *QPF*, 12.
134 Fackenheim's adoption of Strauss's hermeneutic of reading texts – or, more precisely, exploring ideas in their own terms (though Fackenheim vehemently rejects the adoption of the art of esoteric writing) – has led some critics to suggest that Fackenheim's results, his call for a return to midrash, issue only as a result of his hermeneutic. Morgan, Shapiro, and Dray, for instance, critique this hermeneutic from a (broadly speaking) philosophic point of view; Eisen and Seeskin, for their part, critique it from the point of view of a more traditional understanding of midrash. See Morgan, *Dilemmas*, 123–4; Susan E. Shapiro, 'The Recovery of the Sacred: Hermeneutics after the Holocaust,' PhD diss., University of Chicago, 1983, 212, 262–6; Robert Eisen, 'Midrash in Emil Fackenheim's Holocaust Theology,' *Harvard Theological Review* 96, no. 3 (July 2003): 369–92; and Kenneth Seeskin, 'Emil Fackenheim,' in *Interpreters of Judaism in the Late Twentieth Century* (Washington: B'nai Brith, 1993), 55. For a discussion of whether Fackenheim succumbs completely to historicism in *MW*, see Morgan, *Dilemmas*, 117–22. See also below, pp. 237–8.
135 Indeed, Fackenheim points out the particular challenge of historicity to theologians: 'But we must insist that while many – in particular, theologians – might sympathize with the thesis "Being manifests itself differently in different periods," the *total* historicization of philosophy toward which the later Heidegger seems to be moving is open to the same objections as the crudest forms of historicism. The very thesis "Being manifests itself differently in different periods" cannot without self-contradiction be historicized.' *GW*, 228n45, italics in original.
136 At least one scholar – Dray – finds this methodology to issue in a critique that is 'too gentle with the doctrine.' W.H. Dray, 'Historicity, Historicism, and Self-Making,' in *Fackenheim: German Philosophy and Jewish Thought*, ed. Louis Greenspan and Graeme Nicholson (Toronto: University of Toronto Press, 1992), 137. Yet I would argue that Fackenheim's approach is necessary as a means of reaffirming the priority of common sense, in Strauss's sense.

137 Emil L. Fackenheim, 'A Reply to My Critics,' in *Fackenheim: German Philosophy and Jewish Thought*, ed. Louis Greenspan and Graeme Nicholson (Toronto: University of Toronto Press, 1992), 275, italics in original. The sentence continues: 'and whereas (as the book's title said) overtly at issue was "metaphysics," implicitly at issue was also the transcendence required by "Biblical faith."'

138 Strauss, however, is referred to directly only twice in the lecture; both times this is to his 'What Is Political Philosophy?' See *GW*, 224n35 and 225n37. As mentioned, Fackenheim sent the lecture to Strauss for the latter's evaluation.

139 *GW*, 122. One might, of course, trace this as well to Rosenzweig's argument for the need for 'eternity-in-time.' See above, pp. 133–40. Fackenheim ascribes the error of basing knowledge exclusively on the experience of the history of thought to the choice, understood as comprehensive, between Fichte and Hegel, not to revelatory thought. See *MW*, 157–8.

140 *GW*, 122.

141 Fackenheim works from Kant, through Fichte, Schelling, and Hegel, to Heidegger.

142 *GW*, 122.

143 Ibid.

144 Ibid., 122–3.

145 Ibid., 123.

146 Fackenheim suggests that the situation of pragmatic make-believe not be confused with existentialism, which seeks the true from within commitment. Ibid., 216n4. Strauss seems to deny this distinction in his suggestion that 'if a Jew cannot believe in miracles and all of the "old faith," he or she can still be dedicated to what can be seen as the "noblest of all delusions."' In Deutsch and Nicgorski, *Leo Strauss*, 14. Strauss's position may seem not to take seriously enough the claims of revelation, although Deutsch and Nicgorski suggest that Fackenheim recognizes Strauss's position in this matter as a 'third way of life that can be chosen other than strict philosophy or simple religious orthodoxy.' Ibid.

In an essay published the same year as 'Metaphysics and Historicity' (1961), Strauss suggests that 'the only way out seems to be that one … voluntarily choose life-giving delusion instead of deadly truth, that one fabricate a myth. But this is patently impossible for men of intellectual probity.' Strauss, 'Relativism,' 152. I do not know which paper appeared first, and whether Fackenheim adopted Strauss's insight and responded to Strauss's rejection of existentialism. See ibid., esp. 151–5.

147 *GW*, 123. Fackenheim later suggests that 'ideological fanaticism' is an allusion to Nazism. At the same time he recognizes that he had failed to account adequately for the particularity of the Nazi evil. *MW*, xvi–xvii.

148 *GW*, 123. In an allusion to Nazism, Fackenheim suggests that this fanaticism can be avoided if the ideology retains one belief beyond itself: belief in democratic tolerance. See ibid., 216–17n5.

149 But his thought does not on this account move within the realm of philosophy. See below, pp. 209–24: Fackenheim's method is to begin his paper within the human situation, so to speak, then to move to philosophy, then to return to the human situation.

150 *GW*, 124.

151 Ibid.

152 Ibid.

153 Like Strauss, Fackenheim recognizes a strong connection between Nietzsche and Heidegger. According to Fackenheim, Nietzsche by proclaiming that God is dead destroyed the basis of metaphysics. Ibid., 124. Furthermore, Heidegger recognized Nietzsche's historicization of thought: the will to power for Nietzsche does not simply constitute truth; rather, truth is constituted by 'will-to-power willing something *beyond* itself which will itself creates.' Ibid., 217n7, italics in original. The basis of this difference between Strauss and Fackenheim is Strauss's affirmation, and Fackenheim's denial, of esoteric writing. Fackenheim denies not necessarily the existence but the viability of esoteric writing for human thought: according to him, esoteric writing in, for example, Spinoza's work might very often have disastrous consequences.

154 This view is held in common by, for instance, Nietzsche, Collingwood, Dilthey, Croce, Dewey, and Heidegger. Ibid., 124.

155 Ibid., 125. Fackenheim points out that, while Aristotle would agree that man's potentialities are disclosed only through their actualization, he would disagree that these potentialities change over time. For Aristotle, any difference in what is disclosed through the actualization of man's potentialities is a result of the fact that man has both essential and non-essential potentialities. See ibid., 218n10.

156 Ibid., 125. Interestingly, Fackenheim here appends a footnote in which he suggests that non-metaphysicians are unable to address the question of what the doctrine of historicity means. Ibid., 218n11. Has he learned from Strauss the fatal necessity of distinguishing between the philosopher and the 'intellectual'/sophist? See above, pp. 159–71.

157 Ibid., 124.

158 Ibid.

159 Ibid., 125.

160 Ibid. Although the immediate source of Fackenheim's return to common sense was likely Étienne Gilson, whom Fackenheim had cited previously (ibid., 217n6), it is reminiscent of Strauss's concept of common sense, or the surface of things. Interestingly, in the 'Acknowledgments' to the Marquette edition of the lecture, Fackenheim commends his audience for recognizing that one cannot affirm the validity of metaphysical language outside of the practice itself of metaphysics. See, Fackenheim, 'Metaphysics and Historicity.' Fackenheim also writes: 'To ask these questions [about the extent to which a self-making process is intelligible], one need not share the fashionable fear of taking leave of ordinary language even in metaphysical discourse.' GW, 129.

161 Ibid., 126. See R.G. Collingwood, The Idea of History (Oxford: Clarendon Press, 1946), 213ff. et passim, as cited in ibid., 218n12. In making this distinction, Collingwood accepts the nature of modern science. For Aristotle, nature is an internal discipline: Collingwood's 'outside' is the body; his 'inside' is the soul; both are 'natural.'

162 Ibid., 218–19n13. Fackenheim suggests further that the division between natural event and human action is not exhaustive: there might also be a third category of God's action in history. This third category, however, does not commit the believer to the doctrine of historicity because one may affirm both divine action in history and also a fixed human nature. See ibid., 219n14.

163 Ibid., 219n15.

164 Aristotle, Poetics 1451b, as cited in ibid., 127.

165 Ibid., italics in original.

166 Ibid., 128.

167 Fackenheim argues, however, that the doctrine of historicity denies neither that man is 'largely the product of natural processes,' nor that he is created and thereafter influenced by God. Ibid., 128.

168 Ibid.

169 Ibid., 220n19.

170 Ibid., 128.

171 Ibid.

172 This is why Fackenheim insists on the use of 'ordinary language' (ibid., 129): only by beginning with what is evident can the doctrine of historicity be validly assessed.

173 Ibid. Me on, meaning 'not being' or 'nothing.'

174 Ibid.

175 Ibid., 220–1n21.

176 Aquinas, *Summa Contra Gentiles*, as cited in ibid., 220–1n21.
177 Hegel, *Logic*, trans. W. Wallace (London: and Oxford, 1904), section 87, as cited in ibid., 220–1n21.
178 See Aristotle, *Physica*, in *The Basic Works of Aristotle*, ed. Richard McKeon (New York: Random House, 1941), 194b16–195b30 (II:3); and *The Metaphysics*, trans. Hugh Lawson-Tancred (New York: Penguin, 1998), 1025b4–18.
179 *GW*, 220–1n21.
180 Ibid., 129.
181 Ibid., 130. Fackenheim acknowledges the limitations of this undertaking by suggesting that some 'metaphysical assertions' are so radically unintelligible that they do not constitute a metaphysics. Ibid., 221n22.
182 Fackenheim suggests that Hegel, too, recognized the validity of this logic and suggests that his book of that name is 'an attempt to explicate it.' Ibid., 222n23.
183 Ibid., 130.
184 Ibid.
185 From the perspective of traditional metaphysics, one may recognize this process as a movement from potential *aliquid* to actual *aliquid*. The process is neither out of nothing nor non-temporal. Fackenheim seems rather to want to suggest its beginnings in a mystery-miracle: the process is both out of nothing and non-temporal because it is eternally in the fore- and after-knowledge of an omniscient God.
186 In one of his two longest footnotes devoted to Hegel's thought, Fackenheim cites the latter's Absolute Spirit as an example of this quasi-historical process: the logic that arises from both Nature and History returns to its priority to Nature and History, even as it retains both. Hegel's Absolute Spirit may be said to be quasi-historical in the same sense as the process defined by the meontological position. See ibid., 221–2n25. On the other hand, the process by which human being becomes Absolute Spirit in Hegel's thought differs from the meontological process: while Absolute Spirit in Hegel's thought is human being rising above situatedness, the meontological process takes place 'beyond all situatedness.' Ibid., 223n32.
187 Ibid., 131.
188 Ibid.
189 Ibid. Fackenheim is careful to distinguish the 'hope and fear' that might accompany the temporal present from the hope and fear that accompany the historical present: in the temporal present, hope and fear accompany the present only insofar as they are simply 'present effects of past events.' Ibid. In the historical present – Fackenheim implies – hope and fear may

exist in the present insofar as they accompany the appropriation and reenactment of the past.

190 Ibid.
191 Ibid.
192 Ibid.
193 Ibid.
194 Ibid., 132.
195 Ibid.
196 Ibid., italics in original.
197 Ibid.
198 Ibid., 133.
199 Ibid.
200 Ibid. Fackenheim's insistence that idealism be avoided is, of course, comparable to Strauss's critique of idealism. However, for Fackenheim, the critique has an added dimension: because idealism is a form of idolatry, it is the antithesis of Judaism. At the same time, it is definitionally not an idealistic stance to begin in the authority of the rabbinic tradition.
201 Ibid. Fackenheim suggests that Hegel and Schelling, despite arriving at 'idealistic conclusions,' recognize the distinction between situated self-making and situation. Ibid., 222n28. Their idealism stems from their assertion that the self can transcend both nature and itself: temporality and death become ontologically unessential. Furthermore, Fackenheim argues that it is existentialism that 'has brought fully to light the dialectical relation between situation and situated self-making.' Ibid., 223n23.
202 Ibid., 134.
203 Ibid.
204 Ibid.
205 Ibid., 135.
206 Ibid.
207 Ibid.
208 Ibid.
209 Fackenheim points out, however, that the distinction between natural and historical situation is artificial because nowhere does natural situation exist independent of historical situation with regard to man. Ibid., 223n31.
210 This transcendence is, according to Fackenheim, the culmination of Hegel's thought: human being rises to Absolute Spirit and loses its historical aspect. Hegel's transcendence is distinct from the quasi-historical eternity of the meontological process because Hegel presumes a historical situation, which it then transcends, 'while the latter is beyond all situatedness.' Ibid., 223n32. Furthermore, according to Fackenheim, Hegel dispenses

with the otherness of neither nature nor history; he simply relegates them to the unessential. Ibid.

211 Ibid., 136.

212 Ibid. Strauss, we recall, had critiqued the radical historicist on the basis of his complete acquiescence to fate.

213 Ibid.

214 Ibid.

215 Ibid., 137.

216 Ibid., italics in original.

217 Ibid.

218 Ibid.

219 Ibid., 138. Fackenheim notes that, while Collingwood had adopted this position in his *An Essay on Metaphysics*, he later adopted the position that the thesis that 'metaphysics consists of historically changing *Weltanschauungen* itself … spring[s] from a metaphysical thesis of a different order; the thesis being that mind changes through history because it is its own self-constituted functions.' Ibid., 224n34. Collingwood, clarifying the Kantian and Hobbesian grounds of historicism, finds a way to allow metaphysics as the quest for timeless truth to persist, even as he adopts the doctrine of historicity.

220 Ibid., 138. The last sentence is cited by Fackenheim from Strauss, *What Is Political Philosophy?* Ibid., 224n35. This definition of historicism is the first of Fackenheim's two references to Strauss in this lecture. As if to justify his choice of Hegel over Strauss's choice of Plato, Fackenheim suggests that Hegel did in fact retain the fundamental distinction between historical and philosophical questions insofar as the latter never made predictions regarding the future. Ibid., 224n34.

221 Ibid., 138.

222 At this point in the lecture, Fackenheim attempts to distinguish historicism from the doctrine of historicity, historicism being an outgrowth of the doctrine of historicity. Ibid., 224n35. Historicism 'collapses in internal inconsistency' (ibid., 138); the doctrine of historicity does not. Fackenheim defines the distinction between historicism and historicity by historicism's addition to the concept that 'all metaphysical assertions are historically true,' the concept that 'this is so because these assertions are part of a historically situated process of self-making.' Ibid., 225n37. While historicism may collapse in self-contradiction as a result of its posited indifference to the distinction in logical type between the assertion that 'all truth is relative' and the assertion that the statement '"all truth is relative" is true,' the doctrine of historicity, because it does not assert that all

metaphysical assertions are necessarily 'part of an historically situated self-making,' need not collapse. Ibid.

223 In the second and final reference to Strauss in the lecture, Fackenheim points to Strauss's comments on Dewey (ibid., 225n37), where Strauss concludes that 'historicism merely replaced one kind of finality with another kind of finality, by the final conviction that all human answers are essentially and radically "historical."' Strauss, *What Is Political Philosophy?* 72.

224 Indeed this suspicion is verified elsewhere: in his gentle critique of the relevance of Strauss's critique of Spinoza as a sage who 'can reach or approximate the "blessedness of Eternity,"' despite his Machiavellian techniques, Fackenheim suggests that '"Human nature" after the Holocaust is not what it was before … Historicity – whether a curse, a blessing, or something of both, emerges as inescapable.' *MW*, 99.

225 *GW*, 139.

226 *NRH*, 15.

227 *GW*, 139.

228 Ibid. One recognizes here what I characterize below as Fackenheim's philosophizing within the context of the rabbinic framework, or what Fackenheim refers to as within the stance of 'covenantal affirmation.' *QPF*, 8. Furthermore, Fackenheim points out that the impact of the result that transcendence must remain a possibility even within historicity also affects art. He writes: '[A]ny work of genius is a living witness testifying that the total historicization of the arts is absurd.' Ibid.

229 *GW*, 225n39. The parallel of this procedure is, of course, the procedure outlined in the beginning of the lecture, to go beneath the different logics that emerge from the metaphysics based on timeless truths and the metaphysics based on historicity in order to compare, not the interpretations of the two metaphysics, but the metaphysics themselves.

230 Ibid., 139.

231 Ibid.

232 Ibid.

233 Ibid., 140.

234 There were for Hegel, according to Fackenheim, other considerations, arising from his Christian convictions, that encouraged him to abandon this 'struggle.' Ibid., 226n13.

235 Ibid., 140. Fackenheim suggests that he had not thought about the Holocaust directly prior to 1967 and that he had used philosophy and theology as the means of his avoidance. Ibid., xix. Here, though, he refers, if not to the event itself, then to the *idea* of the Holocaust: we must confront

the horror of the Holocaust with a horror of our own. *MW*, 263. The Holocaust has indelibly changed 'human nature' (ibid., 99), making any synthesis of the finite and infinite aspects of man mere escapism from historical reality. Fackenheim's reasons for positing this indelible change in human nature are complex, but one may point to his argument that the event is unique, insofar as its goal was exclusively death. At another time, Fackenheim formulates it as a battle between philosophy and history: philosophy has been rendered impotent by its having lost its battle with history. Hegel was unable to conquer history philosophically. Fackenheim, personal interview, August 2003.

236 Jean Amery, as cited in *MW*, 99.

237 Hegelianism cannot be brought 'up to date'; historically situated self-constituting cannot correct the error posited initially as historical situation. This is not to say that Hegelianism, as the seeking and fleeing of man's finite and infinite aspects, cannot be returned to.

238 *GW*, 226n41.

239 Ibid., 140–1, italics in original.

240 Ibid., 141. Fackenheim lists Kierkegaard, Jaspers, Heidegger, Kuhn, and Buber as existentialist thinkers involved in understanding the 'attempt-at-transcendence.' Ibid., 226–7n43. Fackenheim notes that while Heidegger in his later work returned to historicism, in his earlier work he 'explicitly repudiates' it. Ibid., 227n45. Fackenheim wrote 'The Historicity and Transcendence of Philosophic Truth,' *GW*, in response to Strauss's criticism that he had disposed too quickly of the later Heidegger's historicism, and that a mere 'formal-dialectical "refutation," ' which was in fact anticipated by Heidegger himself,' was inadequate. Ibid., 151.

Strauss, we recall, suggests that 'the root of existentialism must be sought in Nietzsche rather than in Kierkegaard: existentialism emerged by virtue of the "reception" of Kierkegaard on the part of a philosophic public that had begun to be molded by Nietzsche.' Strauss, 'Relativism,' 151. The implication would be that by returning to Kierkegaard, Fackenheim's return to the root of Heidegger's thinking is not a full return.

241 *GW*, 141.

242 Ibid.

243 Ibid., italics in original.

244 Ibid.

245 Ibid., 142.

246 Ibid., italics added.

247 Ibid.

248 Ibid.

249 Ibid.

250 One might characterize this situation as what Strauss referred to as self-delusion.

251 To characterize human self-making as wholly autonomous is to deny the possibility of its humanity, its connections to both nature and history.

252 *GW*, 143, italics in original.

253 Kierkegaard, as cited in ibid., 229n48.

254 Kierkegaard, as cited in ibid.

255 While Fackenheim suggests that he is 'indebted to Professor Strauss ... for his tireless insistence that the eternal verities of the *philosophia perennis* must not be lightly or thoughtlessly dismissed,' he disagrees with him. Ibid., 151. In response to Strauss's conviction that a return to the timeless truths is not escapism, or, alternatively, that one need not adopt historicity even in part, Fackenheim writes: 'This result [that Heidegger's assault fails to destroy transcendent philosophic truth] calls for a renewed philosophic quest, if not for the timeless in an eternal world, then for the non-temporal and non-historical in the human *Lebenswelt*. The philosopher may be unable to escape from the cave of history. He does find, however, that a light from beyond the cave shines into the cave itself, and that it lights up both the lives of men who must live in history and the philosophic thought which seeks to understand it.' Ibid., 163.

256 Ibid., 229n48.

257 Ibid. Fackenheim, who counts himself among Buber's students, traces Buber's thought to Kierkegaard. Ibid., 227n43. But according to Fackenheim, the shortcoming of Kierkegaard's existentialism is his single-minded goal of becoming a Christian. Kierkegaard's thought lacks an understanding of Abraham as anything other than a 'proto-Christian'; it also, more generally, lacks an 'existential openness to Jewish existence.' *EJM*, 201.

258 *GW*, 143.

259 Ibid., 144. In his footnote – his final citation of Hegel – Fackenheim suggests that Hegel, who understood philosophy as both 'the realization and part of the self-realization of the Absolute,' explored this possibility – that the realm of metaphysics is partially, at least, humanly self-created. Ibid., 231n49.

260 Ibid., 144.

261 See *JPCM*, 329; and above, pp. 155–9.

262 *GW*, 144.

263 Ibid.

264 Ibid., 231n50.
265 See Buber, *Eclipse of God*, 50, as cited by ibid., 231n50.
266 Ibid., 144.
267 Ibid., 231n51. For a more detailed description of why his successors – specifically Fichte – accepted the doctrine, and regarded Idealism as the only means of explaining the possibility of 'metaphysical cognition of the self by the self,' see ibid., 231–2n51.
268 This includes both 'the kind of substantialism which, regarding the human self as no less ready-made than matter, offered a mere caricature of selfhood' and 'the Humean kind of mental process which, being a simple rather than a self-constituting process, does not deserve to be called mental at all.' Ibid., 145.
269 It is Fackenheim's failure to deal adequately with this confrontation that Strauss critiques in a personal letter (2 May 1961), and that prompted Fackenheim to write 'The Historicity and Transcendence of Philosophic Truth.' See Morgan, *Dilemmas*, 174n25; and *GW*, 150–1.
270 *GW*, 145.
271 Ibid. See above, pp. 91–111.
272 Ibid.
273 Ibid.
274 Ibid.
275 Ibid., 146.
276 Fackenheim, in keeping with his insistence on the rupture in philosophical thought and the consequent need for fragmentation – or a fundamental openness – in post-Holocaust thought, omits himself from the list.
277 *GW*, 146.
278 Ibid., 232–3n54.
279 Ibid., 146.
280 Ibid.
281 Ibid., 147.
282 Ibid.
283 Ibid.
284 For a discussion of why Fackenheim rejects the return to Plato, see below, pp. 224–9.
285 *GW*, 228n45.
286 One of Fackenheim's most fundamental – and most controversial – suggestions is that Hegel has altered subsequent history by bringing philosophical models into history. Fackenheim, personal interview, August 2003. It might be that *Weltanschauungen*, ideologies and public opinion have been brought into history but not into philosophy.

287 For a discussion of the role of hope in Fackenheim's thought, see below, pp. 224–9.

288 By 'possibility,' I mean to imply Fackenheim's recognition that, while the relationship between the Jew and God can be reaffirmed, this in no way guarantees the existence of God.

289 *QPF*, 9.

290 Strauss seems to imply as much in his one reference to revealed religion in his lecture. See *NRH*, 15.

291 Strauss suggests that 'for a philosopher or philosophy there can never be an absolute sacredness of a particular or contingent event. This particular or contingent is called, since the eighteenth century, the "historical." Therefore people have come to say that revealed religion means historical religion as distinguished from natural religion, and that philosophers could have a natural religion, and furthermore, that there is an essential superiority of this historical to the natural ... What is called "existentialism" is really only a more elaborate form of this interpretation.' *JPCM*, 117. The interpretation to which Strauss refers understands the Bible to be 'in an emphatic sense historical.' Ibid., 117. The misunderstanding is profoundly based: it fails to recognize the ultimate distinctions between the Bible and philosophy. And the results can be, according to Strauss, devastating because if Judaism fails, in deference to current philosophical movements, to remain profoundly connected to its teachings – for instance, of piety – then first, it no longer remains Judaism, and second, Jewish piety cannot serve as a limitation on action. Both Judaism and Jewish piety are susceptible to dissolution in the face of contemporary thought. Fackenheim, as we shall see below, agrees with this assessment of the danger posed to Judaism through its assimilation with current philosophical movements, yet he limits the application of Strauss's critique of existentialism.

292 Fackenheim looks to the rabbinic tradition – for him, during this moment in history, an elastic term – rather than to the Bible, because the Bible cannot account for the authority of a covenant between God and the Jewish people that is ongoing in and through history. See above, pp. 121–9.

293 Sheppard, for instance, tries to understand 'Strauss's thought as adapted to shifting historical contexts.' Eugene Sheppard, 'Leo Strauss and the Politics of Exile,' PhD diss., UCLA, 2001, 6. Whether such an examination can issue in knowledge appropriate to Strauss as a thinker depends on whether one can, after the introduction of the historical sense, be wholly anti-historicist. See David N. Myers, *Resisting History: Historicism and Its Discontents in German-Jewish Thought* (Princeton: Princeton University

Press, 2003), 106–29. Indeed, Myers suggests that Strauss had himself suggested that 'critical historical method, or *Wissenschaft* ... really knows nothing of the central tenets of Judaism: God's existence, God's presence in the world, God's presence in Jewish history. Nor does it speak of God except as an object of historical or psychological interest.' Ibid., 123, in reference to a review by Strauss of Dubnow, Leo Strauss, 'Biblische Geschichte und *Wissenschaft*,' *Jüdische Rundschau* 30 (10 November 1945). In the same essay, however, Strauss suggests that the critical historical method is 'necessary' and 'not revolutionary.' Ibid., 123.

294 *GW*, 219n15.

295 *QPF*, 10.

296 Fackenheim refers to the thought that takes place within 'covenantal affirmation' (ibid., 8) as something akin to philosophical thinking (ibid., 10). He later concludes that his essays that predate 1957 (1) did not defend what is right in liberalism; (2) disregarded the internal criticism in classical Judaism; and (3) were polemical in their distinction between the extremes of humanism and supernaturalism. See *QPF*, 8–9. This change in stance, by the way, marks the first shift in Fackenheim's stance. See above, pp. 121–9; and Michael Oppenheim, *What Does Revelation Mean for the Modern Jew: Rosenzweig, Buber, Fackenheim* (Lewiston: Edwin Mellon Press, 1985), 91–2.

297 Also Strauss, as a theoretical matter, does not choose philosophy over theology; rather, he chooses to stand outside covenantal affirmation, even with a fundamental openness to revelation, in his philosophical work. See below, pp. 209–24.

298 *QPF*, 10, italics added.

299 See above, pp. 209–24.

300 *QPF*, 207.

301 Ibid., 12.

302 The central tenets of Judaism, the tenets that cannot be deviated from without loss of Judaism itself, according to Strauss, are to 'uphold unreservedly a belief in the creation of the world, in the reality of biblical miracles, and in the absolute obligation and the essential immutability of the law as based on the revelation at Sinai ... the very foundation of the Jewish tradition.' Allan Arkush, 'Leo Strauss and Jewish Modernity,' in *Leo Strauss and Judaism: Jerusalem and Athens Critically Revisited*, ed. David Novak (Lanham: Rowman and Littlefield, 1996), 123.

303 Fackenheim concludes that the twentieth-century protests of, for instance, Buber and Rosenzweig, had as their target only caricatures of Judaism's essence. *QPF*, 12–13. 'Neither Rosenzweig nor any other respectable ex-

istentialist thinker misuses his personal commitments in order to escape the rigours of logic and system.' Fackenheim, *The Jewish Thought of Emil Fackenheim*, 62–3.

Although, following Rosenzweig and Buber, Fackenheim understands Judaism to be experiential, there is an inner structure, or a structured openness (*QPF*, 13), that he, following Buber, recognizes as its total rejection of idolatry or false gods. See *EJM*, 221. Not all varieties of religious experience are assimilable to Judaism: the 'essence' of Judaism as Fackenheim understands it is not in Schelling or Hegel's sense of the word. For the latter, essence is an abstraction; whereas for Jews, although it pre-exists experience, it is at the same time experiential. Jews, because they have been singled out, know initially that there is no humanity – or religion – in general.

304 *QPF*, 12–13.

305 Again, Fackenheim looks to the rabbinic tradition, or what he conceives as salvageable from the rabbinic tradition. For the most part, it is midrash that speaks profoundly to him and that provides for him a means . by which to perpetuate, even while doubting, the tradition of the ancient rabbis. Fackenheim does not turn to the Bible exclusively because the Bible cannot account for the authority of a covenant between God and the Jewish people that is ongoing in and through history. See above, pp. 121–9.

306 See above, pp. 60–5; and below, pp. 209–24.

307 That is to say, not all historical events are assimilable to Judaism. At times, the later Fackenheim seems to suggest that only one tenet remains central to Judaism after the Holocaust: hope for the incursion of the one true God. Even so, if hope alone persists from God's initial promise at Sinai to post-Holocaust secular consciousness, it would be enough to safeguard rabbinic historicity, so to speak, from secularist historicism. Fackenheim, personal interview, August 2003.

308 Elsewhere, Fackenheim writes: 'The Jewish theologian would be ill-advised were he, in an attempt to protect the Jewish faith in the God of history, to ignore contemporary history. For the God of Israel cannot be God of either past or future unless He is still God of the present.' Emil L. Fackenheim, *God's Presence in History: Jewish Affirmations and Philosophical Reflections* [*GPH*]. First Jason Aronson Edition (Northvale: Jason Aronson, 1997), 31.

309 Later, in *MW*, it is not clear that Fackenheim does not accept historicism wholeheartedly. If one understands as philosophically objective Fackenheim's transition from his conception of Judaism's essence to resistance

as an ontological category, then the structured openness of Judaism's essence endures.

310 *EJM*, 220. However, Fackenheim concludes that Heidegger in some ways adopts Christian thought, at least insofar as his starting point is that salvation has been completed already. So, for instance, he wonders whether Heidegger's later thought, in order to re-establish a radical insecurity dismissed by Christianity in its having had already salvation, is not '*exclusively post-Christian* thinking.' Ibid., 262n49, italics in original. This position was first suggested by Strauss in his Preface to *SCR*.

311 Ibid., 263n58. Heidegger's later thought does not encounter or confront the possibility that Jewish prophecy might mistake false gods for the true God. Strauss, according to Fackenheim, overlooks the distinction between Jewish insecurity with regard to the prophets and Heidegger's insecurity with regard to 'a future God as yet wholly unknown.' Ibid., 262n51.

312 Fackenheim repudiates the aspect of his earlier theological work (i.e., *QPF*, chapters 2 to 6) in which he makes an ultimate distinction between faith and despair. On the basis of this thesis, he had concluded that only faith can resolve existential questions. By 1957, however, he had come to see that faith *and* despair exist in both secular and rabbinic thought. See *QPF*, 9. From the perspective of his stance within covenantal affirmation, he determines that the distinction between secular and rabbinic thought is not analogous to the distinction between despair and faith; rather, secular thought and rabbinic thought each requires the insights of the other.

313 *QPF*, 244–62.

314 Ibid., 317n11.

315 The 'inmost essence, the Holocaust world ... to the extent it reveals itself at all, [reveals itself] only ... to a thinking confronting it, shattered by it, and saved from total destruction only if it opposes its horror with a sense of horror of its own.' *MW*, 263.

316 *QPF*, 244.

317 Ibid.

318 Ibid.

319 Ibid. Compare Fackenheim's position with Strauss's. The latter, in his critique of Guttmann, writes: 'There is no inquiry into the history of philosophy that is not at the same time a *philosophic* inquiry.' Strauss, 'Preface to Isaac Husik,' as cited by Green, *JPCM*, 75n59, italics in original. Analogously, according to Strauss, the inquiry into the history of theology must be based in philosophic *detachment*, not merely philosophic *objectivity*, if it is not to become yet another instance of the experience of the history of thought.

320 *QPF*, 244.

321 Ibid., 245.

322 Ibid.

323 Ibid.

324 Ibid.

325 Ibid.

326 Ibid.

327 Ibid., 246.

328 I have been intentionally brief here because as we have seen, Fackenheim changes his position with regard to the meaning of the commandments from the time of this essay. See Laurie McRobert, 'Kant and Radical Evil,' in *Fackenheim: German Philosophy and Jewish Thought*, ed. Louis Greenspan and Graeme Nicholson (Toronto: University of Toronto Press, 1992), 34–5; and above, pp. 84–91. So, for instance, while Fackenheim's pre-1967 work recognized Judaism's essence as the divine–human encounter, his post-1967 work reduces the essence even further: the hope of a future encounter between the Sinaitic God and the singled-out man.

329 *QPF*, 251.

330 According to Fackenheim, radical openness of a comprehensive system depends on a reality that is both unity and radically open. See Emil L. Fackenheim, *The Religious Dimension in Hegel's Thought* [*RD*] (Bloomington: Indiana University Press, 1967), 21–2.

331 As formulated elsewhere: 'The Hebraic believer confronts the future with a present knowledge coming from the past; the word from the past is judging justice and accepting love. He who revealed himself to Moses as "I shall be who I shall be" may disclose himself in the future by yet unknown names. He will be the same already-known "I."' *QPF*, 290.

332 Ibid., 251.

333 See above, pp. 91–106.

334 Furthermore, because Judaism's core is both fundamentally paradoxical and also its meaning is in one sense fundamentally historical, Judaism's openness to historical events is understood by Fackenheim as confronting the present always with a temporally comprehensive knowledge of God as Other and of self as identity appropriated through God's grace. Fackenheim's understanding in this matter is not merely theological: Schelling detected the same problem with German Idealism; German Idealism did not recognize that the dialectic between the data of empirical history and the ideal is not a one-to-one ratio. A datum of empirical history can at no point lose its particularity, cannot be translated adequately into idea. See above, pp. 107–11.

335 Fackenheim suggests that the Book of Judges 'can see an exact correlation between Israel's obedience and national victories, and between
Israel's defiance and national defeats: the victories are given by God and
the defeats are sent by Him.' *QPF*, 252. His choice of the Book of Judges
to illustrate the biblical view of history is motivated by that book's ability to harmonize Divine lordship of history with human freedom to rebel
against this authority: it limits itself to Israel's needs and God's relationship to Israel's needs. Later, this view of history was modified in three
primary respects. First, unilateral Divine action is incorporated into it:
in addition to the mutuality of Divine–human, human–Divine action, it
was recognized that God acts separately from his relationship with human beings. Second, the paradox implicit in the coexistence of Divine
omnipotence and human freedom leads to the affirmation that 'history
is wholly in Divine hands even while man has a share in making it; that,
whereas righteousness makes man a partner in the realization of the Divine plan, sin, for all its reality and power, is unable to disrupt or destroy
it.' Ibid., 254. Third are the complaints of Job and Jeremiah – that the
wicked prosper. To resolve the contradiction that history is both worldly
and also wholly in Divine hands, rabbinic thought will allow neither
escapism into a purely spiritual realm, nor the admonition that virtue is
its own reward. Its solution is to affirm that 'the events of the present,
although *disclosing* no meaning, nevertheless *possess* meaning.' Ibid., 255,
italics in original.

336 'The affirmation of revelation,' Fackenheim writes elsewhere, '...
presuppose[s] a commitment, which in turn permeates the religious
thinking which springs from it.' Ibid., 204.

337 In this earlier essay, Fackenheim is more concerned with the rabbinic tradition than he comes to be in his later work. But even in the later work,
he remains committed to the rabbinic tradition, even as it becomes more
elastic. Paradoxically, his commitment to remain within the covenant
forces him to take seriously not only the changes in Jewish self-concep-
tion from the Bible to the Talmud, but also the ultimate change to the covenant – its rupture – as effectuated by the Holocaust.

338 *QPF*, 253.

339 Elsewhere, Fackenheim formulates it in the following way. The 'defining
characteristic' of Jewish theological thought is a 'stubbornness [which]
consists of resisting all forms of thought that would remove the contradictions of the root experiences of Judaism [God's transcendence *and* His
involvement; divine power *and* human freedom; divine involvement with
history] at the price of destroying them. Positively, it consists of develop-

ing logical and literary forms which can preserve the root experiences of Judaism despite their contradictions.' *GPH*, 18.

340 *QPF*, 254.

341 As we have seen, Fackenheim finds in the midrashic framework the structure of Judaism insofar as it manifests, and refuses to resolve, the paradox at the heart of Jewish meaning. See above, pp. 91–106. Both Katz and Eisen have considered whether Fackenheim's understanding of midrash, and the possibility of modern midrash, as it varied over his career, was consonant with philosophic and/or rabbinic understanding. Katz addresses the question in relation to his philosophy; Eisen, in relation to his theology. Eisen concludes that Fackenheim was unable to either resolve or sustain the tension between the past forms of midrash and any possible future forms. See Steven T. Katz, *Post-Holocaust Dialogues: Critical Studies in Modern Jewish Thought* (New York: New York University Press, 1983), 205–47; and Eisen, 'Midrash in Emil Fackenheim's Holocaust Theology.'

342 For a discussion of the dynamic by which Fackenheim joins together philosophy and Judaism in 'Metaphysics and Historicity,' *EJM*, and (primarily) *MW*, see Morgan, *Dilemmas*, 111–24.

343 *PW*, 158.

344 See above, pp. 65–72 and 155–9.

345 So, for instance: 'Historicism culminated in nihilism'; or '[t]he contemporary rejection of natural right leads to nihilism – nay, it is identical with nihilism.' *NRH*, 18 and 5 respectively. Strauss's act of will, however, to doubt all doctrines should not be understood as nihilism, but rather as the means by which to return to recognition of the distinction between philosophy and political philosophy, or to the assertion of the possibility of natural right. For an argument for Strauss as nihilist, see S.B. Drury, 'The Esoteric Philosophy of Leo Strauss,' *Political Theory* 13, no. 3 (August 1985): 315–37.

346 See *PW*, 155. By suggesting here that 'pseudo-philosophers' have the advantage of correcting the mistakes of their predecessors, and that philosophers must attempt to 'foresee which pseudo-philosophies will emerge,' Strauss implies a connection between these pseudo-philosophies and the historical sense. Ibid., 155.

347 See below, pp. 209–24.

348 This present point is beyond the scope of this book, but one reference might perhaps be made. After suggesting that the Bible itself teaches that the mind is insufficient to understand things beyond a certain boundary – for instance, by falsely claiming, on the literal level, God's corporeality –

Maimonides writes that 'philosophers likewise assert the same, and perfectly understand it, without having regard to any religion or opinion.' Maimonides, *The Guide for the Perplexed*, trans. Shlomo Pines (Chicago: University of Chicago Press, 1963), I:31. Maimonides reads the Bible outside the rabbinic framework in order to define the boundary of thought.

Fackenheim's essay 'The Possibility of the Universe in Al-Farabi, Ibn Sina, and Maimonides' (in *JPJP*) suggests that on this point he does not deviate far from Strauss. As Maimonides suggests, the philosopher exceeds his bounds by claiming 'to derive from the nature of things which actually exist what is *absolutely* possible, impossible, and necessary already presupposes the *absolute* metaphysical validity of the laws by which these things are governed.' *JPJP*, 16, italics in original. Fackenheim, 'completely under Strauss's influence' (Fackenheim, personal interview, August 2003), recognizes the need to philosophically validate any deviation from the conclusions of the philosophers. He identifies in Maimonides a 'genuine loyalty to religious doctrine' and an adherence to a religion 'whose prime character was not contemplation, absolute simplicity, or the function of being Prime Mover, but the free giving of *existence* to all that is.' Ibid., 17, italics in original.

349 Arnaldo Momigliano, 'Hermeneutics and Classical Political Thought in Leo Strauss,' in *Essays on Ancient and Modern Judaism*, ed. Silvia Berti, trans. Maura Masella-Gayley (Chicago: University of Chicago Press, 1994), 186.

350 See, for instance, ibid., 179.

351 Ibid., 180.

352 According to Strauss, Heidegger returns to *Sein*, which the latter conceives of as the 'ground of grounds.' Strauss, 'Relativism,' 156. *Sein*, however, as Heidegger conceives it, cannot be the ground of grounds because it blinds the latter to the phenomena as recognized, and communicated, in philosophical texts. Strauss critiques Heidegger for being so presumptive as to claim that 'all thinkers prior to him have been oblivious of *Sein*,' that he 'understands the great thinkers of the past in the decisive respect better than they understood themselves.' Ibid., 156.

353 Momigliano, 'Hermeneutics,' 181.

354 Ibid., 179.

355 See *NRH*, 89.

356 See below, pp. 209–24.

357 Fackenheim's historicism is not, according to him, radical. He gives two reasons for saying so. First, as in the thought of Hegel, the activity of overreaching includes Otherness as an absolute principle – the grasping

of the divine is the self-othering of the human. Second, the finite persists through the infinite. See above, pp. 91–106.

358 For qualifications of the starkness of Strauss's dilemma, see below, pp. 209–24.

359 For Fackenheim's understanding of the 'midrashic framework,' see *GPH*, 20–1; and above, pp. 91–106.

360 One may suggest that Fackenheim preserves the tradition begun with Saadya and Halevi by breaking with that very tradition. Strauss, who is concerned with the break between the ancients and the moderns, denies history at its root: the only possible restoration of tradition is through a return to its pre-history, so to speak.

361 This is the source of Fackenheim's often cited statement that Hegel today would not be a Hegelian. According to him, Hegel understands Spinoza as the beginning of modern philosophy insofar as the latter dissolves the self. Hegel, however, corrects Spinoza through his understanding that there must be a self in place in order to have open dialogue. Because Heidegger does not deal with Spinoza, he implicitly dismisses Hegel's mediation between Spinoza and Judaism. In Heidegger, there is no setting and therefore no dialogical openness. Fackenheim, personal interview, August 2003.

362 *MW*, 129.

363 Again, the question ultimately is whether to contextualize Fackenheim within the philosophical tradition as, in a sense, a follower of Heidegger, insofar as he recognizes history as the fundamental means of exiting the cave; or within the rabbinic framework, insofar as he recognizes history as a means to both retain and transform the doubt implicit in the human experience.

364 In suggesting a corrective hermeneutics to Spinoza's hermeneutics, Strauss writes: 'We remain in perfect accord with Spinoza's way of thinking as long as we look at the devising of a more refined historical method as a desperate remedy for a desperate situation, rather than as a symptom of a healthy and thriving "culture."' *PW*, 154. The modern mind is in a 'deep pit beneath the cave' of Plato, a situation that requires both the invention of formerly unnecessary tools and also the recognition that the utilization of those tools represents only a return to the beginning, not a progress from it. Ibid., 155.

365 Strauss, 'Relativism,' 139.

366 Ibid., 151.

367 Hegel's primary criticism of Plato's political philosophy as described in the *Republic* is that Plato does not allow for the 'subjective element'

among the ruled. Hegel's criticism may be justified insofar as he refers to Plato's concept of justice, but may not be valid when one considers that this criticism may itself be implicit already in Plato. See M.B. Foster, *The Political Philosophies of Plato and Hegel* (Oxford: Clarendon Press, 1968), 72–109. One may suggest that, in the sense that each thinker asks the permanent question, What is justice?, the continuity between Plato and Hegel is as vivid as the discontinuity. Strauss, however, rejects 'Heidegger's judgment that subjectivity and modern metaphysics had their origin in Plato.' Olivier Sedeyn, 'The Wisdom of Jacob Klein,' trans. Brother Robert Smith, *St. John's Review* 47, no. 2·(2003): 5–10. He focuses instead on the discontinuity, the break, between the ancients and the moderns.

5. Reason and Revelation: Jewish Thought after Strauss and Fackenheim

1 Fackenheim told the present writer that when he was a student in Toronto, he went to Strauss, not to learn the thought of any particular philosopher, but rather because he wanted 'to know whether it was true or not' (Fackenheim, personal interview, August 2003). His implication seemed to be that, while one must understand what a particular philosopher is really saying in order to judge its truth, there is also something else that one must understand.

2 See above, pp. 155–9.

3 See above, pp. 159–71.

4 See Emil L. Fackenheim, *God's Presence in History: Jewish Affirmations and Philosophical Reflections* [GPH], First Jason Aronson Edition (Northvale: Jason Aronson, 1997), 20–1; and above, p. 285n107. By 'quasi-adoption,' I mean Fackenheim's turn to midrash as the primary source of contemporary rabbinic Jewish sensibility, a turn necessitated by the contemporary experience of secularism (or alternatively, by the fact that we live in a post-Hegelian world).

5 Leo Strauss, *Natural Right and History* [NRH] (Chicago: University of Chicago Press, 1965), 3.

6 While Strauss promotes the ideals of philosophy, he remains aware that the ideals of philosophy and the God of revelatory theology are within 'hailing distance' of each other. See above, pp. 155–9.

7 Note the resonance of this proscription with the proscription in *Pirke Avot* to avoid intimacy with the ruling powers (I:10; see also *Pirke Avot* II:3).

8 Strauss recognizes that the Bible, in its self-understanding, provides guidance for the whole of a person's life. Leo Strauss, *Jewish Philosophy and the Crisis of Modernity: Essays and Lectures in Modern Jewish Thought* [JPCM],

ed. Kenneth Hart Green (Albany: SUNY Press, 1997), 106. He chooses the life of a philosopher, which necessitates the reduction – at least primarily – of Torah ('instruction') to Law. He writes: 'For the Christian, the sacred doctrine is revealed theology, for the Jew and the Muslim, the sacred is, at least primarily, the legal interpretation of the Divine Law (talmud or fiqh).' Leo Strauss, *Persecution and the Art of Writing* [PW] (Chicago: University of Chicago Press, 1980), 19.

9 See, for instance, Plato, *The Laws,* trans. Trevor J. Saunders, reprinted with minor revisions (New York: Penguin Books, 1975), 731e–732a; *Symposium,* trans. Michael Joyce, in *The Collected Dialogues of Plato, Including the Letters,* ed. Edith Hamilton and Huntington Cairns, Bollingen Series LXXI (Princeton: Princeton University Press, 1980), 206a; and Aristotle, *Politica,* in *The Basic Works of Aristotle,* ed. Richard McKeon (New York: Random House, 1941), 1262b22–23, Book III, esp. chapters 1 to 5. *The Laws* is the only dialogue that does not mention Socrates and that is set far away from Athens (in Crete).

10 See, among other places, Plato, *The Republic,* trans. Desmond Lee, 2nd rev. ed. (New York: Penguin Books, 1987), 375a–376c and 429c–d.

11 Consider, for instance, this in Strauss: 'There is no surer protection against the understanding of anything than taking for granted or otherwise despising the obvious and the surface. The problem inherent in the surface of things, and only in the surface of things, is the heart of things.' Leo Strauss, *Thoughts on Machiavelli* (Chicago: University of Chicago Press, 1978), 13.

12 Leo Strauss, *The Argument and the Action of Plato's 'Laws,'* as cited by Thomas L. Pangle, 'On the Epistolary Dialogue between Leo Strauss and Eric Voegelin,' in *Leo Strauss: Political Philosopher and Jewish Thinker,* ed. Kenneth L. Deutsch and Walter Nicgorski (Lanham: Rowman and Littlefield, 1994), 256.

13 Ibid., 256. See also S.B. Drury, 'The Esoteric Philosophy of Leo Strauss,' *Political Theory* 13, no. 3 (August 1985): 315–37 at 319–20.

14 On more than one occasion, Fackenheim suggested that Strauss's insistence on the need for esoteric speech was 'dirty politics.' Fackenheim, personal interviews, August 2003. For him, the use of esoteric writing cannot be validated in the modern context because its use precludes the possibility of establishing existence as an ontological category. Also, Dannhauser asks: 'What is the point of writing esoterically so late in the twentieth century?' Werner J. Dannhauser, 'Athens and Jerusalem or Jerusalem and Athens?' in *Leo Strauss and Judaism,* ed. David Novak (Lanham: Rowman and Littlefield, 1996), 169. Strauss might respond: 'What is the point of writing esoterically ever?'

338   Notes to pages 207–9

15 Emil L. Fackenheim, *Quest for Past and Future: Essays in Jewish Theology* [*QPF*] (Boston: Beacon Press, 1968), 317n11. See above, pp. 194–201.
16 See above, pp. 91–106.
17 See *JPCM*, 110. In this again we see Maimonides's influence on Strauss.
18 Fackenheim critiques Heidegger's conception of commitment because his philosophy cannot issue in what the content of that commitment might be. See also Leo Strauss, *The City and Man* (Chicago: University of Chicago Press, 1978), 240–1.
19 One sees in this translation – or at any rate, attempt at translation – the paradoxical nature of Jewish philosophy. Can one translate what has not been personally experienced into what has been personally experienced?
20 Note that Strauss recognizes the specificity of religious faith: the problem of how to define Christian and Jewish faith 'is not a "universal-human" one. That means that it presupposes a *specific* faith, which philosophy as philosophy does not and cannot do.' Strauss, as cited in Pangle, 'On the Epistolary Dialogue,' 239–40, italics in original.
21 Natural theology is not identical to atheism; but neither is it neutral to Judaism and Christianity because it precludes the singled-out Jewish experience accomplished by Jewish revelation. For a view of Strauss as an atheist, see Stanley Rosen, *Hermeneutics as Politics* (New York: Oxford University Press, 1987).
22 *JPCM*, 379–80.
23 See above, pp. 155–9.
24 See, for instance, *ma'aseh bereshit* and *ma'aseh merkavah*.
25 So, for instance, Pangle argues that for Strauss, Judaism is inferior to philosophy; just as, for Plato, all poetry is inferior to philosophy. In contrast, Susan Orr argues that Jerusalem is prior to Athens. See Susan Orr, 'Strauss, Reason, and Revelation: Unraveling the Essential Question,' in *Leo Strauss and Judaism: Jerusalem and Athens Critically Revisited*, ed. David Novak (Lanham: Rowman and Littlefield, 1996). On the Catholic side, Frederick D. Wilhelmsen considers Strauss to be a 'Hellenized Jew,' while Ernest Fortin considers many of Strauss's teachings to be 'close to, if not actually identical with, those of any number of orthodox theologians.' See Kenneth L. Deutsch and Walter Nicgorski, Introduction, in *Leo Strauss: Political Philosopher and Jewish Thinker*, ed. Kenneth L. Deutsch and Walter Nicgorski (Lanham: Rowman and Littlefield, 1994), 16. On the Jewish side, Stanley Rosen argues – in contradistinction to Harry Jaffa – that Strauss revealed no authentic care for revelation. See, Rosen, *Hermeneutics as Politics*, 112; and Harry V. Jaffa, 'Leo Strauss, the Bible, and Political Philosophy,' as cited by Deutsch and Nicgorski in *Leo Strauss: Political Philosopher and Jewish Thinker*, 16–7.

26 According to at least one scholar, however, Strauss's development of his textual hermeneutics was 'under the influence of traditional methods of Talmudic exegesis.' Arnaldo Momigliano, 'Hermeneutics and Classical Political Thought in Leo Strauss,' in *Essays on Ancient and Modern Judaism*, ed. Silvia Berti, trans. Maura Masella-Gayley (Chicago: University of Chicago Press, 1994), 188.

27 Strauss, for instance, recognized the importance of religious education as the necessary preparation for philosophical education. See Deutsch and Nicgorski, *Leo Strauss*, 27–8.

28 Albert Keith Whitaker, 'The Bible and Philosophy: Reviews of *The Beginning of Wisdom: Reading Genesis* by Leon R. Kass, and *Political Philosophy and the God of Abraham*, by Thomas L. Pangle,' Claremont Institute, 25 November 2003, 6.

29 Or Strauss recognizes that the only means by which to recover Jewish orthodoxy, the only valid and/or relevant form of Judaism, is through a refutation of Spinoza. See above, pp. 65–72.

30 *JPCM*, 380.

31 Ibid., 126.

32 Leo Strauss, *Spinoza's Critique of Religion* [*SCR*] (New York: Schocken Books, 1982), 213.

33 See Emil L. Fackenheim, *Encounters between Judaism and Modern Philosophy: A Preface to Future Jewish Thought* [*EJM*] (New York: Schocken Books, 1973), 7–29. Strauss suggests that the response to the problem of miracles that suggests 'that miracles presuppose faith; they are not meant to establish faith' (*JPCM*, 126) may yet be inadequate if one could establish criteria 'equally accessible to the sense perception of believers as well as nonbelievers' (ibid., 126).

34 Ibid., 125.

35 Ironically, however, as Zuckert points out, Strauss's emphasis on the irrefutability of reason and revelation follows a 'long Jewish tradition.' See Catherine H. Zuckert, *Postmodern Platos: Nietzsche, Heidegger, Gadamer, Strauss, Derrida* (Chicago: University of Chicago Press, 1996), 127.

36 Strauss writes that in order to clarify the antagonism between the Bible and Greek thought, 'I think it is easier to start from philosophy, for the simple reason that the question which I raise here is a scientific or philosophic question. We have to move in the element of conceptual thought, as it is called, and this is of course the element of Greek philosophy.' *JPCM*, 111.

37 Ibid. Strauss does not provide the details of this derivation, and I have been unable to locate it either in his other essays or apart from his work.

38 See, for instance, Kenneth Hart Green, 'How Leo Strauss Read Judah Ha-levi's *Kuzari*,' *Journal of the American Academy of Religion* 61, no. 2 (Summer 1993): 225–73 at 227; and above, pp. 159–71.
39 Momigliano, 'Hermeneutics,' 187.
40 This refers to Al-Farabi, the tenth-century Islamic philosopher whose com-mentaries were largely responsible for transmitting Plato and Aristotle to later Moslem and Jewish philosophers, including Avicenna and Maimo-nides.
41 *JPCM*, 210. Note that Strauss suggests also that Maimonides may not have gone so far: there was to this thinker a rational component to Judaism, as evidenced, for example, in Deuteronomy 4:6.
42 Of course, this is also connected to Strauss's insistence on the need for esoteric writing: to maintain political stability, one must observe and not undermine the laws of one's state.
43 George Anastaplo, 'Leo Strauss and Judaism Revisited,' expanded version, in *The Great Ideas Today* (1998), 13 April 2004, http://anastaplo.wordpress .com/2011/03/21/leo-strauss-and-judaism-revisted, accessed 31 May 2011.
44 Leo Strauss, correspondence to Erwin A. Glikes, president and publisher, Basic Books, 3 March 1973, reprinted on the back cover of Emil L. Facken-heim, *To Mend the World: Foundations of Post-Holocaust Jewish Thought* [MW], First Midland Edition (Bloomington: Indiana University Press, 1994).
45 *NRH*, 74.
46 Ibid.
47 Ibid.
48 Ibid.
49 Ibid., 74–5.
50 Ibid., 75.
51 See above, pp. 155–9.
52 *NRH*, 75.
53 Ibid.
54 Ibid.
55 Ibid.
56 Ibid.
57 Ibid. As we shall see below, Strauss rejects this argument as based on a misunderstanding of the nature of classical philosophy: classical philoso-phy did not understand itself as a completed system; rather, in its proposal of the right way of life, it left open the possibility that its proposal was not wholly correct. The antagonism between the Bible and philosophy is irresoluble. Fackenheim, for instance, who begins his thought within the

stance of covenantal affirmation, and whose thought moves in the realm of revelatory theology, spoke to the present writer toward the end of his life on more than one occasion of Aristotle's Prime Mover. Fackenheim, personal interviews, August 2003.

58 *JPCM*, 104, italics added.
59 Ibid.
60 Ibid., italics in original.
61 Ibid., 107.
62 See ibid., 100-4.
63 Ibid., 105.
64 Ibid.
65 Ibid.
66 Ibid. Green refers the reader to Aristotle, *Nicomachean Ethics*, 1138a8; Deuteronomy 8:10; Leviticus 25:19; and Genesis 1:28. Throughout this section of 'Progress and Return,' Green provides textual citations of Plato and Aristotle in conjunction with biblical texts. See ibid., 134–5nn21–44.
67 Ibid., 106.
68 Ibid.
69 Ibid., 106–7.
70 One may have noted, for instance, in Strauss's ascription to Greek philosophy the praise of humility, an at least superficial contradiction with Aristotle's great-souled man. See below.
71 *JPCM*, 107.
72 Ibid.
73 Ibid.
74 Ibid.
75 Ibid. Deutsch and Nicgorski suggest that he whom Strauss calls the 'gentleman' is the 'liberally educated person.' Deutsch and Nicgorski, *Leo Strauss*, 27.
76 *JPCM*, 108.
77 Ibid.
78 Ibid.
79 Ibid.
80 Ibid.
81 Strauss qualifies this statement by reminding the reader that 'tragedy is replaced by songs praising the virtuous.' Ibid.
82 Ibid.
83 Ibid.
84 Ibid.
85 Ibid., 109.

86 Ibid. Strauss subsequently refines this position to argue that the morality of the Bible is completed not through understanding, but rather through the fulfilment of God's commands. See ibid., 116. At this point in the lecture (which, incidentally, is its centre), Strauss reveals how his thought moves in the realm of philosophy.

87 Ibid., 109.

88 Ibid.

89 Ibid.

90 Ibid., 109–10. Fackenheim, I suspect, noting along with Strauss that the issue of evil was not itself addressed, would label this 'serenity' escapism. See below, pp. 224–9.

91 Ibid., 110.

92 Ibid.

93 Ibid., 111.

94 Ibid., 110.

95 Ibid.

96 Ibid.

97 See, for instance, Plato's *Laws*, 891c–900b, as directed by Green. Ibid., 135n44.

98 Fackenheim picks up this very point, from the biblical point of view, elucidating the non-validity of modern thought's dismissal of revelation in the biblical story of Elijah on Carmel. See 'Elijah and the Empiricists' in *EJM*; see also below, where Strauss himself makes the same suggestion. *JPCM*, 126.

99 Ibid., 119.

100 Ibid.

101 Ibid., 120.

102 Ibid.

103 Ibid., 112.

104 Ibid., 113.

105 Ibid.

106 Ibid.

107 Ibid., 114.

108 Ibid. Strauss notes also that the concept of divine law in the strict sense is accepted in Greek thought only politically, that is, exoterically. Ibid.

109 Strauss writes that 'mythology is characterized by the conflict between gods and impersonal powers behind the gods.' Ibid., 119.

110 Ibid., 114.

111 Ibid.

112 'I shall be What I shall be' is, according to Strauss, the most radical for-
    mulation of God's unknowability. Ibid.
113 Ibid.
114 Ibid., 115.
115 Ibid.
116 Ibid.
117 Ibid., 116.
118 Ibid. In Fackenheim's formulation, following Strauss on this point, Juda-
    ism, because it must acknowledge the realities of secularism and the
    Holocaust, must adapt itself to be religio-secular. Furthermore, the living
    out of the tension between the biblical and Greek ways of life is character-
    ized by what Borowitz calls Fackenheim's 'action-concepts.' See Eugene
    B. Borowitz, 'Emil Fackenheim as Lurianic Philosopher,' *Sh'ma – A Journal
    of Jewish Responsibility* 13, no. 254 (13 May 1983): 109-111. The ruptures
    in philosophy, in Christianity and in Judaism are mended, according to
    Fackenheim, only through a redefinition of the foundation of thought as
    'action-concepts,' concepts that at once permeate and establish the truth
    of human existence. Fackenheim finds these action-concepts in Jewish
    theology as *t'shuvah* and *tikkun*; and while in his earlier thought the State
    of Israel provides the means for Jewish redemption, action-concepts – the
    tikkun that took place in the death camps – become in his later work the
    foundation for his thought.
119 See above, pp. 155–9.
120 *JPCM*, 121.
121 Ibid.
122 Ibid., 122.
123 Ibid.
124 Ibid.
125 For a discussion of whether Strauss's reading of Plato is entirely valid,
    and what might motivate Strauss to make this reading, see Neil Robert-
    son, 'Leo Strauss's Platonism,' *Animus: A Philosophical Journal for Our Time*
    4 (22 December 1999), http://www.mun.ca/animus/1999vol4/roberts4.
    htm, accessed 31 May 2011.
126 As in modern philosophy, Strauss traces what he considers to be the mis-
    understanding of Platonic thought to its incorporation into Neo-Platonic
    (i.e., Christian-influenced) thought.
127 See *JPCM*, 122.
128 Ibid., 120.
129 Ibid., 123.
130 Fackenheim makes a parallel argument against Buber: it is not enough to

posit the possibility of revelation; one must *prove* its possibility. See above, pp. 140–8.

131 It is here, perhaps, that one sees Strauss's influence on Fackenheim most dramatically: just as Strauss seeks to begin in the common ground of revelation and reason, Fackenheim seeks to establish a religio-secular Judaism. For Strauss, the common ground is permanent; for Fackenheim, it is in flux insofar as the human condition is in dialogue with God. See above, chapter 4.

132 Leo Strauss, *An Introduction to Political Philosophy: Ten Essays by Leo Strauss*, ed. Hilail Gildin (Detroit: Wayne State University Press, 1989), 86.

133 See Plato, *Phaedrus*, trans. Benjamin Jowett, in *The Collected Dialogues of Plato, Including the Letters*, ed. Edith Hamilton and Huntington Cairns, Bollingen Series LXXI (Princeton: Princeton University Press, 1980), 1247e and 1248a1–6.

134 Deutsch and Nicgorski go a step further: 'Strauss views the potential of Jerusalem from the perspective of Athens. Strauss's own ultimate trust and faith is so placed.' Deutsch and Nicgorski, *Leo Strauss*, 28.

135 Leo Strauss, *What Is Political Philosophy? and Other Studies* (Westport: Greenwood Press, 1959), 10. Fackenheim suggests that Strauss's inclusion of an essay on Hermann Cohen in his *Studies in Platonic Political Philosophy* 'proves that Strauss never gave up on Jerusalem any more than on Athens.' *JPJP*, 104.

136 Momigliano, 'Hermeneutics,' 188–9.

137 Ibid., 189. As Green formulates it, Strauss is a philosopher, but since his philosophy is based in beginning with and ascending from the surface of things, as a philosopher he is always a Jew.

138 Strauss writes, for instance: 'I know very well that [the small city-state] cannot be restored.' Letter to Karl Löwith, 15 August 1946, as cited in Deutsch and Nicgorski, *Leo Strauss*, 9. At the same time, though, it might provide the standard by which to judge all polities. See *NRH*, 130–7. According to Fackenheim, Strauss suggested that a return to Athens or Jerusalem is 'possible because it is necessary! And why is it necessary? Because the shadow of Nazism hung over us all.' Emil L. Fackenheim, 'Strauss and Modern Judaism,' *JPJP*, 102, as cited in Deutsch and Nicgorski, *Leo Strauss*, 15.

Again, Strauss conceives of this return as preconditioned by the necessity of ascending from the pit beneath Plato's cave, that is, from the belief or surety in progress and the belief that truth could not have been discovered in ancient times. See *PW*, 154–8; and above, pp. 159–71. So, for instance, 'a "return" to ancient philosophy is not a nostalgic return to

Athens. Rather, it is a contemporary reflection on the fundamental alternative of ancient and modern natural right in the context of the contemporary crisis of liberal democratic regimes. It is required by the present crisis since the progression in the history of the West from nature to reason to history to will as the standard of thinking and acting has produced an intellectual and moral vacuum.' Deutsch and Nicgorski, *Leo Strauss,* 19–20. Strauss's 'return,' because it is motivated by a particular historical context, may be ultimately too narrow for philosophy. Note that Strauss effectuates this return through an act of will. See ibid., 11; and above, pp. 159–71. For a discussion of Strauss's departure from and/or adoption of Nietzsche's thought, and a rejection of the suggestion that Strauss esoterically teaches Nietzschean nihilism, see Zuckert, *Postmodern Platos,* 105; and Drury, 'The Esoteric Philosophy of Leo Strauss,' 333–5.

139 So, for instance, Sheppard, Myers, and Gunnell all place Strauss in historical context. See Eugene R. Sheppard, 'Leo Strauss and the Politics of Exile,' PhD diss., University of California, Los Angeles, 2001; *Leo Strauss and the Politics of Exile: The Making of a Political Philosopher* (Waltham: Brandeis University Press, 2006); David N. Myers, *Resisting History: Historicism and Its Discontents in German-Jewish Thought* (Princeton: Princeton University Press, 2003); and John G. Gunnell, 'Strauss before Straussianism: Reason, Revelation, and Nature,' in *Leo Strauss: Political Philosopher and Jewish Thinker,* ed. Kenneth L. Deutsch and Walter Nicgorski (Lanham: Rowman and Littlefield, 1994).

Deutsch and Nicgorski suggest that '[Strauss's] research, whether into medieval or ancient thought, was given focus and meaning by his concern with the modern context that he saw enveloping himself as well as his listeners and readers.' Deutsch and Nicgorski, *Leo Strauss,* 23. In support of this, the authors cite Strauss's *The City and Man:* 'It is not self-forgetting and pain-loving antiquarianism nor self-forgetting and intoxicating romanticism which induces us to turn with passionate interest, with unqualified willingness to learn, toward the political thought of classical antiquity. We are impelled to do so by the crisis of our time, the crisis of the West.' As cited in ibid., 24.

Fackenheim's recognition of the conflict as action (Bible) contra thought (philosophy) lends this study of the influence of Strauss on his thought an added dimension.

140 Robertson, 'Leo Strauss's Platonism,' 6. Strauss writes that 'Socrates, then, viewed man in the light of the mysterious character of the whole. He held therefore that we are more familiar with the situation of man as man than with the ultimate causes of that situation. We may also say he viewed

man in the light of the unchangeable ideas, i.e., of the fundamental and permanent problems.'

141 Robertson, 'Leo Strauss's Platonism,' 1.

142 *PW*, 158. This position is adopted by M.F. Burnyeat ('Sphynx Without a Secret,' *New York Review of Books*, 30 May 1985, 30–6); and David Myers in *Resisting History;* as well as by others. The passion with which the Straussians and the anti-Straussians defend or attack him may be one indication that Strauss's way of life as filtered through Plato is very much a contemporary way of life.

143 Leo Strauss, 'Perspectives on the Good Society: A Jewish-Protestant Colloquium,' *Criterion* (Summer 1963): 2–9, as cited by Momigliano, 'Hermeneutics,' 187n2. Reprinted in Leo Strauss, *Liberalism, Ancient and Modern*, foreword by Allan Bloom (Chicago: University of Chicago Press, 1995).

144 Leviticus 26:40, 41.

145 *EJM*, 3–4..

146 *NRH*, 75.

147 See *EJM*; and above, pp. 111–20.

148 Elias Bickerman, 'The Maccabees,' in *From Esra to the Last of the Maccabees* (New York: Schocken Books, 1962), 162–4, as cited in *EJM*, 109.

149 Fackenheim characterized Strauss's work as a 'return to Plato.' Personal interviews, August 2003. But one might consider whether 'return' accurately characterizes Strauss's relationship to Greek philosophy. While one might argue that his looking into these texts is motivated by a will to 'return' to pre-modern (or non-anthropocentric) thought, what he finds in these texts is more accurately described as *recovered* or *discovered* – things perhaps that were always there. The need for historical studies is the temporary measure necessary to dig ourselves out of the pit beneath the cave into the cave itself – it is a history of philosophy that has to understand its objects in their own (if ancient, non-historicist) terms.

150 Leo Strauss, *On Tyranny: Including the Strauss–Kojeve Correspondence*, rev. and exp., ed. Victor Gourevitch and Michael S. Roth (New York: The Free Press, 1991), 105–6.

151 See, for instance, *GPH*, esp. chapter 3.

152 We note, however, that this definition might preclude Maimonides as a Jew.

153 Though again, Fackenheim insisted that Strauss himself never abandoned Jerusalem. Fackenheim, personal interview, August 2003.

154 See above, pp. 84–91.

155 Fackenheim 'chastizes Strauss for being at once too optimistic and not optimistic enough. Like Cohen, Strauss was too sanguine about evil, even

though he wrote about Cohen after the death camps and all their horrors. And he was also not optimistic enough about what Jewish philosophy could achieve, a recognition of duty that supports a post-Holocaust Jewish will to survive.' Michael L. Morgan, Introduction to Part I of Emil L. Fackenheim, *Jewish Philosophers and Jewish Philosophy* [*JPJP*] ed. Michael L. Morgan (Bloomington: Indiana University Press, 1996), 4.

Strauss's optimism shows itself in his suggestion, after the Holocaust, that Jews might still be philosophers within whatever political tyranny might accidentally arise.

Strauss's lack of optimism was not, I imagine, lost on Strauss himself. He writes that because there is in Greek philosophical thought no divine promise to back up the demand for morality, 'according to Plato, for example, evil will never cease on earth, whereas according to the Bible the end of days will bring perfect redemption.' *JPCM*, 109.

156 Fackenheim's single-minded hopefulness, and the related insistence that one begin and end one's thought in the historical realm, is manifest in a comment he made to this writer several times. According to him, Strauss did not take evil adequately into account in his thought because 'he did not live long enough.' Fackenheim, personal interview, August 2003.

157 *NRH*, 86–9.

158 We note the distinction between Fackenheim and Saadya on this point: Fackenheim suggests that a reliable tradition of witnesses from Sinai to his present time verifies the Sinaitic revelation; Saadya stresses the primacy of experience to the verification of revelation.

159 See 'The Possibility of the Universe in Al-Farabi, Ibn Sina, and Maimonides,' in *JPJP*. Fackenheim suggests, for instance, in accordance with Strauss, that for Maimonides the laws of nature do not become custom or way: for Maimonides, 'that which is impossible even by miracle must be defined in terms of logical contradiction, not of nonconformity with the "custom" of nature (*minhag hatevah*).' Ibid., 235n61.

160 See *GW*, esp. 181–5.

161 *EJM*, 166.

162 Ibid.

163 For a discussion of the problems of Fackenheim's conception of 'empirical history,' see W.H. Dray, 'Historicity, Historicism, and Self-Making,' in *Fackenheim: German Philosophy and Jewish Thought*, ed. Louis Greenspan and Graeme Nicholson (Toronto: University of Toronto Press, 1992), 133–7.

164 *EJM*, 132.

165 Here we see what Fackenheim characterizes as Strauss's lack of optimism.

166 Emil L. Fackenheim, *The Jewish Thought of Emil Fackenheim: A Reader*, ed. Michael L. Morgan (Detroit: Wayne State University Press, 1987), 60–1.

167 See, for instance, above, pp. 107–11 and 172–94, for the roots of Fackenheim's understanding of theology as a pointing.

168 Fackenheim prefers, for instance, Christian to secularist (or 'semi-, crypto-, or quasi-Christian') philosophers with regard to their relation to Jews because Hegel, while *explicitly* Christian, 'does greater justice to Judaism than any other modern philosopher of the first rank.' *MW*, 107.

169 *GPH*, 54.

170 See above, pp. 84–91; and Laurie McRobert, 'Kant and Radical Evil,' in *Fackenheim: German Philosophy and Jewish Thought*, ed. Louis Greenspan and Graeme Nicholson (Toronto: University of Toronto Press, 1992). Fackenheim writes: 'I think Plato – and maybe I should say both Athens and Jerusalem – is not quite adequate when it comes to confronting the diabolical evil that is the Holocaust.' *JPJP*, 103.

171 *JRH*, 4, italics in original. Judaism must make room within itself for secularism in order to make room both for those who lost faith during the Holocaust and for the possibility that historical action or experience can destroy faith or 'disprove' God. In Ecclesiastes, Fackenheim finds within the revelatory tradition the doubt from which secularism can organically emerge. See *JPJP*, 226.

172 See *JPCM*, esp. 93. Strauss suggests that this problem cannot be resolved; one might ask if philosophy – the quest for the right way of life – might persist if it is resolved.

173 Michael Oppenheim, *What Does Revelation Mean for the Modern Jew: Rosenzweig, Buber, Fackenheim* (Lewiston: Edwin Mellon Press, 1985), 109.

174 See, among other sources, *Republic* 8 and *Timeaus*. Strauss might counter that this position is a confusion of the practical – which, as public opinion, is not within philosophy's scope – and the theoretical.

175 The rupture in philosophy has directed post-Holocaust philosophy to be either immobilized or escapist. For philosophy to continue, it must confront the Holocaust: the idea of humanity has been overturned by both the barbarity of the perpetrators and the living death of the victims. Through this confrontation, philosophy may mend itself at least in part by looking to experience – by looking, for instance, to Kurt Huber, a philosopher who resisted Nazism in the name of Kantian philosophy. *MW*, 273–7.

   The rupture in Christianity is manifested as the loss of trust in the guidance of the Holy Spirit or the saving in Christ. This rupture, too, may be partially mended by, for instance, the public prayer for Jews by Bernhard

Lichtenberg in 1938. Ibid., 289–93. Elsewhere, Fackenheim suggests that what is needed is a 'total self-exposure' of Christianity to secularism. *QPF*, 279.

The rupture within Judaism, between Jews and Christians, and between post-Holocaust Jews and the Jewish tradition, can be partially mended through resistance both to threats to Jewish survival and to the absolute autonomy and exclusive universalism of the post-Christian world. See Oppenheim, *What Does Revelation Mean*, 108–12.

176 Ibid., 108, italics in original.
177 See, 'Auschwitz as Challenge to Philosophy and Theology,' in *MW*, esp. xl–xlviii. Fackenheim writes: 'Jews ... must read their old-new book as if they had never read it before.' Ibid., xlviii.
178 See Borowitz, 'Emil Fackenheim as Lurianic Philosopher,' 109–11.
179 Fackenheim's conception of 'action concepts' is not unlike Strauss's conception of the right way of life as defined by the moral quest for wisdom. However, because Fackenheim works within the stance of covenantal affirmation, his action concepts add to Strauss's conception a beginning in and focus on particularism and individuality. For a discussion of whether the redefinition of Judaism can remain within the boundaries of normative Judaism, or whether Fackenheim's adoption of midrash remains authentically midrashic in structure, see Robert Eisen, 'Midrash in Emil Fackenheim's Holocaust Theology,' *Harvard Theological Review* 96, no. 3 (July 2003): 369–92. Seeskin and Shapiro also suggest that Fackenheim's midrash is pushed too far. See Kenneth Seeskin, 'Emil Fackenheim,' in *Interpreters of Judaism in the Late Twentieth Century* (Washington: B'nai Brith, 1993), 55; and Susan E. Shapiro, 'The Recovery of the Sacred: Hermeneutics after the Holocaust,' PhD diss., University of Chicago, 1983, 212, 262–6. One might look also to Michael L. Morgan, *Interim Judaism: Jewish Thought in a Century of Crisis* (Bloomington: Indiana University Press, 2001), in which he describes the contemporary Jewish situation as one of openness or fragmentation in which older conceptions of Judaism have been abandoned while new conceptions are being sought.
180 Strauss had recognized that the problem of Jewish return is that after Spinoza's break, Jews no longer have anything to which to return. He argues that the only option that can be validated – and that is not inherently self-destructive – is a recovery of an unqualified orthodoxy, a recovery of Judaism as (primarily) Law. While Fackenheim follows Strauss in recognizing the problem of return, he finds in the rabbinic tradition a means of returning that in his thought is both a return and a new beginning – in

other words, that sustains Jewish categories, even as they are open to re-formulation.

181 See above, pp. 194–201.

182 *QPF*, 206.

183 Oppenheim, *What Does Revelation Mean*, 92.

184 Ibid., 93.

185 *QPF*, 15. This statement, written during his earlier work as a theologian, remains valid in his later work, which includes not only the singling out of Jews by God but also their singling out by the Nazis.

186 This is why Heidegger does not reappear in the second half, the 'mending' half, of *MW*.

187 *EJM*, 212.

188 Ibid., 202.

189 Ibid., 248n93.

190 'Preface to the Second Edition' of *MW*, italics in original.

191 Fackenheim's return to the root of revelation is, on the one hand, a reaction to nineteenth-century German-Jewish Liberalism, which was driven to retain the Jewish concept of election even as it discarded the *actuality* of that election, and on the other, a reaction to orthodoxy in forms that insist on the *actuality* of revelation, even as they deny its active role in the subsequent history that it defined. See above, pp. 133–40.

192 See above, pp. 194–201.

193 See *GPH*, 20–1; and above, p. 285n107.

194 For an understanding of how Fackenheim's historicism here may distort traditional midrash, consider Strauss's observation mentioned above: 'there is no Hebrew-biblical term for nature, the Hebrew word being derived very indirectly from a Greek word which is an equivalent of "nature" in Greek, *charakter*, *teva* in Hebrew.' *JCPM*, 111.

195 See above, pp. 207ff.

196 Deutsch and Nicgorski suggest that according to Strauss, 'the one thing needful in contemporary liberal democracies is a viable notion of natural right.' Deutsch and Nicgorski, *Leo Strauss*, 19. Strauss's affirmation of the practical need for natural right is found in the pit beneath Plato's cave, not in the philosophy itself; or alternatively, in the need to secede at present from the world.

197 *JPCM*, 138.

198 See ibid., 90.

199 Like Fackenheim's, however, Strauss's rediscovery remains to an extent unresolved insofar as it both begins in an act of will (see Deutsch and Nicgorski, *Leo Strauss*, 11; and above, pp. 159–71 and 224–9) and also de-

fines a return to the pit beneath the cave. As Fackenheim puts it, Strauss's 'return to the "old" thinking, manifesting as it does an ultimately unarguable commitment, is itself an act of "new" thinking.' *MW*, 264.

200 *MW*, 263–4, italics in original.

201 This is the central thesis of *GPH*.

202 *MW*, xlviii. Fackenheim points out that he attempts to initiate this project in *The Jewish Bible after the Holocaust*. Ibid., xlix, note 16.

203 Hannah Arendt, as cited by Carol Brightman, 'The Metaphysical Couple,' Review of *Letters 1925–1975: By Hannah Arendt and Martin Heidegger,' The Nation* 278, no. 22 (7 June 2004), 30.

204 Fackenheim, personal interview, August 2003.

205 Ibid., December 2002.

206 Novak, 'Philosophy and the Possibility of Revelation,' 184.

207 Ibid., 185.

208 Jenny Strauss Clay, Afterword, in *Leo Strauss and Judaism: Jerusalem and Athens Critically Revisited*, ed. David Novak (Lanham: Rowman and Littlefield, 1996), 194.

209 *JPJP*, 104–5.

210 *JPCM*, 327.

211 See Martin D. Yaffe, 'Historicism and Revelation in Emil Fackenheim's Self-Distancing from Leo Strauss,' in *Emil L. Fackenheim: Philosopher, Theologian, Jew*, ed. Sharon Portnoff, James A. Diamond, and Martin D. Yaffe (Boston: E.J. Brill, 2008).

212 Following Spinoza, Strauss may suggest that because Christian medieval thought did not retain the opposition between philosophy and religion, it imposed upon philosophy ecclesiastical supervision – that is, it destroyed philosophy. See Drury, 'The Esoteric Philosophy of Leo Strauss,' 321–2. Furthermore, 'the Christian belief in the possibility of a synthesis between Athens and Jerusalem is responsible for the naive trust in philosophy that is the hallmark of modernity.' Ibid., 331.

213 See *JPCM*, 90.

214 Although Fackenheim abandoned the label the '614th commandment' after *GPH*, he did not abandon the concept.

215 Kenneth Seeskin, 'Fackenheim's Dilemma,' in *Jewish Philosophy in a Secular Age* (New York: SUNY Press, 1990), 192–3.

216 Wyschogrod criticizes the idea in Fackenheim's earlier thought in which he argues for the possibility of an absolute command without a Divine Commander. And Borowitz asks: 'Can Jews who know no living God long be expected to attach ultimacy to the Jewish people? And how would Fackenheim's sort of Jewish Hegelianism avoid the right-ish

dangers of identifying the State of Israel with the Absolute and thus rendering it immune from criticism and willed transformation?' Eugene Borowitz, 'Review of *The Jewish Return into History* by Emil L. Fackenheim,' *Sh'ma: A Journal of Jewish Responsibility* 8, no. 160 (13 October 1978), 191–2. As to Borowitz's critique of Fackenheim's description of the Holocaust as 'an "orgy of death and destruction"' in favour of the possibility that the Holocaust was a 'misdirected "rational" pursuit of a highest good ... which was actually a hideous evil' (ibid., 192), I can only suggest that Strauss's influence on Fackenheim seems to indicate that the latter was able to recognize the rational as distinct from the ideal.

217 *Making Peace with Religion* was Fackenheim's working title for what became *Religious Dimension*.

218 See Robert Penn Warren, 'Pure and Impure Poetry,' in *Perspectives on Poetry*, ed. James L. Calderwood and Harold E. Toliver (New York: Oxford University Press, 1968), 69–92.

219 For instance, Fackenheim writes: 'It is both naive and un-Jewish to distill, as still binding, "eternal" commandments from a complex composed of both eternal and "time-bound" ones, the latter simply to be discarded. (This is done by old-fashioned liberalism ... [which] considers the standards by which it judges [i.e., Plato, Kant, Jefferson, etc.] to be superior to what is judged by them; this is an inversion of the Jewish view in which a God speaking through the Torah does the judging).' Emil L. Fackenheim, Answer, in *The Condition of Jewish Belief: A Symposium Compiled by the Editors of* Commentary *Magazine*, intro. Milton Himmelfarb, 2nd printing (New York: American Jewish Committee, 1969), 52 (originally appeared in *Commentary* 2, no. 42, August 1966).

220 This post-Hegelian understanding of the relationship between the eternal and the contingent is the source of Fackenheim's response to Shapiro's critique of *MW*: 'Her error in [suggesting that I denigrate the *Muselmaenner*] is due to her failure to recognize that post-Hegelian thought, like Hegel's own, *moves*. Hence the *Muselmaenner* are not left behind as this thought reaches the resistance that mends its own ontological foundations: it can reach, come to possess, and continue to possess these foundations only as it, ever again, *moves* through the mute testimony of the *Muselmaenner* by which it is paralyzed.' *MW*, 336n13, italics in original.

221 See, for instance, Shapiro, *The Recovery of the Sacred*, chapter 4. Both Shapiro and Seeskin suggest that Fackenheim too quickly mends the ruptures he identifies, or in Seeskin's terms, that he is forced to reappropriate the tradition as a result of his hermeneutics. See ibid.; as well as Seeskin, 'Fackenheim's Dilemma,' 201. One might suggest, however, that because

the event of the Holocaust may 'prove' the non-existence of God, the journey that defines the writing and reading of *MW* offers its own 'proof' of the possibility of God's continued existence.

222 *QPF*, 302.
223 Morgan, *Interim Judaism*, 44.
224 Fackenheim, *The Condition of Jewish Belief*, 51. Fackenheim's rejection of Strauss's esotericism is apparent.
225 See Yaffe, 'Historicism and Revelation.'
226 Strauss, correspondence to Glikes, reprinted on back cover, *MW*.
227 See *GPH*, esp. chapters 1 and 3.

Bibliography

List of Source Abbreviations

EJM   Emil L. Fackenheim. *Encounters between Judaism and Modern Philosophy: A Preface to Future Jewish Thought*. New York: Schocken Books, 1973.

GPH   – *God's Presence in History: Jewish Affirmations and Philosophical Reflections*. First Jason Aronson Edition. Northvale: Jason Aronson, 1997.

GW   – *The God Within: Kant, Schelling, and Historicity*. Edited by John Burbidge. Toronto: University of Toronto Press, 1996.

JPCM   Leo Strauss. *Jewish Philosophy and the Crisis of Modernity: Essays and Lectures in Modern Jewish Thought*. Edited by Kenneth Hart Green. Albany: SUNY Press, 1997.

JPJP   Emil L. Fackenheim. *Jewish Philosophers and Jewish Philosophy*. Edited by Michael L. Morgan. Bloomington: Indiana University Press, 1996.

JRH   – *The Jewish Return into History: Reflections in the Age of Auschwitz and a New Jerusalem*. New York: Schocken Books, 1978.

MW   – *To Mend the World: Foundations of Post-Holocaust Jewish Thought*. First Midland Edition. Bloomington: Indiana University Press, 1994.

NRH   Leo Strauss. *Natural Right and History*. Chicago: University of Chicago Press, 1953.

PW   – *Persecution and the Art of Writing*. Chicago: University of Chicago Press, 1980.

QPF   Emil L. Fackenheim. *Quest for Past and Future: Essays in Jewish Theology*. Boston: Beacon Press, 1968.

RD   – *The Religious Dimension in Hegel's Thought*. Bloomington: Indiana University Press, 1967.

SCR   Leo Strauss. *Spinoza's Critique of Religion*. New York: Schocken Books, 1982.

WJ   Emil L. Fackenheim. *What Is Judaism? An Interpretation for the Present Age*. New York: Summit Books, 1987.

Primary Sources

Emil L. Fackenheim

Answer. In *The Condition of Jewish Belief: A Symposium Compiled by the Editors of Commentary Magazine*. Introduction by Milton Himmelfarb. Second printing. New York: American Jewish Committee, 1969. (Originally appeared in *Commentary* 2, no. 42 [August 1966]).

'A Reply to My Critics.' In *Fackenheim: German Philosophy and Jewish Thought*. Edited by Louis Greenspan and Graeme Nicholson. Toronto: University of Toronto Press, 1992.

Encounters between Judaism and Modern Philosophy: A Preface to Future Jewish Thought [*EJM*]. New York: Schocken Books, 1973.

God's Presence in History: Jewish Affirmations and Philosophical Reflections [*GPH*]. First Jason Aronson Edition. Northvale: Jason Aronson, 1997.

The God Within: Kant, Schelling, and Historicity [*GW*]. Edited by John Burbidge. Toronto: University of Toronto Press, 1996.

The Jewish Bible after the Holocaust: A Re-Reading. Bloomington: Indiana University Press, 1990.

'Jewish-Christian Relations after the Holocaust: Toward Post-Holocaust Theological Thought.' The Joseph Cardinal Bernard in Jerusalem Lecture. Chicago: Emil L. Fackenheim, 1996.

Jewish Philosophers and Jewish Philosophy [*JPJP*]. Edited by Michael L. Morgan. Bloomington: Indiana University Press, 1996.

Jewish Philosophy and the Academy. Edited by Emil L. Fackenheim and Raphael Jospe. Teaneck: Fairleigh Dickinson University Press, 1996.

The Jewish Return into History: Reflections in the Age of Auschwitz and a New Jerusalem [*JRH*]. New York: Schocken Books, 1978.

The Jewish Thought of Emil Fackenheim: A Reader. Edited by Michael L. Morgan. Detroit: Wayne State University Press, 1987.

'Metaphysics and Historicity.' The Thomas Aquinas Lecture. Under the auspices of the Aristotelian Society of Marquette University. Milwaukee: Marquette University Press, 1961.

Personal Interviews with the author, Jerusalem, December 2002 and August 2003.

Quest for Past and Future: Essays in Jewish Theology [*QPF*]. Boston: Beacon Press, 1968.

To Mend the World: Foundations of Post-Holocaust Jewish Thought [MW]. First Midland Edition. Bloomington: Indiana University Press, 1994.

The Religious Dimension in Hegel's Thought [RD]. Bloomington: Indiana University Press, 1967.

What Is Judaism? An Interpretation for the Present Age [WJ]. New York: Summit Books, 1987.

Leo Strauss

An Introduction to Political Philosophy: Ten Essays by Leo Strauss. Edited by Hilail Gildin. Detroit: Wayne State University Press, 1989.

'An Unspoken Prologue to a Public Lecture at St. John's College (in Honor of Jacob Klein, 1899–1978).' *Interpretation: A Journal of Political Philosophy* 7, no. 3 (Fall 1978): 1–3.

The City and Man. Chicago: University of Chicago Press, 1978.

Correspondence to Erwin A. Glikes, President and Publisher, Basic Books, 3 March 1973, reprinted on back cover, *MW*.

Jewish Philosophy and the Crisis of Modernity: Essays and Lectures in Modern Jewish Thought [JPCM]. Edited by Kenneth Hart Green. Albany: SUNY Press, 1997.

Leo Strauss: The Early Writings (1921–1932). Translated and edited by Michael Zank. Albany: SUNY Press, 2002.

Liberalism, Ancient and Modern, foreword Allan Bloom. Chicago: University of Chicago Press, 1995.

Natural Right and History [NRH]. Chicago: University of Chicago Press, 1965.

On Tyranny: Including the Strauss–Kojeve Correspondence. Revised and expanded edition. Edited by Victor Gourevitch and Michael S. Roth. New York: The Free Press, 1991.

Persecution and the Art of Writing [PW]. Chicago: University of Chicago Press, 1980.

'Perspectives on the Good Society: A Jewish–Protestant Colloquium.' *Criterion* (Summer 1963): 2–9.

Philosophy and Law: Essays toward the Understanding of Maimonides and His Predecessors. Translated by Eve Adler. Albany: SUNY Press, 1995.

The Political Philosophy of Hobbes: Its Basis and Its Genesis. Translated by Elsa M. Sinclair. Oxford: Clarendon Press, 1936.

'Relativism.' In *Relativism and the Study of Man*. Edited by Helmut Schoeck and James W. Wiggins. New York: Van Nostrand, 1961.

Spinoza's Critique of Religion [SCR]. New York: Schocken Books, 1982.

Studies in Platonic Political Philosophy. Introduction by Thomas L. Pangle. Chicago: University of Chicago Press, 1983.

Thoughts on Machiavelli. Chicago: University of Chicago Press, 1978.

What Is Political Philosophy? and Other Studies. Westport: Greenwood Press, 1959.

'Why We Remain Jews.' In *Leo Strauss: Political Philosopher and Jewish Thinker.* Edited by Kenneth L. Deutsch and Walter Nicgorski. Lanham: Rowman and Littlefield, 1994.

Miscellaneous Primary Sources

Aquinas, Thomas. *Introduction to St. Thomas Aquinas: The* Summa Theologica, *the* Summa Contra Gentiles. Edited by Anton C. Pegis. New York: Random House, 1948.

– *Treatise on Law.* Introduction by Stanley Parry. Chicago: Henry Regnery, n.d.

Aristotle. *The Metaphysics.* Translated by Hugh Lawson-Tancred. New York: Penguin, 1998.

– *Nicomachean Ethics.* Translated by Joe Sachs. Newburyport: Focus Publishing, 2002.

– *Physica.* In *The Basic Works of Aristotle.* Edited by Richard McKeon. New York: Random House, 1941.

– *Politica.* In *The Basic Works of Aristotle.* Edited by Richard McKeon. New York: Random House, 1941.

Arnold, Matthew. *Matthew Arnold: Prose and Poetry.* Edited by Archibald L. Bouton. New York: Charles Scribner's Sons, 1927.

Bacon, Francis. *The New Organon and Related Writings.* Edited by Fulton H. Anderson. Indianapolis: Bobbs-Merrill Educational Publishing, 1980.

– *The Masculine Birth of Time: Or the Interpretation of Nature.* Translated from the Latin manuscript by Laurence Berns (unpublished).

Buber, Martin. *Eclipse of God: Studies in the Relation between Religion and Philosophy.* Introduction by Robert M. Seltzer. Atlantic Highlands: Humanities Press International, 1988.

– *I and Thou.* Translated by Walter Kaufmann. New York: Charles Scribner and Sons, 1970.

Cohen, Hermann. *Religion of Reason out of the Sources of Judaism.* Translated by Simon Kaplan. New York: Frederick Ungar, 1972.

Dante (Alighieri). *The Divine Comedy.* Translated by Laurence Binyon. Notes by C.H. Grandgent. In *The Portable Dante.* Edited by Paolo Milano. New York: Viking Press, 1947.

Hegel, Georg Wilhelm Friedrich. *Lectures on the Philosophy of Religion.* Edited by Peter C. Hodgson. Translated by R.F. Brown, P.C. Hodgson, and J.M.

Stewart with the assistance of H.S. Harris. Berkeley: University of California Press, 1998.

– *Phenomenology of Spirit.* Translated by A.V. Miller. Analysis and Foreword by J.N. Findlay. New York: Oxford University Press, 1977.

– *Reason in History.* Translated by Robert S. Hartman. New York: Macmillan Publishing, 1953.

Heidegger, Martin. *Introduction to Metaphysics.* Translated by Gregory Fried and Richard Polt. New Haven: Yale University Press, 2000.

– 'What Is Metaphysics?' In *Basic Writings from* Being and Time *(1927) to* The Task of Thinking *(1964).* Revised and expanded edition. Edited by David Farrell Krell. New York: HarperCollins Publishers, 1993.

Hobbes, Thomas. *Leviathan.* New York: Liberal Arts Press, 1958.

– *The Elements of Law Natural and Politic, Part I: Human Nature, Part II: De Corpore Politico with Three Lives.* Edited by J.C.A. Gaskin. New York: Oxford University Press, 1999.

Kant, Immanuel. 'Conjectural Beginnings.' Translated by Emil L. Fackenheim. In *On History.* Edited by Lewis White Beck. Translated by Lewis White Beck, Robert E. Anchor, and Emil L. Fackenheim. Englewood Cliffs: Macmillan Publishing, 1963.

– *Critique of Practical Reason.* Translated by Werner S. Pluhar. Cambridge, MA: Hackett Publishing, 2002.

– 'Idea for a Universal History from a Cosmopolitan Point of View.' Translated by Lewis White Beck. In *On History.* Edited by Lewis White Beck. Englewood Cliffs: Macmillan Publishing, 1963.

– *Grounding for the Metaphysics of Morals, with On a Supposed Right to Lie Because of Philanthropic Concerns.* 3rd ed. Translated by James W. Ellington. Indianapolis: Hackett Publishing, 1993.

– *The Philosophy of Kant: Immanuel Kant's Moral and Political Writings.* Edited by Carl J. Friedrich. New York: Random House, 1949.

Lincoln, Abraham. 'President Lincoln: First Inaugural Address, March 4, 1861.' In *A Documentary Portrait through His Speeches and Writings.* Edited by Don E. Fehrenbacher. Stanford: Stanford University Press, 1964.

– 'With Malice Toward None: Second Inaugural Address, March 4, 1865.' In *A Documentary Portrait through His Speeches and Writings.* Edited by Don E. Fehrenbacher. Stanford: Stanford University Press, 1964.

Machiavelli, Niccolo. *The Prince.* Translated by Harvey Mansfield. Chicago: University of Chicago Press, 1998.

Maimonides, Moses (Rambam). *Mishneh Torah. Yad Hachzakah.* 'The Laws of the Fundamentals of the Torah (4:13).' Translated and annotated by Rabbi Abraham Yaakov Finkel. Scranton: Yeshivath Beth Moshe, 2001.

– *The Guide for the Perplexed.* Translated by Shlomo Pines. Chicago: University of Chicago Press, 1963.

Paine, Thomas. *Common Sense.* Introduction by Isaac Kramnick. New York: Penguin Books, 1986.

Plato. *The Laws.* Translated by Trevor J. Saunders. Reprinted with minor revisions. New York: Penguin Books, 1975.

– *Phaedrus.* Translated by Benjamin Jowett. In *The Collected Dialogues of Plato, Including the Letters.* Edited by Edith Hamilton and Huntington Cairns. Bollingen Series LXXI. Princeton: Princeton University Press, 1980.

– *The Republic.* Translated by Desmond Lee. 2nd ed. (revised). New York: Penguin Books, 1987.

– *Symposium.* Translated by Michael Joyce. In *The Collected Dialogues of Plato, Including the Letters.* Edited by Edith Hamilton and Huntington Cairns. Bollingen Series LXXI. Princeton: Princeton University Press, 1980.

– *Timaeus.* Translated by Benjamin Jowett. In *The Collected Dialogues of Plato, Including the Letters.* Edited by Edith Hamilton and Huntington Cairns. Bollingen Series LXXI. Princeton: Princeton University Press, 1980.

Rosenzweig, Franz. *The New Thinking.* Edited and translated by Alan Udoff and Barbara E. Galli. Syracuse: Syracuse University Press, 1999.

– *The Star of Redemption.* Translated by William W. Hallo. Boston: Beacon Press, 1972.

Sartre, Jean-Paul. *Anti-Semite and Jew.* Translated by George J. Becker. New York: Schocken Books, 1965.

Spinoza, Benedict de. *A Theologico-Political Treatise and A Political Treatise.* Translated by R.H.M. Elwes. Bibliographical Note by Francesco Cordasco. New York: Dover Publications, 1951.

Tolstoy, Leo. *Anna Karenina.* Translated by Rochelle S. Townsend. Volume 1 (of 2 volumes). Everyman's Library. New York: E.P. Dutton, 1943.

Yeats, W.B. 'The Second Coming.' In *The Collected Poems of W.B. Yeats.* New York: Macmillan, 1959.

Secondary Sources

Adler, Eve. Translator's Introduction. In Leo Strauss, *Philosophy and Law: Essays toward the Understanding of Maimonides and His Predecessors.* Translated by Eve Adler. Albany: SUNY Press, 1995.

Anastaplo, George. 'Leo Strauss and Judaism Revisited.' Expanded version. In *The Great Ideas Today* (1998). 13 April 2004. http://anastaplo.wordpress.com/2011/03/21/leo-strauss-and-judaism-revisted. Accessed 31 May 2011.

Arkes, Hadley. 'Athens and Jerusalem: The Legacy of Leo Strauss.' In *Leo*

Strauss and Judaism: Jerusalem and Athens Critically Revisited. Edited by David Novak. Lanham: Rowman and Littlefield, 1996.

Arkush, Allan. 'Leo Strauss and Jewish Modernity.' In *Leo Strauss and Judaism: Jerusalem and Athens Critically Revisited.* Edited by David Novak. Lanham: Rowman and Littlefield, 1996.

Baum, Gregory. 'Fackenheim and Christianity.' In *Fackenheim: German Philosophy and Jewish Thought.* Edited by Louis Greenspan and Graeme Nicholson. Toronto: University of Toronto Press, 1992.

Berns, Laurence. 'Kenneth Hart Green's *Jew and Philosopher: The Return to Maimonides in the Jewish Thought of Leo Strauss.' Jewish Political Studies Review* 9, nos. 3–4 (Fall 1997): 91–8.

– 'Leo Strauss 1899–1973.' In *The College*, January 1974. Annapolis: St. John's College.

– 'The Prescientific World and Historicism: Some Reflections on Strauss, Heidegger, and Husserl.' In *Leo Strauss's Thought: Toward a Critical Engagement.* Edited by Alan Udoff. Boulder: Lynne Rienner, 1991.

– 'Putting Things Back Together Again in Kant.' *Interpretation: A Journal of Political Philosophy* 28, no. 3 (Spring 2001): 201–18.

– 'The Relation between Philosophy and Religion: Reflections on Leo Strauss' Suggestion Concerning the Source and Sources of Modern Philosophy.' *Interpretation: A Journal of Political Philosophy* 19, no. 1 (Fall 1991): 43–60.

Bickerman, Elias. 'The Maccabees.' In *From Esra to the Last of the Maccabees.* New York: Schocken Books, 1962.

Blanchard, Jr, Kenneth C. 'Philosophy in the Age of Auschwitz: Emil Fackenheim and Leo Strauss.' In *Remembering for the Future: Working Papers and Addenda.* 'The Impact of the Holocaust on the Contemporary World.' Vol. II. New York: Pergamon Press, 1989.

Bloom, Allan. 'Leo Strauss: September 20, 1899–October 18, 1973.' In *Giants and Dwarfs: Essays 1960–1990.* New York: Simon and Schuster, 1990.

Borowitz, Eugene B. 'Emil Fackenheim as Lurianic Philosopher.' In *Sh'ma – A Journal of Jewish Responsibility* 13, no. 254 (13 May 1983): 109–11.

– 'Review of *The Jewish Return into History* by Emil L. Fackenheim.' In *Sh'ma – A Journal of Jewish Responsibility* 8, no. 160 (13 October 1978): 191–2.

Braiterman, Zachary. *Theodicy and Antitheodicy: Tradition and Change in Post-Holocaust Jewish Theology.* PhD diss., Stanford University, 1995.

Brightman, Carol. 'The Metaphysical Couple.' Review of *Letters 1925–1975: By Hannah Arendt and Martin Heidegger. The Nation* 278, no. 22 (7 June 2004): 29–33.

Burbidge, John. Preface. In *The God Within: Kant, Schelling, and Historicity.* Edited by John Burbidge. Toronto: University of Toronto Press, 1996.

– 'Reason and Existence in Schelling and Fackenheim.' In *Fackenheim: German Philosophy and Jewish Thought*. Edited by Louis Greenspan and Graeme Nicholson. Toronto: University of Toronto Press, 1992.

Burnyeat, M.F. 'Sphynx Without a Secret.' *New York Review of Books*, 30 May 1985: 30–6.

Clay, Jenny Strauss. Afterword. In *Leo Strauss and Judaism*. Edited by David Novak. Lanham: Rowman and Littlefield, 1996.

Cohen, Jonathan. 'Strauss, Soloveitchik, and the Genesis Narrative: Conceptions of the Ideal Jew as Derived from Philosophical and Theological Readings of the Bible.' *Journal of Jewish Thought and Philosophy* 5, no. 1 (1995): 99–143.

Collingwood, R.G. *The Idea of History*. Oxford: Clarendon Press, 1946.

Dannhauser, Werner J. 'Athens and Jerusalem or Jerusalem and Athens?' In *Leo Strauss and Judaism*. Edited by David Novak. Lanham: Rowman and Littlefield, 1996.

Deutsch, Kenneth L., and Walter Nicgorski. Introduction. In *Leo Strauss: Political Philosopher and Jewish Thinker*. Edited by Kenneth L. Deutsch and Walter Nicgorski. Lanham: Rowman and Littlefield, 1994.

Donat, Alexander. *Holocaust Kingdom: A Memoir*. New York: Holocaust Library, 1978.

Dray, W.H. 'Historicity, Historicism, and Self-Making.' In *Fackenheim: German Philosophy and Jewish Thought*. Edited by Louis Greenspan and Graeme Nicholson. Toronto: University of Toronto Press, 1992.

Drury, S.B. 'The Esoteric Philosophy of Leo Strauss.' *Political Theory* 13, no. 3 (August 1985): 315–37.

Eisen, Robert. 'Midrash in Emil Fackenheim's Holocaust Theology.' *Harvard Theological Review* 96, no. 3 (July 2003): 369–92.

Elton, William. *A Guide to the New Criticism*. Chicago: Modern Poetry Association, 1950.

Fortin, Ernest L. 'Rational Theologians and Irrational Philosophers: A Straussian Perspective.' In *Classical Christianity and the Political Order: Reflections on the Theologico-Political Problem*. Edited by J. Brian Benestad. Lanham: Rowman and Littlefield, 1996.

Foster, M.B. *The Political Philosophies of Plato and Hegel*. Oxford: Clarendon Press, 1968.

Fradkin, Hillel. 'Leo Strauss.' In *Interpreters of Judaism in the Late Twentieth Century*. Edited by Steven T. Katz. Washington: B'nai B'rith, 1993.

– 'Philosophy and Law: Leo Strauss as a Student of Medieval Jewish Thought.' In *Leo Strauss: Political Philosopher and Jewish Thinker*. Edited by Kenneth L. Deutsch and Walter Nicgorski. Lanham: Rowman and Littlefield, 1994.

Germino, Dante. 'Blasphemy and Leo Strauss's Machiavelli.' In *Leo Strauss: Political Philosopher and Jewish Thinker*. Edited by Kenneth L. Deutsch and Walter Nicgorski. Lanham: Rowman and Littlefield, 1994.

Gildin, Hilail. 'Deja Jew All Over Again: Dannhauser on Leo Strauss and Atheism.' *Interpretation: A Journal of Political Philosophy* 25, no. 1 (Fall 1997): 125–33.

Gillman, Neil. *Sacred Fragments: Recovering Theology for the Modern Jew*. Philadelphia: Jewish Publication Society, 1990.

Gilson, Étienne. 'Homage to Maimonides.' In *Essays on Maimonides: An Octocentennial Volume*. Edited by Salo Wittmayer Baron. New York: Columbia University Press, 1941.

Green, Kenneth Hart. 'Editor's Introduction: Leo Strauss as a Modern Jewish Thinker.' In *Jewish Philosophy and the Crisis of Modernity: Essays and Lectures in Modern Jewish Thought*. Edited by Kenneth Hart Green. Albany: SUNY Press, 1997.

– 'How Leo Strauss Read Judah Halevi's *Kuzari*.' *Journal of the American Academy of Religion* 61, no. 2 (Summer 1993): 225–73.

– *Jew and Philosopher: The Return to Maimonides in the Jewish Thought of Leo Strauss*. Albany: SUNY Press, 1993.

Greenspan, Louis, and Graeme Nicholson. Introduction. In *Fackenheim: German Philosophy and Jewish Thought*. Edited by Louis Greenspan and Graeme Nicholson. Toronto: University of Toronto Press, 1992.

Guignon, Charles B. 'Martin Heidegger.' In *The Cambridge Dictionary of Philosophy*. 2nd ed. Robert Audi, General Editor. New York: Cambridge University Press, 1999. 370–3.

Gunnell, John G. 'Strauss before Straussianism: Reason, Revelation, and Nature.' In *Leo Strauss: Political Philosopher and Jewish Thinker*. Edited by Kenneth L. Deutsch and Walter Nicgorski. Lanham: Rowman and Littlefield, 1994.

Jaffa, Harry V. 'Leo Strauss, the Bible, and Political Philosophy.' In *Leo Strauss: Political Philosopher and Jewish Thinker*. Edited by Kenneth L. Deutsch and Walter Nicgorski. Lanham: Rowman and Littlefield, 1994.

Janssens, David. *Between Athens and Jerusalem: Philosophy, Prophecy, and Politics in Leo Strauss' Early Thought*. Albany: SUNY Press, 2008.

Kass, Leon R. *The Beginning of Wisdom: Reading Genesis*. New York: The Free Press, 2003.

Katz, Steven T. *Post-Holocaust Dialogues: Critical Studies in Modern Jewish Thought*. New York: New York University Press, 1983.

Klein, Jacob. 'History and the Liberal Arts.' *St. John's Review* 47, no. 2 (2003): 11–23.

Krell, Marc A. 'Post-Holocaust vs. Postmodern: Emil Fackenheim's Dialogue with Christianity.' *Journal of Jewish Thought and Philosophy* 12, no. 1 (2003): 69–96.

Lawrence, Frederick G. 'Leo Strauss and the Fourth Wave of Modernity.' In *Jerusalem and Athens Critically Revisited*. Edited by David Novak. Lanham: Rowman and Littlefield, 1996.

Lerner, Ralph. 'Leo Strauss (1899–1973).' In *American Jewish Year Book* 76. New York: American Jewish Committee, 1976: 91–7.

McRobert, Laurie. 'Kant and Radical Evil.' In *Fackenheim: German Philosophy and Jewish Thought*. Edited by Louis Greenspan and Graeme Nicholson. Toronto: University of Toronto Press, 1992.

Meier, Heinrich. *Leo Strauss and the Theologico-Political Problem*. Translated by Marcus Brainard. Cambridge: Cambridge University Press, 2006.

Momigliano, Arnaldo. 'Hermeneutics and Classical Political Thought in Leo Strauss.' In *Essays on Ancient and Modern Judaism*. Edited by Silvia Berti. Translated by Maura Masella-Gayley. Chicago: University of Chicago Press, 1994.

Morgan, Michael L. *Dilemmas in Modern Jewish Thought: The Dialectics of Revelation and History*. Bloomington: Indiana University Press, 1992.

– E-mail to the author, 14 September, 2004.

– *Interim Judaism: Jewish Thought in a Century of Crisis*. Bloomington: Indiana University Press, 2001.

– Introduction to Part I. In *Jewish Philosophers and Jewish Philosophy*. Edited by Michael L. Morgan. Bloomington: Indiana University Press, 1996.

– Introduction to Part II. The Early Stage: From 1945 to 1967. In *Jewish Philosophers and Jewish Philosophy*. Edited by Michael L. Morgan. Bloomington: Indiana University Press, 1996.

– 'Philosophy, History, and the Jewish Thinker: Philosophy and Jewish Thought in *To Mend the World*.' In *Fackenheim: German Philosophy and Jewish Thought*. Edited by Louis Greenspan and Graeme Nicholson. Toronto: University of Toronto Press, 1992.

– 'Teaching Leo Strauss as a Jewish and General Philosopher.' In *Jewish Philosophy and the Academy*. Edited by Emil L. Fackenheim and Raphael Jospe. Teaneck: Fairleigh Dickinson University Press, 1996.

Myers, David N. *Resisting History: Historicism and Its Discontents in German-Jewish Thought*. Princeton: Princeton University Press, 2003.

Nicholson, Graeme. 'The Passing of Hegel's Germany.' In *Fackenheim: German Philosophy and Jewish Thought*. Edited by Louis Greenspan and Graeme Nicholson. Toronto: University of Toronto Press, 1992.

Novak, David. 'Introduction.' In *Leo Strauss and Judaism: Jerusalem and Athens*

Critically Revisited. Edited by David Novak. Lanham: Rowman and Little-
field, 1996.
– 'Philosophy and the Possibility of Revelation: A Theological Response to the
Challenge of Leo Strauss.' In *Leo Strauss and Judaism: Jerusalem and Athens
Critically Revisited.* Edited by David Novak. Lanham: Rowman and Little-
field, 1996.
Oppenheim, Michael. *What Does Revelation Mean for the Modern Jew: Rosenz-
weig, Buber, Fackenheim.* Lewiston: Edwin Mellon Press, 1985.
Orr, Susan. *Jerusalem and Athens: Reason and Revelation in the Work of Leo
Strauss.* Lanham: Rowman and Littlefield, 1995.
– 'Strauss, Reason, and Revelation: Unraveling the Essential Question.' In *Leo
Strauss and Judaism: Jerusalem and Athens Critically Revisited.* Edited by David
Novak. Lanham: Rowman and Littlefield, 1996.
Pangle, Thomas L. 'On the Epistolary Dialogue between Leo Strauss and Eric
Voegelin.' In *Leo Strauss: Political Philosopher and Jewish Thinker.* Edited by
Kenneth L. Deutsch and Walter Nicgorski. Lanham: Rowman and Little-
field, 1994.
Portnoff, Sharon, James A. Diamond, and Martin D. Yaffe, eds. *Emil L. Facken-
heim: Philosopher, Theologian, Jew.* Boston: E.J. Brill, 2008.
Robertson, Neil. 'Leo Strauss's Platonism.' *Animus: A Philosophical Journal for
Our Time* 4 (22 December 1999). http://www.mun.ca/animus/1999vol4/
roberts4.htm. Accessed 31 May 2011.
Rosen, Stanley. *Hermeneutics as Politics.* New York: Oxford University Press,
1987.
– 'Leo Strauss and the Quarrel between the Ancients and the Moderns.' In
Leo Strauss's Thought: Towards a Critical Engagement. Edited by Alàn Udoff.
Boulder: Lyenne Rienner, 1991.
Sedeyn, Olivier. 'The Wisdom of Jacob Klein.' Translated by Brother Robert
Smith. In *St. John's Review* 47, no. 2 (2003): 5–10.
Seeskin, Kenneth. 'Emil Fackenheim.' In *Interpreters of Judaism in the Late Twen-
tieth Century.* Washington: B'nai Brith, 1993.
– 'Fackenheim's Dilemma.' In *Jewish Philosophy in a Secular Age.* New York:
SUNY Press, 1990.
Seltzer, Robert M. 'Judaism According to Emil Fackenheim.' *Commentary* 86,
no. 3 (September 1988): 30–4.
Shapiro, Susan E. 'For Thy Breach Is Great Like the Sea: Who Can Heal Thee.'
Religious Studies Review 13, no. 3 (July 1987): 210–13.
– 'The Recovery of the Sacred: Hermeneutics after the Holocaust.' PhD diss.,
University of Chicago, 1983.
Shearson, W.A. 'The Fragmented Middle: Hegel and Kierkegaard.' In *Facken-*

heim: German Philosophy and Jewish Thought. Edited by Louis Greenspan and Graeme Nicholson. Toronto: University of Toronto Press, 1992.

Shell, Susan. 'Taking Evil Seriously: Schmitt's "Concept of the Political" and Strauss' "True Politics."' In *Leo Strauss: Political Philosopher and Jewish Thinker.* Edited by Kenneth L. Deutsch and Walter Nicgorski. Lanham: Rowman and Littlefield, 1994.

Sheppard, Eugene R. 'Leo Strauss and the Politics of Exile.' PhD diss., University of California, Los Angeles, 2001.

– *Leo Strauss and the Politics of Exile: The Making of a Political Philosopher.* Waltham: Brandeis University Press, 2006.

Smith, Steven B. 'Leo Strauss: Between Athens and Jerusalem.' In *Leo Strauss: Political Philosopher and Jewish Thinker.* Edited by Kenneth L. Deutsch and Walter Nicgorski. Lanham: Rowman and Littlefield, 1994.

– *Reading Leo Strauss: Politics, Philosophy, Judaism.* Chicago: University of Chicago Press, 2006.

– *Spinoza, Liberalism, and the Question of Jewish Identity.* New Haven: Yale University Press, 1997.

Tanguay, Daniel. *Leo Strauss: An Intellectual Biography.* Translated by Christopher Nadon. New Haven: Yale University Press, 2007.

Tolstoy, Leo. *Anna Karenina.* Translated by Rochelle S. Townsend. Vol. 1. New York: E.P. Dutton, 1943.

Umphrey, Stewart. 'Natural Right and Philosophy.' In *Leo Strauss: Political Philosopher and Jewish Thinker.* Edited by Kenneth L. Deutsch and Walter Nicgorski. Lanham: Rowman and Littlefield, 1994.

Warren, Robert Penn. 'Pure and Impure Poetry.' In *Perspectives on Poetry.* Edited by James L. Calderwood and Harold E. Toliver. New York: Oxford University Press, 1968. 69–92.

Whitaker, Albert Keith. 'The Bible and Philosophy: Reviews of *The Beginning of Wisdom: Reading Genesis* by Leon R. Kass, and *Political Philosophy and the God of Abraham,* by Thomas L. Pangle.' Claremont Institute, 25 November 2003. http://www.claremont.org/writings/crb/winter2003/whitaker.html.

Wimsatt, Jr, W.K., and M.C. Beardsley. 'The Affective Fallacy.' *Sewanee Review* 57 (Winter 1949): 31–55.

Yaffe, Martin D. 'Autonomy, Community, Authority: Hermann Cohen, Carl Schmitt, Leo Strauss.' In *Autonomy and Judaism: The Individual and the Community in Jewish Philosophical Thought.* Edited by Daniel H. Frank. Albany: SUNY Press, 1992.

– 'Historicism and Revelation in Emil Fackenheim's Self-Distancing from Leo Strauss.' In *Emil L. Fackenheim: Philosopher, Theologian, Jew.* Edited by

Sharon Portnoff, James A. Diamond, and Martin D. Yaffe. Boston: E.J. Brill, 2008.
- 'Leo Strauss's "Maimonideanism" in His Interpretation of Spinoza's *Theologico-Political Treatise.'* Annual Conference, Association for Jewish Studies, Boston, 22 December 2003.
Zuckert, Catherine H. *Postmodern Platos: Nietzsche, Heidegger, Gadamer, Strauss, Derrida.* Chicago: University of Chicago Press, 1996.

Index

Abraham, 116, 325n257; action-concepts, 149, 231, 343n118, 349n179; affective fallacy, 78, 277n232; Akeda, 216

anthropocentrism: in emergence of natural law in early modern philosophy, 11; Fackenheim on, 234; of Heidegger, 56, 60; of Hobbes, 53, 54, 202; ideas of progress and history associated with, 265n93; of Kant, 12, 82, 87; of Machiavelli, 46, 49–50, 202; revelation associated with, 294n231; Strauss on, 57, 233; of synthesis of revelatory religion and philosophy, 153; Torah and, 236

Anti-Semite and Jew (Sartre), 232

Aquinas, Thomas: on man rising above predicament of history, 175; on natural law, 11, 255n157; natural rights doctrine of, 43; in ontological tradition, 179

Aristotle: on actualization of human potentialities, 193, 318n155; on beginning from what is known, 258n24; and biblical injunction against rebellion against God, 219; as classic conventionalist, 45; Collingwood's idea of nature distinguished from that of, 319n161; *Ethics*, 51, 214; on existence of natural right, 161; Fackenheim on return to, 194; on fear and pity, 215; Hegel and, 91; Heidegger compared with, 267n114; on history and poetry, 178; on knowledge and obedience, 220; knowledge as aim of, 5; looking to what is true for most men in most cases, 160; Machiavelli and, 48, 51–2; Maimonides and, 256n5; on natural law, 213; and natural religion, 273n194; on natural right, 43, 45, 260n36, 263n83; on pleasure and perfection, 45; Strauss on commonalities between Plato and, 257n9; Strauss on understanding his problems as he saw them, 43; on tragedy, 215; on universally valid rules of action, 257n12

Arkush, Allan, 8

Arnold, Matthew, 269n141

assimilationism, 70, 71, 250n97

atheism: attributed to Strauss, 62;

from ecclesiastical authority, 11, 12, 13, 31, 39, 40, 42–3, 69; Strauss and Fackenheim as two options to restore reason and revelation, 23–30; Strauss on Jewish, 60–79; Strauss on Western, 38–60; Strauss's formulation of relationship between reason and revelation in modern thought, and his rejection of a practical synthesis, 38–80; tension between revelatory theology and, in Jewish thought, 16–20; tension between revelatory theology and, in modern Western thought, 10–16; traditions of, 40, 46, 56, 57, 58; as unable to verify its own truth, 79; usurpation by science, 156; as way of life, 39, 45–6, 80, 205–6, 208, 221, 222, 226, 340n57. *See also* empiricism; existentialism; Greek philosophy; idealism; metaphysics; political philosophy

Philosophy and Law (Strauss), 4, 5

Plato: cave analogy of, 31, 43, 45, 154, 162, 275n209, 310n61, 344n138, 350n196; Cohen on, 72; connects the intelligible with the good, 230; on dialectic as logical, 192; divided line simile of, 257n12; on divinity, 20; esoteric writing of, 43, 257n8; Fackenheim sees Holocaust as evil beyond philosophy of, 7; forms, 59; Hegel and, 92, 95, 335n367; Heidegger and, 13, 114; on human nature and political action, 54; knowledge as aim of, 5; *Laws*, 9, 206, 207, 259n29; on love of one's own, 206–7; natural rights doctrine of, 43, 53, 259n31; noble lie of, 168; on philosophy

and myth, 9; *The Republic*, 9, 206–7, 275n211, 335n367; on the state, 25; Strauss bases his philosophy on, 27; Strauss on, 41–3, 223, 248n75; Strauss on commonalities between Aristotle and, 257n9; Strauss's return to, 27, 35, 42, 186, 207, 225, 234; on the surfaces indicating the intelligibles, 224; on tragedy, 215; on universally valid rules of action, 222, 257n12

poetry, 117, 178

pointing-to-the-Other, 191

political philosophy: Cohen and, 72; as exoteric writing, 39; Hegel on philosophy and modern form of, 172; of Hobbes, 54; as necessary for acquiring wisdom, 54; political science distinguished from, 25; private sphere of philosophy in dialectical relationship with, 31; revelation translated into terms of, 13; understanding the faith of the fathers as essential for, 223

political science, political philosophy distinguished from, 25

positivism, 164, 177, 200

pragmatic make-believe, 112, 175, 317n146

progress: anthropocentrism and belief in, 265n93; Bacon's science as progressive, 31; Heidegger on, 56; historical sense in eighteenth-century idea of, 310n63; Hobbes on, 53; idealistic concept of progressive history, 46; in Judaism, 230; and meaning of Jewish history, 199; as at odds with Judaism, 76; secular messianism, 229; Spinoza introduces idea to Jews, 17; Strauss